International Technical Support Organization

IBM AIX 5L Reference for HP-UX System Administrators

March 2006

SG24-6767-00

Note: Before using this information and the product it supports, read the information in "Notices" on page xv.

First Edition (March 2006)

This edition applies to AIX 5L Version 5.3 and HP-UX 11i Version 1 [HP-UX 11.11] (with a bit of Version 2 [HP-UX 11.23].

Contents

Figures

Notices

This information was developed for products and services offered in the U.S.A.

IBM may not offer the products, services, or features discussed in this document in other countries. Consult your local IBM representative for information on the products and services currently available in your area. Any reference to an IBM product, program, or service is not intended to state or imply that only that IBM product, program, or service may be used. Any functionally equivalent product, program, or service that does not infringe any IBM intellectual property right may be used instead. However, it is the user's responsibility to evaluate and verify the operation of any non-IBM product, program, or service.

IBM may have patents or pending patent applications covering subject matter described in this document. The furnishing of this document does not give you any license to these patents. You can send license inquiries, in writing, to:
IBM Director of Licensing, IBM Corporation, North Castle Drive Armonk, NY 10504-1785 U.S.A.

The following paragraph does not apply to the United Kingdom or any other country where such provisions are inconsistent with local law: INTERNATIONAL BUSINESS MACHINES CORPORATION PROVIDES THIS PUBLICATION "AS IS" WITHOUT WARRANTY OF ANY KIND, EITHER EXPRESS OR IMPLIED, INCLUDING, BUT NOT LIMITED TO, THE IMPLIED WARRANTIES OF NON-INFRINGEMENT, MERCHANTABILITY OR FITNESS FOR A PARTICULAR PURPOSE. Some states do not allow disclaimer of express or implied warranties in certain transactions, therefore, this statement may not apply to you.

This information could include technical inaccuracies or typographical errors. Changes are periodically made to the information herein; these changes will be incorporated in new editions of the publication. IBM may make improvements and/or changes in the product(s) and/or the program(s) described in this publication at any time without notice.

Any references in this information to non-IBM Web sites are provided for convenience only and do not in any manner serve as an endorsement of those Web sites. The materials at those Web sites are not part of the materials for this IBM product and use of those Web sites is at your own risk.

IBM may use or distribute any of the information you supply in any way it believes appropriate without incurring any obligation to you.

Information concerning non-IBM products was obtained from the suppliers of those products, their published announcements or other publicly available sources. IBM has not tested those products and cannot confirm the accuracy of performance, compatibility or any other claims related to non-IBM products. Questions on the capabilities of non-IBM products should be addressed to the suppliers of those products.

This information contains examples of data and reports used in daily business operations. To illustrate them as completely as possible, the examples include the names of individuals, companies, brands, and products. All of these names are fictitious and any similarity to the names and addresses used by an actual business enterprise is entirely coincidental.

COPYRIGHT LICENSE:
This information contains sample application programs in source language, which illustrates programming techniques on various operating platforms. You may copy, modify, and distribute these sample programs in any form without payment to IBM, for the purposes of developing, using, marketing or distributing application programs conforming to the application programming interface for the operating platform for which the sample programs are written. These examples have not been thoroughly tested under all conditions. IBM, therefore, cannot guarantee or imply reliability, serviceability, or function of these programs. You may copy, modify, and distribute these sample programs in any form without payment to IBM for the purposes of developing, using, marketing, or distributing application programs conforming to IBM's application programming interfaces.

Trademarks

The following terms are trademarks of the International Business Machines Corporation in the United States, other countries, or both:

@server®	IBM®	POWER5™
@server®	Language Environment®	POWER6™
Redbooks (logo) ™	Micro Channel®	Redbooks™
eServer™	Power Series®	Requisite®
pSeries®	PowerPC 750™	RISC System/6000®
AIX 5L™	PowerPC®	RS/6000®
AIX®	POWER™	SecureWay®
CICS®	POWERserver®	Tivoli®
DB2®	POWER2™	Virtualization Engine™
HACMP™	POWER3™	WebSphere®
Infoprint®	POWER4™	

The following terms are trademarks of other companies:

CacheFS, Java, Power Management, Sun, and all Java-based trademarks are trademarks of Sun Microsystems, Inc. in the United States, other countries, or both.

Microsoft, Windows, and the Windows logo are trademarks of Microsoft Corporation in the United States, other countries, or both.

Chips, Itanium, Intel logo, Intel Inside logo, and Intel Centrino logo are trademarks or registered trademarks of Intel Corporation or its subsidiaries in the United States, other countries, or both.

UNIX is a registered trademark of The Open Group in the United States and other countries.

Linux is a trademark of Linus Torvalds in the United States, other countries, or both.

Other company, product, and service names may be trademarks or service marks of others.

Preface

The *AIX 5L Differences Guide Version 5.2,* SG24-5765-02, and *AIX 5L Differences Guide Version 5.3,* SG24-7463-00, are excellent references for learning about AIX® 5L™. No matter what your skill level of UNIX® is, you will be able to use the AIX 5L Differences Guides as a starting point into many of the newest features of AIX 5L.

This book concentrates on providing an experienced systems administrator in one flavor of UNIX (either HP-UX or AIX 5L) with a jump start into easy administration of the other. We concentrate on HP-UX 11i Version 1 (also known as HP-UX 11.11), as we had no access to the Integrity platform (Itanium® family of processors) to allow any hands-on testing with HP-UX 11i Version 2 (also known as HP-UX 11.23). There are sections of this book that touch on HP-UX 11i Version 2 to explain, where possible, the differences in concepts between Version 11, Version 2, and AIX 5L.

Many of the examples given for both HP-UX and AIX 5L concentrate on the actual command line rather than the available GUIs for the respective operating systems. The command line provides a closer feel for what is actually happening on the machine.

The team that wrote this redbook

This redbook was produced by a team of specialists from around the world working at the International Technical Support Organization, Austin Center.

Dino Quintero is a Consulting IT Specialist at the ITSO in Poughkeepsie, New York. Before joining the ITSO, he worked as a Performance Analyst for the Enterprise Systems Group and as a Disaster Recovery Architect for IBM® Global Services. His areas of expertise include disaster recovery and pSeries® clustering solutions. He is certified in pSeries system administration and pSeries clustering technologies. He is also an IBM Senior Certified Professional on pSeries technologies. Currently, he leads teams delivering Redbooks™ solutions on pSeries clustering technologies and delivering technical workshops worldwide.

Harrison Leal is a Technical Support Analyst for HSBC Bank Brazil. He has five years of experience in UNIX Systems Management. His areas of expertise include AIX 5L, HP-UX, HACMP™, MC/Service Guard, and Storage solutions.

Geoffrey Mattes is a Senior IT Specialist for IBM Global Services Australia and has had more than 10 years if experience in the administration of a mix of UNIX flavors. He has worked in IBM Global Services for seven years. His areas of expertise include HP-UX, AIX 5L, and Linux® Systems Administration, troubleshooting, automation, system customization, and scripting.

Manoj Sooka is an advisory IT Specialist for IBM Global Services in South Africa. He has been working for IBM SA for 11 years and has five years of experience in HP-UX system administration and two years in AIX 5L system administration. He is certified as an HP-UX CSA and IBM CATE pSeries and AIX 5L.

Thanks to the following people for their contributions to this project:

Octavian Lascu
International Technical Support Organization, Austin Center

Julie Czubik
International Technical Support Organization, Poughkeepsie Center

Lisa Case, John McBride, Tom Burke
IBM Poughkeepsie

Anthony (Red) Steel
IBM Australia

Become a published author

Join us for a two- to six-week residency program! Help write an IBM Redbook dealing with specific products or solutions, while getting hands-on experience with leading-edge technologies. You'll team with IBM technical professionals, Business Partners and/or clients.

Your efforts will help increase product acceptance and client satisfaction. As a bonus, you'll develop a network of contacts in IBM development labs, and increase your productivity and marketability.

Learn more about the residency program, browse the residency index, and apply online at:

ibm.com/redbooks/residencies.html

Comments welcome

Your comments are important to us!

We want our Redbooks to be as helpful as possible. Send us your comments about this or other Redbooks in one of the following ways:

► Use the online **Contact us** review redbook form found at:

  ibm.com/redbooks

► Send your comments in an email to:

  redbook@us.ibm.com

► Mail your comments to:

  IBM Corporation, International Technical Support Organization
  Dept. JN9B Building 905
  11501 Burnet Road
  Austin, Texas 78758-3493

Overview

In this chapter the following topics are covered:

- ▶ "HP-UX and AIX 5L quick feature summaries" on page 2
- ▶ "Systems administration overview" on page 5
- ▶ "Introduction to pSeries (and RS/6000) architectures" on page 11

1.1 HP-UX and AIX 5L quick feature summaries

This section is an overview of the main features of HP-UX and AIX 5L operating systems.

1.1.1 Overview of features for HP-UX 11i

HP-UX 11i has strong functionality in:

► Management
► Security
► High performance and scalability
► Reliability, availability, and serviceability (RAS)
► Applications compatibility
► Programming and processing
► Web page http authoring and Web site construction
► HP invent value-added features
► Availability and support

1.1.2 Overview of features of AIX 5L

Support for 64-bit architecture is provided by AIX 5L. This support provides improved performance for specialized applications with:

► Large address spaces (up to 16,384,000 terabytes)

► Access to large datasets for data warehousing, scientific, and multimedia applications

► Long integers in computations

A major enhancement in AIX 5L Version 5.1 is the introduction of the 64-bit kernel. The primary advantage of a 64-bit kernel is the increased kernel address space, allowing systems to support increased workloads. This ability is important for a number of reasons:

► Data sharing and I/O device sharing are simplified if multiple applications can be run on the same system.

► More powerful systems will reduce the number of systems needed by an organization, thereby reducing the cost and complexity of system administration.

Server consolidation and workload scalability will continue to require higher capacity hardware systems that support more memory and additional I/O devices. The 64-bit AIX 5L Version 5.1 kernel is designed to support these requirements.

AIX Version 4.3.3 features

Overview of the features of AIX Version 4.3.3:

- ► Significant AIX scalability enhancements for 24-way SMP systems
- ► AIX Workload Management system with a policy-based method for managing system workload and system resources
- ► AIX exploitation of SecureWay® Directory for users and groups
- ► Increased network performance and scalability for e-business
- ► Improved system availability with support for online Journaled File System (JFS) backup and concurrent mirroring and striping
- ► Enhanced RAS and improved serviceability features
- ► NIS+ network information management system
- ► Enhanced file and print capability
- ► Mechanical Computer-Aided AIX Developer Kit, Java™ Technology Edition, Version 1.1.8
- ► Enhanced ease-of-use capabilities, including additional Web-based System Manager Task Guides and SMIT support

AIX 5L Version 5.1 features

Overview of AIX 5L Version 5.1 features:

- ► New Journal File System 2 (JFS2) File System
- ► Selectable Logical Track Group (LTG): Helps administrators tune disk storage for optimum performance
- ► Virtual IP Address (VIPA): Helps applications remain available if a network connection is lost
- ► IP Multipath Routing: Improves network availability by providing multiple routes to a destination
- ► Multiple Default Gateways and Routers: Keeps traffic moving through a network by detecting and routing around dead gateways
- ► Extended Memory Allocator: Helps improve performance of applications that request large numbers of small memory blocks
- ► Native Kerberos V5 Authentication (POWER™ only)
- ► /proc file system: Helps system administrators more easily review system workloads and processes for corrective action
- ► RMC: Automates system monitoring, thereby helping to improve system availability and performance

- UNIX System V Release 4 (SVR4): Printing allows users comfortable with SVR4 print utilities to more easily use AIX 5L
- Accounting in Workload Manager: Allows users to collect system resource usage information for billing or reporting purposes

AIX 5L Version 5.2 features

This list is not an exhaustive list of enhancements to AIX 5L Version 5.2, but a list of the key features introduced.

- Flexibility and Affinity with Linux
- System scalability with JFS2 file system and Large pages
- Logical partition support for p670/p690
- e-business and network performance
- Security
- Java
- Systems and resource management
- Storage
- Reliability, availability, serviceability (RAS)
- CPU-Gard
- Debugging and performance tools

AIX 5L Version 5.3 features

AIX 5L Version 5.3 offers new levels of innovative self-management technologies. It continues to exploit current 64-bit system and software architectures to support advanced virtualization options, as well as POWER5™ processors with simultaneous multi-threading capability for improve performance and system utilization.

Highlights for AIX 5L Version 5.3:

- Scalable, open, standards-based UNIX operating system with Linux affinity.
- POWER5 and IBM Virtualization Engine™ enablement helps deliver power, increase utilization, and ease administration.
- Rock-solid security and availability to help protect IT assets and keep businesses running.
- Accounting and chargeback.
- Enhance scalability and performance.
- Systems management and development tools.
- Security.
- Open Source flexibility.
- AIX 5L Expansion Pack.

For more information about AIX 5L releases and upgrade benefits, contact your IBM representative or visit the following Web sites:

► ibm.com/servers/aix
► ibm.com/eserver/pseries
► ibm.com/common/ssi

1.2 Systems administration overview

Both HP-UX and AIX 5L have different tools for the system administrator. For HP-UX, there is a range of products, such as Admin tool, Admin suite, Admin wizard, Management console, Management center, and so on. In the following section we describe the main administrator tools for AIX 5L.

1.2.1 System Management Interface Tool (SMIT)

For AIX 5L, there are basically two powerful tools for the system administrator. The System Management Interface Tool (SMIT) is the most used administration tool for AIX 5L system managers today. SMIT offers the following features:

► Two modes of operation
► An interactive, menu-driven user interface
► User assistance
► System management activity logging
► Fast paths to system management tasks
► User-added SMIT screens

Modes of operation

SMIT runs in two modes: ASCII (non-graphical) and Xwindows (graphical). ASCII SMIT can run on both terminals and graphical displays. The graphical mode, which supports a mouse and point-and-click operations, can be run only on a graphical display and with Xwindows support. The ASCII mode is often the preferred way to run SMIT, because it can be run from any display. To start the ASCII mode, type the following command:

```
# smitty or smit -C
```

To start the graphical mode, type:

```
# smit or smit -m
```

Note that the function keys used in the ASCII version of SMIT do not correspond to actions in the graphical SMIT. We describe the details in Table 1-2 on page 8.

SMIT selector screen

Example 1-1 shows the SMIT selector screen.

Example 1-1 SMIT selector screen

```
+----------------------------------------------------------------------+
|                       Available Network Interfaces                   |
|                                                                      |
|  Move cursor to desired item and press Enter.                        |
|                                                                      |
|    en0    10-80    Standard Ethernet Network Interface               |
|    et0    10-80    IEEE 802.3 Ethernet Network Interface             |
|    tr0    10-88    Token Ring Network Interface                      |
|                                                                      |
|  F1=Help              F2=Refresh              F3=Cancel              |
|  F8=Image             F10=Exit                Enter=Do               |
|  /=Find               n=Find Next                                    |
+----------------------------------------------------------------------+
```

A selector screen is a special version of a dialog screen in which there is only one value to change. This value of the object is used to determine which subsequent dialog to display.

SMIT dialog screen

Example 1-2 shows the SMIT dialog screen.

Example 1-2 SMIT dialog screen

```
                               Add a Group

Type or select values in entry fields.
Press Enter AFTER making all desired changes.

                                                    [Entry Fields]
* Group NAME                                        []
  ADMINISTRATIVE group?                             false +
  Group ID                                          []  #
  USER list                                         []  +
  ADMINISTRATOR list                                []  +




F1=Help              F2=Refresh         F3=Cancel            F4=List
F5=Reset             F6=Command         F7=Edit             F8=Image
F9=Shell             F10=Exit           Enter=Do
```

A dialog screen allows you to enter input values for the selected operation. Some fields will already be filled in with default values in the system. Usually, you can change this value.

To enter data, move the highlighted bar to the value you want to change and then either enter a value or select one from a pop-up list. Fields that you can type in are indicated by square brackets ([]). Fields that have data that is larger than the space available to display it are indicated by angle brackets (<>), to indicate that there is data further to the left or right (or both) of the display area.

Table 1-1 shows the different SMIT symbols.

Special symbols on the screen are used to indicate how data is to be entered.

Table 1-1   SMIT symbols

Symbols in SMIT dialog screens	Explanation
*	A required field.
#	A numeric value is required for this field.
/	A path name is required for this field.
X	A hexadecimal value is required for this field.
?	The value entered will not be displayed.
+	A pop-up list or ring is available.

An * symbol in the left-most column of a line indicates that the field is required. A value must be entered here before you can commit the dialog and execute the command.

In the ASCII version, a plus sign (+) is used to indicate that a pop-up list or ring is available. To access a pop-up list, use the F4 key. A ring is a special type of list. If a fixed number of options are available, the Tab key can be used to cycle through the options.

In the Motif version, a List button is displayed. Either click the button or press Ctrl+L to get a pop-up window to select from.

The following keys can be used while in the menus and dialog screens. Some keys are only valid in particular screens. Those valid only for the ASCII interface are marked (A) and those valid only for the Motif interface are marked (M). Table 1-2 on page 8 gives an overview of all function keys.

Table 1-2 SMIT function keys

Function keys	Explanation
F1 (or ESC+1)	Help: Show contextual help information.
F2 (or ESC+2)	Refresh: Redraw the display (A).
F3 (or ESC+3)	Cancel: Return to the previous screen (A).
F4 (or ESC+4)	List: Display a pop-up list of possible values (A).
F5 (or ESC+5)	Reset: Restore the original value of an entry field.
F6 (or ESC+6)	Command: Show the AIX 5L command that will be executed.
F7 (or ESC+7)	Edit: A field in a pop-up box or select from a multi-selection pop-up list.
F8 (or ESC+8)	Image: Save the current screen to a file (A) and show the current fast path.
F9 (or ESC+9)	Shell: Start a sub-shell (A).
F9	Reset all fields (M).
F10 (or ESC+0)	Exit: Exit SMIT immediately (A).
F10	Go to command bar (M).
F12	Exit: Exit SMIT immediately (M).
Ctrl-L	List: Give a pop-up list of possible values (M).
PgDn (or Ctrl+V)	Scroll down one page.
PgUp (or ESC+V)	Scroll up one page.
Home (or ESC+<)	Go to the top of the scrolling region.
End (or ESC+>)	Go to the bottom of the scrolling region.
Enter	Do the current command or select from a single-selection pop-up list.
/text	Finds the text in the output.
n	Finds the next occurrence of the text.

SMIT output screen

Example 1-3 shows the SMIT output screen.

Example 1-3   SMIT output screen

```
                          COMMAND STATUS

Command: OK              stdout: yes            stderr: no

Before command completion, additional instructions may appear below.

system   0        true     root      files
staff    1        false    invscout,snapp,daemon    files
bin      2        true     root,bin         files
sys      3        true     root,bin,sys     files
adm      4        true     bin,adm files
uucp     5        true     nuucp,uucp       files
mail     6        true     files
security          7        true     root    files
cron     8        true     root      files
printq   9        true     lp        files
audit    10       true     root      files
ecs      28       true     files
nobody   -2       false    nobody,lpd       files
usr      100      false    guest     files
perf     20       false    files
shutdown          21       true     files
lp       11       true     root,lp,printq   files
imnadm   188      false    imnadm    files




F1=Help              F2=Refresh          F3=Cancel          F6=Command
F8=Image             F9=Shell            F10=Exit           /=Find
n=Find Next
```

The Command field can have the following values: OK, RUNNING, and FAILED. Note that in the Motif version there is a running man icon in the top right-hand corner of the screen that is used to indicate this value.

stdout is the standard output, that is, there is output produced as a result of running the command. The output will be displayed in the body section of this screen. stderr is the error messages, if there are any. In Example 1-3 there is no error message.

The body of the screen holds the output/error messages of the command output in Example 1-3.

To read an in-depth article about SMIT, go to the following Web site:

```
http://www.ibm.com/servers/aix/products/aixos/whitepapers/smit.html
```

1.2.2 Web-based System Manager

The Web-based System Manager is a graphical user interface administration tool for AIX 5L. This is a Java-based comprehensive suite of system management tools for AIX 5L. To start the Web-based System Manager, type the following command at the command line of the graphical console:

```
# wsm
```

Figure 1-1 shows the Web-based System Manager.

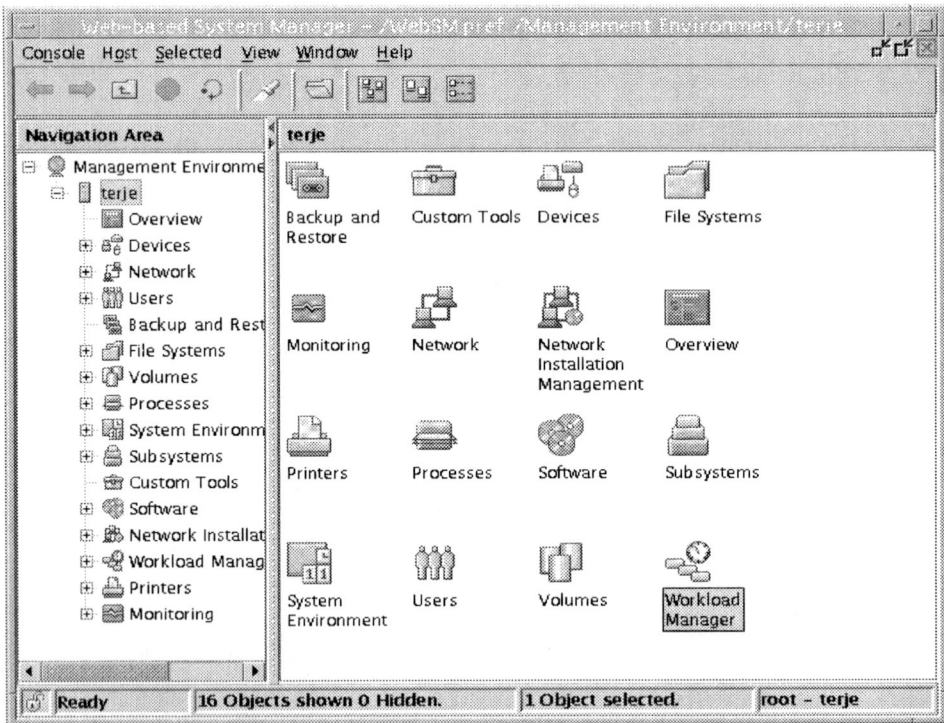

Figure 1-1   Web-based System Manager

The AIX 5L release of Web-based System Manager utilizes a management console capable of administering multiple AIX 5L hosts on POWER hardware.

The Web-based System Manager can be run in stand-alone mode, that is, you can use this tool to perform system administration functions on the AIX 5L system you are currently running on. However, the Web-based System Manager also supports a client-server environment. In this environment, it is possible to administer an AIX 5L system from a remote PC or from another AIX 5L system using a graphics terminal. In this environment, the AIX 5L system being administered is the server and the system you are performing the administration functions from is the client.

The client can operate in either application mode on AIX 5L with Java 1.42 or in applet mode on platforms that support Java 1.42. Thus, the AIX 5L system can be managed from another AIX 5L system or from a PC running Microsoft® Windows® 95 or Windows NT.

The objectives of the Web-based System Manager are:

► Simplification of AIX 5L administration by a single interface.

► Enable AIX 5L systems to be administered from almost any client platform (client must have a browser that supports Java 1.42).

► Enable AIX 5L systems to be administered remotely.

► Provide a system administration environment that provides a similar look and feel to the Windows and AIX 5L CDE environments.

The Web-based System Manager provides a comprehensive system management environment and covers most of the tasks in the SMIT user interface. The Web-based System Manager can only be run from a graphics terminal, so SMIT will need to be used in the ASCII environment.

1.3 Introduction to pSeries (and RS/6000) architectures

In February 1990, IBM introduced the first RISC System/6000® (RS/6000®) with the first Performance Optimization With Enhanced RISC (POWER) architecture. Since that date, several POWER architectures have been designed for the RS/6000 models.

The PowerPC® family of microprocessors, a single-chip implementation jointly developed by Apple, IBM, and Motorola, established a rapidly expanding market for RISC-based hardware and software. IBM has many successful lines of PowerPC-based products for workstations and servers.

Motorola introduced a broad range of desktop and server systems, and other companies such as Bull, Canon, and FirePower have announced or shipped PowerPC-based systems. Apple has Power Macintosh systems, and companies such as Daystar, Pioneer, Power Computing, and Radius also have announced Power Macintosh-compatible systems.

With these successes the alliance ended, leaving IBM to continue building on its CPU architecture and design, which can be seen with the introduction of the powerful copper technology deployed in the S80 and 690 servers.

RS/6000 system bus types

The job of the bus is to provide the highway for information to flow between the RS/6000 system elements and the optional I/O feature cards (for example, SCSI adapters and Ethernet cards) that are plugged into the adapter slots.

PCI Based RS/6000 systems

Peripheral Component Interconnect (PCI) buses are an open industry specification that supports complete processor independence. The PCI bus works across multiple operating system platforms. IBM uses this technology in all of its RS/6000s.

RS/6000s also contain an Industry Standard Architecture (ISA) bus for use with some built-in devices, such as the diskette drive and keyboard.

Some older model PCI systems also contain ISA slots that would accept standard ISA cards. Newer models no longer support this.

The first RS/6000s were based on IBM's Micro Channel® Architecture (MCA). The MCA systems are sometimes referred to as classical systems. These were very popular. MCA machines can be easily recognized by the physical key on the front of the machines. PCI and MCA are basically the same from an administrative viewpoint. There are differences primarily in the startup procedure.

Architecture types

AIX 5L Version 5.1 supports three architecture types (see Table 1-3).

Table 1-3 Architecture types

Architecture	Processor	Description
rs6k	POWER	This is the original or "classic" RS/6000 workstation, based on the microchannel bus.
rspc	POWER	POWER Reference Platform, based on the PCI bus.
chrp	POWER	Common Hardware Reference Platform, based on the PCI bus.

The **bootinfo -p** command returns the system architecture type.

1.3.1 POWER2 Super Chip

The next microprocessor launched by IBM was the POWER2™ Super Chip (P2SC) processor. This microprocessor was first introduced in the RS/6000 Model 595. Currently, the P2SC processors are employed only in the RS/6000 SP Thin4 nodes, where they run at a clock speed of 160 MHz, with a theoretical peak speed of 640 MEGAFLOPS.

The POWER2 Super Chip (P2SC) is a compression of the POWER2 eight-chip architecture into a single chip with increased processor speed and performance. It retains the design of its predecessor, the POWER2. The initial models had clock speeds of 120 MHz and 135 MHz. High-density CMOS-6S technology allows each to incorporate 15,000,000 transistors.

1.3.2 POWER3

POWER3™ was the next microprocessor developed by IBM. The POWER3 microprocessor introduces a generation of 64-bit processors especially designed for high performance and visual computing applications. POWER3 processors are the replacement for the POWER2 and POWER2 Super Chips® (P2SC) in high-end RS/6000 workstations and technical servers.

The POWER3 processor was designed to provide high performance floating point computation. This type of microprocessor is widely used in such areas as the oil and gas industry, reservoir simulation and seismic processing, and weather forecast prediction.

The POWER3 is designed for frequencies of up to 600 MHz when fabricated with advanced semiconductor technologies, such as copper metallurgy and silicon-on-insulator (SOI). In contrast, the P2SC design has reached its peak operating frequency at 160 MHz. The first POWER3 based system, RS/6000 43P 7043 Model 260, runs at 200 MHz.

1.3.3 POWER3 II chip

The POWER3 II is a third generation super scalar design that is used for 64-bit technical and scientific applications. The POWER3 and POWER3 II microprocessors are very similar; the use of chopper and increased number of transistors in POWER 3 II is the main difference. This processor operates between 333 and 400 MHz.

1.3.4 PowerPC

The PowerPC family of processors was started by the alliance between Apple, Motorola, and IBM in 1991. This alliance established a rapidly expanding market for RISC-based hardware and software.

The IBM PowerPC architecture has a whole range of variants, most of them still used in workstation and server products. Both processors have a 32-bit architecture, and both processors give the performance needed to support graphics, computation, and multimedia-intensive applications.

The 604e is a 32-bit implementation of the PowerPC architecture, with clock speeds of 233-375 MHz. PowerPC 750™ is another model of the PowerPC chip. This is a second 32-bit implementation, clocked between 300–466 MHz.

1.3.5 RS64 processor family

The RS64 processor is a second 64-bit implementation, clocked at 262 MHz and 340 MHz. There are four generations of this processor.

The main characteristic of the RS64-II processor is that it will run at 262 MHz, compared with 125 MHz for the previous RS64 processor. This chip also has an 8 MB cache, which is double the previous amount.

In summary, the RS64 Series processors are very robust, delivering real performance on real applications for the next generation of 64-bit RISC commercial and server processors, all while retaining optimum chip size and power. They achieve high performance on real applications because of their low latency design and IBM's superior silicon technology. The RS64 Series can be expected to lead the commercial and server benchmarks for years to come.

Additional information may be obtained from the following Web site:

```
http://www.ibm.com/servers/eserver/pseries/library/wp_systems.html
```

1.3.6 POWER4

The POWER4™ processor was designed to operate at speeds of over 1 GHz and can handle commercial and technical workloads.

Business applications include attributes from both commercial and technical workloads. Binary compatibility with 64-bit PowerPC architecture is maintained. One of the main characteristics is that one single POWER4 processor chip contains two POWER4 processors. The IBM @server pSeries 690 is the first pSeries model that utilizes this microprocessor.

In April 2002, IBM disclosed information about its future server chips. IBM plans to endow its POWER5 and POWER6™ processors with an ability called *Fast Path* to take over tasks that software currently handles more slowly. POWER5 will be able to take over software tasks commonly used in the operating system, such as packaging data to be sent to networks. POWER6 will extend its reach further, taking over tasks now handled by higher-level software, such as IBM or Oracle database software or IBM's WebSphere® e-commerce software.

Additional information may be obtained from the following Web site:

```
http://www.chips.ibm.com
```

1.3.7 POWER5

The primary design objectives of POWER5 technology are:

► Maintain binary and structural compatibility with existing POWER4 systems.
► Enhance and extend SMP scalability.
► Continue superior performance.
► Provide additional server flexibility.
► Deliver power efficient design.
► Enhance reliability, availability, and serviceability.

2

Software packaging

This chapter contains the following topics:

2.1 Overview

In this chapter we discuss how the installables are named in HP-UX and AIX 5L operating systems. We also discuss the naming conventions and the package definitions of HP-UX and AIX 5L.

2.2 Software packaging in HP-UX

HP-UX uses the *Software Distributor* (SD-UX) product bundled with HP-UX for managing software (and patches), both from local and remote sources. The basic SD-UX packaging concepts are fileset, product, bundle, and depot.

The following sections contain high-level overviews of the different definitions. For more details, issue the command **man 4 sd**.

Fileset

A fileset is a collection of files that are contained in a product. Usually, you do not directly install these filesets, as shown in Example 2-1.

Example 2-1 Filesets

```
# swlist -l fileset OnlineDiag | head
# Initializing...
# Contacting target "coffee"...
#
# Target:  coffee:/
#

# OnlineDiag                          B.11.11.13.14  HPUX 11.11 Support
Tools Bundle, Dec 2003
# OnlineDiag.Sup-Tool-Mgr             B.11.11.13.14  Support Tools Manager
for HPUX systems
  OnlineDiag.Sup-Tool-Mgr.RELEASE-NOTES B.11.11.13.14  HPUX Support Tools
Manager Release Notes
  OnlineDiag.Sup-Tool-Mgr.STM-CATALOGS  B.11.11.13.14  HPUX Support Tools
Manager Catalogs
```

Product

A product is a collection of filesets. It is installable in its own right and contains all the information needed to install and configure itself. Refer to Example 2-2 on page 19.

Example 2-2   Collection of filesets

```
# swlist -l product OnlineDiag
# Initializing...
# Contacting target "coffee"...
#
# Target:  coffee:/
#

# OnlineDiag                  B.11.11.13.14  HPUX 11.11 Support Tools Bundle,
Dec 2003
  OnlineDiag.Sup-Tool-Mgr     B.11.11.13.14  Support Tools Manager for HPUX
systems
  OnlineDiag.EMS-KRMonitor    A.11.11.04     EMS Kernel Resource Monitor
  OnlineDiag.EMS-Core         A.04.00.01     EMS Core Product
  OnlineDiag.EMS-Config       A.04.00.01     EMS Config
  OnlineDiag.Contrib-Tools    B.11.11.13.14  Contributed Tools
  OnlineDiag.LIF-LOAD         B.11.11.13.14  HP LIF LOAD Tools
```

Bundle

From the sd (4) man page:

Bundle   A bundle is a way of encapsulating products, subproducts and filesets into a single software object. More than one bundle can contain the same software objects. A bundle can be thought of as a particular "configuration" of software. It is a convenient way to group software objects together for easy selection. Bundle is NOT a super-set of product.

From our point of view, a bundle is a logical grouping of products that you install to receive a certain set of functions. Refer to Example 2-3.

Example 2-3   Bundles

```
# swlist -l bundle OnlineDiag
# Initializing...
# Contacting target "coffee"...
#
# Target:  coffee:/
#

  OnlineDiag   B.11.11.13.14  HPUX 11.11 Support Tools Bundle, Dec 2003
```

Depot

A SD-UX depot is a location where bundles, products, and filesets reside. For example, this could be a tape, a local directory, a CD-ROM, a DVD, or even a directory on a remote machine defined as a depot.

Remote machine depots give SD-UX the ability to pull products (or patches) across the network without administrator intervention (and there is no need for NFS file systems using this form of SD-UX). This means that it is possible to have a central point of distribution for products and patches for multiple systems.

Software specification

The hierarchy of a specific piece of software is in the form:

```
bundle[.product[.subproduct][.fileset]][,version]
product[.subproduct][.fileset][,version]
The version component has the form:
[r= revision][,a= arch][,v= vendor][,c= category]
```

For example, to list the files within the fileset of PERL-RUN in the product of Perl5 in the bundle of Perl run the command shown in Example 2-4.

Example 2-4   Listing the files in the fileset PERL-RUN

```
# swlist perl.Perl5.PERL-RUN|head -15
# Initializing...
# Contacting target "coffee"...
#
# Target:  coffee:/
#

# perl                    B.5.6.1.F      Perl Programming Language
  perl.Perl5.PERL-RUN     B.5.6.1.F      The Perl Programming Language with
Extensions
  /opt/perl
  /opt/perl/bin
  /opt/perl/bin/GET
  /opt/perl/bin/HEAD
  /opt/perl/bin/POST
  /opt/perl/bin/SOAPsh.pl
  /opt/perl/bin/XMLRPCsh.pl
```

Operating environments and HP-UX

When HP-UX introduced HP-UX 11i, they also introduced the concept of *Operating Environments* (OEs). An OE is a configuration of software products and bundles aimed at simplifying installation and setup. These OEs may contain software that may include otherwise locked items (for example, GlancePlus or MirrorDisk-UX).

There are three commercial server OEs, each being a super-set of the other. The major components of each are:

▶ 11i Mission Critical Operating Environment

  – ECM Toolkit
  – MC/ServiceGuard
  – ServiceGuard NFS
  – Workload Manager

▶ 11i Enterprise Operating Environment

  – MirrorDisk/UX
  – Online JFS
  – OV GlancePlus Pak
  – Process Resource Manager
  – EMS HA Monitors

▶ 11i Operating Environment

Refer to 3.13, "Installing and removing additional software" on page 54, for additional information.

For a detailed list of what is in each Operating Environment refer to:

    http://docs.hp.com/en/oshpux11i.html

Software updates

HP-UX regularly releases patch bundles for both the operating system products and HP-UX's supplied application products. For example:

Gold Base Bundle	A stable, tested, and recommended set of patches for the operating system and environment.
Gold Application Bundle	A stable, tested, and recommended set of patches for the applications that were installed from the HP Application CD/DVD.
HWE Bundle	The Hardware Enablement Bundle. Updates and supplies new drivers for different hardware components.
Bundle11i	Critical must-install patches.

The Gold bundles are updated every six months. The HWE Bundle is updated every three months. Bundle11i is updated as needed.

You can also download patches individually directly from the HP-UX support Web site:

```
http://www2.itrc.hp.com/service/patch/mainPage.do
```

2.3 Software packaging in AIX 5L

Similar to HP-UX, AIX 5L also has a specific terminology related to installable software. In this section we describe the different AIX 5L terminology for installable software. When translating to/from HP-UX and AIX 5L terminologies, it might get confusing, as there are some terms used in both that have quite different meanings.

Let us take a look at the packaging terminology. There are four basic package concepts in AIX 5L: fileset, package, LPP, and bundle.

Fileset

A fileset is the smallest individually installable unit. It is a collection of files that provides a specific function. For example, the bos.net.tcp.client is a fileset in the bos.net package.

Fileset naming convention

Filesets follow this standard naming convention:

```
LPP.msg[.lang].package.fileset
```

The LPP is the first part of every fileset name. For example, all filesets within the BOS program product will have *bos* at the beginning of their name.

If a package has only one installable fileset, then the fileset name may be the same as the package name, for example, bos.INed.

The following are the standard fileset suffixes:

.adt	Application Development Toolkit for the Licensed Program Product
.com	Common code between two similar filesets
.compat	Compatibility code that will be removed in a future release of the License Program Product
.data	/usr/share portion of a fileset
.dev	Device support for that Licensed Program Product
.diag	Diagnostics for a fileset
.fnt	Font portion of a fileset

.help[lang]	Translated help files for that Licensed Program Product
.loc	Locale for that Licensed Program Product
.mp	Multi-processor specific code for a fileset
.msg[lang]	Translated messages
.rte	Run time or minimum set
.smit	SMIT tools and dialogs for a fileset
.ucode	Microcode for a fileset
.up	Uniprocessor specific code for a file set

With the message libraries associated with LPPs, the language is also part of the naming convention.

Package

A package contains a group of filesets with a common function. This is a single installable image, for example, bos.net.

Package names

The following are examples of the major packages in the AIX 5L Basic Operating System:

bos.acct	Accounting Services: Contains accounting services that support or enhance the base operating system (BOS).
bos.adt	Base Application Development Toolkit: Contains commands, files, and libraries required to develop software applications.
bos.diag	Hardware Diagnostics: Contains the Diagnostic Controller for the hardware diagnostics package.
bos.docregister	Documentation Registration Tools: Contains the utilities used in the administration of the HTML documentation options and their associated search indexes.
bos.docsearch	Documentation Library Service: Provides functions that allow users to navigate, read, and search HTML documents that are registered with the library service.
bos.dosutil	DOS Utilities: Contains DOS file and disk utilities for handling DOS diskettes.
bos.iconv	AIX 5L Language Converters: Converts data from one code set designation to another code set that might be used to represent data in a given locale.

bos.INed	INed Editor: Contains a full-screen text editor that supports viewing, entering, and revising text at any location in the editor window.
bos.loc	AIX 5L Localization: Contains support for applications to run using the cultural conventions of a specific language and territory. These conventions include date and time formatting, collation order, monetary and numeric formatting, language for messages, and character classification. Where applicable, additional software such as input methods and fonts, which is required to display and process characters of a specific language, is also included.
bos.mh	Mail Handler (MH): Contains commands to create, distribute, receive, view, process, and store mail messages.
bos.net	Base Operating System Network Facilities: Provides network support for the operating system. Includes Transmission Control Protocol/Internet Protocol (TCP/IP), Point-to-Point Protocol (PPP), Network File System (NFS), Cache File System (CacheFS™), Automount File System (AutoFS), Network Information Services (NIS), Network Information Services+ (NIS+), UNIX-to-UNIX Copy (UUCP), and Asynchronous Terminal Emulator (ATE).
bos.perf	Base Performance Tools: Contains two filesets for identifying and diagnosing performance problems.
bos.powermgt	Power Management™ Software: Controls electric power consumption features, such as system standby, device idle, suspend, and hibernation on models that support these features.
bos.rte	Base Operating System RunTime: Contains the set of commands needed to start, install, and run AIX 5L.
bos.sysmgt	System Management Tools and Applications: Contains system management functions related to installation, system backup, error logging, and trace.
bos.terminfo	Base AIX 5L Terminal Function: Contains description files, used by curses libraries, for various terminals.
bos.txt	Text Formatting Services: Contains services for formatting and printing documents.

Licensed Program Product (LPP)

This is a complete software product collection, including all the packages and filesets required. Licensed Program Products are separately orderable products that run on the AIX 5L operating system, for example, DB2®, CICS®, Tivoli® Storage Manager, and so on.

Filesets name have been designed to describe the contents of the fileset. For instance, all filesets within the BOS program product will have *bos* at the beginning of their name.

Bundles

However, it will be a difficult task to figure out which individual fileset you want to install on your machine. So, AIX 5L offers a collection of filesets as a bundle that match a particular purpose. For example, if you are developing applications, the App-Dev bundle would be the logical choice to install.

A bundle is a collection of packages and filesets suited for a particular environment. AIX 5L's bundles are quite comparable to HP-UX's bundles.

The following are the predefined system bundles in AIX 5L Version 5.3:

- ► App-Dev
- ► CDE
- ► GNOME
- ► KDE
- ► Media-Defined
- ► Netscape
- ► Devices
- ► wsm-remote

When you install a bundle, some of the filesets are installed if the prerequisite hardware is available. For example, a graphic adapter is needed to run CDE.

In some cases, bundles are equivalent to product offerings. Often, however, they are a subset of a product offering or a separate customized bundle. The bundles available may vary from configuration to configuration.

The standard bundle definitions that control what selections appear in SMIT or the Web-based System Manager are stored in /usr/sys/inst.data/sys_bundles.

AIX 5L Base Operating System

The AIX 5L Base Operating System licensed program includes the AIX 5L operating system, languages, device drivers, system management tools, utilities, and other filesets as listed.

The AIX 5L Version 5.1 operating system is delivered on multiple CDs. These are:

► AIX 5L Base Operating System (5 CDs)
► Bonus Pack
► Expansion Pack
► AIX 5L Documentation
► AIX 5L Toolbox for Linux Applications

Bonus and expansion packs

The contents of these bonus and expansion packs vary from time to time. The main purpose of these packs is to acquaint users with tools and products that may be valuable in their business environment. For example, the AIX 5L Version 5.1 Expansion and Bonus packs contain tools to build secure Java application Data Encryption Standard (DES) library routines, software security and encryption support, Network Authentication Service, IBM HTTP Server, and so on.

Software updates

As new software is created for AIX 5L, you will want to upgrade your system to maintain the latest features and functionality.

A *maintenance level* (ML) consists of one file set update for each fileset that has changed since the base level of AIX 5L Version 5.1. Each of these fileset updates is cumulative, containing all fixes for that fileset since AIX 5L Version 5.1 was introduced, and supersedes all previous updates for the same file set.

With the `oslevel` command, you can obtain the operating system (OS) level you are running. For example:

```
# oslevel
5.1.0.0
```

The above command outputs indicate that the current maintenance level is Version 5, Release 1, Modification 0, and Fix 0.

The `oslevel -r` command tells you which maintenance level you have:

```
# oslevel -r
5100-02
```

In the above examples, the command output shows that you are at maintenance level 2.

> **Note:** All versions and release levels must be purchased. However, modification and fix-level upgrades are available at no charge.

To learn about version and release upgrades, refer to Chapter 3, "Installing and upgrading tasks" on page 29.

> **Tip:** To perform software and patch installation/updates without needing to manually transfer the packages to each system, you can configure one server as a Network Installation Manager (NIM) Master. You can then define machines as clients of this master. With the appropriate configuration, you can use the NIM master as a single push or pull point for installation of software packages or patches. This eliminates the need to manually move the installation media from machine to machine, either physically or via direct NFS.

Installing and upgrading tasks

This chapter describes how to install, configure, and set up HP-UX 11i and AIX 5L Version 5.x. This chapter covers the following topics:

3.1 Hardware requirements

This section describes the hardware requirements for AIX 5L Version 5.x. and HP-UX 11i.

3.1.1 Supported platforms for HP-UX 11i

For more information about supported platforms, refer to *HP-UX 11i Installation and Updating Guide HP Part Number 5990-7279* from the Web site:

`http://www.docs.hp.com`

Memory requirements
HP-UX 11i requires 1 GB of physical memory and 1 GB swap space.

Disk requirements
For the installation of the HP-UX11i Foundation Operating Environment (FOE), 14 GB are allocated, but only 37 percent of the allocation is used.

3.1.2 Supported platforms for AIX 5L Version 5.x

These are the supported platforms for AIX 5L Version 5.x:

- ▶ IBM Power (IBM @server pSeries and RS/6000)
- ▶ POWER2
- ▶ Personal Computer Power Series® 830 and 850 desktop systems
- ▶ IBM PowerPC systems or POWER3 systems, with the following exceptions:
  - – RS/6000 7016 POWERserver® Model 730
  - – RS/6000 7007 Notebook Workstation Model N40
  - – POWERnetwork Dataserver 7051
  - – RS/6000 7249 Models 851 and 860
  - – RS/6000 7247 Models 821, 822, and 823
- ▶ POWER4
- ▶ POWER5

The 64-bit kernel is available for 64-bit POWER systems. Older 32-bit architecture is supported by the 32-bit kernel. The 64-bit POWER hardware gives you the choice of running 32-bit or 64-bit kernels.

Memory requirements
AIX 5L Version 5.2 and AIX 5L Version 5.3 require 128 MB of memory.

Disk requirements

AIX 5L Version 5.2 and AIX 5L Version 5.3 require 2.2 GB of physical disk space.

3.2 Software terminology in AIX 5L

In this section we describe software terminology that is specific to the AIX 5L environment.

Software terminology shown in Table 3-1 is applicable in this section.

Table 3-1   Software terminology for AIX 5L

Terminology	Description
Apply	When a service update is installed or applied, it enters the applied state and becomes the currently active version of the software. When an update is in the applied state, the previous version of the update is stored in a special save directory. This allows you to restore the previous version, if necessary, without having to reinstall it. Software that has been applied to the system can be either committed or rejected. The `installp -s` command can be used to get a list of applied products and updates that are available to be either committed or rejected.
Base Operating System (BOS)	The base operating system (BOS) is the collection of programs that controls the resources and the operations of the computer system
Boot device	The device that assigns the fixed disk within the root volume group (rootvg) that contains the startup (boot) image.
bosinst.data	The file that controls the actions of the BOS installation program.

Terminology	Description
Clean up	The clean-up procedure instructs the system to attempt to remove software products that were partially installed. The system also attempts to revert to the previous version of the removed product. If the system successfully reverts to the previous version, it becomes the currently active version. If this cannot be done, then the software product is marked as broken. After the clean-up procedure is complete, you can attempt to install the software again.
Commit	When you commit software updates, you are making a commitment to that version of the software product. When you commit a product update, the saved files from all previous versions of the software product are removed from the system, thereby making it impossible to return to a previous version of the software product. Software updates can be committed at the time of installation by using either the Web-based System Manager or SMIT interface (or by using the -ac flags with the `installp` command). Note that committing already applied software does not change the currently active version of the software product. It merely removes saved files for the previous version of the software product. Once you commit a new version of a product update, you must force a reinstall of the base level of the software product and reapply the latest level of updates desired.
Complete overwrite installation	An installation method that completely overwrites an existing version of the Base Operating System that is installed on your system. This procedure might impair recovery of data or destroy all existing data on your hard drives. Be sure to back up your system before doing a complete overwrite installation.

Terminology	Description
Configuration Assistant	A graphical interface application used to perform post-installation system configuration tasks.
Console device	During the installation of the Base Operating System (BOS), the system console is the display device at the system on which you are installing the software.
Fileset update	An individually installable update. Fileset updates either enhance or correct a defect in a previously installed fileset.
Installation Assistant	An ASCII interface application used to perform post-installation system configuration tasks.
Maintenance level update	The service updates that are necessary to upgrade the Base Operating System or an optional software product to the current release level.
Migration installation	An installation method for upgrading AIX Version 3.2 or later to the current release while preserving the existing root volume group. This method preserves the /usr, /tmp, /var, and / (root) file systems, as well as the root volume group, logical volumes, and system configuration files. Migration is the default installation method for any machine that is running AIX Version 3.2 or later.
Optional software products	Software that is not automatically installed on your system when you install the Base Operating System (BOS). Software products include those shipped with the operating system and those purchased separately. The BOS is divided into subsystems that can be individually updated, such as bos.rte.install. Any update that begins with bos.rte updates a BOS subsystem.

Terminology	Description
Preservation installation	An installation method used when a previous version of the Base Operating System is installed on your system and you want to preserve the user data in the root volume group. However, this method overwrites the /usr, /tmp, /var, and / (root) file systems, so any user data in these directories is lost. System configuration must be done after doing a preservation installation.
Reject	To keep portions of applied updates from becoming permanent parts of the product, based on the results of a test period. When you reject an applied service update, the update's files are deleted and the software vital product data (SWVPD) information is changed to indicate that the update is no longer on the system. The previous version of the software, if there is one, is restored and becomes the active version of the software.
Remove	For a software option, the deletion of the option and all of its applied or committed updates from the system. The software vital product data (SWVPD) information is changed to indicate that the option has been removed from the system. Depending on the option, system configuration information is also cleaned up, although this is not always complete. If a previous version, release, or level of the option is on the system, the system does not restore the previous version. Only an option with its updates can be removed. Updates cannot be removed by themselves.
Root volume group (rootvg)	A volume group containing the Base Operating System.

Terminology	Description
Service update	Software that corrects a defect in the BOS or in an optional software product. Service updates are organized by filesets. This type of update always changes part of a fileset.
System Management Interface Tool (SMIT)	A set of menu-driven services that facilitates the performance of system tasks such as software installation and configuration, device configuration and management, problem determination, and storage management. SMIT is provided in both a character-based curses interface and an AIX 5L graphical user interface.
Verify	The verify procedure instructs the system to verify the software you are installing. The system confirms that your software files are the correct length and contain the correct number of digits and characters. If any errors are reported, it might be necessary to install the software product again. The verification process can add a significant amount of time to the installation process.
Web-based System Manager	A graphical user interface (GUI) tool for managing systems. Based on the Object Oriented (OO) model, Web-based System Manager enables users to perform administration tasks by manipulating icons representing objects in the system, as an alternative to learning and remembering complex commands.

3.3 Installation methods

The following section describes the possible installation methods for HP-UX 11i and IBM AIX 5L.

HP-UX 11i

The system administrator can choose between three different ways to install the operating system. Table 3-2 on page 36 describes the different methods.

Table 3-2   HP-UX 11i installation methods

Installation methods	Overall description
Cold-Install from CD	Install directly from the CDs or DVDs. This installation can be default or advanced.
Cold-Install from Golden Image	A golden image is a copy of another operation system, installed and configured. This image is used for installing other servers.
Cold-Install from Network Depot	Depots need to be created containing the operating system and other software bundles. Then install the software from the depot using Ignite-UX.

For more information about installation methods, refer to *HP-UX 11i Installation and Updating Guide HP Part Number 5990-7279,* which can be found on the Web site:

```
http://www.docs.hp.com
```

AIX 5L

The Base Operating System (BOS) installation program first restores the run-time bos image, then installs the appropriate filesets, depending on whether you are installing from a graphical or an ASCII system. The installation program automatically installs required message filesets and devices filesets, according to the language you choose and the hardware configuration of the installed machine.

Table 3-3 gives an overview of the different ways to install AIX 5L.

Table 3-3   AIX 5L installation methods

Installation method	Overall description
Interactive installation	This is the most common way to install AIX 5L, and only the Base Operating System will be installed. Additional software must be installed after the installation. The user can choose between an initial installation that overwrites all previous software or an upgrade installation, which will preserve most configuration settings. CD media is the most common.

Installation method	Overall description
Install from system backup	Create a bootable backup copy or mksysb image of your root volume group. This backup or image is used for installing other servers. It can be used by NIM, tape, or CD and DVD.
Preinstallation option for a new system order	The preinstall option is only valid if accompanied by a hardware order that includes the preinstalled AIX 5L Version 5.x
Network Installation Management (NIM)	Network installations are carried out using the AIX 5L Network Installation Management, which is a system management tool in AIX 5L. This allows the user to manage the installation of the BOS and optional software on one or more machines in a network environment. The NIM environment is made of client and server machines, where it is the server machine that makes the resources available to the other machines; for example, installation has to be initiated from the server to the client. An existing server with AIX 5L installed is required to set up NIM environment. This is a complete unattended installation method.
Alternate Disk Install	More details are in 3.14, "Installing the operating system on another disk" on page 62.

3.4 AIX 5L installation process from product CD-ROM

This section focuses on the installation of AIX 5L on a stand-alone system, that is, a system that can boot and start up by itself. Later we discuss how to perform a NIM installation.

It is beyond the scope of this document to cover, in detail, the installation of the operating system for HP-UX 11i. Refer to *HP-UX 11i Installation and Updating Guide HP Part Number 5990-7279* at the following Web site for more information about how to install the HP-UX 11i operating system:

```
http://www.docs.hp.com
```

Step 1

For step 1:

1. Insert CD 1 into the CD-ROM driver.
2. Power on the peripheral SCSI devices.
3. Power on the system.

Insert the installation media into the drive. If it is an external device, you must power it on before powering on the system; otherwise, the system will not recognize it. It is best to power on all peripheral devices anyway, because during the installation, all recognized devices will be configured.

Power on the system to start the boot sequence. The LEDs will display numbers, indicating that the system components are being tested. Also, if you are using a graphical display, you will see the icons (or words) of the hardware devices appear on the screen. The system is completing a power-on self test (POST).

Once the POST completes, the system will search the boot list for a bootable image. When it finds the bootable image, you will see the installation menu.

Note: The system will attempt to boot from the first entry in the boot list. Pressing the F5 key (or the 5 key on newer models) during boot will invoke the service boot list, which includes the CD-ROM. It may take some time before the system reaches the installation menu.

Step 2: Console and language definition

Each native display and all the ASCII terminals attached to the built-in serial ports will display the console message. Whichever display you respond to will become the console during the installation. The console display can be changed at a later time, if required.

Graphic displays will ask you to press the F1 key and then the Enter key to set the system console (see Example 3-1). If you are using an ASCII terminal as the system console, you will need to press another key, such as 2, which indicates a specific terminal, and then press Enter.

Upon installation, the AIX 5L kernel displays the system console define message to all the console and attached native serial ports. If you are using an ASCII terminal as your console, make sure that it powered on and correctly configured before you begin installation. If your terminal was not correctly configured, you can still type (for example) 2 and press Enter to continue, once you have corrected the problem.

Example 3-1   Console definition

```
****** Please define the System Console ******
```

```
Type F1 key and press Enter
to use this display as the System Console.
```

The screen shown in Example 3-1 on page 38 will be displayed in seven different languages, and will be written to all native (graphics) displays or the built-in serial ports.

The terminal characteristics for serial ports should be same as the default, in order to display this message:

```
Terminal type=dumb
Speed=9600
Parity=none
Bits per character=8
Stop bits=1
Line Control=IPRTS
Operation mode=echo
Turnaround character=CR
```

You will also be prompted to select the language to be used for the messages and the status information during the installation process. This language needs to be the same as the language intended for the primary environment of the system.

Select the language that is to be used during the installation process. After the definition of the console and the language, the Welcome to the Base Operating System Installation and Maintenance menu will be displayed.

Step 3: Installation and Maintenance menu

Example 3-2 shows the Installation and Maintenance menu.

Example 3-2   Installation and Maintenance menu

```
              Welcome to Base Operating System
                Installation and Maintenance


Type the number of your choice and press Enter. Choice  indicated by >>>

          >>> 1 Start Install now with Default Setting
              2 Change/Show Installation Setting and Install
              3 Start Maintenance Mode for System Recovery


88 Help ?
99 Previous Menu
>>>Choice [1]:2
```

The first option will start the installation using the default settings. If, however, you wish to view and alter the current settings, then you need to select the second option, which is discussed later in this chapter.

The third option allows for maintenance tasks, such as going into the maintenance shell, copying the system dump, carrying out an image backup, and so on.

For an initial installation, we recommend that you choose option 2 to verify that the settings are what you want.

Installation Settings menu

Example 3-3 shows the Installation Settings menu.

Example 3-3   Installation Settings menu

```
                    Installation Settings


Either type 0 or press Enter to install current settings, or type the number of
the settings you want to change and press Enter.

    1 System Settings:
        Method of installation..........New and Complete Overwrite
        Disk where you want to Install.......hdisk0

    2 Primary Language Environment Settings (AFTER) Install:
        Cultural Convention...................C (POSIX)
        Language..............................C (POSIX)
        Keyboard..............................C (POSIX)
        Keyboard Type........................Default

    3 Advanced Options

    0 Install with the settings listed above

    88 Help ?
    99 Previous Menu

>>>Choice[1]:
```

3.5 Option 1 of the Installation and Maintenance menu

When you select option 1 to change the method of installation, a sub menu will be displayed, the contents of which depends on the current state of the machine. Example 3-4 on page 41 shows this menu.

Example 3-4   Change Method of Installation menu

```
                    Change Method of Installation

              Type the number of your choice and press Enter.

1 New and Complete Overwrite
  Overwrites EVERYTHING on the disk selected for installation.
  Warning: Only use this method if the disk is totally empty or there is
  nothing on the disk you want to preserve.

2 Preservation Install
  Preserves SOME of the existing data on the disk selected for installation.
  Warning: This method overwrites the usr (/usr), variable (/var), temporary
  (/tmp), and root (/) file systems. Other product (application) files and
  configuration data will be destroyed.

3 Migration Install
  Upgrades the Base Operating System to current release. Other product
  (application) files and configuration data will be spared.

  88 Help ?
  99 Previous Menu

>>>Choice [2]:1
```

New and complete overwrite installation

The new and complete overwrite installation overwrites all data on the selected destination disk. The only times to use the new and complete overwrite installation method are:

► If you have a new machine. In this case, the hard disk or disks on which you are installing the BOS are empty.

► If your root volume group has become corrupted and you do not have a backup to restore it. This can be indicated by serious ODM problems and hangs for **lslpp** and **oslevel** commands. The only choice would then be to install onto a hard disk that contains an existing root volume group that you wish to completely overwrite.

► You want to reassign your hard disks to make rootvg smaller.

After the installation is complete, you will have to configure your system using the Configuration Assistant application, SMIT, or the command line.

Migration installation

Use the migration installation method to upgrade AIX 5L to a different version or release while preserving the existing root volume group.

The following describes some traits of a migration installation:

▶ During a migration installation, the installation process determines which optional software products must be installed on AIX 5L. Previous versions of AIX 5L software that exist on the system are replaced by the new software in AIX 5L.

▶ This method preserves all file systems except /tmp, as well as the root volume group, logical volumes, and system configuration files. In most cases, user configuration files from the previous version of a product are saved.

▶ Non-software products remain on the system.

▶ When migrating from Version 3.2, all files in /usr/lib/drivers, /usr/lib/microcode, /usr/lib/methods, and /dev are removed from the system, so software support for non-IBM device drivers must be reinstalled.

Preservation installation

Use the preservation installation method when a version of BOS is installed on your system and you want to preserve user data in the root volume group. The following describes some traits of a preservation installation:

▶ The /etc/preserve.list file contains a list of system files to be copied and saved during a preservation BOS installation. The /etc/filesystems file is listed by default. Add the full path names of any additional files that you want to save during the preservation installation to the /etc/preserve.list file. You must create the /etc/preserve.list file on an AIX Version 3.1 machine. On an AIX Version 4.1 or later system, this file already exists on your system and can be directly edited.

▶ Ensure that you have sufficient disk space in the /tmp file system to store the files listed in the /etc/preserve.list file.

▶ This method overwrites the /usr, /tmp, /var, and / (root) file systems by default, so any user data in these directories is lost. These file systems are removed and recreated, so any other LPPs or filesets that you installed on the system will also be lost. Think of a preservation install as an overwrite installation for these file systems. System configuration must be done after doing a preservation installation.

3.5.1 Installation disks

This section describes how to set up the target disks. Example 3-5 on page 43 shows the installation disks menu.

Example 3-5   Installation disks

```
              Change Disks Where You Want to Install

    Type one or more numbers for the disk(s) to be used for installation
    and press Enter. To cancel a choice, type the corresponding number and
    press Enter. At least one bootable disk must be selected. The current
    choice is indicated by >>>.

                                    Size      VG
            Name location Code      (MB)     Status       Bootable
    >>> 1 hdisk0 04-C0-00-4,0       2063     rootvg       yes
        2 hdisk1 04-C0-00-5,0       2063     rootvg       no

        >>>0 Continue with choices indicated above
        66 Disks not known to Base Operating System Installation
        77 Display More Disk Information
        88 Help?
        99 Previous Menu

>>>
Choice[0]:
```

The device options are:
► Default disks (previous location)
► Available disk
► Disks not known to BOS

Having selected the type of installation, you must then select the disks that are to be used for the installation. A list of all the available disks will be displayed, similar to the one shown.

This screen also gives you the option to install to an unsupported disk by adding the code for the device first.

When you have finished selecting the disks, type 0 in the Choice field and press Enter (or just press Enter if the default selection is already 0, as shown in Example 3-5).

3.6 Option 2 of the Installation and Maintenance menu

Example 3-6 on page 44 shows how the language selection screen looks.

Example 3-6   Primary language environment

```
Type the number for the Cultural Convention (such as date, time, and money),
Language and Keyboard for this system and press Enter, or type 75 and press
Enter to create your own combination.

        Cultural Convention      Language                 Keyboard

>> 1.C (POSIX)                   C (POSIX)                C (POSIX)
   2.Albanian                    English (United States)  Albanian
   3.Arabic                      Arabic (Bahrain)         Arabic (Bahrain)

            ... several screens later ...

106. Create your own combination of Cultural Convention, Language and
     Keyboards.

     88 Help?
     99 Previous menu

     Choice[1]:
```

At this point in the installation process, you can change the language and cultural convention that will be used on the system after installation. This screen may actually display a number of language options, such as French, German, Italian, Byelorussian, Ukrainian, and so forth.

You can create your own combination of cultural conventions, language, and keyboard, as you can see in Example 3-6.

Cultural convention determines the way numeric, monetary, and date and time characteristics are displayed.

It is recommended that if you are going to change the language, change it at this point rather than after the installation is complete. Whatever language is specified at this point is pulled off the installation media.

The Language field determines the language used to display text and system messages.

3.7 Option 3 of the Installation and Maintenance menu

The Advanced Options menu, shown in Example 3-7 on page 45, will be slightly different if you are installing on a 32-bit system. You will not have the option to choose the 64-bit kernel and JFS2 support.

Example 3-7   Advanced Options menu

```
                      Advanced Options

Either type 0 and press Enter to install with current settings, or type the
number of the setting you want to change and press Enter.

1 Desktop..........................................CDE
2 Install Trusted Computing Base......................No
3 Install 64-bit Kernel and JFS2 Support.............. No

>>> 0 Install with the current settings listed above.

88 Help ?
99 Previous Menu
>>> Choice [0]: _
```

For an ASCII console or a system with a graphical console where the desktop selected is NONE, a minimal configuration is installed, which includes X11, Java, Perl, SMIT, and the Web-based System Manager.

For a system with a graphical console, if you choose CDE, GNOME, or KDE, the desktop and documentation service libraries are also installed. This is considered a default installation configuration. If you choose GNOME or KDE, the interface prompts you for the Toolbox for Linux Applications CD. If this CD is not available, you can type q to continue the installation without it.

The default installation configuration may prompt for additional CD volumes during the BOS installation. When prompted, if you decide not to continue with additional volumes or if a volume is not available, you can type q and press Enter to continue the installation process. The system will have enough of the BOS loaded to be usable.

Install Trusted Computing Base (TCB)

When you install the Trusted Computing Base, the trusted path, the trusted shell, and system integrity checking are installed. The trusted path protects your system in case a program is masquerading as the program you want to use. The trusted path tries to ensure that the programs you run are trusted programs. If you want to install the TCB, you must indicate Yes now. The TCB cannot be installed later.

Install 64-bit kernel and JFS2 support

If you have a 64-bit system and select Yes for this option, the 64-bit kernel is linked so that it becomes the running kernel on the system after the installation is complete. If you choose No, the 64-bit kernel is still installed on the system, but the running kernel after installation is either the up or mp kernel, depending on the system. To toggle the choice between no (the default) and yes, type 3 and press Enter.

If you choose Yes and are installing with the New and Complete Overwrite method, the file systems are created with JFS2 (Journaled File System 2), instead of JFS. will discuss JFS2 in "JFS2 rootvg support for 64-bit systems" on page 187.

If you want the 64-bit kernel to be the running kernel, but do not want JFS2 file systems, then select No. This menu will not appear in 32-bit systems.

3.8 Begin installation

A number of tasks are performed to complete the installation, including creating a new boot logical volume and customizing the locale and console information into the newly installed operating system. While the BOS is installing, the status indicator screen is displayed, as in Example 3-8. The screen reports what percentage of the tasks are complete. Note that the percentage indicator and the elapsed time are not linear, that is, if it reports that 50 percent has completed in four minutes, this does not indicate that the total installation time will be eight minutes.

During the installation phase, only the software for the devices that are connected and powered on will be installed. All other device software will be installed on demand.

Example 3-8   Begin installation

```
                    Installing Base Operating System

If you need the system key to select SERVICE mode, turn the system key to the
NORMAIL position anytime before installation ends

    Please wait......

          Approximate                     Elapsed Time
        % tasks completed                 (in minutes)


              16                               1
```

The installation media contains information stored on it to determine the sizes that the standard AIX 5L file systems will have. These will be set large enough for the installation to succeed but will not leave much free space after installation. You can dynamically increase the size of any of the file systems once AIX 5L has been installed. If you are installing from a system image backup tape, the file systems created will be the same sizes and names as those on the system when the tape was created.

The files are restored from the media and then verified. This will take some time but can be left unattended. After the BOS has installed, the appropriate locale optional program will also be installed. At any stage before the installation process completes, if your system has a system key, turn it to the Normal position (only on older microchannel machines).

Once the installation has completed, the system will automatically reboot from the newly installed operating system on disk.

3.9 Installation flow chart

Figure 3-1 on page 48 gives an overview over the installation process.

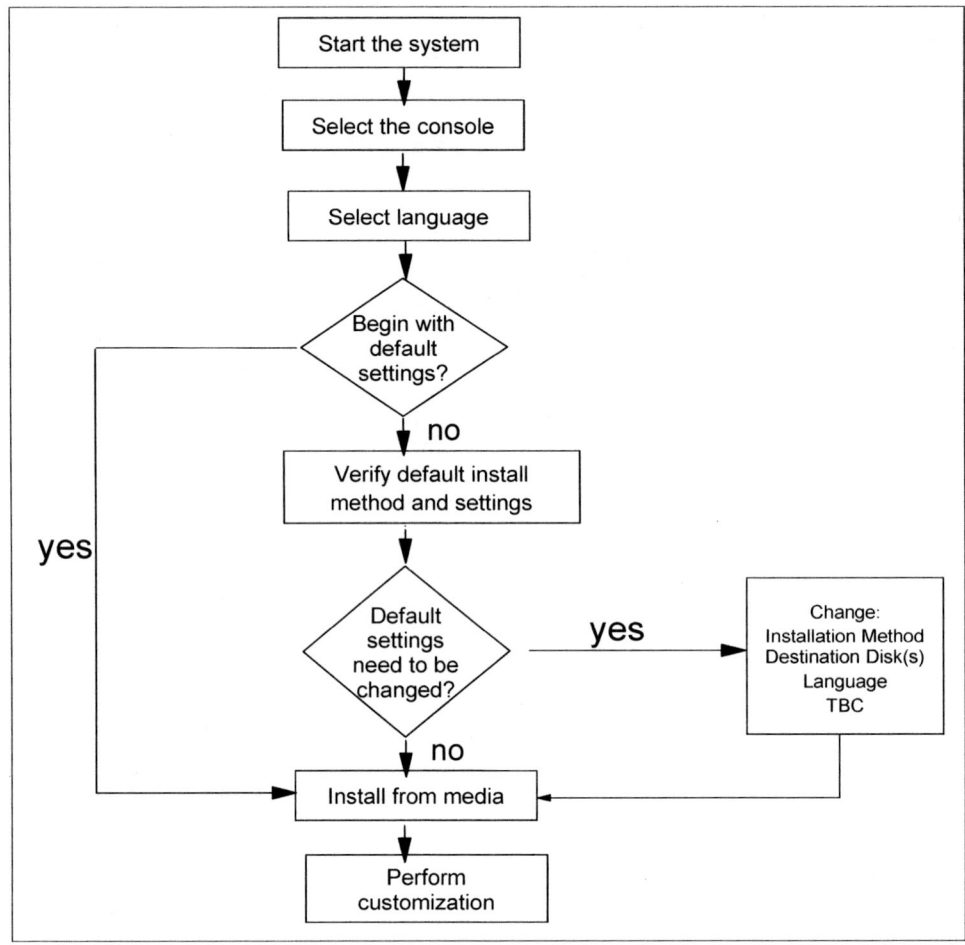

Figure 3-1   Installation flow chart

3.10 Configuration Assistant menu

After installing AIX 5L, you will see the screen requesting that a user accepts AIX 5L licensing to continue. Once you accept it, you will see the Configuration Assistant menu if your console is a graphical console, as shown in Figure 3-2 on page 49.

At this time, the operating system will run with the default setting: one user (root), the date and time set for where the system was manufactured, and other very general settings. You will probably want to change some or all of these settings. Note that you do not have to set all of these settings. You can change any of these settings once you log in after finishing this step.

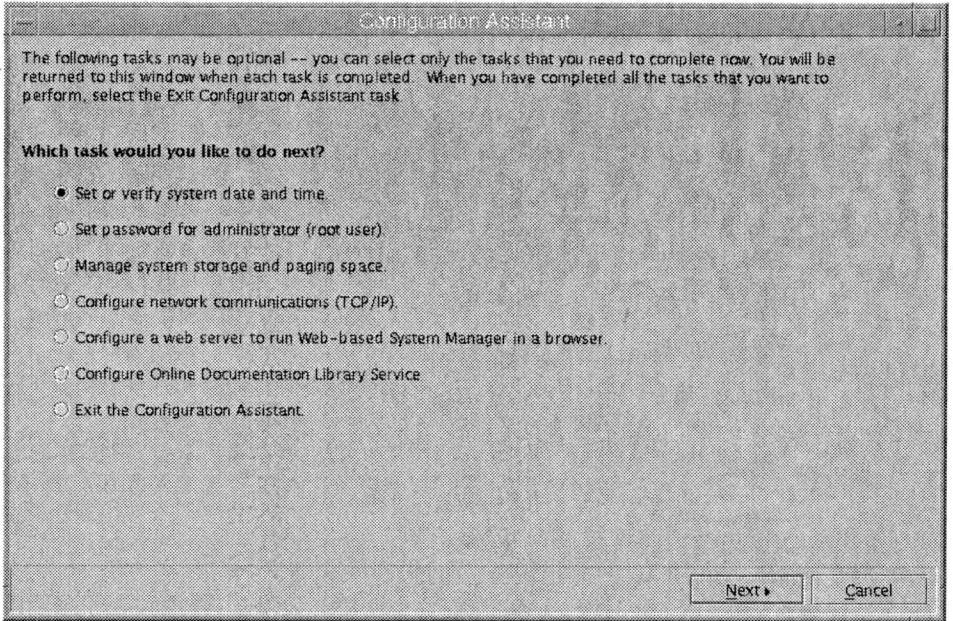

Figure 3-2   Configuration Assistant menu

If using a graphic terminal for the installation, the newly installed BOS reboots and starts the Configuration Assistant, which guides you through the customization tasks. When you use the Configuration Assistant immediately after BOS installation, only the tasks that apply to your type of installation display. If an ASCII terminal was used for the installation, an ASCII-based Installation Assistant is displayed instead. Both the graphics-based Configuration Assistant and the ASCII-based Installation Assistant provide comparable support.

When you have completed your work using the Configuration Assistant/Installation Assistant, you can indicate that you are done working with the program. This will prevent this program from being displayed the next time the root user logs in.

The Configuration Assistant/Installation Assistant provide step-by-step instructions for completing each customization task. Examples of tasks that can be performed are setting the system date and time, setting root's password, and configuring the network.

Complete the tasks in the order that the Configuration Assistant/Installation Assistant lists them. It is helpful to complete all customization tasks before you use your system. After you exit the Configuration Assistant/Installation Assistant, you can log in.

You must have root user authority to use the Configuration Assistant/Installation Assistant. From a graphics terminal, type `install_assist` to access the Configuration Assistant. From AIX 5L, the command `configassist` can also be used to access the Configuration Assistant. From an ASCII terminal, use the `install_assist` command to access the Installation Assistant.

This concludes the installation of AIX 5L.

3.11 Verifying correct installation

Once the installation is complete, the system administrator can verify the installation by using the `lppchk` command. This is similar to the `swverify` command in HP-UX 11i. The `lppchk` command verifies that files for an installable software product (fileset) match the Software Vital Product Data (SWVPD) database information for file sizes, checksum values, or symbolic links. A fileset is the smallest separately installable option of a software package.

To verify that all filesets have all the required requisites and are completely installed, enter the following command:

```
# lppchk -v
```

The `lppchk` command returns a return code of zero if no errors were found. Any other return value indicates an error was found.

For more information, see the `lppchk` manual pages.

3.12 Maintenance updates and patching

This section describes maintenance and patching procedures for HP-UX 11i and AIX 5L.

HP-UX 11i

HP-UX has two main options for patching updates:

Standard HP-UX Patch Bundles   Two patches packages are available, Quality Pack (QPK) patch bundle and Hardware Enablement (HWE) bundle. The first package has all stable defect-fix patches for core HP-UX, graphics, and networking drivers. The second package is required for new systems and add-on hardware.

Individual Patches   This option is used when you occasionally need to install one individual patch.

In order to install a Maintenance Update (MU), the HP-UX 11i administrator has to log into the IT Resource Center (ITRC) Web site:

    http://www.itrc.hp.com

After the HP-UX administrator has downloaded the patches, he can install using the command `swinstall`.

For more information about patch management, refer to *Patch Management User Guide* HP Part Number 5991-0686 at the following Web site:

    http://www.docs.hp.com

AIX 5L

As new software is created for AIX 5L, you want to upgrade your system to maintain the latest features and functionality.

The numerical information that shows what level of software you currently have installed is broken into four parts: Version, release, modification, and fix. You can see this information using the `oslevel` command. For example, 5. 3. 0. 0 means Version 5, Release 3, Modification 0, Fix 0.

> **Note:** Version and release upgrades must be purchased. Modification and fix-level upgrades are available at no charge.

Maintenance levels

A maintenance level (ML) consists of one fileset update for each fileset that has changed since the base level of AIX 5L Version 5.x. Each of these fileset updates is cumulative, containing all the fixes for that fileset since AIX 5L Version 5.x was introduced, and supersedes all previous updates for the same fileset.

You can determine which maintenance level is installed using the `oslevel -r` command. At the time of writing, the current maintenance level for AIX 5L Version 5.3 is 5300-01.

Recommended maintenance

A recommended maintenance level is a set of fileset updates that apply to the last maintenance level. Recommended maintenance packages are made up of field-tested fileset updates, and provide a mechanism for delivering preventive maintenance packages between full maintenance levels.

3.12.1 Obtaining maintenance levels

The easiest way to obtain maintenance level and fix packages is to log into one of the fixdist servers; however, this method is only supported in AIX Version 4.3.3.

For AIX 5L, you must download fixes from the following IBM Web site:

```
http://techsupport.services.ibm.com/server/support?view=pSeries
```

3.12.2 Installing maintenance levels and fixes

There are two ways to install ML and fixes. The easiest way to install them is to use the System Management Interface Tool (SMIT).

Procedure

To install the maintenance levels and fixes, use the following procedure:

1. Download the fix from the IBM Web site.

2. Uncompress and untar the software achieve.

3. Type `smitty update_all`.

4. From here, follow the instructions on the screen to install the fix (see Example 3-9).

Example 3-9   update_all screen shot

```
           Update Installed Software to Latest Level (Update All)

Type or select a value for the entry field.
Press Enter AFTER making all desired changes.

                                                      [Entry Fields]
* INPUT device / directory for software        []                      +


F1=Help              F2=Refresh           F3=Cancel          F4=List
F5=Reset             F6=Command           F7=Edit            F8=Image
F9=Shell             F10=Exit             Enter=Do
```

A second option is to use the **instfix** command. The **instfix** command allows you to install a fix or set of fixes without knowing any information other than the Authorized Program Analysis Report (APAR) number or other unique keywords that identify the fix.

Any fix can have a single fileset or multiple filesets that comprise that fix. Fix information is organized in the Table of Contents (TOC) on the installation media. After a fix is installed, fix information is kept on the system in a fix database.

The **instfix** command can also be used to determine if a fix is installed on your system.

To install a patch with the **instfix** command:

1. Download the fix from the IBM Web site.
2. Uncompress and untar the software archive.

From the current directory, type the following command:

```
# instfix -T -d . | instfix -d . -f -
```

If you want to install only a specific fix, type the following command:

```
# instfix -k <Fileset> -d .
```

3.12.3 Removing a fix

The **swremove** command is used to remove patches installed on a HP-UX 11i system. This process is known as patch rollback. But this procedure only is possible if certain files were saved as part of the patch installation process. During installation, the HP-UX 11i saves all patches that are replaced by a new patch. These saved patches are rollback files. For example, the following removes the patch PHCO_29566 from a HP-UX 11i.

```
# swremove PHCO_29566
```

The option -p also can be used to preview it.

For more information, see the swremove (1M) man page.

On AIX 5L, you can either use the **installp -r** command or use the **smitty reject** fast path (see Example 3-10 on page 54).

When you reject an applied service update, the update files are removed from the system and the previous version of the software is restored. Only service updates in the applied state can be rejected.

To reject a service update using SMIT, type the **smitty reject** fast path on the command line.

Example 3-10   Reject Applied Software screen

```
            Reject Applied Software Updates (Use Previous Version)

Type or select values in entry fields.
Press Enter AFTER making all desired changes.

                                                      [Entry Fields]
* SOFTWARE name                                       []                    +
  PREVIEW only? (reject operation will NOT occur)     no                    +
  REJECT dependent software?                          no                    +
  EXTEND file systems if space needed?                yes                   +
  DETAILED output?                                    no                    +


F1=Help          F2=Refresh         F3=Cancel          F4=List
F5=Reset         F6=Command         F7=Edit            F8=Image
F9=Shell         F10=Exit           Enter=Do
```

In the input field, specify the package, for example, IY19375, and press Enter. This will bring up another window where you can control the deletion process.

You can also use the **installp -r** command to remove a fix, but this is a complex command, and if you are not familiar with AIX 5L, it is not recommended.

3.13 Installing and removing additional software

This section covers the process of installing and maintaining optional software products and updates.

3.13.1 Installing software under HP-UX 11i

Software Distributor (SD-UX) is used to manage software in the HP-UX. This software is included with the HP-UX Operating System. The HP-UX has one daemon responsible by this management; the daemon is called swagentd.

The command used to install software and patches is **swinstall**. This command can be used with the GUI interface or command line.

Example 3-11 shows the **swinstall** command from the command line.

Example 3-11   swinstall command

```
#swinstall -s /var/opt/mx/depot11 AgentConfig

=======  06/24/05 10:39:01 CDT  BEGIN swinstall SESSION
```

```
                    (non-interactive) (jobid=brazil-0018)

          * Session started for user "root@brazil".
          * Beginning Selection
          * Target connection succeeded for "brazil:/".
          * Source connection succeeded for "brazil:/var/opt/mx/depot11".
          * Source:              /var/opt/mx/depot11
          * Targets:             brazil:/
          * Software selections:
              AgentConfig.SD-CONFIG,a=HP-UX_B.11.00_32/64,v=HP
          * Selection succeeded.

          * Beginning Analysis and Execution
          * Session selections have been saved in the file
            "/.sw/sessions/swinstall.last".
          * The analysis phase succeeded for "brazil:/".
          * The execution phase succeeded for "brazil:/".
          * Analysis and Execution succeeded.

NOTE:     More information may be found in the agent logfile using the
          command "swjob -a log brazil-0018 @ brazil:/".

=======   06/24/05 10:39:39 CDT   END swinstall SESSION (non-interactive)
          (jobid=brazil-0018)
```

The option -s is the path of the depot, and the last parameter the software name. To use the GUI interface, the option -i is used.

```
#swinstall -i -s /var/opt/mx/depot11 AgentConfig
```

For more information go to 2.2, "Software packaging in HP-UX" on page 18, and the swinstall (1M) man page.

3.13.2 Removing software under HP-UX 11i

To delete software that has been installed on your system, the command **swremove** is used. This command is the same as that used to remove patches, and also can be used with the GUI interface and command line.

Example 3-12 shows the **swremove** command from the command line.

Example 3-12   swremove command

```
# swremove  AgentConfig

=======   06/24/05 11:37:01 CDT   BEGIN swremove SESSION
          (non-interactive) (jobid=brazil-0026)
```

```
* Session started for user "root@brazil".
* Beginning Selection
* Target connection succeeded for "brazil:/".
* Software selections:
    AgentConfig.SD-CONFIG,l=/,a=HP-UX_B.11.00_32/64,v=HP
* Selection succeeded.
* Beginning Analysis
* Session selections have been saved in the file
  "/.sw/sessions/swremove.last".
* The analysis phase succeeded for "brazil:/".
* Analysis succeeded.
* Beginning Execution
* The execution phase succeeded for "brazil:/".
* Execution succeeded.

NOTE:    More information may be found in the agent logfile using the
         command "swjob -a log brazil-0026 @ brazil:/".

=======  06/24/05 11:37:13 CDT   END swremove SESSION (non-interactive)
         (jobid=brazil-0026)
```

To use the GUI interface, option -i is used, and option -p is used to preview.

For more information go to 2.2, "Software packaging in HP-UX" on page 18, or the **swremove** (1M) man page.

3.13.3 Software states under AIX 5L

In an AIX 5L environment, it is important to know about the different software states.

Applied state

When a service update is installed or applied, it enters the applied state and becomes the currently active version of the software. When an update is in the applied state, the previous version of the update is stored in a special save directory. The applied state gives you the opportunity to test the newer software before committing to its use. If it works as expected, then you can commit the software that will remove the old version from the disk.

Commit state

When you commit a product update, the saved files from all previous versions of the software product are removed from the system, thereby making it impossible to return to a previous version of the software product. This means there is only one level of that software product installed on your system.

With committed (or applied) software products, you can also remove them. This will cause the product's files to be deleted from the system. Requisite software (software dependent on this product) will also be removed unless it is required by some other software product on your system. If you want to use the software again, you would need to reinstall it.

3.13.4 Installing software under AIX 5L

The following section describes how we install additional software in the AIX 5L environment.

Use the `smitty install_update` fast path to access this menu. Example 3-13 shows the software installation screen.

Example 3-13   Install and Update Software menu

```
                    Install and Update Software

Move cursor to desired item and press Enter.

  Install Software
  Update Installed Software to Latest Level (Update All)
  Install Software Bundle
  Update Software by Fix (APAR)
  Install and Update from ALL Available Software


F1=Help              F2=Refresh           F3=Cancel            F8=Image
F9=Shell             F10=Exit             Enter=Do
```

Install software

This option enables you to install all the latest software or selectively install some or all of the individual software products that exist on the installation media (or directory). This menu also can be used if you are reinstalling a currently installed software product. If a product is reinstalled at the same level or at an earlier level, only the base product (no updates) will be installed. This is most commonly used to install optional software not currently installed on you system.

Update Installed Software to Latest Level

This option enables you to update all currently installed filesets to the latest level available on the installation media. Only the existing installed products are updated; no new optional software will be installed. This is the most commonly used method to install a maintenance level update.

Install Software Bundle

This option installs and updates software using a bundle as a template. A bundle is a list of software products that are suited for a particular use.

For example, the App-Dev bundle is a list of software products that an application developer probably would want to install. The actual software is not contained in the bundle; you still have to select the input device where the installation medium resides.

Update Software by Fix (APAR)

This enables you to install fileset updates that are grouped by some relationship and identified by a unique keyword, such as an APAR number. An APAR number is used to identify reported problems caused by a suspected defect in a program. A fix to an APAR can be made up of one or more fileset updates.

This menu option allows you to selectively install fixes identified by keyword. After a fix is installed, fix information is kept on the system in a fix database.

A fix to an APAR can be made up of one or more fileset updates, and can be downloaded from the following IBM Web site:

http://www.ibm.com/servers/eserver/support/unixservers/aixfixes.html

Install and Update from ALL Available Software

This enables you to install or update software from all software available on the installation media. This menu can be used when none of the other menus, which limit the available software in some way, fit your needs. In general, the software list from this menu will be longer than on the menus that are tailored to a specific type of installation.

After selecting Install Software, the screen shown in Example 3-14 appears.

Example 3-14   Install software

```
                       Install Software


Type or select values in entry fields.
Press Enter AFTER making all desired changes.

                                               [Entry Fields]
* INPUT device / directory for software        /dev/cd0
* SOFTWARE to install                          [_all_latest]          +
  PREVIEW only? (install operation will NOT occur)   no                +
  COMMIT software updates?                     yes                     +
  SAVE replaced files?                         no                      +
  AUTOMATICALLY install requisite software?    yes                     +
  EXTEND file systems if space needed?         yes                     +
```

```
OVERWRITE same or newer versions?                      no               +
VERIFY install and check file sizes?                   no               +
Include corresponding LANGUAGE filesets?               yes              +
DETAILED output?                                       no               +
Process multiple volumes?                              yes              +
ACCEPT new license agreements?                         no               +
Preview new LICENSE agreements?                        no               +


F1=Help            F2=Refresh         F3=Cancel          F4=List
F5=Reset           F6=Command         F7=Edit            F8=Image
F9=Shell           F10=Exit           Enter=Do
```

You can specify the software to install either by choosing the default setting (_all_latest) or by selecting from a list. Press F4 to access the list, provided the CD-ROM is inserted in the CD drive. It is also possible to install software from disk.

The Preview option indicates whether you want to preview the installation of the selected software products and updates without actually performing software installation. A preview identifies requirements for the software installation to be successful.

Committing software has two effects: It frees up disk space that was used to store older versions of that software, and it eliminates the possibility of being able to reject the update and go back to the previous version.

Selecting No instructs the system not to commit the software updates you are installing. The software you are installing will be applied. When software is applied to the system, it becomes the active version of the software. If it is replacing a previous version of the software, the previous version is saved in a special directory on the disk. The previous version can be retrieved, if necessary, by rejecting the current version. Once you are satisfied with the updates, you should commit them to free up disk space used by the saved files. If you select No, the you must select SAVE replaced files.

3.13.5 Listing installed software

The following section describes how to list installed software in HP-UX 11i and AIX 5L.

HP-UX 11i

HP-UX 11i has different definitions for software: Product, bundle, fileset, and depot. For more information see 2.2, "Software packaging in HP-UX" on page 18.

You can list the installed software products by using the **swlist** command with the option -l product. The options bundle, fileset, and depot can also be used with this command. For example:

```
# swlist -l product
```

For more information about the **swlist** command, see the swlist (1M) man page.

AIX 5L

The easiest way to list already installed software is to use the **smitty list_installed** fast path. Example 3-15 shows what the resulting menu.

Example 3-15   List Installed Software and Related Information menu

```
          List Installed Software and Related Information

Move cursor to desired item and press Enter.

   List Installed Software
   List Applied but Not Committed Software Updates
   Show Software Installation History
   Show Fix (APAR) Installation Status
   List Fileset Requisites
   List Fileset Dependents
   List Files Included in a Fileset
   List Fileset Containing File
   Show Installed License Agreements


F1=Help              F2=Refresh          F3=Cancel         F8=Image
F9=Shell             F10=Exit            Enter=Do
```

This menu provides information about the software and fixes installed on a system. Instead of using the **smitty list_installed** fast path, you can also use the **lslpp** command.

The **lslpp** command displays information about installed filesets or fileset updates. The FilesetName parameter is the name of a software product. The FixID (also known as PTF or program temporary fix ID) parameter specifies the identifier of an update to a formatted fileset. For example:

► To display all files in the inventory database, which includes **vmstat**, type the following command:

```
# lslpp -w "*vmstat*"
```

► To list the installation state for the most recent level of installed filesets for all of the bos.rte filesets, type the following command:

```
# lslpp -l "bos.rte.*"
```

▶ To display the names of the files added to the system during installation of the bos.perf.perfstat fileset, type the following command:

```
# lslpp -f "*perf*"
```

Important command options include:

-l	Displays the name, level, state, and description of the fileset
-h	Displays the installation and update history for the fileset
-p	Displays requisite information for the fileset
-d	Displays dependent information for the fileset
-f	Displays the names of the files added to the system during installation of the fileset
-w	Lists the fileset that owns a file

3.13.6 Software maintenance

The following sections describe software maintenance procedures for HP-UX 11i and AIX 5L.

HP-UX 11i

For software maintenance in the HP-UX 11i operating environment, you can use the following commands: `swinstall`, `swcopy`, `swremove`, `swlist`, `swreg`, `swmodify`, `swpackage`, `swverify`, and `swconfig`. SAM can also be used.

AIX 5L

Use the `smitty maintain_software` fast path to access the Software Maintenance and Utilities menu, as shown in Example 3-16.

Example 3-16   Software Maintenance and Utilities menu

```
                   Software Maintenance and Utilities

Move cursor to desired item and press Enter.

  Commit Applied Software Updates (Remove Saved Files)
  Reject Applied Software Updates (Use Previous Version)
  Remove Installed Software

  Copy Software to Hard Disk for Future Installation

  Check Software File Sizes After Installation
  Verify Software Installation and Requisites
```

F1=Help	F2=Refresh	F3=Cancel	F8=Image
F9=Shell	F10=Exit	Enter=Do	

Software maintenance is important in AIX 5L because it allows you to delete unnecessary software and thus preserve disk space. From here you can reject, commit, and remove software.

You can copy filesets from the installation media to the hard drive without actually performing an installation. This allows you to install it later without needing the original installation media. The default directory for doing this is /usr/sys/inst.images.

3.14 Installing the operating system on another disk

Only AIX 5L Version 5.x has the ability to install a complete new operating system on another disk or part of a disk while the production environment is up and running. The result is a significant reduction in downtime. It also allows large facilities to better manage an upgrade because systems can be installed over a longer period of time. While the systems are still running at the previous version, the switch to the newer version can happen at the same time.

This concept is called *alternate disk installation*.

3.14.1 Benefits of alternate disk installation

If you already have an AIX 5L version installed, you can choose an alternate disk installation to transition your site through the upgrade process more smoothly.

► Alternate disk installation lets you install a new version of the operating system while your current version is still running.

► You can retain the flexibility of reverting to the earlier version of AIX 5L if the new installation is not compatible with your existing applications or customizations.

► Using an alternate destination disk, you can install the new version to different machines over time, then, when it is convenient, reboot to implement the new installations.

► You can test your applications against the new version on an alternate disk. With this option, you can stabilize your environment before implementing the installation on other machines.

The **mksysb** command creates a backup of the operating system (the root volume group). You can use this backup to reinstall a system to its original state after it has been corrupted. If you create the backup on tape, the tape is bootable and includes the installation programs needed to install from the backup. This is a very important and useful command.

3.14.2 System requirements

Table 3-4 shows the required filesets to run an alternate disk installation.

Table 3-4   System requirement

Fileset name	Description	Requisite software
bos.alt_disk_install.rte	This fileset ships the **alt_disk_install** command, which allows cloning of the rootvg and installing an AIX 5L mksysb to an alternate disk.	bos.sysmgt.sysbr
bos.alt_disk_install.boot_images	This fileset ships the boot images, which is required to install mksysb images to an alternate disk.	bos.alt_disk_install.rte

The bos.alt_disk_install package requires approximately 12 MB of disk space in /usr.

Although one additional disk is required, the system recommendation is four disks to use the alternate disk installation—two drivers for the primary rootvg mirrored and two for the **alt_disk_install** implementation.

Once you have installed these filesets, the alternate disk installation functions are available to you in the Software Installation and Maintenance menu. Use the following SMIT fast path:

```
# smitty alt_install
```

Example 3-17   Alternate Disk Installation menu

```
Alternate Disk Installation

Move cursor to desired item and press Enter.

  Install mksysb on an Alternate Disk
  Clone the rootvg to an Alternate Disk
  NIM Alternate Disk Migration
```

```
F1=Help          F2=Refresh          F3=Cancel          F8=Image
F9=Shell         F10=Exit            Enter=Do
```

Alternate disk installation can be used in one of three ways:

- ► Cloning the current running rootvg to an alternate disk
- ► Installing a mksysb image on another disk
- ► Upgrading the Base Operating System to current release

3.14.3 Alternate disk rootvg cloning

Cloning the rootvg to an alternate disk can have many advantages:

- ► Having an online backup available in case of disaster. Keeping an online backup requires that an extra disk or disks be available on the system.

- ► Applying new maintenance levels or updates. A copy of the rootvg is made to an alternate disk, then updates are applied to that copy. Finally, the boot list is updated to boot from the new device. The system runs uninterrupted during this time. When it is rebooted, the system will boot from the newly updated rootvg for testing. If the updates cause problems, the old rootvg can be retrieved by resetting the bootlist and rebooting.

In the following example, we show how to use the alternate disk installation: primary rootvg currently running on hdisk0 and hdisk1, and we will make a clone to the second set of drives, hdisk2 and hdisk3

We are also upgrading the clone disks from AIX 5L Version 5.2 ML 2 to AIX 5L Version 5.2 ML 3.

Example 3-18 shows the menu for cloning rootvg. Start the clone procedure by issuing the following smitty fastpath:

```
# smitty alt_clone
```

Example 3-18   Cloning the rootvg

```
                    Clone the rootvg to an Alternate Disk

Type or select values in entry fields.
Press Enter AFTER making all desired changes.

                                                     [Entry Fields]
* Target Disk(s) to install                       [hdisk2 hdisk3]          +
  Phase to execute                                all                      +
  image.data file                                 []
```

```
Exclude list                                    []
Bundle to install                               [update_all]        +
  -OR-
Fileset(s) to install                           []
Fix bundle to install                           []
  -OR-
Fixes to install                                []
Directory or Device with images                 [/tmp/update]
(required if filesets, bundles or fixes used)

installp Flags
COMMIT software updates?                         yes                 +
SAVE replaced files?                            no                  +
AUTOMATICALLY install requisite software?       yes                 +
EXTEND file systems if space needed?            yes                 +
OVERWRITE same or newer versions?               no                  +
VERIFY install and check file sizes?            no                  +

Customization script                            []
Set bootlist to boot from this disk
on next reboot?                                 yes                 +
Reboot when complete?                           no                  +
Verbose output?                                 no                  +
Debug output?                                   no                  +


F1=Help          F2=Refresh       F3=Cancel        F4=List
F5=Reset         F6=Command       F7=Edit          F8=Image
F9=Shell         F10=Exit         Enter=Do
```

In this example, the following facts are presumed:

▶ We are cloning to disks hdisk2 and hdisk3.

▶ We are running an update_all operation installation of the software in /tmp/update. It is here that the new MLs are located.

▶ We are specifying that this operation should change the current bootlist to hdisk2 and hdisk3 after completion.

▶ We are not asking the process to complete an immediate reboot upon completion of the upgrade because this is something we want to schedule in an appropriate maintenance window.

After completion of the operation, we can verify the bootlist with the following command:

```
bootlist -m normal -o
```

The bootlist will be set to hdisk2 hdisk3, and issuing an **lspv** command will show the following:

```
# lspv
hdisk0        0001615fa41bf87a      rootvg
hdisk1        0001615fcbc1a83f      rootvg
hdisk2        0001615fcbc1a86b      altinst_rootvg
hdisk3        0001615fcbea5d16      altinst_rootvg
```

At this point, we have cloned and installed AIX 5L Version 5.2 ML 3. The changes will be activated on the next reboot.

After reboot

After the reboot, issue the **oslevel** command or complete the appropriate verifications to ensure the upgrade occurred as expected. Issuing the **lspv** command will give you the following output:

```
# lspv
hdisk0        0001615fa41bf87a              old_rootvg
hdisk1        0001615fcbc1a83f              old_rootvg
hdisk2        0001615fcbc1a86b                rootvg
hdisk3        0001615fcbea5d16                rootvg
```

We have booted AIX 5L Version 5.2 ML3 from the hdisk2 and hdisk3, and the disks recognized as the new rootvg hdisks (0 and 1) now show a volume group of old_rootvg and are not active

The recommendation now is to leave disk 0 and disk 1 with AIX 5L Version 5.2 ML 2 in case you need to fall back to the old system.

Cloning back to hdisk0 and hdisk1

To complete the cloning of hdisk 2 and 3 back to hdisk 0 and 1, you must issue the following commands:

1. **alt_disk_install -W hdisk0 hdisk1**

   Wakes up the old_rootvg.

2. **alt_disk_install -S**

   Puts the old_rootvg back to sleep.

3. **alt_disk_install -X altinst_rootvg**

   Removes the old_rootvg volume group name associated with hdisk0 and hdisk1 from the ODM and assigns them a value of none, which will allow the cloning to recur cleanly.

4. **smitty alt_clone**

   Reclones back to hdisk0 and hdisk1 using the previous example.

3.14.4 Alternate mksysb install

An alternate mksysb install involves installing a mksysb image that has already been created from another system onto an alternate disk of the target system. The mksysb image (AIX Version 4.3 or later) would be created on a system that was either the same hardware configuration as the target system or would have all the device and kernel support installed for a different machine type or platform or different devices.

To create the alternate mksysb system, use the following SMIT fast path:

```
# smitty alt_mksysb
```

Example 3-19 shows the alternate mksysb installation screen.

Example 3-19   Install mksysb

```
                  Install mksysb on an Alternate Disk

Type or select values in entry fields.
Press Enter AFTER making all desired changes.

                                                [Entry Fields]
* Target Disk(s) to install                     []                      +
* Device or image name                          []                      +
  Phase to execute                              all                     +
  image.data file                              [] /
  Customization script                         [] /
  Set bootlist to boot from this disk
  on next reboot?                               yes                     +
  Reboot when complete?                         no                      +
  Verbose output?                               no                      +
  Debug output?                                 no                      +
  resolv.conf file                             [] /

F1=Help            F2=Refresh        F3=Cancel         F4=List
F5=Reset           F6=Command        F7=Edit           F8=Image
F9=Shell           F10=Exit          Enter=Do
```

Enter the name of the disk on which you want to install the mksysb in the "Target Disk(s) to install" field.

Enter the name of the device or the image name from which you will be restoring the mksysb in the "Device or image name" field. Press Enter.

Once the mksysb image is restored to the new disk, the system reboots from the new alternate rootvg. This completes your alternate mksysb installation.

3.14.5 Alternate disk migration

Alternate disk migration installation allows the user to create a copy of rootvg to a free disk (or disks) and simultaneously migrate it through Network Installation Management (NIM) to a new release level. Using alternate disk migration installation over a conventional migration provides the following advantages:

► Reduced downtime

The migration is performed while the system is up and functioning. There is no requirement to boot from install media, and the majority of processing occurs on the NIM master.

► Quick recovery in the event of migration failure

Because you are creating a copy of rootvg, all changes are performed to the copy (altinst_rootvg). In the event of serious migration installation failure, the failed migration is cleaned up, and there is no need for the administrator to take further action. In the event of a problem with the new (migrated) level of AIX 5L, the system can be quickly returned to the premigration operating system by booting from the original disk.

► High degree of flexibility and customization in the migration process

This is done with the use of optional NIM customization resources: image_data, bosinst_data, exclude_files, premigration script, installp_bundle, and post-migration script.

Alternate disk migration installation has the following requirements:

► Configured NIM master running AIX 5L Version 5.3 or later with AIX 5L recommended maintenance level 5100-03 or later.

► The NIM master must have bos.alt_disk_install.rte installed in its rootvg and the SPOT that will be used.

► The level of the NIM master rootvg, lpp_source, and SPOT must be at the same level.

► The client (the system to be migrated) must be at AIX 4.3.3 or later.

► The client must have a disk (or disks) large enough to clone the rootvg and an additional 500 MB (approximately) of free space for the migration. The total amount of required space will depend on original system configuration and migration customization.

► The client must be a registered NIM client to the master.

► The NIM master must be able to execute remote commands on the client using the rshd protocol.

► The client must have a minimum of 128 MBs of memory.

- A reliable network, which can facilitate large amounts of NFS traffic, must exist between the NIM master and the client.
- The client's hardware should support the level it is migrating to and meet all other conventional migration requirements.

To create the alternate disk migration, use the following SMIT fast path:

```
# smitty nimadm_migrate
```

Example 3-20 shows the alternate disk migration.

Example 3-20   Alternate disk migration

```
Perform NIM Alternate Disk Migration

Type or select values in entry fields.
Press Enter AFTER making all desired changes.

[TOP]                                                    [Entry Fields]
* Target NIM Client                             []                        +
* NIM LPP_SOURCE resource                       []                        +
* NIM SPOT resource                             []                        +
* Target Disk(s) to install                     []
  DISK CACHE volume group name                  []                        +

  NIM IMAGE_DATA resource                       []                        +
  NIM BOSINST_DATA resource                     []                        +
  NIM EXCLUDE_FILES resource                    []                        +
  NIM INSTALLP_BUNDLE resource                  []                        +
  NIM PRE-MIGRATION SCRIPT resource             []                        +
  NIM POST-MIGRATION SCRIPT resource            []                        +

  Phase to execute                              [all]                     +
  NFS mounting options                          []
  Set Client bootlist to alternate disk?        yes                       +
  Reboot NIM Client when complete?              no                        +
  Verbose output?                               no                        +
  Debug output?                                 no                        +

  ACCEPT new license agreements?                no                        +
[BOTTOM]

F1=Help            F2=Refresh          F3=Cancel          F4=List
F5=Reset           F6=Command          F7=Edit            F8=Image
F9=Shell           F10=Exit            Enter=Do
```

For more information about the fields go to the `smitty nimadm_migrate` and press F1 or ESC+1.

3.15 Ignite-UX

Both operating systems offer the possibility to automate the installation process without operator intervention, for example, when a large number of clients or servers are to be installed. This process is called Ignite-UX in the HP-UX environment. In AIX 5L, this is called Network Installation Management. An automated installation process gives the system administrator many advantages:

► Simplifies installations
► Speed - Faster than CD-ROM installation
► Allows unattended installation
► Replication - Same systems across the enterprise

In this section, we briefly discuss how this process is done on the HP-UX environment.

Requirements
The following list shows the prerequisites for Ignite-UX:

► Server PA-RISC or Itanium-based running HP-UX 11i or HP-UX11.

► Disk space needed for HP-UX 11i, 4 GB (Depot of HP-UX).

► Ignite-UX installation requires 250 MB of disk space when the full product is installed in /opt.

► TFTP available in /etc/inetd.conf.

► Boot server on the same subnet.

3.15.1 Installing the boot server

Before is necessary, install *Ignite-UX-11-11* in the server. This software is bundle.

Ignite-UX, when initialized via the command /opt/ignite/bin/ignite, asks whether the user wants to configure the Ignite server with the server setup wizard. Configuring the Ignite server with the server setup wizard is much easier, but the user can choose to configure it via the command line.

For more information about Ignite-UX, refer to *Ignite-UX Administration Guide* HP Number B2355-90872 at the Web site:

```
http://www.docs.hp.com
```

3.15.2 Install server on same subnet as client

If the client exists on the subnet as the install server, add the client as an install client of the install server using the following command:

```
# /opt/ignite/bin/bootsys
```

For more information see the bootsys (1M) manual pages.

The Ignite GUI interface can also be used.

3.15.3 Boot install clients

It is recommended that HP-UX clients be booted in manual boot mode when system maintenance and administration is required. Refer to "Single-user and manual boot" on page 85.

The following command is used for PA-RISC:

```
BOOT ADMIN> boot lan.n.n.n.n install
```

The following command is used for Itanium:

```
EFI shell> lanboot
```

3.16 Network Installation Management (NIM)

NIM permits the installation, maintenance, and upgrade of AIX 5L, its basic operating system, and additional software and fixes that may be applied over a period of time over token-ring, Ethernet, FDDI, and ATM networks. NIM also permits the customization of machines both during and after installation. As a result, NIM has eliminated the reliance on tapes and CD-ROMs for software installation; the bonus, in NIM's case, is in the network. NIM will allow one machine to act as a master in the environment. This machine will be responsible for storing information about the clients it supports, the resources it or other servers provide to these clients, and the networks on which they operate.

Some of the benefits of NIM are:

- ► Manageability: It allows central localization of software installation images, thus making backup and administration easier.

- ► Central Administration: Administrators can install remote AIX 5L machines without having to physically attend them.

- ► Scalability: You can install more than one machine at a time, implement a group strategy of machines and resources, and choose how many machines to install at a time.

- Availability: Where server down time means loss of profits, NIM provides you with a backup image of all your servers. A new server can be set up and running in just over an hour.

- High availability of NIM Server: The most significant single point of failure in a NIM environment is the NIM master. AIX 5L Version 5.3 introduces a way to define a backup NIM master, take over to the backup master, and then fail back to the primary master. This helps to create more reliable NIM environments.

- Non-prompted installation: NIM provides a function to install systems without having to go to the machine.

- Installations can be initiated by either the client or master at a convenient time. For example, if a client is unavailable at the time of the install, you can initiate an install when it is back online, or, if there is less traffic on your network at a certain time, you can have the installations occur then.

- It is a relatively faster means of installation than tape or CD-ROM.

- NIM provides greater functionality than CD-ROM or tape. Among other things, it allows you to customize an install, initiate a non-prompted install, or install additional software.

3.16.1 NIM environments

A NIM environment is typical of any client-server environment. You have client machines accessing resources that are remotely held on servers. In the NIM environment, there is also the additional requirement that these resources bring stand-alone, dataless, and diskless machines to a running state. It is obvious, then, that certain resources are required to support the operation of systems within the NIM environment. This capability is dependent upon the functionality of the network.

All information about the NIM environment is stored in three ODM databases (this data is located in files in the /etc/objrepos directory):

- nim_object: Each object represents a physical entity in the NIM environment.
- nim_attr: Stores individual characteristics of physical entities.
- nim_pdattr: Contains predefined characteristics.

The objects that compose the ODM database are machines, networks, resources, and groups. When we speak of their characteristics, we are referring to their attributes that are part of their initial definition. In this definition, we also assign the objects a name. This name is for NIM purposes only and may be totally different from any defining physical characteristic it may have. To have a functioning environment, the following conditions must be met:

- NFS and TCP/IP must be installed.

- ► TCP/IP must be configured.
- ► TCP/IP communications must be established between machines.
- ► Name resolution must be configured.

3.16.2 NIM setup

This section describes the NIM master setup.

NIM master

To configure NIM master, the better way is by EZNIM. The `smitty eznim` menu helps the system administrator by organizing the commonly used NIM operations and simplifies frequently used advanced NIM operations.

Follow these steps to set up NIM:

- ► Prepare the AIX 5L operating system, and install CD-ROMs that are the same levels that are currently installed.
- ► Configure the NIM master server. Execute the `smitty setup_eznim_master` fast path.

Example 3-21   Easy NIM server configuration

```
                    Easy NIM - Setup the NIM Master environment

Type or select values in entry fields.
Press Enter AFTER making all desired changes.

                                                    [Entry Fields]
    Select or specify software source              [cd0]                    +
    to initialize environment


    Select Volume Group for resources              [rootvg]                 +


    Select Filesytem for resources                 [/export/eznim]

    Options
        CREATE system backup image?                [yes]                    +
        CREATE new Filesystem?                     [yes]                    +
        DISPLAY verbose output?                    [no]                     +

F1=Help             F2=Refresh          F3=Cancel           F4=List
F5=Reset            F6=Command          F7=Edit             F8=Image
F9=Shell            F10=Exit            Enter=Do
```

You can select the software source to configure from, select the volume group to use for the NIM resources, and select the file system to use for the NIM resources. When the NIM master environment is configured, the basic NIM resources are created, for example, lpp_source and spot.

To view the NIM resources created by EZNIM, select **Show the NIM environment** or run the lsnim command on the NIM master.

lpp_source

An lpp_source resource represents a directory in which software installation images are stored. If the lpp_source contains the minimum set of support images required to install a machine, it is given the simages attribute and can be used for BOS installation (bos_inst) operations.

NIM uses an lpp_source for an installation operation by first mounting the lpp_source on the client machine. The **installp** commands are then started on the client using the mounted lpp_source as the source for installation images. When the installation operation has completed, NIM automatically unmounts the resource.

In addition to providing images to install machines, lpp_source resources can also be used to create and update SPOT resources.

Shared Product Object Tree (SPOT)

The SPOT is a fundamental resource in the NIM environment. It is required to install or initialize all machine configuration types. A SPOT provides a /usr file system for diskless and dataless clients, as well as the network boot support for all clients.

Everything that a machine requires in a /usr file system, such as the AIX 5L kernel, executable commands, libraries, and applications are included in the SPOT. Machine-unique information or user data is usually stored in the other file systems. A SPOT can be located on any standalone machine within the NIM environment, including the master. The SPOT is created, controlled, and maintained from the master, even though the SPOT can be located on another system.

NIM client

EZNIM also allows you to manage a NIM client. On a client system, use the **smitty setup_eznim_client** fast path (but only if your NIM client system is already installed). If you have a new machine, it is necessary to configure the boot by network using NIM master; see 3.16.4, "Booting a machine over the network" on page 76.

Example 3-22   Easy NIM client configuration

```
Easy NIM - Client Configuration

Type or select values in entry fields.
Press Enter AFTER making all desired changes.

                                                      [Entry Fields]
* Machine Name                                        []
* Primary Network Install Interface                   []                    +
* Host Name of Network Install Master                 []

  Hardware Platform Type                              chrp
  Kernel to use for Network Boot                      [mp]                   +


F1=Help            F2=Refresh        F3=Cancel         F4=List
F5=Reset           F6=Command        F7=Edit           F8=Image
F9=Shell           F10=Exit          Enter=Do
```

You need to select the hostname of the NIM client, select the primary network interface, select the hostname of the NIM master, and others fields can be default values.

3.16.3 Install the Base Operating System (BOS) on a NIM client

In this method, using installation images to install BOS on a NIM client is similar to the traditional BOS installation from a tape or CD-ROM device, because the BOS image is installed from the installation images in the lpp_source resource.

Prerequisites:

► The NIM master must be configured, and lpp_source and SPOT resources must be defined.

► The NIM client to be installed must already exist in the NIM environment. If your system does not exist in an NIM environment, it is necessary to configure the boot by network using the NIM master. For more details see 3.16.4, "Booting a machine over the network" on page 76.

The steps to install the Base Operating System (BOS) on a NIM client are:

1. Use the `smitty nim_bosinst` fast path from the NIM master.

2. Select the TARGET for the operation.

3. Select **rte** as the installation TYPE.

4. Select the SPOT to use for the installation.

5. Select the LPP_SOURCE to use for the installation.

6. In the displayed dialog fields, supply the correct values for the installation options or accept the default values. Use the help information and the LIST option to help you.

7. If the client machine being installed is not already a running, configured NIM client, NIM will not automatically reboot the machine over the network for installation. If the client was not rebooted automatically from SMIT, initiate a network boot from the client to install it.

8. After the machine boots over the network, the display on the client machine will begin prompting for information about how the machine should be configured during installation. Specify the requested information to continue with the installation.

A command line can also be used for this procedure. For more information see the nim (1M) manual pages.

3.16.4 Booting a machine over the network

It is the platform and kernel type of a client that determine the procedure required to boot the machine over the network. To determine the platform of a running machine, use the **bootinfo -p** command. To determine the kernel type of a running machine, use the **bootinfo -z** command.

If you are using an rs6k machine with an *up* kernel, use Method A. If you are booting an rs6k machine with an *mp* kernel, use Method B. For models of *rspc* machines, you may use Method C. For all other platform and kernel types, follow the procedures in your hardware documentation to perform the network boot.

Older model rs6k-platform machines may require IPL ROM emulation to boot over the network. To determine whether a running rs6k machine requires emulation, enter the command **bootinfo -q** *AdapterName*, where *AdapterName* is the network adapter over which the client will be installed. If the adapter is network-boot enabled, the **bootinfo** command will return 1, and no emulation is required. For example, enter:

```
# bootinfo -q tok0
```

Use this procedure to create the IPL ROM emulation media on the NIM master for machines that do not have a BOOTP-enabled IPL ROM:

1. Insert a formatted diskette or a tape into the appropriate drive on the NIM master.

2. Enter the following command:

```
# bosboot -T rs6k -r /usr/lpp/bos.sysmgt/nim/methods/IPLROM.emulation -d
DeviceName -M both
```

Where *DeviceName* can be fd0, /dev/fd0, rmt0, or /dev/rmt0. This operation requires that the devices.base.rte fileset be installed on the machine upon which the emulation media is being created

3. Insert the IPL ROM emulation media in the appropriate drive on the target machine.

Method A (booting an rs6k uniprocessor machine)

Follow these steps to boot a rs6k uniprocessor machine:

1. Begin with your machine powered off.

2. If your client requires IPL-ROM emulation, insert the media into the appropriate drive of the client, and turn on the machine with the hardware key in the Service position. When the bootp menus display, continue with step 3. If your client does not require emulation, turn the key to the Secure position and turn on the machine. Note the LEDs on the front of the machine. They will eventually stop changing and display 200. When this happens, turn the key to the Service position and quickly press the yellow Reset button. When the bootp menus display, continue with step 3.

3. From the bootp main menu, choose the Select BOOT (Start-up) Device option.

4. In the next menu that appears, select the boot device.

5. Select the network adapter to be used. Choose the adapter with the correct network type (Ethernet, token-ring, and so on) and adapter characteristics (thick cable, twisted pair for Ethernet, 4 MB and 16 MB data rates for token-ring, and so on).

6. Set or change the network addresses. Specify the IP addresses of:
   - The client machine you are booting
   - Your SPOT server in the bootp server address field
   - Your client's gateway in the gateway address field
   - The subnet mask value getting set in the IPL_ROM

After you determine the addresses and save the addresses, return to the main menu.

> **Note:** You do not need to type the period (.) characters in the IP addresses, but you must specify any leading zero (0) characters that make up parts of the addresses.

7. From the main menu, select the Send Test Transmission (PING) option.

8. Verify that the displayed addresses are the same as the addresses you specified for your boot device. If the addresses are incorrect, return to the main menu. Then go back to step 3. If the addresses are correct, select the Start the ping test option. If the ping test fails, verify that the addresses are correct, and perform network problem determination if necessary. If the ping test completes successfully, return to the main menu.

9. From the main menu, select the Exit Main Menu and Start System (BOOT) option.

10. Turn the hardware key to the Normal position, and press Enter to boot your client over the network.

Method B (booting an rs6k multiprocessor machine)

Follow these steps to boot a rs6k multiprocessor machine:

1. Begin with the machine switched off.

2. Turn the key mode switch to the Secure position.

3. Turn the power switch on the system unit to the On position.

4. When the LED displays 200, turn the key mode switch to the Service position.

5. Press the Reset button once.

6. When the SMS menu appears, select the System Boot option.

7. Select the Boot from Network option from the sub-menu.

8. Choose the Select BOOT (Start-up) Device option.

9. Select the network adapter from which the machine will boot. If there are multiple network adapters displayed, press the Enter key to view the other entries. Type a number from the list and press the Enter key.

10. If a network adapter is selected, the Set or Change Network Addresses screen is displayed next. The hardware address for the network adapter is displayed in the hardware address field. Record the hardware address for defining the NIM machine object. If you want to attempt the broadcast style install, leave the IP address fields as zeros for the bootp request over the LAN. If there are multiple bootp servers on the LAN or the client is on a different network than the server, enter the client and server IP addresses. Type in the IP addresses using leading zeros to pad the network address fields, for example, 10.166.133.004. If this machine must use a gateway to reach the server, enter the IP address for the gateway. Save the address information and return to the main menu.

11. Select the Sent Test Transmission (PING) option on the main menu to test the network connection between the client and the server systems.

Press the Enter key to start the ping test. If the ping test was not successful, check that the IP addresses are correct and that the physical network connections are sound. If the ping test was successful, return to the main menu.

12. Select the Exit Main Menu and Start System (BOOT) option.

13. Follow the instructions on the screen to turn the key mode switch to the Normal position and press the Enter key.

The bootp request will be issued, followed by a TFTP transfer of the network boot image.

Method C (booting a rspc machine)

Follow these steps to boot a rspc machine:

1. Begin with your machine powered off.

2. Bring the machine up to System Management Services using the SMS diskette, or, once the graphic images start appearing on the screen, press the F1 key.

> **Note:** For ASCII terminals, press the F4 key as words representing the icons appear. The relevant function key will depend on the type and model of rspc machine; refer to your User Guide.
>
> If the last icon or keyword is displayed prior to pressing the F4 or F1 key, the normal mode boot list is used instead of the Systems Management Services diskette.
>
> For later models of rspc, the functionality of the SMS diskette is incorporated into the firmware, which is accessed by pressing the F1 or 1 key.

3. The System Management Services (SMS) menu is displayed. Select the Utilities option.

4. From the Utilities menu, select the Remote Initial Program Load Setup option.

5. From the Network Parameters screen, select the IP parameters option.

6. Set or change the values displayed so they are correct for your client system.

7. Specify the IP address of:

   - The client machine you are booting in the client address field.
   - Your SPOT server in the bootp server address field.
   - Your client's gateway in the gateway address field.

8. Specify the subnet mask for your client machine if you are prompted for one in the subnet mask field.

9. After you determine the addresses, press Enter to save the addresses and continue.

10. The Network Parameters screen is displayed. Select the Ping option.

11. Select the network adapter to be used as the client's boot device and verify that the displayed addresses are the same as the addresses you specified for your boot device. If the addresses are incorrect, press the Esc key until you return to the main menu, and then go back to Step 5.

12. If the addresses are correct, press Enter to perform the ping test. The ping test may take several seconds to complete.

13. If the ping test fails, verify that the addresses are correct, and perform network problem determination if required. If the ping test completes successfully, you will see a success sign and will be returned to the SMS menu.

14. From the Systems Management Services menu, choose the Select Boot Devices option.

15. Select the network adapter to be used for the network boot list from the list of displayed bootable devices. Be sure to select the correct network type and adapter characteristics. Once you are happy with the devices listed in the boot list, exit from SMS and continue the boot process. Sometimes you may find it better to power the machine off and then back on again.

> **Note:** When performing a BOS installation on a NIM client with an rspc platform, the machine may fail to boot if network traffic is heavy.
>
> If the network boot was initiated from the NIM master, the machine will eventually boot from the disk. If the network boot was initiated from the SMS menus on the NIM client, the machine will return control to the SMS menus.
>
> For multiple interfaces, select the interface that has been specified in the NIM client definition so that NIM master can allocate the correct boot image.

3.17 Quick reference

Table 3-5 on page 81 shows the comparison between AIX 5L and HP-UX 11i for installation and upgrade tasks.

Table 3-5   Quick reference for installing and upgrading tasks

Task	AIX 5L	HP-UX 11i
Install packages.	`installp -a` or the `smitty install_latest` fast path	`swinstall`
Display installed packages.	`lslpp -L` or the `smitty list_installed_sw` fast path	`swlist`
Remove software package.	`installp -r` (for applied package) or the `smitty reject` fast path `installp -u` (for committed package) or the `smitty remove` (fast path)	`swremove`
Upgrade a package.	`installp -a`	`swinstall`
Verify correct installation.	`lppchk` or the `smitty check_files` fast path	`swverify`
Install a patch.	`instfix` or the `smitty update_by_fix` fast path	`swinstall`
Remove a patch.	`installp -r` or the `smitty reject` fast path	`swremove`
Display installed patches.	`instfix -ia`	`swlist`
Install OS on another disk (alternate disk installation).	`alt_disk_install`	N/A
Create an installation server for network installation.	`smitty setup_eznim_master`	`/opt/ignite/bin/ignite` by Server Setup Wizard
Set up a client for network installation.	`smitty setup_eznim_client`	`bootsys`

System startup and shutdown

This chapter describes system startup and shutdown procedures. The following topics are covered:

83

4.1 The system startup process

This section describes the system startup process.

4.1.1 HP-UX

In the HP-UX operating system, the boot process consists of a sequence of phases. The boot process is also called the bootstrap process. In the following section, we list the phases and then briefly describe each of them:

- ► Processor Dependent Code (PDC)
- ► Initial System Loader (ISL)
- ► hpux

PDC

The PDC is pre-installed firmware that runs when the system is powered on or when it is reset. It runs self-tests to verify and initialize the system hardware components. It also finds the path to the console and initializes the console device. It then begins the autoboot sequence. The user is allowed to interrupt the autoboot sequence by pressing any key within 10 seconds. If it is not interrupted, the PDC loads the ISL and transfers control to it. Messages similar to Example 4-1 appear.

Example 4-1   PDC boot messages

```
Firmware Version  39.43

Duplex Console IO Dependent Code (IODC) revision 4

-------------------------------------------------------------------------------
    (c) Copyright 1995-1998, Hewlett-Packard Company, All rights reserved
-------------------------------------------------------------------------------

    Processor   Speed            State              CoProcessor State  Cache Size
    ---------   --------   --------------------     -----------------  ----------
        0       180  MHz   Active                   Functional         1  MB
        1       180  MHz   Idle                     Functional         1  MB
        2       180  MHz   Idle                     Functional         1  MB
        3       180  MHz   Idle                     Functional         1  MB

    Central Bus Speed (in MHz)  :        120
    Available Memory            :    2097148  KB
    Good Memory Required        :     169384  KB

      Primary boot path:     10/0.3      (dec)
      Alternate boot path:   10/0.6      (dec)
      Console path:          10/8.0      (dec)
```

```
Keyboard path:          10/12/7.0      (dec)


Processor is booting from first available device.

To discontinue, press any key within 10 seconds.
```

ISL

The initial system loader starts the operating system independent part of the boot process. If the autoboot flag is enabled, an autoboot process allows a complete boot operation to occur with no intervention from the user. ISL executes commands from an autoexec file that initiates *hpux*, the HP-UX specific boot loader.

hpux

hpux is the HP-UX secondary system loader (SSL) bootstrap utility. It is responsible for loading and passing control to the HP-UX kernel, which is also called the image.

The loaded image or kernel then displays numerous configuration and status messages, and passes control to the init process and begins normal operation.

Single-user and manual boot

Single-user and manual boot mode is used when system maintenance and administration is required. This mode ensures that other users cannot log and impact what you are doing.

By pressing any key within the 10 second autoboot delay period, during the PDC phase, the autoboot sequence is interrupted. The Boot Console Handler (BCH), which is an interface to the PDC commands, displays its main menu (Example 4-1 on page 84) and allows interaction with the PDC.

From the main menu, the following can be done:

► Boot from available paths.
► Display or modify paths.
► Search for boot devices.
► Display or set boot values.
► Display hardware information.
► Display service commands.
► Restart the system.
► Display help for menu and commands.

Example 4-2   PDC main menu

```
---- Main Menu ------------------------------------------------------------------

    Command                         Description
    -------                         -----------
    BOot [PRI|ALT|<path>]           Boot from specified path
    PAth [PRI|ALT] [<path>]         Display or modify a path
    SEArch [DIsplay|IPL] [<path>]   Search for boot devices

    COnfiguration menu              Displays or sets boot values
    INformation menu                Displays hardware information
    SERvice menu                    Displays service commands

    DIsplay                         Redisplay the current menu
    HElp [<menu>|<command>]         Display help for menu or command
    RESET                           Restart the system
```

Select the boot path you want to boot from by typing the following command:

```
boot pri or boot p1
```

This boots from the primary boot path or the p1 option, which is a specific boot path to a boot device.

The PDC responds by asking the user whether they want to interact with IPL. Reply *y*, as shown in Example 4-3.

Example 4-3   PDC interactive command line

```
Main Menu: Enter command or menu > bo pri

Interact with IPL (Y, N, or Cancel)?> y
 Booting...
Boot IO Dependent Code (IODC) revision 152


HARD Booted.
```

The ISL prompt will then be displayed. To boot the kernel into single-user mode type:

```
 hpux -is
```

The -i option tells the system to come up in *run level s* for single user mode of operation:

```
ISL> hpux -is
Boot
: disc(10/0.3.0;0)/stand/vmunix
```

10371072 + 2019328 + 1424792 start 0x1f6a68

Autoboot and autosearch flags

There are two flags, autoboot and autosearch, that also affect the autoboot sequence.

To have the system boot without any user intervention, the autoboot flag should be enabled. For interaction with the boot process, the flag should be disabled. The values of these flags can be changed in two ways:

► From a running system, use the `setboot` command.
► From the PDC phase, use the configuration menu.

Table 4-1 on page 90 describes how the settings of these flags affect the boot sequence.

Boot Process on Itanium systems

The boot process on the Itanium server family is different from the boot process on the PA-Risc systems. We very briefly describe the process below.

For a more detailed and in-depth description of this process, refer to the *boot (1M)* and *efi manual pages* and the following reference documentation on the HP documentation Web site at:

http://www.docs.hp.com/

► *Installing and Managing HP-UX Virtual Partitions (vPars)*

► *Managing Systems and Workgroups, A Guide for HP-UX System Administrators, Edition 7,* Manufacturing Part Number 5990-8172 E0904

► *Managing Superdome Complexes: A Guide for HP-UX System Administrators, HP9000 Computers, Edition 1,* Manufacturing Part Number B2355-90702 E1200

The boot process consists of the following software components: CMOS, option ROM, EFI (Extensible Firmware Interface), Boot Manager, and the hpux.efi.

The EFI is an interface between HP-UX and the Itanium-based platform firmware. After the system is reset or powered on, the firmware is initialized and all the hardware is tested and verified. The user can interrupt the firmware initialization phase and make configuration changes to the CMOS and option ROMs.

Control is then transferred to the EFI. The EFI itself initializes the EFI boot and runtime services and launches the boot manager. The boot manager allows the loading of EFI applications or drivers from the EFI file system. It then loads and transfers control to hpux.efi, which is the HP-UX specific bootstrap loader. Hpux.efi then loads the kernel object file from the HP-UX file system to memory and transfers control to the loaded kernel image.

Single-user mode

This is a brief process to boot into single-user mode. For a detailed procedure refer to the HP reference documentation at:

```
http://www.docs.hp.com/
```

Stop the boot process at the hpux.efi interface, which is the HP-UX boot loader prompt, HPUX>, by entering the following command:

```
boot −is vmunix
```

Where vmunix is the kernel loaded from /stand/vmunix and the −is option is used to invoke single-user mode.

4.1.2 AIX 5L

When you power on an IBM @server pSeries (or RS/6000) machine, one of the first things it will do is determine which device it should use to boot the machine. It also activates the disks, sets up access to the files and directories, starts networking, and completes other machine-specific configurations.

The following sequence of events takes place when an IBM @server pSeries (or RS/6000) is powered on or reset:

1. ROS IPL (Read Only Storage Initial Program Load). This phase includes a power-on self-test (POST), the location of a boot device, and loading of the boot kernel into memory.

2. Phase 1 (Base Device Configuration Phase): This phase runs /etc/rc.boot with an argument of 1. rc.boot builds the Object Data Manager (ODM) database, makes sure that base devices are configured, initializes the Logical Volume Manager (LVM), activates the root volume group (rootvg), and checks and mounts the root file system.

3. Phase 2: Here /etc/rc.boot is run with an argument of 2. This merges the ODM data and device files into the root file system and configures any devices not configured by Phase 1.

4. Phase 3: This phase starts /etc/init with the process ID (pid) of 1.

5. Phase 4 (run-time phase): Here init runs the entries in /etc/inittab and invokes /etc/rc.boot 3. The /tmp file system is mounted, the ODM database is saved for future boots, and the run state is set to multi-user, at which time various subsystems such as TCP/IP and NFS, if found in /etc/inittab, are started.

Up until the run-time phase, all you have as an indicator of how the boot sequence is going is the LED display on the front panel of the machine. Three-digit codes flash as the sequence progresses, and if you want to know the meaning of the codes, you have to look them up in either *RS/6000 & eServer pSeries Diagnostics Information for Multiple Bus Systems*, SA38-0509, or *RS/6000 Diagnostics Information for Micro Channel Bus System*, SA38-0532.

At a certain point, however, you will see either code c32 or c33, which indicates that the run-time phase is assigning the console. c32 is for high-function terminal devices (hfts) and c33 is for serial-line terminals (ttys). After that, the boot output goes to the display until, finally, the Console Login message appears, at which time the machine is completely up and in multi-user mode.

In AIX 5L, there are three different startup modes: Normal, System Management Service (SMS), and maintenance mode. In this section we describe the three startup modes.

Normal mode

By default, the machine will use the "normal" boot list, which usually contains one or more hard drives. When the machine does a normal boot, it will complete the full AIX 5L boot sequence and start processes, enable terminals, and generate a login prompt to make it available for multi-user access.

System Management Services (SMS)

Another boot option for the IBM @server pSeries (or RS/6000) is to boot machine-specific code called the System Management Services (SMS) programs. These programs are not part of AIX 5L. This code is shipped with the hardware and is built in to the firmware. This can be used to examine the system configuration and set boot lists without the aid of AIX 5L operating system. It is invoked during the initial stages of the boot sequence using the F1 or 1 key.

> **Tip:** To start SMS, you must reboot the system. As a rule of thumb you must press the F1 or 1 key once the monitor light turns green. You have approximately 15 seconds to press F1 or 1. Once all device icons (or words) display in the monitor, it is too late to interrupt the boot sequence, and the system will boot from the default boot list, for example, hdisk0.

The SMS menu will vary depending on the model. But generally there are four main services, as shown in Table 4-1 on page 90.

Table 4-1   SMS services

SMS menu	Explanation
Config	View the hardware configuration on the system.
Boot	View or change the boot list.
Utilities	Set power on and supervisory passwords, updating firmware, select console, and so on.
Exit	Return to previous screen.

Maintenance mode

A machine is started from a hard disk, network, tape, or CD-ROM with the key set in the service position. This condition is also called maintenance mode. In maintenance mode, a system administrator can perform tasks such as installing new or updated software and running diagnostic checks.

All machines have a normal boot list and one or more service boot lists. The normal boot list is the default boot list.

When connecting to systems via TTYs and with newer models like F80, M80, and H80, you have to use the 1, 5, and 6 keys instead of function keys.

To view the normal boot list, at an AIX 5L command prompt, type:

```
# bootlist -m normal -o
```

The boot list can be changed using the same command:

```
# bootlist -m normal hdiskX "2nd device"
```

PCI RS/6000 systems use sounds and graphics to show the different phases of the boot process. For example, as soon as you power on the system, an audio beep is produced when the processor is found to be active, the PowerPC logo is shown (or text is presented) when the system memory checking is completed, and device logos are shown for all devices that have a valid address. At the end of the device logo display, if the system ROS is not damaged, an audio beep is again produced.

Several MCA-based RS/6000 systems have LED displays to show what phase of the boot process the system is going through. If something goes wrong, you can interpret the LED codes and take the appropriate action to rectify the problem.

The boot process

During a hard disk boot, the boot image is found on a local disk created when the operating system was installed. During the boot process, the system configures all devices found in the machine and initializes other basic software required for the system to operate (such as the Logical Volume Manager). At the end of this process, the file systems are mounted and ready for use.

The LED panel will provide information during the boot progress. Some values displayed are model specific. These values can be found in the Service Guide for that specific model.

The boot process can be divided into four steps: Hardware initialization, loading the boot image, device configuration, and starting the init process.

Hardware initialization

The initial step in booting a machine completes a Power-on Self Test (POST). This step initializes the memory, the keyboard, communication adapters, and audio components. This is the same point where you would press a function key to choose a different boot list. This test is run by chips on the I/O board and a special part of the CPU. The system will refuse to boot if a failure is found here. Trivial errors to check for in this case are loose cables and defective cards. Errors on the power supply will also terminate the boot process. On large systems, this phase will take some time. The LED values displayed during this part are model specific.

Loading the boot image

Once the POST is completed, the system will locate and load bootstrap code. This part is completed by System ROS (Read Only Storage) stored in the firmware. The bootstrap code, sometimes referred to as Software ROS or level 2 firmware, takes control and builds AIX 5L-specific boot information, then locates, loads, and turns control over to the AIX 5L boot logical volume (BLV). Because these machines can run different operating systems, the System ROS is generic boot information for the machine and is operating system independent.

Device configuration

The kernel completes the boot process by configuring devices and starting the init process. Some LED codes displayed during the boot process are model specific. The initial phases during the POST and loading the AIX 5L kernel will have the model-specific codes. This is because this phase provides hardware checks and initialization and is unique to each model. Once the kernel is loaded, the LED codes are AIX 5L codes. These will be the same across all AIX 5L systems.

4.1.3 Useful commands

The commands that are used to manage system startup, shutdown, and related tasks are discussed in the following sections.

Using the alog command

There may be instances when you must trace the boot process and obtain if something went wrong with the system during the boot process. AIX 5L provides you with an excellent tool to monitor these problems through the help of the **alog** command.

The **alog** command can maintain and manage logs. It reads standard input, writes to standard output, and copies the output into a fixed-size file. This file is treated as a circular log. If the file is full, new entries are written over the oldest existing entries.

The **alog** command works with log files that are specified on the command line or with logs that are defined in the **alog** configuration database.

The most common flags used with the **alog** command and their descriptions are given in Table 4-2.

Table 4-2   Command flags for the alog command

Flag	Description
-f *LogFile*	Specifies the name of a log file. If the specified log file does not exist, one is created. If the **alog** command is unable to write to the log file, it writes to /dev/null.
-L	Lists the log types currently defined in the **alog** configuration database. If you use the -L flag with the -t LogType flag, the attributes for a specified LogType are listed.
-o	Lists the contents of the log file; writes the contents of the log file to standard output in sequential order.
-q	Copies standard input to the log file, but does not write to standard output.
-t	Identifies a log defined in the **alog** configuration database. The **alog** command gets the log's file name and size from the **alog** configuration database.

Some examples of the **alog** command are:

► To view the boot log, run:

```
# alog -o -t boot
```

- To record the current date and time in a log file named /tmp/mylog, enter:

  # date | alog -f /tmp/mylog

- To see the list the logs defined in the alog database, run:

  # alog -L

Using the bootlist command

The **bootlist** command allows you to display and alter the list of boot devices from which the system may be booted. When the system is booted, it will scan the devices in the list and attempt to boot from the first device it finds containing a boot image. This command supports the updating of the following boot lists:

- Normal boot list: The normal list designates possible boot devices for when the system is booted in normal mode.

- Service boot list: The service list designates possible boot devices for when the system is booted in service mode.

- Previous boot device: This entry designates the last device from which the system booted. Some hardware platforms may attempt to boot from the previous boot device before looking for a boot device in one of the other lists.

Support of these boot lists varies from platform to platform. Some platforms do not have boot lists. When searching for a boot device, the system selects the first device in the list and determines if it is bootable. If no boot file system is detected on the first device, the system moves on to the next device in the list. As a result, the ordering of devices in the device list is extremely important.

The general syntax of the command is as follows:

bootlist [{{-m *Mode* }[-r][--o] [[--i]| [[--f *File*]
[*Device* [Attr=*Value* ...] ...]]]

The most common flags used with the **bootlist** command are provided in Table 4-3.

Table 4-3 Command flags for the bootlist command

Flag	Description
-m *mode*	Specifies which boot list to display or alter. Possible values for the mode variable are normal, service, both, or prevboot.
-f *File*	Indicates that the device information is to be read from the specified file name.
-i	Indicates that the device list specified by the -m flag should be invalidated.

Flag	Description
-o	Displays bootlist with the -m flag. Applies only to AIX Version 4.2 or later.
-r	Indicates whether to display the specified bootlist after any specified alteration is performed.

Some examples of the bootlist command are:

► To display a boot list (AIX Version 4.2 or later), use the following command:

```
# bootlist -m normal -o
fd0
cd0
hdisk0
```

► If you want to make changes to your normal boot list, use the following command:

```
# bootlist -m normal hdisk0 cd0
```

4.2 The /etc/inittab file

There is a difference in the way the startup scripts are initialized and executed in HP-UX and AIX 5L.

HP-UX starts subsystems as per the Open Software Foundation (OSF/1) industry standards. AIX 5L uses the Berkeley Software Distribution (BSD) standard. AIX 5L also has the option of using the System V standard for the initialization files startup. The following sections describe the startup methods in more detail.

4.2.1 Startup process in HP-UX

After the kernel is loaded into memory, control is taken over by it. The kernel loads device drivers for hardware attached to the system. The swapper process is started and the file system checks are done before control is passed onto the init process.

The init process is always started with a process ID of one, and it starts the rest of the of the process by reading its configuration file, /etc/inittab. The initdefault entry in the /etc/inittab file tells init the run level the system will default to after completing the boot process. The default run level on HP-UX is run level 3. Example 4-1 on page 84 shows an /etc/inittab file.

Example 4-4   /etc/inittab file

```
init:3:initdefault:
ioin::sysinit:/sbin/ioinitrc >/dev/console 2>&1
tape::sysinit:/sbin/mtinit > /dev/console 2>&1
muxi::sysinit:/sbin/dasetup    </dev/console >/dev/console 2>&1 # mux init
stty::sysinit:/sbin/stty 9600 clocal icanon echo opost onlcr ixon icrnl ignpar
</dev/systty
vxen::bootwait:/sbin/fs/vxfs/vxenablef -a
vol1::sysinit:/sbin/init.d/vxvm-sysboot </dev/console >/dev/console 2>&1 ##vxvm
vol2::sysinit:/sbin/init.d/vxvm-startup start </dev/console >/dev/console 2>&1
##vxvm
brc1::bootwait:/sbin/bcheckrc </dev/console >/dev/console 2>&1 # fsck, etc.
link::wait:/sbin/sh -c "/sbin/rm -f /dev/syscon; \
                        /sbin/ln /dev/systty /dev/syscon" >/dev/console 2>&1
cprt::bootwait:/sbin/cat /etc/copyright >/dev/syscon          # legal req
sqnc::wait:/sbin/rc </dev/console >/dev/console 2>&1          # system init
#powf::powerwait:/sbin/powerfail >/dev/console 2>&1          # powerfail
cons:123456:respawn:/usr/sbin/getty console console          # system console
#ttp1:234:respawn:/usr/sbin/getty -h tty0p1 9600
#ttp2:234:respawn:/usr/sbin/getty -h tty0p2 9600
#ttp3:234:respawn:/usr/sbin/getty -h tty0p3 9600
#ttp4:234:respawn:/usr/sbin/getty -h tty0p4 9600
#ttp5:234:respawn:/usr/sbin/getty -h tty0p5 9600
krsd:123456:respawn:/sbin/krsd -i
sfd:123456:respawn:/sbin/sfd
#ups::respawn:rtprio 0 /usr/lbin/ups_mond -f /etc/ups_conf
```

The format of the entries in the configuration file is as follows:

```
id:rstate:action:process
```

id	Unique one-to-four character identifier, used for each entry.
rstate	The run level in which the entry will be processed. An entry can have multiple run levels specified.
action	This value instructs init how to action the process in the next field. The values are boot, bootwait, initdefault, off, once, ondemand, powerfail, powerwait, respawn, sysinit, and wait. Refer to the inittab (4) man page for the actions init will take for each of the above values.
process	The process or shell command to be executed.

The following are some of the other important events that take place when the inittab file is processed:

▶ The /sbin/ioinitrc shell script calls the **ioinit** command. This tests and maintains consistency between the kernel data structures and the

/etc/ioconfig file. The ioconfig file is used to retain the IO configuration across reboots. Refer to the *ioinit and ioconfig manual pages* for more details.

▶ The /sbin/bcheckrc shell script runs the **fsck** command to check and repair file systems. It also starts the LVM if it is being used on the system.

▶ The /sbin/rc shell script runs when the run level of the system is changed. The processes for the run level are started when moving to a higher run level or stopped when moving to a lower run level.

Run levels

A run level can be explained as the system operational state. A run level itself is defined as a specific set of processes currently running on a specific run level. In HP-UX, there are various different run levels, as Table 4-4 shows.

Table 4-4   HP-UX run levels

Run level	Description
0	System shutdown level. All processes and the system are stopped.
s	Single user mode; used for system maintenance. Only the system console is active. Only kernel processes and daemons are active.
S	Same as run level s, except that the terminal being used temporarily acts as the console.
1	Certain essential processes are started. It is also single user mode and used for system maintenance.
2	Most system daemons and login processes are started. Called the multi-user level. Logins are possible locally and remotely.
3	Network services are started and NFS file systems are exported.
4	Activates graphical processes for CDE.
5	Can be used for user-defined services.
6	Can be used for user-defined services.

The run level can be changed with the **init** command with the desired run level as the argument to the command. For example, to change to run level 3 from a lower level or from single user mode the command is:

```
init 3
```

Please note that changing down to a single user mode, *run level s or S*, does not stop all system activity. We therefore recommend that you use the shutdown command from a running system to bring the system down into single user mode in an orderly manner.

To see the current run level of the system, use the command **who** **−r**.

The last three fields indicate the current run level, the number of times the system has been in this level and the previous system level:

```
# who -r
       .       run-level 3  Jun  9 16:52    3    0    S
```

System startup files

After being invoked from inittab, the /sbin/rc script calls execution startup and shutdown scripts to start and stop the various subsystems. This section briefly explains the mechanism and files used in this process.

Sequencer script

The /sbin/rc is called the startup and shutdown sequencer script. Depending on which run level the system is changed to, this script invokes the execution scripts as either startup or shutdown (kill) scripts. This script reads the variable values from the configuration variable script, /etc/rc.config.

Execution scripts

The execution scripts are startup and shutdown scripts and are located in the /sbin/init.d directory.

The execution scripts should be able to recognize the following four arguments:

start   The script names beginning with S should perform its start actions.

stop   The script names beginning with K should perform its stop actions.

start_msg The argument is passed to script names beginning with S so that the script can report back a short message indicating what the start action will do.

stop_msg The argument is passed to script names beginning with K so that the script can report back a short message indicating what the stop action will do.

Configuration variable files

The configuration variable files are contained in the /etc/rc.config.d directory. The variables in these files are updated to allow or prevent the execution scripts from starting. All these files are called by the /etc/rc.config script and the variables stored for use by the /sbin/rc script (see Example 4-5). The files, by convention, are usually named the same as the execution scripts in the /sbin/init.d directory.

Example 4-5   Example of /etc/rc.config.d/clean

```
##!/sbin/sh
# @(#)B.11.11_LR
```

```
# Clean up configuration
#
# CLEAN_ADM:    Set to 1 to move old log files out of the way.  See
#               /sbin/init.d/clean_adm.
# CLEAN_UUCP:   Set to 1 to clean up uucp spool directory.
#
CLEAN_ADM=1
CLEAN_UUCP=1
```

In Example 4-5 on page 97, the value of one for the variables, CLEAN_ADM and CLEAN_UUCP, enables the scripts to start.

Sequencer directories

These directories contain symbolic links to the execution script files in /sbin/init.d. The link files follow a naming convention, for example, /sbin/rc2.d/S900samba:

rc2.d   The sequencer directory is numbered to reflect the run level for which its contents will be executed. In this case, start scripts in this directory will be executed upon entering run level 2 from run level 1, and kill scripts will be executed upon entering run level 2 from run level 3.

S   The first character of a sequencer link name determines whether the script is executed as a start script (if the character is S) or as a kill script (if the character is K).

900   A three-digit number is used for sequencing scripts within the sequencer directory. Scripts are executed by type (start or kill) in alphabetical order as defined by the shell. Although it is not recommended, two scripts may share the same sequence number.

samba   The name of the startup script follows the sequence number. The startup script name, by convention, should be the same name as the 'script to which this sequencer entry is linked. In this example, the link points to /sbin/init.d/samba.

Scripts are executed in alphabetical order. The entire file name of the script is used for alphabetical ordering purposes. When ordering start and kill script links, note that subsystems started in any given order should be stopped in the reverse order to eliminate any dependencies between subsystems. This means that kill scripts will generally not have the same numbers as their start script counterparts.

/etc/rc.log

The console displays messages (as shown in Example 4-6 on page 99) for each of the subsystems as they are started. All startup scripts messages and return values are logged to the /etc/rc.log file. You can view this file if a problem is suspected with one of the startup scripts.

Example 4-6   HP-UX startup messages

Rights for non-DOD U.S. Government Departments and Agencies are as set
forth in FAR 52.227-19(c)(1,2).

/sbin/auto_parms: DHCP access is disabled (see /etc/auto_parms.log)

                    HP-UX Start-up in progress
        _____

        Configure system crash dumps .... OK
        VxVM device node check... OK
        VxVM general startup ... . OK
        VxVM reconfiguration recovery.. OK
        Mount file systems... OK
        Update kernel and loadable modules.................................... N/A
        Initialize loadable modules.. OK
        Setting hostname... OK
        Start Kernel Logging facility... N/A
        Set privilege group... N/A
        Display date.. N/A
        Copy processor logs to /var/tombstones................................. OK
        Save system crash dump if needed...................................... N/A
        Enable auxiliary swap space.. OK
        Start syncer daemon.. OK
        Configure Loopback interfaces (lo0).................................... OK
        VxVM volume recovery start... OK
        Configuring all unconfigured software filesets......................... OK
        Recover editor crash files... OK
        Clean UUCP... OK
        List and/or clear temporary files..................................... OK
        Clean up old log files... OK
        Start system message logging daemon.................................... OK
        Start pty allocator daemon... OK
        Configuring OLA/R interface... N/A
        Start network tracing and logging daemon............................... OK

For more information about the startup process in HP-UX, refer to the manuals
mentioned earlier in this chapter, which can be located at:

    http://www.docs.hp.com

4.2.2 Startup process in AIX 5L

The /etc/inittab file (see Example 4-7 on page 100) lists the processes that init
will start, and it also specifies when to start them. If this file gets corrupted, the

system will not boot properly. It is useful to keep a backup of this file. The default run level on AIX 5L is run level 2.

The fields are:

▶ identifier: Up to 14 characters that identify the process. Terminals use their logical device name as an identifier.

▶ runlevel: Defines what run levels the process is valid for. AIX 5L uses run levels of 0–9. If the **telinit** command is used to change the run level, a SIGTERM signal will be sent to all processes that are not defined for the new run level. If after 20 seconds a process has not terminated, a SIGKILL signal is sent. The default run level for the system is 2, which is AIX 5L multiuser mode.

▶ action: How to treat the process. Valid actions are:

  − respawn: If the process does not exist, start it.
  − wait: Start the process and wait for it to finish before reading the next line.
  − once: Start the process and do not restart it if it stops.
  − sysinit: Commands to be run before trying to access the console.
  − off: Do not run the command.
  − command: The AIX 5L command to run to start the process.

Example 4-7   Example of /etc/inittab file

```
init:2:initdefault:
brc::sysinit:/sbin/rc.boot 3 >/dev/console 2>&1 # Phase 3 of system boot
powerfail::powerfail:/etc/rc.powerfail 2>&1 | alog -tboot > /dev/console #
Power Failure Detection
load64bit:2:wait:/etc/methods/cfg64 >/dev/console 2>&1 # Enable 64-bit execs
rc:23456789:wait:/etc/rc 2>&1 | alog -tboot > /dev/console # Multi-User checks
fbcheck:23456789:wait:/usr/sbin/fbcheck 2>&1 | alog -tboot > /dev/console # run
/etc/firstboot
srcmstr:23456789:respawn:/usr/sbin/srcmstr # System Resource Controller
rctcpip:23456789:wait:/etc/rc.tcpip > /dev/console 2>&1 # Start TCP/IP daemons
ihshttpd:2:wait:/usr/HTTPServer/bin/httpd > /dev/console 2>&1 # Start HTTP
daemon
rcnfs:23456789:wait:/etc/rc.nfs > /dev/console 2>&1 # Start NFS Daemons
cron:23456789:respawn:/usr/sbin/cron
piobe:2:wait:/usr/lib/lpd/pio/etc/pioinit >/dev/null 2>&1  # pb cleanup
qdaemon:23456789:wait:/usr/bin/startsrc -sqdaemon
writesrv:23456789:wait:/usr/bin/startsrc -swritesrv
uprintfd:23456789:respawn:/usr/sbin/uprintfd
shdaemon:2:off:/usr/sbin/shdaemon >/dev/console 2>&1 # High availability daemon
l2:2:wait:/etc/rc.d/rc 2
l3:3:wait:/etc/rc.d/rc 3
l4:4:wait:/etc/rc.d/rc 4
l5:5:wait:/etc/rc.d/rc 5
l6:6:wait:/etc/rc.d/rc 6
```

```
17:7:wait:/etc/rc.d/rc 7
18:8:wait:/etc/rc.d/rc 8
19:9:wait:/etc/rc.d/rc 9
ctrmc:2:once:/usr/bin/startsrc -s ctrmc > /dev/console 2>&1
logsymp:2:once:/usr/lib/ras/logsymptom # for system dumps
pmd:2:wait:/usr/bin/pmd > /dev/console 2>&1 # Start PM daemon
itess:23456789:once:/usr/IMNSearch/bin/itess -start search >/dev/null 2>&1
diagd:2:once:/usr/lpp/diagnostics/bin/diagd >/dev/console 2>&1
dt:2:wait:/etc/rc.dt
cons:0123456789:respawn:/usr/sbin/getty /dev/console
httpdlite:23456789:once:/usr/IMNSearch/httpdlite/httpdlite -r
/etc/IMNSearch/httpdlite/httpdlite.conf & >/dev/console 2>&1
```

There are new entries in the inittab that have been added with AIX 5L Version 5.1. Look for ctrmc (Resource Monitoring and Control subsystem) and shdaemon (system hang detection daemon) in the inittab listing in Example 4-7 on page 100.

The format in the /etc/inittab is:

```
id:runlevel:action:command
```

The inittab file is reread by the init daemon every 60 seconds. The **telinit q** command is only needed if you cannot wait for the next 60-second check.

To add records into the inittab file, you should use the **mkitab** command. For example, to add an entry for tty4, enter the following command:

```
# mkitab "tty4:2:respawn:/usr/sbin/getty /dev/tty4"
```

You can use the -i option to add records after a particular entry.

To change currently existing entries from this file, use the **chitab** command. For example, to change tty4's run level, enter the following command:

```
# chitab "tty4:23:respawn:/usr/sbin/getty /dev/tty4"
```

AIX 5L run levels

AIX 5L uses a default run level of 2. This is the normal multi-user mode. AIX 5L does not follow the System V R4 run level specification with special meanings for run levels 0, 3, 5, and 6. In AIX 5L, run levels of 0–1 are reserved, 2 is the default, and 3–9 can be defined according to the system administrator's preference.

The **telinit** command can be used to change the run level for the system. This can also be accomplished using the **smitty telinit** fast path. Once the **telinit** command is used to change the run level, the system will begin to respond by telling you which processes are terminating or starting as a result of the change in the run level.

Use the **shutdown -m** command to enter maintenance mode. When the system enters maintenance mode from another run level, only the system console is used as the terminal.

System Resource Controller (SRC)

Many lines in the /etc/inittab file contain one or several SRC statements. The System Resource Controller provides a set of commands to make it easier for the administrator to control subsystems.

A subsystem group is a group of any specified subsystems. Grouping systems together allows the control of several subsystems at one time, for example, TCP/IP, SNA Services, NIS, and NFS.

A subserver is a program or process that belongs to a subsystem. A subsystem can have multiple subservers and is responsible for starting, stopping, and providing the status of subservers.

Subservers are started when their parent subsystems are started. If you try to start a subserver and its parent subsystem is not active, the **startsrc** command starts the subsystem as well. The relationship between the group and subsystem is easily seen from the output of **lssrc -a**.

Some examples of the command are shown below:

► To list SRC status run:

```
# lssrc -g nfs
Subsystem        Group        PID      Status
 biod            nfs          11354    active
 rpc.lockd       nfs          11108    active
 nfsd            nfs                   inoperative
 rpc.statd       nfs                   inoperative
 rpc.mountd      nfs                   inoperative
```

► To list a long status of a subsystem run:

```
# lssrc -ls inetd
Subsystem        Group        PID          Status
 inetd           tcpip        10322        active

Debug          Not active

Signal         Purpose
 SIGALRM        Establishes socket connections for failed services.
 SIGHUP         Rereads the configuration database and reconfigures services.
```

```
SIGCHLD          Restarts the service in case the service ends abnormally.
```

```
Service        Command                     Description            Status
cmsd           /usr/dt/bin/rpc.cmsd        cmsd 100068 2-5        active
ttdbserver     /usr/dt/bin/rpc.ttdbserver rpc.ttdbserver 100083 1 active
dpclSD         /etc/dpclSD                 dpclSD /etc/dpcld      active
pmv4           /etc/pmdv4                  pmdv4                  active
dtspc          /usr/dt/bin/dtspcd          /usr/dt/bin/dtspcd    active
time           internal                                          active
daytime        internal                                          active
time           internal                                          active
daytime        internal                                          active
ntalk          /usr/sbin/talkd             talkd                 active
exec           /usr/sbin/rexecd            rexecd                active
login          /usr/sbin/rlogind           rlogind               active
shell          /usr/sbin/rshd              rshd                  active
telnet         /usr/sbin/telnetd           telnetd -a            active
ftp            /usr/sbin/ftpd              ftpd                  active
```

► To start a subsystem, run:

```
# startsrc -s lpd
0513-059 The lpd Subsystem has been started. Subsystem PID is 24224.
```

► To stop a subsystem, run:

```
# stopsrc -s lpd
0513-044 The lpd Subsystem was requested to stop.
```

For more information about the AIX 5L boot and startup process, refer to the following publications:

► *AIX 5L Version 5.3 System Management Guide: Operating System and Devices,* SC23-4910-01

```
http://publib.boulder.ibm.com/infocenter/pseries/topic/com.ibm.aix.doc/aixb
man/baseadmn/baseadmn.pdf
```

► *IBM @server Certification Study Guide - pSeries AIX System Administration,* SG24-6191

```
http://www.redbooks.ibm.com/abstracts/sg246191.html
```

► *IBM @server Certification Study Guide - AIX 5L Installation and System Recovery,* SG24-6183

```
http://publib-b.boulder.ibm.com/abstracts/sg246183.html
```

4.3 System shutdown

Critical UNIX servers are made to be left powered on continuously; however, you must halt or shut down the system and sometimes turn the power off when performing several maintenance tasks, such as:

- ► Turning off a system's power due to an anticipated power outage
- ► Adding or removing system hardware that is not hot-pluggable or hot-swappable
- ► Installing a new release of the operating system
- ► Moving a system from one location to another

4.3.1 HP-UX

The system can be shut down using a number of commands. They are listed and described in the following sections.

shutdown

The **shutdown** command is used to terminate all currently running processes. It can be used to take down the system into single user mode for maintenance and administrative purposes, as shown in Table 4-5.

It can be used to halt the system for powering off and for rebooting the system.

```
/sbin/shutdown [-h|-r] [-y] [grace]
```

Table 4-5   Frequently used options of the shutdown command

Flags	Explanation
-h	Shuts the system down and does a halt.
-r	Shuts the system down and reboots automatically.
-y	Does not require any response from the user.
grace	Duration in seconds in which users are allowed to log off before system shutdown. The default period is 60.

To take the system down into single-user mode:

```
# shutdown
```

To shut down and reboot the system automatically:

```
# shutdown -r
```

To shut down and halt the system in ten minutes, with no response required from the user:

```
# shutdown -hy 600
```

Please refer to the *shutdown (1M) manual page* for the other arguments, options, and examples of the command.

init changes the system run level to zero, which shuts down the system.

 # init 0 changes the run level to zero, which shuts down the system.

reboot

The **reboot** command can also be used to reboot or halt the system. Unlike the **shutdown** command, it does not terminate all the running processes and it does not run the subsystem shutdown scripts. It is therefore recommended to use the **shutdown** command to stop the system in an orderly manner.

Refer to the manual pages for the above commands for a complete list of arguments and options.

/etc/Shutdown.allow file

The system can only be shutdown by a user if the user name is included in this file. If the file does not exist or is zero length in size, the root user can still shut the system down.

4.3.2 AIX 5L

In AIX 5L, there are three commands you can use to shut down the system: **init**, **halt**, and **shutdown**. The **shutdown** command has more options, as shown in Table 4-7 on page 107.

Using the init command

The following flags can be used to shut down the machine by using the **init** command: S, s, M, and m.

Using these flags tells the **init** command to enter the maintenance mode. When the system enters maintenance mode from another run level, only the system console is used as the terminal.

From maintenance mode, you can use the **init 2** command to enter into multi-user level.

Using the halt or fasthalt command

The **halt** command (Table 4-6) writes data to the disk and then stops the processor. The machine does not restart. Only a root user should run this command. Do not use this command if other users are logged into the system. If no other users are logged in, the **halt** command can be used. Use the **halt** command if you are not going to restart the machine immediately. When the message ....Halt completed.... is displayed, you can turn the power off. On newer systems, **halt** or **fasthalt** will power off the system.

The **halt** command logs the shutdown using the **syslogd** command and places a record of the shutdown in /var/adm/wtmp, the login accounting file. The system also writes an entry into the error log, which states that the system was shut down.

The **fasthalt** command stops the system by calling the **halt** command. The **fasthalt** command provides BSD compatibility. The syntax is:

{ halt | fasthalt } [-l] [-n] [-p] [-q] [-y]

Table 4-6   The halt command

Flags	Explanation
-l	Does not log the halt in the accounting file. The -l flag does not suppress the accounting file update. The -n and -q flags imply the -l flag.
-n	Prevents the sync before stopping.
-p	Halts the system without a power down. The -p flag will have no effect if used in combination with flags not requiring a permanent halt. Power will still be turned off if other operands request a delayed power on and reboot.
-q	Causes a quick halt. Running the **halt** command with the -q flag does not issue sync, so the system will halt immediately.
-y	Halts the system from a dial-up operation.

Using the shutdown command

The **shutdown** command (see Table 4-7 on page 107) is used to shut the system down cleanly. If used with no options, it will display a message on all enabled terminals (using the **wall** command). Then, after one minute, the command will disable all terminals, kill all processes on the system, sync the disks, unmount all file systems, and then halt the system.

You can also use **shutdown** with the -F option for a fast immediate shutdown (no warning), -r to reboot after the shutdown, or -m to bring the system down into maintenance mode.

The -k flag produces a "pretend" shutdown—it will appear to all users that the machine is about to shut down, but no shutdown will actually occur.

Table 4-7   Frequently used options of the shutdown command

Flags	Explanation
-d	Brings the system down from a distributed mode to a multiuser mode.
-F	Does a fast shutdown, bypassing the messages to other users and bringing the system down as quickly as possible.
-h	Halts the operating system completely; same as the -v flag.
-i	Specifies interactive mode. Displays interactive messages to guide the user through the shutdown.
-k	Avoids shutting down the system.
-m	Brings the system down to maintenance (single user) mode.
-r	Restarts the system after being shut down with the **reboot** command.
-l	In AIX 5L Version 5.1, creates a new file (/etc/shutdown.log) and appends the log output to it. This may be helpful in resolving problems with the shutdown procedure. While the output is generally not extensive, if the root file system is full, the log output will not be captured.
-t	Restarts the system on the date specified by mmddHHMM [yy].

Some examples of the **shutdown** command are:

► To turn off the machine, enter the following command:

```
# shutdown
```

This shuts down the system, waiting one minute before stopping the user processes and the init process.

► To give users more time to finish what they are doing and bring the system to maintenance mode, enter the following command:

```
# shutdown -m +2
```

This brings the system down from multi-user mode to maintenance mode after waiting two minutes.

▶ To restart the system, enter the following command:

```
# shutdown -Fr
```

This brings the system down as quickly as possible and then reboots the system.

If you need a customized shutdown sequence, you can create a file called /etc/rc.shutdown. If this file exists, it is called by the **shutdown** command and is executed first. For example, this is useful if you need to close a database prior to a shutdown. If rc.shutdown fails (non-zero return code value), the shutdown cycle is terminated.

For more information about AIX 5L's system shutdown process, refer to *AIX 5L Version 5.3 System Management Guide: Operating System and Devices,* SC23-4910-01, which can be found at:

```
http://publib.boulder.ibm.com/infocenter/pseries/topic/com.ibm.aix.doc/aixb
man/baseadmn/baseadmn.pdf
```

4.4 Manage the system environment

The System Administration Manager (SAM) tool allows many system administration tasks to be performed. It makes many routine tasks easier to work with than doing the same tasks from the command-line interface. Table 4-8 summarizes the main functional areas in SAM.

Table 4-8 shows an overview of the main System Administration Manager menu functions.

Table 4-8   SAM

Functional area	Explanation
Accounts for users and groups	Routine administration of users and groups. Adding, modifying, and removing.
Auditing and security	System security management and setting up of auditing events.
Backup and recovery	Scheduling of automated backups. Interactive backups feature. Performing restores.
Disks and file systems	Management of disks, file systems, logical volumes, volume groups, and swap and devices.
Display	Graphical display configuration.

Functional area	Explanation
Kernel configuration	View and change kernel parameters, drivers, dump devices, and subsystems.
Networking and communications	Configure and modify network applications and interfaces.
Performance monitors	Monitor performance of system components. View system properties.
Peripheral devices	Display and configure interface adapters, devices, and peripherals.
Printers and plotters	Configuration of printer devices.
Process management	Control processes and schedule cron jobs.
Resource management	System resource monitoring.
Routine tasks	Selective file removal; manage system log files and system shutdown.
Run SAM on remote systems	Manage remote systems.
Software management	View, install, remove, and copy software.
Time	Configure Network Time Protocol and system clock setup.

The System Environment selection in SMIT controls many different aspects of the system. Example 4-8 shows the SMIT system environment screen.

Example 4-8   System Environments smitty screen

```
                    System Environments

Move cursor to desired item and press Enter.

  Stop the System
  Assign the Console
  Change / Show Date and Time
  Manage Language Environment
  Change / Show Characteristics of Operating System
  Change / Show Number of Licensed Users
  Broadcast Message to all Users
  Manage System Logs
  Change / Show Characteristics of System Dump
  Change System User Interface
  Internet and Documentation Services
  Enable 64-bit Application Environment
```

```
Manage Remote Reboot Facility
Manage System Hang Detection

F1=Help           F2=Refresh          F3=Cancel          F8=Image
F9=Shell          F10=Exit            Enter=Do
```

Table 4-9 shows an overview for the system environment screen.

Table 4-9   System environments

System entry	Explanation
Stop the system	Runs the **shutdown** command.
Assign the console	Allows assignment or reassignment of the system console. A reboot is required for it to take effect.
Change/show date and time	Runs the **date** command to set the date and time. Time zones are also controlled here. Time in AIX 5L is kept in CUT (GMT) time and is converted and displayed using the local time zone.
Manage language environments	Sets up the language information on your system.
Change/Show Characteristics of the Operating System	Allows dynamic setting of kernel parameters.
Change/Show Number of Licensed Users	Shows status of fixed and floating licenses.
Manage AIX 5L Floating User Licenses for this Server	Sets up floating licenses.
Broadcast Message to all Users	Issues the **wall** command.
Manage System Logs	Displays and cleans up various system logs.
Change/Show Characteristics of System Dump	Manages what happens when your system panics, crashes, and dumps system data.
Internet and Documentation Services	Controls setting up of the Web-based documentation.
Change System User Interface	Determines whether CDE, GNOME, KDE, or command-line login is used.

System entry	Explanation
Enable 64-bit Application Environment	Enables the 64-bit application environment immediately or with restart.
Manage Remote Reboot Facility	Allows you to reboot the system through an integrated serial port.
Manage System Hang Detection	The System Hang Detection alerts the administrator and allows the system to perform several actions when a hang is suspected.

4.5 Quick reference

Table 4-10 on page 112 shows the different system startup and shutdown phases and commands for HP-UX and for AIX 5L.

Table 4-10   Quick reference for system startup and shutdown

Tasks/locations	AIX 5L	HP-UX
Boot process.	Phases: ► Read Only Storage (ROS): Check the system board, perform Power-On Self-Test (POST), locate the boot image, load the boot image into memory, begin system initialization, and execute phase 1 of the /etc/rc.boot script. ► Base Device Configuration: Start Configuration Manager to configure base devices. ► System Boot: Start init process phase 2, switch to hard-disk root file system, start other processes defined by records in the /etc/inittab file, and execute phase 3 of the /etc/rc.boot script.	Phases: ► PDC: When system is reset or powered on, firmware does self tests and initializes hardware. The autoboot sequence is started. User can interrupt the process and interact with PDC. Control is transferred to ISL. ► ISL: Starts operating independent part of the boot process. When autoboot flag is enabled, complete boot process occurs without user intervention. ► hpux: Secondary system loader loads and passes control to the kernel. ► init: Reads /etc/inittab file and starts system in default run level. Then starts the rest of the process defined for the run levels.

Tasks/locations	AIX 5L	HP-UX
System run levels.	Defined run levels: ▶ 0–1: Reserved for future use ▶ 2: Multiuser mode with NFS resources shared (default run level) ▶ 3-9: Defined according to the user's preferences ▶ m,M,s,S: Single-user mode (maintenance level) ▶ a,b,c: Starts processes assigned to the new run levels while leaving the existing processes at the current level running ▶ Q,q: `init` command to reexamine the /etc/inittab file Note: When a level is specified, the `init` command kills processes at the current level and restarts any processes associated with the new run level based on the /etc/inittab file.	Defined run levels: ▶ 0: Power-down state. ▶ s or S: Single-user state system maintenance and administration. ▶ 1: Single-user state system maintenance and administration. ▶ 2: Multiuser state. Local and remote logins possible. ▶ 3: Multiuser state with NFS and network services started (default run level). ▶ 4: Graphical managers activated. ▶ 5: User-defined services. ▶ 6: User-defined services.
Determine a system's run level.	`who -r`	`who -r`
Change a system's run level.	`telinit level number`	`init level number`
Startup script.	/etc/rc	/sbin/rc
Boot process and startup log.	`alog` command	/etc/rc.log
Display or alter the list of boot devices.	`bootlist`	`setboot`
Shut down and reboot.	`shutdown -Fr`	`shutdown -ry 0`
Shut down and halt.	`shutdown` or `halt`	`shutdown -h`

Tasks/locations	AIX 5L	HP-UX
Kernel modules directory.	Kernel and kernel extension modules are stored in two directories: ► /usr/lib/boot ► /usr/lib/drivers	Kernel modules are stored in these directories: ► /stand/system ► /stand/vmunix ► /stand/dlkm

Device management

This chapter provides a description of the most common device management tasks in HP-UX 11i and AIX 5L Version 5.3. We also highlight differences between the two operating systems in relation to devices and device management.

In this chapter, the following topics are discussed for each operating system:

5.1 Overview

Before starting with the topics related to device management, let us review the terminology used by HP-UX 11i and AIX 5L Version 5.3:

Physical device   Actual hardware that is connected in some way to the system.

Ports   The physical connectors/adapters in the system, where the physical devices are attached.

Device driver   Software in the kernel that controls the activity on a port and the format of the data that is sent to a device.

Logical device   This is a software interface that presents a means of accessing a physical device to the user and application programs. Data written to the logical device will be sent to the appropriate device driver. Data read from logical devices will be read from the appropriate device driver.

The following commands are the primary methods of device management in HP-UX 11i:

`insf`	Installs/reinstalls special files
`ioscan`	Displays and modifies the physical to logical device mapping
`lsdev`	Lists all drivers available to the currently running kernel
`lssf`	Lists information about the specified special file
`mksf`	Manually creates a special file
`print_manifest`	Displays hardware and software configuration information
`rad`	Manages hot swap *Remove Add Delete* operations

The following commands are the primary methods of device management in AIX 5L Version 5.3:

`cfgmgr`	Configures devices into the system
`drslot`	Manages a dynamically reconfigurable slot
`lsattr`	Displays attribute characteristics and possible values for devices in the system
`lscfg`	Displays configuration information about logical devices
`lsdev`	Displays logical devices in the system and their characteristics
`lsslot`	Displays dynamically reconfigurable slots

mkdev	Creates a device file
prtconf	Displays system and configuration information
rmdev	Removes logical devices from the system

5.2 Listing devices

On any operating system, it is always good to know what underlying hardware you have connected.

5.2.1 Listing devices in HP-UX

The primary command for listing attached hardware in the HP-UX world is the **ioscan** command. For example, to display all devices in the class of *disk* (so all devices that think they are disks) run the command:

```
# ioscan -funC disk
Class  I  H/W Path    Driver     S/W State H/W Type  Description
=====================================================================
disk   0  10/0.3.0    sdisk      CLAIMED   DEVICE    Quantum XP34361WD
                     /dev/dsk/c1t3d0    /dev/rdsk/c1t3d0
disk   1  10/0.4.0    sdisk      CLAIMED   DEVICE    Quantum XP34361WD
                     /dev/dsk/c1t4d0    /dev/rdsk/c1t4d0
disk   2  10/0.5.0    sdisk      CLAIMED   DEVICE    SEAGATE ST34371W
                     /dev/dsk/c1t5d0    /dev/rdsk/c1t5d0
disk   3  10/0.6.0    sdisk      CLAIMED   DEVICE    SEAGATE ST34371W
                     /dev/dsk/c1t6d0    /dev/rdsk/c1t6d0
disk   4  10/12/5.2.0 sdisk      CLAIMED   DEVICE    TOSHIBA CD-ROM XM-5701TA
                     /dev/dsk/c3t2d0    /dev/rdsk/c3t2d0
```

The more interesting columns from the **ioscan** command are:

H/W Path
The hardware path to the device. Each model of machine uses different logical relationships between the hardware and the software. For more information, see the documentation supplied with the machine.

Driver
The software driver the kernel will use to access this hardware.

S/W State
From the man page for **ioscan** (1m).

> **CLAIMED**   Software bound successfully.
>
> **UNCLAIMED**   No associated software found.
>
> **DIFF_HW**   Software found does not match the associated software.

NO_HW	The hardware at this address is no longer responding.	
ERROR	The hardware at this address is responding but is in an error state.	
SCAN	Node locked, try again later.	
Device	The disk device used to interface with the driver.	

For a particular device file, you can also use the **lssf** command. For example, to display information about /dev/dsk/c3t2d0:

```
# lssf /dev/dsk/c3t2d0
sdisk card instance 3 SCSI target 2 SCSI LUN 0 section 0 at address 10/12/5.2.0
/dev/dsk/c3t2d0
```

The **lsdev** command tells you what device drivers are configured into the kernel and what their corresponding major numbers are, as shown in Example 5-1.

Example 5-1   lsdev command output

```
# lsdev|head
     Character      Block      Driver         Class
        0            -1        cn             pseudo
        2            -1        devkrs         pseudo
        3            -1        mm             pseudo
        4            -1        lpr0           unknown
        5            -1        btlan          lan
        6            -1        ip             pseudo
        7            -1        arp            pseudo
        8            -1        rawip          pseudo
       10            -1        tcp            pseudo

or

# lsdev -d sdisk
     Character      Block      Driver         Class
       188           31        sdisk          disk
```

The **prtconf** command displays a summary of installed hardware and software. Example 5-2 shows an extract of the hardware configuration detail from the **prtconf** command.

Example 5-2   Hardware configuration details from the prtconf command

```
System Hardware

     Model:            9000/889/K460
     Main Memory:      1535 MB
     Processors:       4
```

```
OS mode:            64 bit
HW capability:      32 or 64 bit
LAN hardware ID:    0x0060B0FD2E09
Software ID:        1289854341
Keyboard Language:  Not_Applicable

Storage devices              HW Path    Interface
Quantum XP34361WD 4095 Mb    10/0.3.0   GSC built-in Fast/Wide SCSI Interface
TOSHIBA CD-ROM XM-5701TA     10/12/5.2.0 Built-in SCSI
HP C1533A                    10/12/5.0.0 Built-in SCSI

I/O Interfaces
Class      H/W Path    Driver    Description
ext_bus    8/0         c720      GSC add-on Fast/Wide SCSI Interface
ext_bus    10/0        c720      GSC built-in Fast/Wide SCSI Interface
tty        10/4/0      mux2      MUX
ext_bus    10/8        c720      GSC add-on Fast/Wide SCSI Interface
ext_bus    10/12/0     CentIf    Built-in Parallel Interface
ext_bus    10/12/5     c720      Built-in SCSI
lan        10/12/6     lan2      Built-in LAN
ps2        10/12/7     ps2       Built-in Keyboard/Mouse
```

5.2.2 Listing devices in AIX 5L

The **prtconf** command displays system configuration information. This includes hardware and volume group configuration. It basically comprises **lscfg**, **lsps**, **lsvg -p <vg's>**, and more.

A portion of a **prtconf** command is shown in Example 5-3.

Example 5-3   prtconf command output

```
# prtconf| head -25
System Model: IBM,7038-6M2
Machine Serial Number: 10197AA
Processor Type: PowerPC_POWER4
Number Of Processors: 4
Processor Clock Speed: 1200 MHz
CPU Type: 64-bit
Kernel Type: 32-bit
LPAR Info: 1 NULL
Memory Size: 8192 MB
Good Memory Size: 8192 MB
Platform Firmware level: 3K041029
Firmware Version: IBM,RG041029_d79e00_r
Console Login: enable
Auto Restart: true
Full Core: false
```

```
Network Information
        Host Name: alexander
        IP Address: 22.1.1.199
        Sub Netmask: 255.255.255.0
        Gateway: 22.1.1.1
        Name Server: 22.21.16.7
        Domain Name: thelab.ibm.com
```

The other main command that we use is **lsdev**. This command queries the ODM, so we can use it to locate the customized devices or the predefined devices. Here we have some examples of this command:

```
# lsdev -Cc disk
hdisk0 Available 20-60-00-8,0   16 Bit LVD SCSI Disk Drive
hdisk1 Available 20-60-00-9,0   16 Bit SCSI Disk Drive
hdisk2 Available 20-60-00-10,0  16 Bit SCSI Disk Drive
hdisk3 Available 20-60-00-11,0  16 Bit SCSI Disk Drive
hdisk4 Available 20-60-00-13,0  16 Bit SCSI Disk Drive
```

In this first example, the -C option (upper case) means that we want to query the customized section of ODM, while the -c option (lower case) is used to query a class under the customized section of ODM. The columns are as follows:

First column   This is the name of the logical device (for example, hdisk0).

Second column   This columns shows the state of the device (for example, available or defined).

Third column   This column specifies the location code for the device. The location codes consist of up to four fields of information, and they differ based on model type. The format of the location code is AB-CD-EF-GH. The location code that we describe here is for the CHRP architecture, which means any multiprocessor PCI bus system. To find the architecture type for your system, you may use the **# bootinfo -p** command.

In the CHRP architecture, the location codes are:

AB   Defines the bus type

           00 for processor bus

           01 for ISA buses

           04 for PCI buses

CD   Defines the slot in which the adapter is located; if you find letters in this field instead of numbers, that means that the adapter is built-in (integrated) to the system planar.

EF This field defines the connector ID. It is used to identify the adapter connector to which a resource is attached (for example, a SCSI adapter with two ports). In adapters with only one port, this value is always 00.

GH Defines a port, address, memory module, or device of FRU. GH has several meanings, depending upon the resource type.

- ► For memory cards, this value defines a memory module. Values are 1 through 16. For modules plugged directly to the system planar, the values look like this: 00-00-00-GH.

- ► For L2 Cache, GH defines the cache value.

- ► For async devices, it defines the port on the fanout box. The possible values are 0 through 15.

- ► For diskette drives, H defines which diskette drive (1 or 2). G is always 0.

For SCSI devices, the location code is exactly the same for AB-CD-EF values. The only difference is in G and H:

G Defines the control unit address of the device (SCSI ID). Possible values are 0 to 15.

H Defines the logical unit number (LUN) for the device. Possible values are 0 to 255.

All adapters and cards are identified with only AB-CD.

> **Note:** As mentioned, the actual values in the location codes vary from model to model. For specific values, you need to refer to the Service Guide for your model. It can be found online at:
>
> `http://www.ibm.com/servers/eserver/pseries/library/hardware_docs/index.html`

Fourth column This last column contains the description for the device.

```
# lsdev -Cc adapter
sa0     Available 01-S1    Standard I/O Serial Port
```

```
sa1        Available 01-S2    Standard I/O Serial Port
sa2        Available 01-S3    Standard I/O Serial Port
siokma0    Available 01-K1    Keyboard/Mouse Adapter
fda0       Available 01-D1    Standard I/O Diskette Adapter
scsi0      Available 10-60    Wide SCSI I/O Controller
mga0       Available 20-58    GXT120P Graphics Adapter
scsi1      Available 20-60    Wide/Fast-20 SCSI I/O Controller
scsi2      Available 30-58    Wide SCSI I/O Controller
sioka0     Available 01-K1-00 Keyboard Adapter
ppa0       Available 01-R1    Standard I/O Parallel Port Adapter
tok0       Available 10-68    IBM PCI Tokenring Adapter (14101800)
ssa0       Available 10-70    IBM SSA Enhanced RAID Adapter (14104500)
ent0       Available 10-78    IBM 10/100/1000 Base-T Ethernet PCI Adapter
ent1       Available 10-80    IBM PCI Ethernet Adapter (22100020)
scraid0    Available 30-60    IBM PCI SCSI RAID Adapter
sioma0     Available 01-K1-01 Mouse Adapter
```

As you can see in this example, we make a query in the customized section of the ODM, looking into the adapter class. If you look at the second column, you will find that the location code only has two or three fields, instead of four. This is because it only defines the adapter slot.

Other useful options for the **lsdev** command are:

-P   Queries the predefined section of the ODM.

-H   This flag can be used with -C or -P, and it will provide a long listing output with headers of all the configured or predefined (supported) devices (# **lsdev -PH**).

-s   This can be used with -C or -P to query a specific subclass (# **lsdev -Cs scsi**).

-l   This flag can be used to query a logical device (# **lsdev -Cl scsi0**).

In AIX 5L Version 5.3, there are two more commands to list more information about the devices:

lsattr   This command is used to obtain the specific configuration attributes for a device. For example, to get the attributes of a tape drive, use the command in Example 5-4.

Example 5-4   lsattr -el command and output

```
# lsattr -El rmt0
mode          yes   Use DEVICE BUFFERS during writes        True
block_size    1024  BLOCK size (0=variable length)          True
extfm         no    Use EXTENDED file marks                 True
ret           no    RETENSION on tape change or reset       True
density_set_1 39    DENSITY setting #1                      True
```

```
density_set_2 39    DENSITY setting #2                   True
compress      yes   Use data COMPRESSION                 True
size_in_mb    20000 Size in Megabytes                    False
ret_error     no    RETURN error on tape change or reset True
```

The first column of the **lsattr** command specifies the attribute for the device; the second column specifies the actual value for that attribute; the third column is a brief description; and the last column specifies if the value for that attribute can be changed (true) or not (false).

lscfg

The list configuration command (**lscfg**) displays the information of the vendor name, serial number, type, and model of the device. All of this information its known in AIX 5L Version 5.1 as the Vital Product Data (VPD). For example, to get the VPD for the tape drive (rmt0), use the command in Example 5-5.

Example 5-5   lscfg -vl command and output

```
# lscfg -vl rmt0
  DEVICE            LOCATION            DESCRIPTION
  rmt0              10-60-00-5,0        SCSI 8mm Tape Drive (20000 MB)
        Manufacturer...............EXABYTE
        Machine Type and Model......IBM-20GB
        Device Specific.(Z1)........38zA
        Serial Number..............60089837
        Device Specific.(LI)........A0000001
        Part Number................59H2813
        FRU Number.................59H2839
        EC Level...................E30279
        Device Specific.(Z0)........0180020283000030
        Device Specific.(Z3)........
```

lsattr and **lscfg** can only be run with configured devices.

5.3 Adding devices

The next section describes how to add devices for HP-UX 11i and AIX 5L.

5.3.1 Adding devices in HP-UX 11i

In HP-UX devices are generally self configurable. During a reboot of the machine, HP-UX will attempt to configure all the devices it finds out on the I/O buses.

If it cannot find an appropriate driver, then when you look in **ioscan** it will be UNCLAIMED. If this is the case, you may need to install some drivers for the hardware and go through the hot plug steps below.

The basic high-level steps for adding new hardware devices to a HP-UX system are as follows.

Non hot pluggable

For non hot pluggable additions (for example, a non hotplug LAN card):

1. Verify that the correct driver software is installed in HP-UX.

2. Shut down and power off the machine.

3. Have a qualified technician install the new hardware.

4. Power on the machine.

5. Verify that the device has a driver associated with it using **ioscan**, is in the CLAIMED state, and that there is a device created for it. For example:

```
Class    I  H/W Path  Driver     S/W State H/W Type  Description
==================================================================
lan      2  0/12/0/0/4/0  btlan   CLAIMED    INTERFACE  HP A5506B PCI
10/100Base-TX 4 Port
                        /dev/diag/lan2  /dev/ether2    /dev/lan2
```

Hot pluggable

For a hot pluggable or OLAR capable devices (for example, when you assign more SAN-attached LUNs), the basic high-level steps are:

1. Verify that the correct driver software is installed in HP-UX.

2. Add the additional hardware in the approved manner.

   – If it is the replacement of a hot swap card, first power down the slot either with SAM or by using **rad**. Insert the new card. Then power up the card with SAM or **rad**.

   – If it is adding new LUNs, assign the LUNs from the SAN to the HBA.

3. Perform an **ioscan** that goes out and scans the bus:

   ```
   # ioscan -fn
   ```

4. Create the appropriate device files for any newly added devices. The **insf -e** command will create and recreate any devices required for all the system.

   ```
   # insf -e
   ```

5. Verify that the device has a driver associated with it using **ioscan**, is in the CLAIMED state, and that there is a device created for it. For example:

   ```
   # ioscan -funC disk
   ```

```
Class  I  H/W Path        Driver  S/W State  H/W Type    Description
=========================================================================
disk   33  0/3/0/0.107.35.19.44.0.5  sdisk  CLAIMED    DEVICE  IBM 2105F20
            /dev/dsk/c17t0d5        /dev/rdsk/c17t0d5
```

5.3.2 Adding devices in AIX 5L

As mentioned earlier, all the devices are self configurable except serial and parallel devices. The command that is used to configure the devices is the configuration manager (**cfgmgr**).

This command is run automatically at system boot, but you can run it at any time in a running system. For SCSI devices, the only thing that you have to do is to set a unique SCSI ID on the device before attaching it. If you are going to attach a new device to a running system, be sure that the device is hot-swappable; otherwise, you need to power off the system before.

If **cfgmgr** does not find a device driver, you will be asked to install it. Take a look at Figure 5-1 to understand the cfgmgr function.

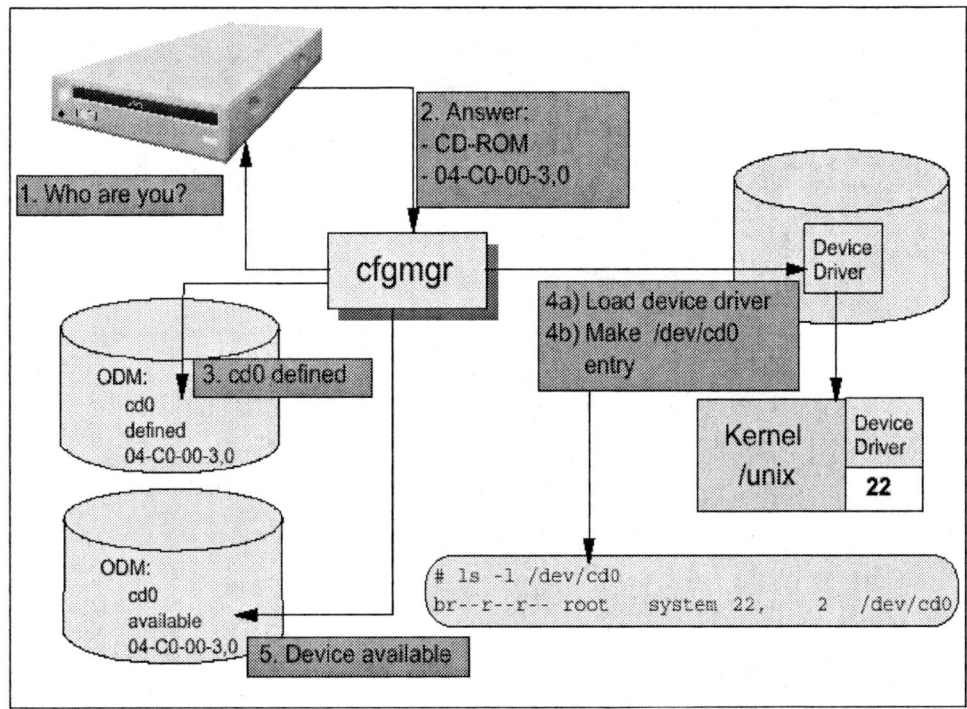

Figure 5-1   The configuration manager

Device configuration is not a difficult task in AIX 5L. In fact, more and more systems are supporting hot plugging a device into a running machine.

To install/replace a hot swappable card into a hot swap capable slot you would follow the basic high-level steps below:

1. Verify that both the slot and the card are indeed hot pluggable.

2. If you are replacing a faulty device, you must first unconfigure it with **rmdev**.

3. Enter either smit or diag to initiate the appropriate task (remove/add/replace).

   – smitty devdrpci (for the PCI hot plug manager)
   – diag -T identifyRemove (for either PCI or SCSI Hot Plug Managers)

4. Follow the bouncing balls of the task you initiated. When you have completed this, the card is in the system. For example, if you have just added a new PCI device and you did a **lsslot -c pci** you would see the following:

```
# Slot      Description                        Device(s)
U0.1-P2-I1  PCI-X capable, 64 bit, 133MHz slot Unknown
```

Notice that the device is Unknown at this stage. This is due to the fact that there is no driver configured for it.

5. Now run the configuration manager (**cfgmgr**) to configure the device driver for the newly added card. Now **lsslot -c pci** should show something similar to:

```
# Slot      Description                        Device(s)
U0.1-P2-I1  PCI-X capable, 64 bit, 133MHz slot fcs0
```

SMIT and adding devices

There are many smitty screens that are used to change the device configuration or to add devices.

Look at Example 5-6 to see the menu of smitty in the devices section. Run the following command to get the menu:

```
# smitty devices
```

Example 5-6   Main menu for devices in smitty

```
                          Devices
Move cursor to desired item and press Enter.
[TOP]
  Install/Configure Devices Added After IPL
  Printer/Plotter
  TTY
  Asynchronous Adapters
  PTY
  Console
  Fixed Disk
  Disk Array
```

```
CD ROM Drive
Read/Write Optical Drive
Diskette Drive
Tape Drive
Communication
Graphic Displays
Graphic Input Devices
Low Function Terminal (LFT)
[MORE...12]
F1=Help           F2=Refresh        F3=Cancel         F8=Image
F9=Shell          F0=Exit           Enter=Do
```

For more information, see the detail within the individual device types.

Other commands related to adding devices

As with many other tasks in AIX 5L, we can also configure a device using the command line. The command that we use is called **mkdev**. The following example is used to configure an additional tape drive in to our system:

```
# mkdev -c tape -s scsi -t scsd -p scsi0 -w 5,0
rmt0 Available
```

In order to configure any device with **mkdev**, we need to know at least the following information:

-c   Class of the device.

-s   Subclass of the device.

-t   Type of the device. This is a specific attribute for the device.

-p   The parent adapter of the device. You have to specify the logical name.

-w   You have to know the SCSI ID that you are going to assign to your new device. If it is a non-SCSI device, you have to know the port number on the adapter.

The **mkdev** command also creates the ODM entries for the device and loads the device driver. Here is another example of the **mkdev** command for a non-SCSI device:

```
# mkdev -c tty -t tty -s rs232 -p sa1 -w 0 -a login=enable -a term=ibm3151
tty0 Available
```

In this example, we are adding a new serial terminal to the parent adapter sa1, using port 0 in the adapter. The -a option is used to assign specific characteristics for the device, such as the terminal type and login attributes.

If the -a option is omitted (for SCSI and non-SCSI devices), then the default values are taken from the ODM (the PdAt "predefined attributes" file).

lsslot shows the list of dynamic slots and what is in them. For example:

```
lsslot -c pci
# Slot      Description                      Device(s)
U0.1-P2-I1  PCI-X capable, 64 bit, 133MHz slot  fcs1
U0.1-P2-I2  PCI-X capable, 64 bit, 133MHz slot  scsi2 scsi3
U0.1-P2-I3  PCI-X capable, 64 bit, 133MHz slot  Empty
U0.1-P2-I4  PCI-X capable, 64 bit, 133MHz slot  Empty
U0.1-P2-I5  PCI-X capable, 64 bit, 133MHz slot  ent1
U0.1-P2-I6  PCI-X capable, 64 bit, 133MHz slot  fcs0
U0.1-P2-I7  PCI-X capable, 32 bit, 66MHz slot   Empty
```

5.4 Removing a device

The next section describes how to remove devices.

5.4.1 Removing a device in HP-UX

To remove a device, use the **rmsf** (rm special file) command. For more information see *man 1m rmsf*. For example, to remove the disk at address 10/0.6.0:

```
# ioscan -fnH 10/0.6.0
Class     I H/W Path  Driver S/W State H/W Type  Description
==================================================================
disk      3 10/0.6.0  sdisk CLAIMED   DEVICE    SEAGATE ST34371W
                      /dev/dsk/c1t6d0   /dev/rdsk/c1t6d0
# rmsf -H 10/0.6.0
# ioscan -fnH 10/0.6.0
#
```

> **Warning:** Removing a device that is currently in use can cause unexpected results.

5.4.2 Removing a device in AIX 5L

For replacing a faulty hot pluggable device, see 5.3.2, "Adding devices in AIX 5L" on page 125.

Removing a device is done with the **rmdev** command. This command will remove all the ODM entries for a configured device. For example:

```
# lsdev -Cc tape
```

```
rmt0 Available 10-60-00-5,0 SCSI 8mm Tape Drive

# rmdev -l rmt0
rmt0 Defined

# lsdev -Cc tape
rmt0 Defined 10-60-00-5,0 SCSI 8mm Tape Drive
```

In the above example, we list first the tape drive configured in the system when we use the **rmdev** command. We only use the -l option, which indicates the logical device name. This command will change the device state only, from available to defined, and it does not delete the ODM or /dev entries; if you would like to remove them from the system, you should also use the -d flag. Use the following example to remove the tape drive from the system:

```
# ls -l /dev/*hdisk5*
brw-------   1 root      system      41,  1 Jun 23 10:22 /dev/hdisk5
crw-------   1 root      system      41,  1 Jun 23 10:22 /dev/rhdisk5
# rmdev -l hdisk5 -d
hdisk5 deleted
# lsdev -Cl hdisk5
# ls -l /dev/*hdisk5*
#
```

5.5 Modifying a device

This section explains how to modify devices in HP-UX and AIX 5L.

5.5.1 Modifying a device in HP-UX

HP-UX does not have a single set of commands to enable you to change device attributes. Particular devices may come with their own commands to allow you to configure them. For example, to change the default time out on a disk see Example 5-7.

Example 5-7   Changing the default time out on a disk

```
# pvdisplay /dev/dsk/c1t6d0
--- Physical volumes ---
PV Name                  /dev/dsk/c1t6d0
VG Name                  /dev/vgabc
PV Status                available
Allocatable              yes
VGDA                     2
Cur LV                   1
PE Size (Mbytes)         4
Total PE                 1023
```

```
Free PE                        998
Allocated PE                   25
Stale PE                       0
IO Timeout (Seconds)           default
Autoswitch                     On

# pvchange -t 120 /dev/dsk/c1t6d0
Physical volume "/dev/dsk/c1t6d0" has been successfully changed.
Volume Group configuration for /dev/vgabc has been saved in
/etc/lvmconf/vgabc.conf
# pvdisplay /dev/dsk/c1t6d0|grep Time
IO Timeout (Seconds)           120
```

5.5.2 Modifying a device in AIX 5L

In this section, use the smitty screens to change the values for a device. It is important to remember that in most cases, when you are going to change a device, the device must not be in use.

You may need to put it into the defined state, which can be done by running **rmdev -l device_name**.

Let us see an example of the smitty screen that is used to change the attributes of a network interface. The fast path to this smitty screen is # **smitty chgenet**. The first screen that appears is shown in Example 5-8, and is used to select the Ethernet adapter that we want to use.

Example 5-8   Selecting the Ethernet adapter

```
                        Ethernet Adapter

    Move cursor to desired item and press Enter. Use arrow keys to scroll.

      ent1 Available 10-80 IBM PCI Ethernet Adapter (22100020)
      ent0 Available 10-78 IBM 10/100/1000 Base-T Ethernet PCI Adapter (1410

    F1=Help              F2=Refresh           F3=Cancel
    F8=Image             F0=Exit              Enter=Do
    /=Find               n=Find Next
```

When you have selected the adapter, then the dialog screen in Example 5-9 will be shown.

Example 5-9   Changing attributes for a network interface

```
        Change / Show Characteristics of an Ethernet Adapter
```

```
Type or select values in entry fields.
Press Enter AFTER making all desired changes.

                                                [Entry Fields]
     Ethernet Adapter                    ent1
     Description                          IBM PCI Ethernet Adapt>
     Status                               Available
     Location                             10-80
     HARDWARE TRANSMIT queue size        [64]                      +#
     HARDWARE RECEIVE queue size         [32]                      +#
     Full duplex                          no                       +
     Enable ALTERNATE ETHERNET address    no                       +
     ALTERNATE ETHERNET address          [0x000000000000]          +
     Apply change to DATABASE only        no                       +

F1=Help          F2=Refresh      F3=Cancel      F4=List
F5=Reset         F6=Command      F7=Edit        F8=Image
F9=Shell         F0=Exit         Enter=Do
```

In Example 5-9 on page 130, we can change some attributes, such as the hardware receive/transmit queue size. These values have a performance impact when they are increased. See Chapter 14, "Performance management" on page 485, for detailed information about these values.

Example 5-10 shows the equivalent command for AIX 5L to change the default time out on an hdisk.

Example 5-10   Equivalent AIX 5L command to change default time out

```
# lsattr -El hdisk5 -a rw_timeout
rw_timeout 30 READ/WRITE time out value True
# chdev -l hdisk5 -a rw_timeout=120
hdisk5 changed
# lsattr -El hdisk5 -a rw_timeout
rw_timeout 120 READ/WRITE time out value True
```

5.6 Alternate paths/MPIO configuration

For both high availability and possibly (depending on the workload profile) performance, both HP-UX and AIX 5L natively provide the capability to allow multiple paths from the OS logical disk layer to the physical disk layer.

In HP-UX's case, this is called *Alternate Links* or *PV Links* and allows a single *alternate path* for failover purposes, which works with all disk subsystems as long as you have the environment configured such that you have two /dev entries for each physical disk/LUN.

In AIX 5L Version 5.2 and later, IBM introduced native MPIO (multi-path IO) support for certain storage subsystems (for example, the ESS range, some Hitachi, SYMMETRIX). MPIO support is configured on supported subsystems at device discovery time.

Certain vendors also provide additional software (for example, RDAC for IBM Fast-T, PowerPath for EMC) with their disk subsystems, which also provide differing capabilities in regard to multi-path redundancy.

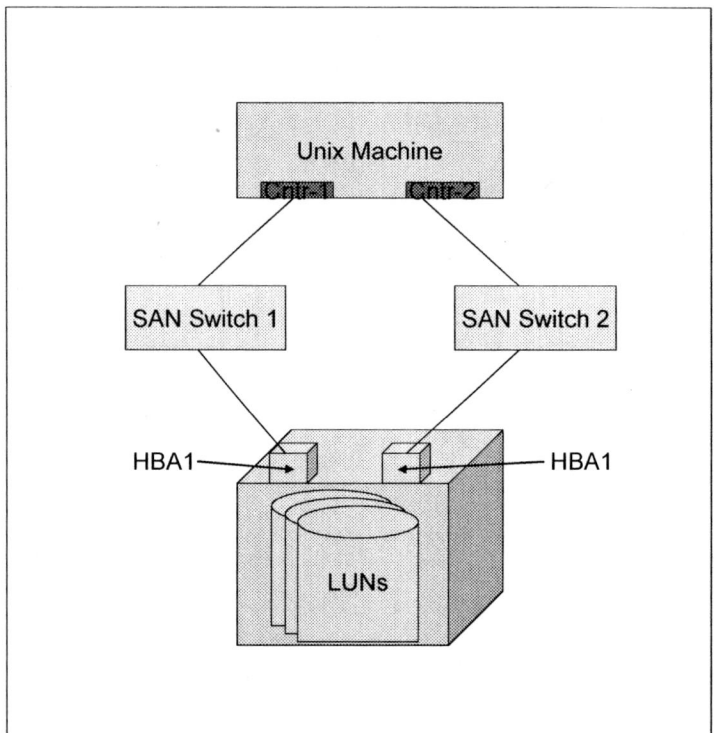

Figure 5-2   Multi path scenario

5.6.1 HP-UX's PV links/alternate paths

For HP-UX, if we take Figure 5-2, and you had one LUN assigned to the machine, you would end up with two /dev/dsk devices. For example:

```
disk      3  10/0.6.0     sdisk      CLAIMED   DEVICE     SEAGATE ST34371W
                          /dev/dsk/c14t1d6 /dev/rdsk/c14t1d6
disk      4  10/12/5.2.0  sdisk      CLAIMED   DEVICE     SEAGATE ST34371W
```

If you added both of these devices to the same volume group, then you would have created failover redundancy for that disk in the VG.

The disk portion of the **vgdisplay -v** command would look similar to the following:

```
--- Physical volumes ---
PV Name       /dev/dsk/c14t1d6
PV Name       /dev/dsk/c19t1d6 Alternate Link
PV Status     available
Total PE      2169
Free PE       0
Autoswitch    On
```

In the HP-UX case, if you do not add both the disks into the VG, then you are not providing redundancy.

The *Alternate Link* is only used in the case of a failure of the *primary* path. The setting of *Autoswitch* determines what action HP-UX will take on recovery of the path. For more information please see the man page for **vgdisplay**.

5.6.2 AIX 5L's MPIO

For a good description of the capabilities of MPIO, please see section 4.1 of *AIX 5L Differences Guide Version 5.2*, SG24-5765-02. The *AIX 5L Differences Guide* has in-depth descriptions of the reservation policy, algorithms, and the commands modified for use with MPIO devices. We only lightly touch on these topics here.

MPIO in AIX 5L provides a couple of different algorithms for multipathing:

fail_over   Only the highest priority path is used. If this fails, then the next highest priority path is used.

round_robin   All paths are used relative to their weighted priority. If one path fails, the others pick up the slack.

Taking Figure 5-2 on page 132 as an example environment, if you had one LUN assigned to the machine you would end up with only one /dev/dsk/hdiskX device, but underneath that, there would be two *paths* to the disk. For example:

```
#lspath -l hdisk4
Enabled hdisk4 fscsi0
Enabled hdisk4 fscsi1
```

So, hdisk4 in this example has redundancy via fscsi0 and fscsi1. At this point, we cannot tell which MPIO algorithm is being used; to do that we need to look at the device *attributes* with **lsattr**, as shown in Example 5-11.

Example 5-11   Checking device attributes with the lsattr command

```
lsattr -El hdisk4
PCM               PCM/friend/fcpother Path Control Module              False
algorithm         fail_over           Algorithm                       True
clr_q             no                  Device CLEARS its Queue on error True
dist_err_pcnt     0                   Distributed Error Sample Time    True
dist_tw_width     50                  Distributed Error Sample Time    True
hcheck_cmd        test_unit_rdy       Health Check Command             True
hcheck_interval   0                   Health Check Interval            True
hcheck_mode       nonactive           Health Check Mode               True
location                              Location Label                   True
lun_id            0x5211000000000000  Logical Unit Number ID           False
max_transfer      0x40000             Maximum TRANSFER Size            True
node_name         0x5005076300c09589  FC Node Name                     False
pvid              none                Physical volume identifier       False
q_err             yes                 Use QERR bit                     True
q_type            simple              Queuing TYPE                     True
queue_depth       1                   Queue DEPTH                      True
reassign_to       120                 REASSIGN time out value          True
reserve_policy    single_path         Reserve Policy                   True
rw_timeout        30                  READ/WRITE time out value        True
scsi_id           0x650b00            SCSI ID                          False
start_timeout     60                  START unit time out value        True
ww_name           0x5005076300c19589  FC World Wide Name               False
```

We can see from the example above that the algorithm is set to *fail_over*. This means that only one path will be in use at a time.

If we wish to change this, the disk must not be in active use. We do not need to move the device to *Defined*, but if it is in use by the LVM we will not be able to modify it.

If the disk is assigned to a volume group, then we need to vary that volume group off before we can perform any changes.

To change the algorithm to round_robin we can use three different methods: **smitty mpio**, WebSM, or **chdev**. For example:

```
# chdev -a reserve_policy=no_reserve -a algorithm=round_robin -l hdisk4
hdisk4 changed
# lsattr -El hdisk4 | grep -E "^PCM|^algorithm|reserve_policy"
PCM               PCM/friend/fcpother Path Control Module              False
algorithm         round_robin         Algorithm                       True
reserve_policy    no_reserve          Reserve Policy                   True
```

Without going into much more depth, a couple of the more useful commands relating to MPIO are:

lspath   Displays information about paths to an Multi Path I/O (MPIO) capable device.

iostat -m   Displays statistics for each path on each disk.

smitty mpio   This gives you all the options you can want for MPIO maintenance, including disabling all activity down a particular parent adapter, enabling/disabling all the paths (though you can never disable the last path to a device), changing path priorities, and so on.

5.7 Changing kernel attributes

The implementation of the HP-UX kernel and the AIX 5L kernel differ significantly. The HP-UX kernel, as of HP-UX 11i Version 1, has 12 *dynamic* parameters that do not require a kernel re-build and reboot to take affect.

The AIX 5L kernel is a much more dynamically extensible kernel where most parameters can be changed without requiring a reboot. In AIX 5L there is no recompilation of the kernel.

Changing tunable kernel attributes can have performance affects, so in this section we talk about how they can be changed, not the affect any of these changes may have. For information about the affect that individual parameters may have, please see *Performance Management Guide,* SC23-4905-01, for AIX 5L and the following Web site for HP-UX 11i:

    http://docs.hp.com/en/hpux11i.html

5.7.1 Changing kernel attributes in HP-UX

The most straightforward way of changing kernel attributes in HP-UX 11i across the different architectures (PA-RISC/Itanium) is via the SAM Kernel Configuration screen.

> **Note:** Due to the different structures of PA-RISC and Itanium kernels, the command set for kernel management and compilation is also different.

Some of the common kernel attributes that a systems administrator may need to change are maxusers, maxdsize, maxtsize, maxssize, maxfiles, maxswapchunks, maxvgs, a lot of "msg", "sem" (semaphore), "shm" (shared memory) parameters, dbc_max_pct, and dbc_min_pct.

Many of these are *static* kernel structures that require a kernel rebuild.

SAM and `kmtune` allow you to update individual parameters either on the fly (if available) or for the next kernel re-build.

5.7.2 Changing kernel attributes in AIX 5L

AIX 5L does not require you to ever *rebuild* the kernel. In fact, nearly all of the tunable kernel parameters can be changed and take affect on the running system.

For a more detailed description of the changes that were made in AIX 5L Version 5.2 please see section 7.2, "AIX Tuning Framework," in the *AIX 5L Differences Guide Version 5.2*, SG24-5765-02.

Prior to AIX 5L Version 5.2, all the performance parameters that can be set by the `vmtune`, `schedtune`, `no`, or `nfso` commands were lost at the next system reboot. The syntax and the output of those commands were also completely different. In AIX 5L Version 5.2, a complete review of the performance management was made and the following enhancements were provided:

► Support of permanent and reboot values for tuning parameters in a new /etc/tunables directory. This directory consists of the following files:

   — /etc/tunables/nextboot ASCII file using a stanza format with one stanza per command and one line per parameter to be changed from its default value. An additional information stanza provides general information about the file.

   — /etc/tunables/lastboot contains values for each parameter set during the last reboot. The default values are marked.

   — /etc/tunables/lastboot.log logs all changes made or impossible to make. The lastboot file contains a checksum for the lastboot.log to detect file corruption.

► Files can be copied from one machine to another, applied, edited, or created using SMIT, Web-based System Manager, or an editor such as vi.

► All the tuning commands have been enhanced to have a consistent syntax and interface. They all interact with the /etc/tunables/nextboot file. These enhancements are part of the bos.perf.tune fileset.

The commands used in AIX 5L Version 5.3 for tuning system parameters are:

`ioo`   Manages input/output tunables

`nfso`   Manages NFS tunables

`no`   Manages network tunables

schedo	Manages CPU schedule tunables
vmo	Manages Virtual Memory Manager (VMM) tunables
smitty tuning	Takes you to the SMIT panel as a single point of modification for all of the above

Please see the relevant man page for more details about each of these commands.

In AIX 5L, we also have a special device named sys0 that is used to manage some kernel parameters. Any change to the sys0 parameters is stored in the ODM and preserved over reboot (and most of them require a reboot to take effect).

The way to change these values is by using **smitty**, the **chdev** command, or the Web-based System Manager. In Figure 5-3, we can see the Web-based System Manager window that is used to change the values of the operating system.

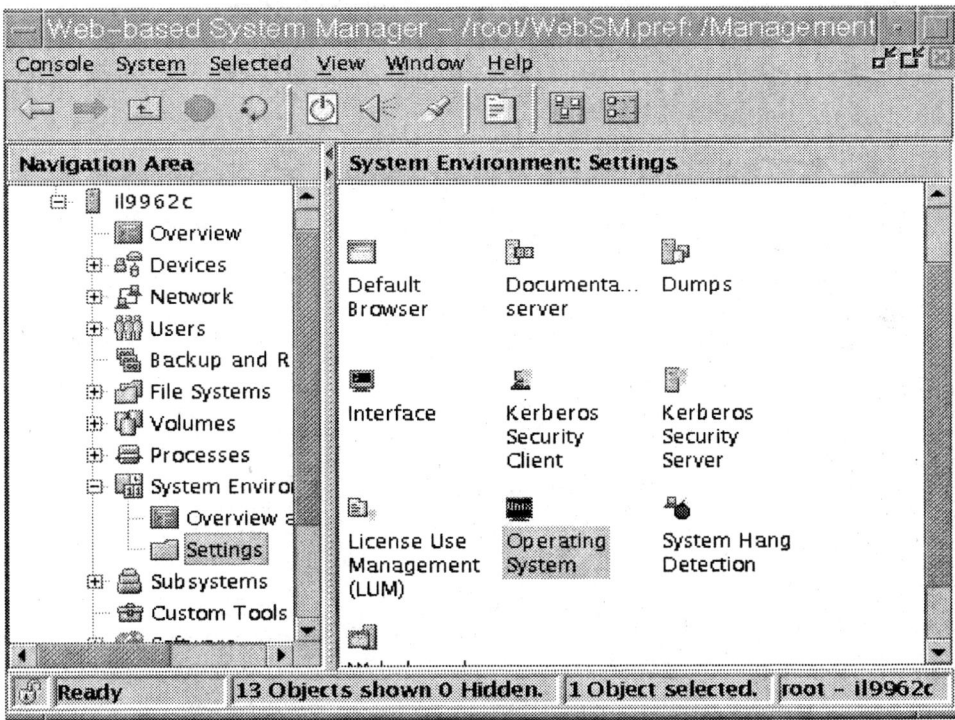

Figure 5-3   Changing operating system parameters

After we select the operating system from the menu window of the Web-based System Manager, the screen shown in Figure 5-4 is presented. Unlike the other tuning commands listed above, most of the values that we can change in that screen need a reboot to take effect.

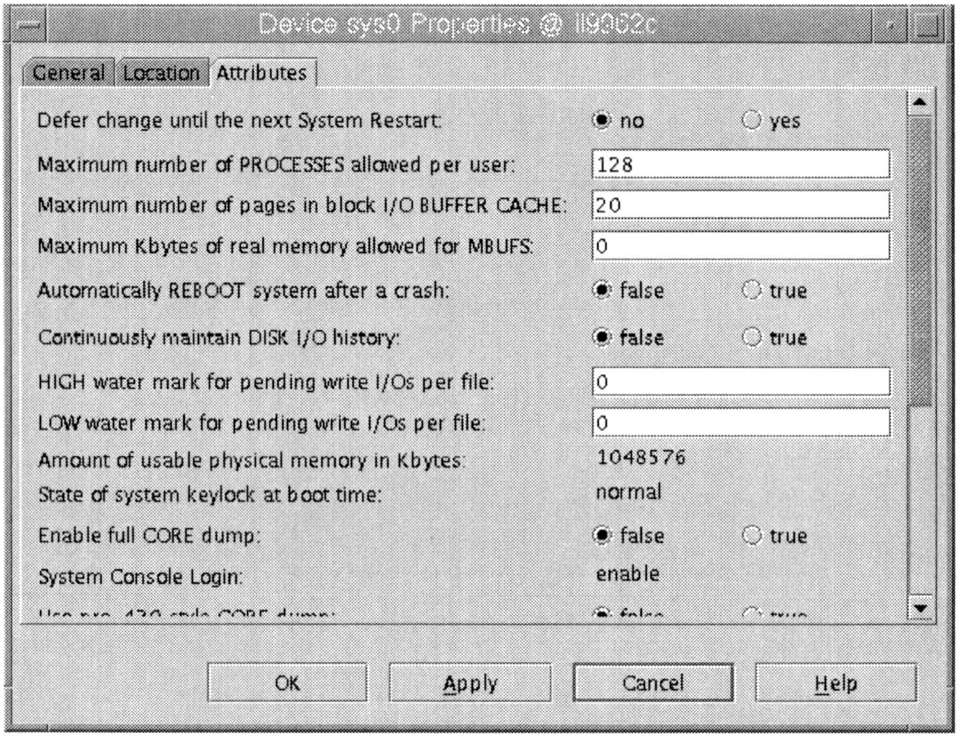

Figure 5-4   Changing the attributes for sys0

If we decide to change the number of processes allowed per user to 500, we just have to indicate the new value into the field and select **Apply** in the screen. Example 5-12 shows the alternate command to make the change. This parameter change will take effect immediately if the number is larger than before, or after a reboot otherwise.

Example 5-12   Changing the number of processes

```
# lsattr -H -E -l sys0 -a maxuproc
attribute value description                                  user_settable
maxuproc 128 Maximum number of PROCESSES allowed per user True

# chdev -l sys0 -a maxuproc=500
sys0 changed
lsattr -H -E -l sys0 -a maxuproc
attribute value description                                  user_settable
```

```
maxuproc  500  Maximum number of PROCESSES allowed per user True
```

or

```
# smitty chgsys
```

5.8 Quick reference

AIX 5L has many different ways to manage devices. For example, it uses a database (ODM) instead of flat files. Look at Figure 5-5 for a summary of device commands, device states, and the related ODM database.

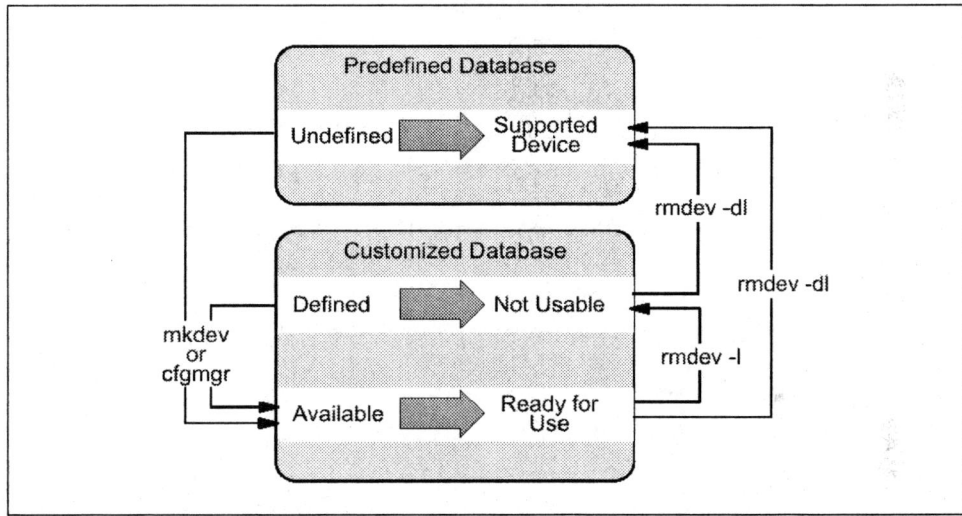

Figure 5-5   AIX 5L Device states and ODM

Table 5-1 shows the comparison between AIX 5L and HP-UX 11i for device management.

Table 5-1   Quick reference for device management

Task	AIX 5L	HP-UX 11i
Run multiple tasks in a GUI environment.	► `smit` ► Web-based System Manager	`sam`
Configure a device (dynamic reconfiguration).	`cfgmgr`	`ioscan & insf -e`

Task	AIX 5L	HP-UX 11i
Add a device with t.he command line	`mkdev`	`mksf`
Remove a SCSI device.	`rmdev` Note: It can change the state of a device from available to defined, or it can delete the ODM entries for a device.	`rmsf`
Change attributes for a device.	`chdev`	`N/A`
List devices.	► `lsdev` Note: Can be used to query configured devices if used with -C option (upper case) or supported devices if used with -P option. ► `prtconf` ► `lscfg`	► `ioscan` ► `print_manifest` ► `lsdev` ► `stm (Support Tools Manager)`
List the configuration attributes for devices.	`lsattr -El`	► `sam` ► `stm`
List VPD (serial number, model, vendor, part number) of a device.	`lscfg -vl`	`stm`
Change kernel attributes.	► `chdev` ► `smitty chgsys`	► `sam - for either` ► For PA-RISC: system_prep, kmtune, kmsystem, kmupdate ► For Itanium: kconfig, kcmodule, kctune, kcweb

6

Logical Volume Manager and disk management

In this chapter we introduce the use of the AIX 5L Logical Volume Manager (LVM) and HP-UX Logical Volume Manager (LVM). We use the following versions of software:

► LVM Version 5.2 to AIX 5L Version 5.2
► LVM Version 5.3 to AIX 5L Version 5.3
► LVM from HP-UX 11i

The following topics are discussed:

6.1 Logical volume management overviews

Traditionally in a UNIX environment, the management of physical disks is always a difficult task because there are a lot of restrictions on allocating the physical space. First of all, you need to define physical partitions, and each physical partition is fixed and cannot be increased. In addition, a physical disk in a traditional UNIX system can only have eight physical partitions, so the client had to select the correct size of each partition before the system could be installed. A major restriction of the physical partition is that each one has to consist of contiguous disk space; this restriction limits the partition to reside on a single physical drive.

Changing the partition size and thus the file system is not an easy task. It involves backing up the file system, removing the partition, creating new ones, and restoring the file system.

For all of those reasons, many of the UNIX systems, such as HP-UX 11i and AIX 5L, have defined a new, flexible technique to manage the storage allocation. It is known as logical volumes.

AIX 5L has its own native Logical Volume Manager (LVM) and introduces several new features for the current and emerging storage requirements with JFS and JFS2.

The HP-UX has the LVM from HP, and for file system, the Veritas File System (VxFS) from VERITAS Software Corporation.

With AIX 5L, you can also implement the Veritas file system. For a good comparison between AIX 5L's JFS file system and the Veritas VxFS file system refer to the redbook *Introducing VERITAS Foundation Suite for AIX*, SG24-6619.

In this chapter we discuss the most frequently used logical volumes tasks using the following software:

AIX 5L	Logical Volume Manager (LVM) from AIX 5L
HP-UX 11i	Logical Volume Manager (LVM) from HP-UX
	MirrorDisk/UX

Some of the benefits of logical volumes are:

- ► Logical volumes solve non-contiguous space problems.
- ► Logical volumes can span disks.
- ► Logical volumes can dynamically increase their size.

6.2 Introducing the logical volume solutions

Before we can start with the logical volume administration tasks, we define and list the characteristics for each software (LVM to HP-UX and LVM to AIX 5L), its naming conventions, and the terminology that is used.

6.2.1 HP-UX 11i LVM

This provides the user with flexibility in configuring and managing mass storage resources. In HP-UX you have one more product used to manage mass storage resources, the MirrorDisk/UX. This product is installed separately.

MirrorDisk/UX   Enable mirroring options in LVM commands.

HP-UX 11i LVM physical components

The HP-UX 11i LVM has three physical components:

Physical volume   A physical volume (PV) is the physical disk and the name for the disk drive. When one disk is added to the system, the operating system creates two files located in the directories /dev/dsk and /dev/rdsk. These files have the name of the disk. The disk must be added to a volume group in order to be used.

Volume group   A volume group (VG) consists of one or more related physical disks that are accessed by a VG name by default. When the operation system is installed, the VG *vg00* is created and contains all the file systems of the operations system. All the information is unique per volume group and is located in the volume group descriptor area (VGDA). All the disks in a volume group contain at least one copy of the VGDA.

Physical extent   A physical extent (PE) is the basic unit of disk space allocation. The size of the physical extent is defined when the VG is created. Your size is expressed in units of megabytes (MB).

There are some rules for LVM from HP-UX 11i, as shown in Table 6-1 on page 144.

Table 6-1 LVM rules in HP-UX 11i

Metric	Value
Number of VGs per system	This value is defined by kernel. The default value is 10.
Number of disks per VG	The default value is 16. The maximum number of physical volumes can be a value in the range of 1 to 255.
Number of physical extents per disk	The default value is 1016, but if you place a PV that exceeds this value, the default value is adjusted to match the physical volume size. The maximum number of the physical extent can be a value in the range of 1 to 65535.
Size of physical extent	The default value is 4 MB. The size can be in the range of 1 to 256.

HP-UX 11i LVM logical components

We have defined the physical storage components for the LVM. Now we will define the logical part. There are two main components:

Logical extent   The logical extent has the same size as the physical extent, defined by VG. It is the smallest unit of allocation of disk space.

Logical volume   This consists of one or more logical extents within a volume group, that are logical partitions of the volume group (VG).

A logical volume can be used to contain one of the following, one at time:

► Journaled File System (JFS)
► Raw device
► Swap area

Naming conventions for LVM from HP-UX

Use Table 6-2 to obtain the names that LVM uses for each of its components.

Table 6-2 Naming conventions for LVM

Description	Naming convention
Volume group	The operating system group is *vg00*. When you create a new one, SAM automatically assigns the name vgnn, but you can choose another name.

Description	Naming convention
Logical volume	The name given by LVM to a newly created LV is lvolnn, but you can choose another one. The name for all the LVs of the operating system start with lvol1 up to lvol8.
Physical volume	In HP-UX, the names of the disks are defined by the physical addresses of the disks.
Swap area	The logical volume default for the swap area is lvol2. To extend the swap area, another logical volume should be created, and added in swap area.

6.2.2 AIX 5L LVM introduction

The Logical Volume Manager (LVM) has been a feature of the AIX 5L operating system since Version 3, and is installed automatically with the operating system. The use of the Logical Volume Manager makes the life of the system administrator so much easier, because you can add disk space dynamically, you can mirror the information or spread the logical volumes to increase performance (RAID 0), you can relocate a logical volume and its content online, and you can move a group of disks from one system to another without losing data. In AIX 5L Version 5.3 a large number of changes and enhancements have been implemented to reduce the command execution time of several Logical Volume Manager (LVM) high-level commands.

Let us begin our look at the LVM by seeing how physical disks are viewed by the operating system.

AIX 5L physical storage components

In AIX 5L, the storage allocation is managed by the LVM. The LVM is divided in two sections: Physical storage and logical storage. Let us review all the physical storage components first.

Physical volume   A physical volume (PV) is the name for the disk drive. When a disk is added to the system, a file called hdiskn is created under /dev. The disk must be added to a volume group in order to be used by LVM.

Volume group   A volume group (VG) consists of one or more related physical disks that are accessed by a VG name by default. When the operating system is installed, the VG *rootvg* is created and contains all the file systems of the operating system. All the information is unique per volume group and its located in the volume group descriptor area (VGDA). All the disks in a volume group contain at least one copy of the VGDA.

Physical Partition A physical partition (PP) is the basic unit of disk space allocation. It is a division of a physical volume. The size of the physical partition is unique for a whole volume group and cannot be changed after the VG is created.

There are some rules for the physical storage for AIX 5L, as shown in Table 6-3.

Table 6-3 Physical storage rules in AIX 5L

Metric	AIX 5L Version 5.2	AIX 5L Version 5.3
Number of VGs per system	255.	255.
Number of physical partitions per disk	The default is 32, but if you change a normal VG into a Big VG, you can have up to 128 PV per VG.	1024, with scalable VG.
Number of physical partitions per disk	By default, you have 1016 PP. You can change it dynamically to the whole VG.	The maximum number of PPs is no longer defined on a per-disk basis, but applies to the entire VG. The maximum number is 2097152, with scalable VG.
Size of physical partition	The default is 4 MB. This value changes in powers of two and its maximum size is 1024 MB. This value cannot be changed dynamically.	128 GB, with scalable VG.

You can increase or decrease the number of physical partitions online, but keep in mind that if you are going to change the number of PPs, the number of total disks per volume group will be decreased. This means that a volume group has a fixed number of physical partitions. For a *normal* volume group, this value is 32512; for a *Big* volume group, the value is 130048; and for a scalable volume group this value is 2097152.

Table 6-4 on page 147 shows how these values can be changed.

Table 6-4   Max number of PPs per disk in a normal VG

Number of disks	Maximum number of PPs/disk
32	1016
16	2032
8	4064
4	8128
2	16256
1	32512

In order to understand why we may need to change the number of PPs per VG, let us analyze the following example:

► Situation

A client has a volume group called datavg that contains two PVs of 9.1 GB each. The physical partition size is 16 MB. The client wants to increase the size of one of the file systems, but does not have enough physical partitions to meet the requirements. The client has a new 18.2 GB disk to include in the datavg VG.

► Result

The client cannot add the new disk, because of the default limit for the number of physical partitions per disk (1016), in this case, 1016 * 16 MB = 16 GB. As you can see, the system cannot make enough PPs in the new disk (16 GB is less than18 GB), so it cannot be added to the volume group datavg, and the physical partition size cannot be changed.

► Solution

We cannot change the physical partition size in the volume group, but we can change the number of physical partitions in a VG. So, if we increase the physical partitions, the client could add the 18.2 GB disk to the datavg VG. Use the **chvg -t** command to change the number of PPs. The command will look like this:

```
# chvg -t2 datavg
```

For the -t option, the number two (2) is a multiplier for the number of physical partitions; in our example, -t2 will allow 2032 PPs (1016*2) per PV.

Doing this change, the 18.2 GB disk of our client can be added to the datavg VG.

There is also another solution in AIX 5L Version 5.3 where you can convert to a scalable VG, for example:

```
# varyoffvg datavg
# chvg -a'y' -Q'y' '-G' datavg
0516-1224 chvg: WARNING, once this operation is completed, volume group
datavg
          cannot be imported into AIX 5.2 or lower versions. Continue (y/n) ?
y
0516-1712 chvg: Volume group datavg changed.  datavg can include up to 1024
physical volumes with 2097152 total physical partitions in the volume
group.
# varyonvg datavg
```

Remember: If you increase the number of PPs per PV with the -t option, the number of maximum disks per VG is decreased.

Logical storage components AIX 5L

We have defined the physical storage components for LVM; now we will define the logical part. There are two main components:

Logical partition This is the smallest unit of allocation of disk space. Each logical partition maps to a physical partition, which physically stores the data. This logical partition only works as a pointer, and the LP size for a volume group is equal to the PP size.

Logical volume This consists of one or more logical partitions within a volume group. A logical volume does not need to be contiguous within a physical volume, because the logical partitions within the logical volume are maintained to be contiguous. The view of the system is the logical one. Thus, the physical partitions they point to can reside anywhere on the physical volumes in the volume group. A graphical view of the logical volume can be seen in Figure 6-1 on page 149.

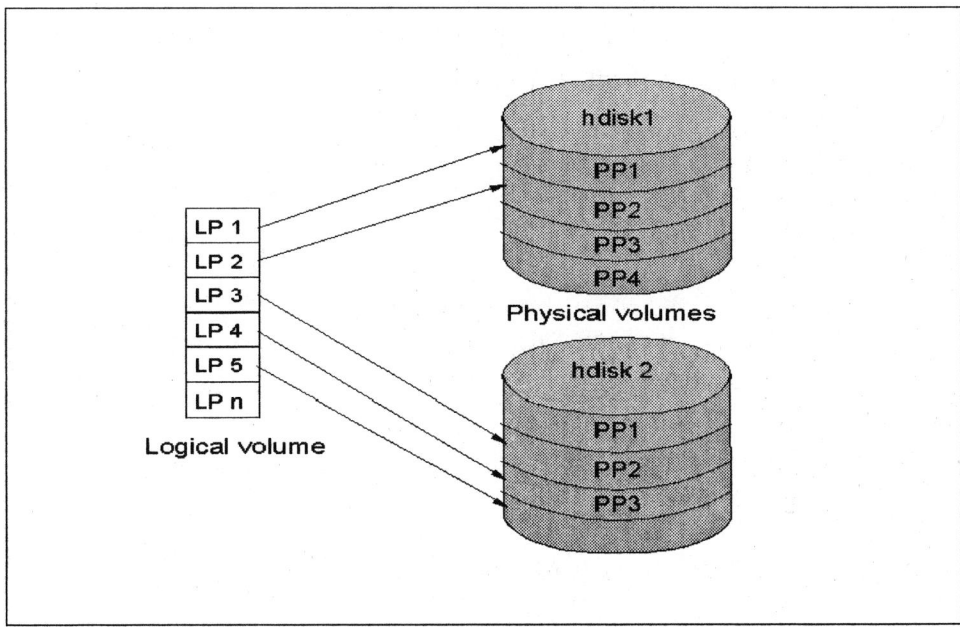

Figure 6-1   Logical storage

A logical volume can be used to contain one of the following, one at time:

- ► Journaled File System (JFS)
- ► Enhanced File System (JFS2)
- ► Paging space
- ► Journal log
- ► Boot logical volume
- ► Raw device (for database use)

Naming conventions for LVM AIX 5L

Use Table 6-5 to obtain the names that LVM uses for each of its components.

Table 6-5   Naming conventions for LVM

Description	Naming convention
Volume group	The operating system group is rootvg. When you create a new one, LVM automatically assigns the name vgnn, but you can choose another name.

Description	Naming convention
Logical volume	The name given by LVM to a newly created LV is lvnn, but you can choose another one. The name for all the LVs of the operating system start with hd.
Physical volume	hdisknn, where *n* represents a digit sequentially assigned.
Paging space	The name for the default paging space is hd6. The name for additional paging space will be pagingnn, and this name cannot be changed.

6.3 Working with Logical Volume Manager

In this section we describe the way to list, create, remove, and change characteristics for volume groups, logical volumes, and physical disks. We mainly use LVM from AIX 5L and LVM from HP-UX 11i.

6.3.1 Volume groups

As defined earlier, a volume group is a collection of physical disks that are related. Let us review the main and most important ways to work with them.

Listing a volume group: HP-UX 11i

When the HP-UX 11i is installed, the volume group default is created for the operation system, your name is *vg00*. For HP-UX we use the **vgdisplay** command.

If you do not specify an option **vgdisplay** will show all volume groups defined in the system. There are two optional parameters for **vgdisplay**, -v and vgname:

vgdisplay <vg name>   Shows basic information about volume group

vgdisplay -v <vg name>   Shows all information about the volume group

Example 6-1 shows the **vgdisplay** command.

Example 6-1   vgdisplay command

```
# vgdisplay
--- Volume groups ---
VG Name                  /dev/vg00
VG Write Access          read/write
VG Status                available
```

```
Max LV                     255
Cur LV                     12
Open LV                    12
Max PV                     16
Cur PV                     2
Act PV                     2
Max PE per PV              2500
VGDA                       4
PE Size (Mbytes)           4
Total PE                   2046
Alloc PE                   1283
Free PE                    763
Total PVG                  0
Total Spare PVs            0
Total Spare PVs in use     0
```

An explanation of the output:

VG Name	Name of the volume group and path.
VG Write Access	Access mode of the volume group. You can have two values, read/write and read/only.
VG Status	State of the volume group, always available; if this volume group is not available, the volume group is not displayed.
Max LV	Maximum number of logical volumes in the volume group.
Cur LV	Current number of logical volumes in the volume group.
Open LV	Logical volumes opened in volume group.
Max PV	Maximum number of physical volumes in the volume group.
Act PV	Number of physical volumes active in the volume group.
Max PE per PV	Maximum number of physical extent (PE) that can be allocated per physical volume.
VGDA	Number of volume group descriptor areas within the volume group.
PE Size	Size of physical extent.
Total PE	Total number of the physical extents in the volume group.

Alloc PE	Number of physical extents allocated to logical volumes.
Free PE	Number of physical extents not allocated in the volume group.
Total PVG	Total number of physical volume groups within the volume group.
Total Spare PVs	Total number of physical volumes that are designated as spares.
Total Spare PVs in user	Total number of spare physical volumes that are active.

Example 6-2   vgdisplay -v command

```
# vgdisplay -v vg00
--- Volume groups ---
VG Name                 /dev/vgignite
VG Write Access         read/write
VG Status               available
Max LV                  255
Cur LV                  12
Open LV                 12
Max PV                  16
Cur PV                  2
Act PV                  2
Max PE per PV           2500
VGDA                    4
PE Size (Mbytes)        4
Total PE                2046
Alloc PE                1283
Free PE                 763
Total PVG               0
Total Spare PVs         0
Total Spare PVs in use  0

    --- Logical volumes ---
    LV Name             /dev/vgignite/lvol1
    LV Status           available/syncd
    LV Size (Mbytes)    300
    Current LE          75
    Allocated PE        75
    Used PV             1

    PV Name             /dev/dsk/c1t3d0
    PV Status           available
    Total PE            1023
    Free PE             763
```

Below are the definitions of the extra fields displayed with **vgdisplay -v** in Example 6-2 on page 152.

A quick explanation of the output:

`--- Logical volumes ---`

LV Name	Name of the logical volume and path.
LV Status	Shows the status of the logical volume.
LV Size	Size of the logical volume.
Current LE	Number of the logical extents (LE) in the logical volume.
Allocated PE	Number of the physical extents used by the logical volume.
Used PV	Number of the physical volumes used by the logical volume.

`-- Physical volumes ---`

PV Name	Name of physical volume allocated in the volume group and path.
PV Status	Shows the status of the physical volume.
Total PE	Number the physical extents in the physical volume.
Free PE	Number of free physical extents in the physical volume.
Autoswitch	This option is used for multiported devices accessed via multiple paths. The option can be On or Off.

If the volume group has the physical volume group PVG, this command also shows information about the PVG.

`-- Physical volumes ---`

PVG Name	Name of the physical volume group
PV Name	Name of the physical volumes in the physical volume group

See the **vgcreate**, **vgextend**, and lvmpvg man pages for more information about the physical volume group.

Listing a volume group: AIX 5L

In AIX 5L, we use **lsvg** to list a volume group. If you do not specify an option, it will show you all the volume groups defined in the system. Some of its useful flags are:

-o	Shows only the active volume groups
-p <vg_name>	Shows all the physical volumes that belong to the requested volume group (vg_name)
-l <vg_name>	Shows all the logical volumes that belong to the requested volume group (vg_name)

Example 6-3 shows some examples of the **lsvg** command.

Example 6-3   lsvg command

```
# lsvg
rootvg
nimvg
# lsvg rootvg
VOLUME GROUP:    rootvg              VG IDENTIFIER:
0003219400004c00000000e
bddebba01
VG STATE:        active              PP SIZE:        16 megabyte(s)
VG PERMISSION:   read/write          TOTAL PPs:      1352 (21632 megabytes)
MAX LVs:         256                 FREE PPs:       1167 (18672 megabytes)
LVs:             13                  USED PPs:       185 (2960 megabytes)
OPEN LVs:        11                  QUORUM:         2
TOTAL PVs:       3                   VG DESCRIPTORS: 3
STALE PVs:       0                   STALE PPs:      0
ACTIVE PVs:      3                   AUTO ON:        yes
MAX PPs per PV: 1016                 MAX PVs:        32
LTG size:        128 kilobyte(s)     AUTO SYNC:      no
HOT SPARE:       no
```

The **lsvg** command output on AIX 5L Version 5.3 has changed to show the maximum physical partitions per volume group for all volume group types. The corresponding number is listed as the value for the MAX PPs per VG field. The **lsvg** output for scalable VGs will not display the maximum number of PPs per PV because for the scalable VG type the limit for PPs is defined per VG and not per PV, as shown in Example 6-4.

Example 6-4   lsvg output

```
#lsvg nimvg
VOLUME GROUP:       nimvg            VG IDENTIFIER:
000a395a00004c00000000ff476dd0b5
VG STATE:           active           PP SIZE:        256 megabyte(s)
```

VG PERMISSION:	read/write	TOTAL PPs:	546 (139776 megabytes)
MAX LVs:	256	FREE PPs:	340 (87040 megabytes)
LVs:	5	USED PPs:	206 (52736 megabytes)
OPEN LVs:	4	QUORUM:	2
TOTAL PVs:	1	VG DESCRIPTORS:	2
STALE PVs:	0	STALE PPs:	0
ACTIVE PVs:	1	AUTO ON:	yes
MAX PPs per VG:	32512		0
MAX PPs per PV:	1016	MAX PVs:	32
LTG size (Dynamic):	256 kilobyte(s)	AUTO SYNC:	no
HOT SPARE:	no	BB POLICY:	relocatable

In the above example, we use the **lsvg rootvg** command without options. In this case, the output of the **lsvg** command shows all the information about the rootvg volume group. An explanation of the output follows:

VG Identifier   This is a unique worldwide identifier for each volume group. This is a 32-bit number in AIX 5L Version 5.x. In earlier versions, this was only a 16-bit number.

VG Permission   This attribute establishes that rootvg has read and write permissions.

MAX LVs   This value is the maximum number of logical volumes per volume group.

LVs   This is the number of already existing logical volumes.

OPEN LVs   This is the number of logical volumes that are in use at this time (mounted FS, paging spaces, and so on).

TOTAL PVs   This is the number of physical volumes that belong to the rootvg volume group.

STALE PVs   When a physical disk has unsync partitions, it becomes a stale physical volume.

ACTIVE PVs   This is the number of active physical volumes.

MAX PPs per PV   This field establishes the maximum number of physical partitions per physical volume.

MAX PPs per VG   This field establishes the maximum number of physical partitions per physical volume (only Scalable volume group and AIX 5L Version 5.3).

LTG   The Logical Track Group Size is a value that helps improve performance for the volume group access.

HOT SPARE	In AIX 5L, you can define a disk as hot spare in the volume group. In this case, when a disk fails, it is replaced by the hotspare disk.
PP size	This is the size for the physical partition of the volume.
TOTAL PPs	This field indicates the number of total PPs for the volume group.
Free PPs	This field indicates the unused PPs for the volume group. These free PPs can be used to increase a file system, a paging space, or a logical volume.
USED PPs	This field indicates the number of allocated or reserved physical partitions. Use the **df** command to obtain the remaining space for the file systems.
QUORUM	This value establishes the minimum number of VGDAs that must be good to keep the VG online.
VG Descriptors	This is the actual number of good VGDAs in the volume group.
Stale PP	This is the number of unsync physical partitions.
AUTO ON	This field indicates that this volume group must be activated on each reboot.
MAX PVs	This value indicates the maximum number of physical volumes per volume group.
Auto sync	This is an attribute of AIX 5L that allows the partitions in a volume group to automatically synchronize.

Here is another example of the **lsvg** command:

```
# lsvg -p nimvg
nimvg:
PV_NAME             PV STATE        TOTAL PPs   FREE PPs    FREE DISTRIBUTION
hdisk3              active          542         462         109..28..108..108..109
hdisk4              active          542         447         109..13..108..108..109
```

The above example uses the -p option. This flag shows the information for each physical disk within the volume group. The meaning for each column is as follows:

PV_NAME	Establishes the name of the physical disk.
PV STATE	This vaiue indicates whether the PV is active.
TOTAL PPS	This is the size of the PV in physical partitions.
Free PPs	Number of unassigned physical partitions.

FREE DISTRIBUTION A physical disk that is divided into five zones (edge, middle, center, inner-middle, and inner-edge). The numbers shown define the location for the free partitions in these five zones.

Example 6-5 shown another example of the **lsvg** command.

Example 6-5   lsvg -l command

```
# lsvg -l rootvg
rootvg:
LV NAME            TYPE      LPs   PPs   PVs   LV STATE       MOUNT POINT
hd5                boot      1     1     1     closed/syncd   N/A
hd6                paging    24    24    1     open/syncd     N/A
hd8                jfslog    1     1     1     open/syncd     N/A
hd4                jfs       4     4     1     open/syncd     /
hd2                jfs       76    76    1     open/syncd     /usr
hd9var             jfs       4     4     1     open/syncd     /var
hd3                jfs       6     6     1     open/syncd     /tmp
hd1                jfs       1     1     1     open/syncd     /home
hd10opt            jfs       2     2     1     open/syncd     /opt
paging00           paging    20    20    1     open/syncd     N/A
paging01           paging    20    20    1     open/syncd     N/A
lv00               jfs2log   1     1     1     closed/syncd   N/A
ptflv              jfs       25    25    1     open/syncd     /ptf
```

Example 6-5 shows all the information for each LV that belongs to the volume group. In this case, we used the -l option. We outline a brief explanation of the fields in Example 6-5:

LV NAME   This field indicates the name of the logical volume.

TYPE   This column establishes the use of this logical volume. It is only a descriptor. By default, we have boot, jfs, jfs2, jfslog, jfs2log, and paging.

LP   This number indicates the size of the logical volume, expressed in logical partitions.

PPs   This is the number of PPs assigned to the logical volume. In most cases, this value must be equal to the LPs value, unless you have a mirror; in this case, the PPs could be twice or triple the size of the LPs because of the mirror.

PVs   As you know, a logical volume could be spread across two or more PVs. This column indicates in how many PVs the logical volume is located.

LV STATE   This column has two values: closed/syncd: This means that this logical volume is not used. If a file system is not mounted, then its logical volume must appear closed/syncd. Also, hd5, which is the boot logical volume, is closed, because it is only read at boot time.

MOUNT POINT   This column is only available for file systems and indicates the mount point for each file system defined in the system.

Adding a volume group: HP-UX 11i

In HP-UX, there are a couple of steps for creating a VG.

▶ The first step is to execute the command **pvcreate**. This command initializes a direct access storage device. After this step, the disk can be used by a volume group.

```
# pvcreate /dev/rdsk/c1t0d0
```

▶ In the second step, you need to create the directory for the volume group under /dev with the special file called group.

```
# mkdir /dev/vgdba
# mknod /dev/vgdba/group c 64 0x030000
```

▶ In the third step, the volume group will be created with the **vgcreate** command.

```
# vgcreate /dev/vgdba /dev/dsk/c1t0d0.
```

See the **vgcreate** man page for more information.

You can also to create a volume group by using System Administration Manager (SAM). If you would like to add a new physical volume to an existing volume group, you must use the **vgextend** command. Here is an example of its use:

```
# vgextend /dev/vgdba /dev/dsk/c2t1d0
```

The command **vgextend** receives two parameters: The first one is the volume group and the second one is the physical volume. You can also to extend a volume group by SAM.

Adding a volume group: AIX 5L

AIX 5L Version 5.3 implements changes to the volume group. In this version, AIX 5L has more options to create volume groups. One of the new options is the scalable volume, and we still have the other two options to create the normal volume group and to create the big volume group. In order to add a new volume group, we need to have available physical volumes.

A PV can be belong only to one volume group. To add a volume group, use the **mkvg** or **smitty** command. The fast path to create a normal volume group is #

smitty mkvg. Example 6-6 shows the dialog screen of SMIT that is used to add a volume group.

Example 6-6   Adding a volume group

```
                       Add a Volume Group

Type or select values in entry fields.
Press Enter AFTER making all desired changes.

                                                  [Entry Fields]
    VOLUME GROUP name                             [informixvg]
    Physical partition SIZE in megabytes          16                    +
  * PHYSICAL VOLUME names                         [hdisk3]              +
    Activate volume group AUTOMATICALLY           yes                   +
      at system restart?
    Volume Group MAJOR NUMBER                     []                   +#
    Create VG Concurrent Capable?                 no                    +
    Auto-varyon in Concurrent Mode?               no                    +
    LTG Size in kbytes                            128                   +

F1=Help          F2=Refresh        F3=Cancel       F4=List
F5=Reset         F6=Command        F7=Edit         F8=Image
F9=Shell         F0=Exit           Enter=Do
```

The first line in Example 6-6 indicates the name that we want for the new volume group.

The second line specifies the size for the physical partitions. This size must be selected according to the size of our disk. Remember that a disk can only have 1016 PPs.

The third line specifies the ability to activate this volume group each time the system is restarted.

If you would like to create a volume group using the **mkvg** command, you should use the following syntax:

```
# mkvg -s 16 -y nimvg hdisk3
```

> **Tip:** Here we have some useful tips to create volume groups:
>
> ► You can change the number of PPs per physical volume by using the -t flag of the **mkvg** or **chvg** commands.
>
> ► If you would like to create a Big volume group, you must do it with the -B option of the **mkvg** or **chvg** commands or by smitty (only in AIX 5L Version 5.3; in AIX 5L Version 5.2 you cannot use SMIT **smitty _mkbvg**).
>
> ► If you would like to create a scalable volume group. You must do it with the -S option of the **mkvg** command or **smitty _mksvg**.
>
> ► If you have a big volume group or you have changed the number of PPs per PV, you cannot import that volume group in versions earlier than AIX 4.3.3.

If you would like to add a new physical volume to an existing volume group, you must use the **extendvg** command or **smitty**. The following is an example of its use:

```
# extendvg nimvg hdisk4
0516-014 linstallpv: The physical volume appears to belong to another
        volume group.
0003219400004c00
0516-631 extendvg: Warning, all data belonging to physical
        volume hdisk4 will be destroyed.
extendvg: Do you wish to continue? y(es) n(o)? y
```

As you can see, the **extendvg** command receives two parameters: The first one is the volume group name (informixvg) and the second one is the name of the new physical volume. If the physical volume you are adding was used by another VG previously, the command prompts you if you would like to delete the information on that disk; if the PV is completely new, then the command does not show this warning.

Removing a volume group: HP-UX 11i

In HP-UX you use the **vgreduce** command to remove all PVs except the final disk. To actually delete the VG (remove the final disk), you must then use the **vgremove** command.

The command to remove a disk from a diskgroup using **vgreduce** is:

```
# vgreduce /dev/vgdba /dev/dsk/c2t1d0
```

The command **vgreduce** receives two parameters: The first one is the volume group and the second one is the physical volume. If you have one disk with missing status, can you use the option -f. This option removes disks with missing status.

Removing a volume group: AIX 5L Version 5.x

Tip: In HP-UX 11i, you can create a volume group in two different ways:
- By using the command line
- By using the SAM

In order to remove a volume group from the system, you must meet the following requirements:

- Your volume group is removed when the last disk is removed.

- A disk can be removed from a VG if it does not have open logical volumes (in use).

- If a disk contains an open logical volume, you need to close it. If it is a file system, just unmount it, and if it is a paging space, you need to deactivate the paging space first.

To remove a disk from a volume group, we use the **reducevg** command. In the following example, we have the informixvg volume group with two disks (hdisk3 and hdisk4), and we are going to remove hdisk4. If the PV contains logical volumes (inactive), we need to use the -d option, which deletes all the allocated physical partitions on the disk before removing the disk. Refer to Example 6-7.

Example 6-7   reducevg command example

```
# reducevg -d informixvg hdisk4
0516-914 rmlv: Warning, all data belonging to logical volume
        lv01 on physical volume hdisk4 will be destroyed.
rmlv: Do you wish to continue? y(es) n(o)?y
rmlv: Logical volume lv01 is removed.
If we do not use the -d option, the following output will occur:
0516-016 ldeletepv: Cannot delete physical volume with allocated
        partitions. Use either migratepv to move the partitions or
        reducevg with the -d option to delete the partitions.
0516-884 reducevg: Unable to remove physical volume hdisk4.
```

When you delete the last disk from a VG, the volume group is also removed. Example 6-8 shows an example of using the **reducevg** command for the informixvg volume group in our system.

Example 6-8   reducevg command example

```
:# reducevg -d informixvg hdisk3
0516-914 rmlv: Warning, all data belonging to logical volume
        lv02 on physical volume hdisk3 will be destroyed.
rmlv: Do you wish to continue? y(es) n(o)? y
rmlv: Logical volume lv01 is removed.
```

```
ldeletepv: Volume Group deleted since it contains no physical volumes.
```

Activating/deactivating a volume group: HP-UX 11i

In the HP-UX, the **vgchange** command it is used to activate and to deactivate the volume group, and other advanced options for high availability. The following are examples with basic options:

▶ To activate:

```
# vgchange -a y /dev/vgdba
```

▶ To deactivate:

```
# vgchange -a n /dev/vgdba
```

Importing/exporting a volume group: HP-UX 11i

Importing and exporting a volume group in the HP-UX is very similar to importing and exporting in AIX 5L, but during export and import, HP-UX does not update /etc/fstab. During import it does not create any mountpoints in the HP-UX 11i.

To import an exported VG, use the **vgimport** command. Unlike AIX 5L, the LV names are not stored within the ondisk data structures, so to maintain the LV names, you need a *mapfile*. The mapfile can be created during the **vgexport** process. The mapfile can also contain the VGID, removing the need to specify all the individual disks in the VG.

The **vgexport** command removes the volume group. But before, the **vgchange** command should be executed to deactivate the volume group as follows:

```
# vgexport /dev/vgdba
```

Next, the map file is created with the -m option, to be used later:

```
# vgexport -p -v -m /tmp/vgdba.map /dev/vgdba
Beginning the export process on Volume Group "vgdba".
vgexport: Volume group "vgdba" is still active.
/dev/dsk/c1t3d0
/dev/dsk/c1t4d0
```

Before executing the **vgimport** command, it is necessary to take the following steps:

```
# mkdir /dev/vgdba
# mknod /dev/vgdba/group c 64 0x030000
# vgimport -p -v -m /tmp/vgdba.map /dev/vgdba /dev/dsk/c1t3d0 /dev/dsk/c1t4d0
```

With these steps, the volume will be created.

Activating/deactivating a volume group: AIX 5L

As you can imagine, the term *activating* means to make available the volume group for use. The command in AIX 5L is called **varyonvg**.

In order to put one volume group online, the **varyonvg** command checks the quorum rule.

The quorum is the percentage of VGDAs that must be good in the volume group in order to activate the volume group, or, if it is already active, to keep it online. This percentage by default must be greater than 51 percent of the total of VGDAs.

The VGDAs are dispersed in the volume groups according to the amount of physical disks:

VG with one PV   The disk contains two VGDAs.

VG with two PVs   The first disk contains two VGDAs and the second disk contains only one VGDA.

VG with 3 or more PVs   Each disk contains only one VGDA.

When you activate a VG, all its resident file systems are mounted by default if they have the flag mount=true in the /etc/filesystems file. The command to activate the volume group should look like this:

```
# varyonvg apachevg
```

If you want to deactivate the volume group, you must use the **varyoffvg** command. To use this command, you must be sure that none of the logical volumes are opened (in use); otherwise, the command will fail. The following example shows the output of the **varyoff** command when it fails. When all the LVs are closed, you will not receive any message on your screen:

```
# varyoffvg apachevg
0516-012 lvaryoffvg: Logical volume must be closed. If the logical
        volume contains a file system, the umount command will close
        the LV device.
0516-942 varyoffvg: Unable to vary off volume group apachevg.
```

Importing/exporting a volume group: AIX 5L

In AIX 5L, the **importvg** command requires only one PV to perform the import. It also updates /etc/filesystems to add all the appropriate file system entries as they were when the export occurred, as well as creating any mountpoints that did not exist.

There may be times where you need to move physical disks from one system to another, so that the volume groups and logical volumes can be accessed directly on the target system. The procedure to remove a volume group without loosing data is called exporting. The necessary command is **exportvg**, which removes all knowledge of a volume group from the operating system, and all the data for a volume group is stored in the Object Data Manager (ODM). The **exportvg** command only removes the information about the volume group from the ODM. It does not remove anything on the disks that belongs to the volume group.

If you want to export a volume group, you must deactivate it (run **varyoffvg**).

Once you have deactivated the volume group, you can use the **exportvg** command. The command to export a VG should look like this:

```
# exportvg apachevg
exportvg apachevg
0516-764 exportvg: The volume group must be varied off
        before exporting.
```

In the previous example, we did not deactivate the volume group apachevg and we received the error message. When you deactivate the VG first, you do not receive any output on the screen.

When a system wants to access an existing volume group in some disks, the system must be aware of it. This procedure is known as import, and the command used is **importvg**. The **importvg** command reads the information about the VGDA of the selected disk, which includes the PP size, number of PVs, number of LVs, name of LVs, and all the characteristics about that volume group. So, once the **importvg** command reads the information about the VGDA, it then builds all the ODM entries. The following example shows how to import a volume group:

```
# importvg -y apachevg hdisk3
apachevg
```

In the example above, the **importvg** command uses the -y flag, which allows us to select the name of the volume group and hdisk3, which is the disk that contains the volume group information. If the volume group has more than one disk, you can select any of those disks, because all of them have a copy of the VGDA.

> **Attention:** The **importvg** command will automatically vary on a volume group unless the -n flag is used when importing a volume group.

6.3.2 Working with logical volumes

At this time, we have only discussed the physical area of both volume managers (HP-UX LVM and AIX 5L LVM). Now we review all the logical concepts involved in the volume management.

In this section we describe the ways in which HP-UX LVM and AIX 5L LVM create, delete, change, and show characteristics of a logical volume.

In HP-UX, the logical volume name needs to be unique within a VG. For example, where do the logical volume special files reside? In HP-UX, the logical volume special files are located in the directory /dev/<vgnmae>/<lvname>. In AIX 5L, the logical volume special files reside in the directory /dev/<lvname>.

Basic functions of logical volumes

In LVM from IBM and LVM from HP-UX, a logical volume is a virtual device that has its own layout defined by the association of logical partitions.

Listing logical volumes: HP-UX 11i

To determine what logical volumes exist in HP-UX, use the **vgdisplay -v** command. For example, to display a list of LVs in vg00:

```
vgdisplay -v vg00|grep "LV Name"
```

Example 6-9 shows information about the logical volumes with the command **lvdisplay**.

Example 6-9 Information about logical volume

```
# lvdisplay /dev/vg_brazil/lv_pr
--- Logical volumes ---
LV Name                   /dev/vg_brazil/lv_pr
VG Name                   /dev/vg_brazil
LV Permission             read/write
LV Status                 available/syncd
Mirror copies             0
Consistency Recovery      MWC
Schedule                  parallel
LV Size (Mbytes)          24
Current LE                6
Allocated PE              6
Stripes                   0
Stripe Size (Kbytes)      0
Bad block                 on
Allocation                strict
IO Timeout (Seconds)      default
```

To show all information with the distribution of the logical volumes in the disks, the -v option is used. Refer to Example 6-10.

Example 6-10   Distribution of the logical volumes in the disks

```
# lvdisplay -v /dev/vg_brazil/lv_pr
--- Logical volumes ---
LV Name                      /dev/vg_brazil/lv_pr
VG Name                      /dev/vg_brazil
LV Permission                read/write
LV Status                    available/syncd
Mirror copies                0
Consistency Recovery         MWC
Schedule                     parallel
LV Size (Mbytes)             24
Current LE                   6
Allocated PE                 6
Stripes                      0
Stripe Size (Kbytes)         0
Bad block                    on
Allocation                   strict
IO Timeout (Seconds)         default

   --- Distribution of logical volume ---
   PV Name           LE on PV  PE on PV
   /dev/dsk/c2t3d0     6          6

   --- Logical extents ---
   LE    PV1               PE1    Status 1
   00000 /dev/dsk/c2t3d0   00000 current
   00001 /dev/dsk/c2t3d0   00001 current
   00002 /dev/dsk/c2t3d0   00002 current
   00003 /dev/dsk/c2t3d0   00003 current
   00004 /dev/dsk/c2t3d0   00004 current
   00005 /dev/dsk/c2t3d0   00005 current
```

Listing logical volumes: AIX 5L

In AIX 5L, we have different ways to know how many logical volumes we do have. You can list the logical volumes per volume group (by running # **lsvg -l vgname**), and you can list the logical volumes by physical volume (by running # **lspv -l hdiskn**). But if you want to see internal characteristics of the logical volume, you must use the **lslv** command.

In Example 6-11 on page 167, we use the **lslv -l** command to see the physical distribution of the logical volume across the physical disk.

Example 6-11 Physical volume map for a LVM

```
# lslv -l lv_pkpsie
lv_pkpsie:N/A
PV              COPIES          IN BAND         DISTRIBUTION
hdisk1          004:000:000     100%            000:004:000:000:000
```

The output fields are defined as follows:

PV   This column shows the physical volume where the LV resides.

COPIES   The output of this column is divided into three fields. As you can see, only the first field has a value (4); this is the number of physical partitions for the first copy of the logical volume. Only when a logical volume is mirrored is the second and third field used.

IN BAND   As mentioned earlier, a physical volume is divided into five sections (edge, middle, center, inner-middle, and inner-edge). When you create the LV, you can select one of the five sections of the disk to allocate the LV. The section that has the fastest response time is the center.

          The % IN BAND defines the percentage of physical partitions that were allocated in the section defined by the administrator.

DISTRIBUTION This column illustrates how the physical partitions are divided across the five sections of the physical disk. In this example, all the partitions are allocated at the center of the disk.

In Example 6-12, we use the **lslv -m** command. The output of this option shows each logical partition and which physical partition it is pointing to. As you can see, only the PP1 and PV1 columns contain information, because we do not have a mirror defined on this logical volume.

Example 6-12 Logical partition map

```
# lslv -m lv_pkpsie
lv_pkpsie:N/A
LP    PP1  PV1               PP2  PV2               PP3  PV3
0001  0117 hdisk1
0002  0118 hdisk1
0003  0119 hdisk1
0004  0120 hdisk1
```

In Example 6-13, we use the **lslv** command. The output of this option shows all information about the logical volume.

Example 6-13   All information about logical volume

```
# lslv lv_pkpsie
LOGICAL VOLUME:      lv_pkpsie              VOLUME GROUP:   rootvg
LV IDENTIFIER:       000197aa00004c00000001047d7b8dd8.11 PERMISSION:
read/write
VG STATE:            active/complete        LV STATE:       closed/syncd
TYPE:                jfs                    WRITE VERIFY:   off
MAX LPs:             512                    PP SIZE:        256 megabyte(s)
COPIES:              1                      SCHED POLICY:   parallel
LPs:                 4                      PPs:            4
STALE PPs:           0                      BB POLICY:      relocatable
INTER-POLICY:        minimum                RELOCATABLE:    yes
INTRA-POLICY:        middle                 UPPER BOUND:    32
MOUNT POINT:         N/A                    LABEL:          None
MIRROR WRITE CONSISTENCY: on/ACTIVE
EACH LP COPY ON A SEPARATE PV ?: yes
Serialize IO ?:      NO
```

For a detailed explanation of all the fields, please see the man page for **lslv**.

Adding a logical volume: HP-UX 11i

In HP-UX 11i, there are two ways to create a logical volume. You can use the command line or SAM.

Example 6-14 shows the **lvcreate** command. The -L option defines the size of the logical volume, the -n option defines the logical name, and the last parameter is the name of the volume group.

Example 6-14   lvcreate command example

```
# lvcreate -L 28 -n lvol222 vg_brazil
Logical volume "/dev/vg_brazil/lvol222" has been successfully created with
character device "/dev/vg_brazil/rlvol222".
Logical volume "/dev/vg_brazil/lvol222" has been successfully extended.
Volume Group configuration for /dev/vg_brazil has been saved in
/etc/lvmconf/vg_brazil.conf
```

Adding a logical volume in AIX 5L

In AIX 5L, there are many ways to create a logical volume. The first method and the easiest one is by using smitty, but we also can use the GUI Web-based System Manager or the **mklv** command. For example:

```
# mklv
0516-606 mklv: Volume group name not entered.
Usage: mklv [-a IntraPolicy] [-b BadBlocks] [-c Copies]
        [-d Schedule] [-e InterPolicy] [-i] [-L Label] [-m MapFile]
        [-r Relocate] [-s Strict][-t Type] [-u UpperBound]
        [-v Verify] [-x MaxLPs] [-y LVname] [-S StripeSize] [-Y Prefix]
        [-o Overlapping IO] [-C StripeWidth] [-T IOoption] VGname NumberOfLPs
[PVname...]
Makes a logical volume
```

Let us work with the smitty screen to create a LV. The fast path is **smitty mklv**, as shown in Example 6-15.

Example 6-15   Creating an LV using smitty

```
Add a Logical Volume

Type or select values in entry fields.
Press Enter AFTER making all desired changes.

                                                [Entry Fields]
   Logical volume NAME                       []
 * VOLUME GROUP name                         rootvg
 * Number of LOGICAL PARTITIONS              []                      #
   PHYSICAL VOLUME names                     []                      +
   Logical volume TYPE                       []                      +
   POSITION on physical volume               middle                 +
   RANGE of physical volumes                 minimum                +
   MAXIMUM NUMBER of PHYSICAL VOLUMES        []                      #
      to use for allocation
   Number of COPIES of each logical          1                       +
      partition
   Mirror Write Consistency?                 active                 +
   Allocate each logical partition copy      yes                    +
      on a SEPARATE physical volume?
   RELOCATE the logical volume during        yes                    +
      reorganization?
   Logical volume LABEL                      []
   MAXIMUM NUMBER of LOGICAL PARTITIONS      [512]                   #
   Enable BAD BLOCK relocation?              yes                    +
   SCHEDULING POLICY for reading/writing     parallel               +
      logical partition copies
   Enable WRITE VERIFY?                      no                     +
   File containing ALLOCATION MAP            []
```

```
Stripe Size?                                          [Not Striped]        +
Serialize IO?                                          no                  +

F1=Help                 F2=Refresh              F3=Cancel               F4=List
F5=Reset                F6=Command              F7=Edit                 F8=Image
F9=Shell                F10=Exit                Enter=Do
```

In Example 6-15 on page 169, we can see all the fields that we use to define a new LV. Before this screen, we need to select the volume group for our LV.

Let us describe the steps in the following lines:

▶ In the first line, you can specify the name of the new logical volume, otherwise the default (lvnn) is used.

▶ In the third line (number of logical partitions), you need to specify the size for this logical volume in LP. Remember that a logical partition points to a physical partition, so the size must be calculated using PPsize * number_of_LPs.

▶ The fourth line (physical volume name) allows you to specify a specific disk within the volume group. If you leave it blank, the system will use the first available disk.

▶ The logical volume type is only a tag that is used to recognize the type of our logical volume in an easy way. The default is jfs.

▶ The position indicates the section where you want to allocate the logical volume within the disk. Remember that the center of the disk is the fastest section.

▶ Number of copies indicates if you would like to make a mirror. If you leave one copy, there is no mirror, with one LP point to one PP. When you select two, then one LP points to two PPs.

The same task can be done by using the **mklv** command. Here is the syntax:

```
# mklv -cl -t jfs -y weblv rootvg 6
```

Note: If you do not define a mirror on a logical volume when you create it, the mirror can be established later, but you cannot define a stripe layout after the creation of a LV.

Removing a logical volume: HP-UX 11i

To remove a logical volume, you can use SAM or the **lvremove** command. In both operating systems, a logical volume cannot be deleted if you have a mounted file system.

Two examples are shown in Example 6-16. The second example shows a logical volume mounted.

Example 6-16   lvremove command example

```
# lvremove /dev/vg_brazil/lvol222
The logical volume "/dev/vg_brazil/lvol222" is not empty;
do you really want to delete the logical volume (y/n) : y
Logical volume "/dev/vg_brazil/lvol222" has been successfully removed.
Volume Group configuration for /dev/vg_brazil has been saved in
/etc/lvmconf/vg_brazil.conf

# lvremove /dev/vg_brazil/lvol222
The logical volume "/dev/vg_brazil/lvol222" is not empty;
do you really want to delete the logical volume (y/n) : y
lvremove: Couldn't delete logical volume "/dev/vg_brazil/lvol222":
The specified logical volume is open, or
a sparing operation is in progress.

Volume Group configuration for /dev/vg_brazil has been saved in
/etc/lvmconf/vg_brazil.conf
```

Removing a logical volume in AIX 5L

To remove a logical volume, you can use smitty or the **rmlv** command. A logical volume cannot be deleted if you have a mounted file system.

Do not use the **rmlv** command to delete a logical volume that contains a file system or a paging space, because this command will delete the ODM definition for this volume. The file system structure also has its own definition in the ODM and in the /etc/filesystems file. So, if you use the **rmlv** command, the file system information will not be deleted. In this case, you must use the **rmfs** command instead of **rmlv**.

Here is an example of the **rmlv** command:

```
# rmlv lv01
Warning, all data contained on logical volume lv01 will be destroyed.
rmlv: Do you wish to continue? y(es) n(o)? y
rmlv: Logical volume lv01 is removed.
```

Changing characteristics of a volume in HP-UX 11i

You can use the command **lvchange** or SAM to change logical volume characteristics.

If you want to change the name of a LV in HP, umount the file system (if appropriate), and then rename both the /dev/vgxx/lvBLAH and /dev/vgxx/rlvBLAH to whatever you want. Then update /etc/fstab and remount.

In this example, the logical volume is changed to read-only permission:

```
# lvchange -p r /dev/vg_brazil/lv_usa
Logical volume "/dev/vg_brazil/lv_usa" has been successfully changed.
Volume Group configuration for /dev/vg_brazil has been saved in
/etc/lvmconf/vg_brazil.conf
```

In SAM, choose the options Disks and File Systems, then Logical Volumes; choose the logical volume, and finally select the Actions and Modify option.

Changing characteristics of a volume: AIX 5L

In AIX 5L, you can change most of the characteristics of a logical volume, you can add a mirror, and you can move the logical volume to another physical disk.

Example 6-17 shows you how to change the attributes of a LV by using the **smitty chlv** fast path.

```
Change a Logical Volume

Move cursor to desired item and press Enter.

    Change a Logical Volume
    Rename a Logical Volume
```

In the following screen, we can select between changing the name of the logical volume or changing its attributes. The next screen that we will see when we select option 1, "Change a logical volume", allows us to select the logical volume that we want to change. Finally, the dialog screen to change the attributes of a logical volume will look like Example 6-17.

Example 6-17   Changing attributes of a logical volume

```
Change a Logical Volume

Type or select values in entry fields.
Press Enter AFTER making all desired changes.
[Entry Fields]
* Logical volume NAME                           lv_harr
  Logical volume TYPE                           [jfs2]            +
  POSITION on physical volume                   middle            +
  RANGE of physical volumes                     minimum           +
  MAXIMUM NUMBER of PHYSICAL VOLUMES            [32]               #
      to use for allocation
  Allocate each logical partition copy          yes               +
```

```
              on a SEPARATE physical volume?
RELOCATE the logical volume during              yes              +
   reorganization?
Logical volume LABEL                            [/HML]
MAXIMUM NUMBER of LOGICAL PARTITIONS            [512]                       #
SCHEDULING POLICY for reading/writing           parallel         +
   logical partition copies
PERMISSIONS                                     read/write       +
Enable BAD BLOCK relocation?                    yes              +
Enable WRITE VERIFY?                            no               +
Mirror Write Consistency?                       active           +
Serialize IO?                                   no               +
```

Any attribute that we change with this smitty screen can also be changed by the **chlv** command.

6.3.3 Working with physical disks

In this section we review the common tasks on the physical disk management.

Listing a physical volume in HP-UX 11i

In HP-UX 11i, the command to list information about a physical volume is **pvdisplay**, as shown in Example 6-18.

Example 6-18   The pvdisplay command

```
# pvdisplay /dev/dsk/c1t4d0
--- Physical volumes ---
PV Name                     /dev/dsk/c1t4d0
VG Name                     /dev/vg00
PV Status                   available
Allocatable                 yes
VGDA                        2
Cur LV                      2
PE Size (Mbytes)            4
Total PE                    1023
Free PE                     745
Allocated PE                278
Stale PE                    0
IO Timeout (Seconds)        default
Autoswitch                  On
```

With the **pvdisplay** command, you can see size, status, free space, and other information. With the option -v, you have information about the physical extent and the logical volumes allocated in the physical volumes, as shown in Example 6-19.

Example 6-19   The pvdisplay command with option -v

```
# pvdisplay -v /dev/dsk/c2t3d0 | more
--- Physical volumes ---
PV Name                   /dev/dsk/c2t3d0
VG Name                   /dev/vg_brazil
PV Status                 available
Allocatable               yes
VGDA                      2
Cur LV                    2
PE Size (Mbytes)          4
Total PE                  1023
Free PE                   1010
Allocated PE              13
Stale PE                  0
IO Timeout (Seconds)      default
Autoswitch                On

   --- Distribution of physical volume ---
   LV Name             LE of LV  PE for LV
   /dev/vg_brazil/lv_usa  6          6

   --- Physical extents ---
   PE   Status   LV                     LE
   0000 current  /dev/vg_brazil/lv_usa  0000
   --- Distribution of physical volume ---
   LV Name             LE of LV  PE for LV
   /dev/vg_brazil/lv_usa  6          6
   /dev/vg_brazil/lvol444 7          7

   --- Physical extents ---
   PE   Status   LV                     LE
   0000 current  /dev/vg_brazil/lv_usa  0000
   0001 current  /dev/vg_brazil/lv_usa  0001
   0002 current  /dev/vg_brazil/lv_usa  0002
   0003 current  /dev/vg_brazil/lv_usa  0003
   0004 current  /dev/vg_brazil/lv_usa  0004
   0005 current  /dev/vg_brazil/lv_usa  0005
   0006 free                            0000
   0007 free                            0001
   0008 free                            0002
   0009 free                            0003
   0010 free                            0004
Standard input
```

Listing a physical volume: AIX 5L

In AIX 5L, the `lspv` command shows the status of the physical volumes. Let us review some examples of this command in Example 6-20.

Example 6-20   lspv command

```
# lspv
hdisk0          000321941dc75aeb                rootvg
hdisk1          00032194faa00f1f                rootvg
hdisk2          000321944957d438                rootvg
hdisk3          000321944957d841                apachevg
hdisk4          000321946f05b508                None
hdisk5          000321946f05bc04                None
hdisk6          000321946f05ae03                None
hdisk7          000321946235b50a                None
hdisk8          000321946212b304                None
```

As you can see, the `lspv` command without options shows us a complete list of the physical disks that belong to our systems. The first column contains the name of the physical disk, the second column is the PV identifier, and the third one indicates whether the physical volume belongs to a volume group. In Example 6-20, rootvg has three PVs, apachevg has one PV, and hdisk4 is not assigned to any volume group.

Example 6-21   Listing the PV information

```
# lspv hdisk3
PHYSICAL VOLUME:    hdisk3                  VOLUME GROUP:       apachevg
PV IDENTIFIER:      000321944957d841 VG IDENTIFIER
0003219400004c00000000edd
0bc0e1f
PV STATE:           active
STALE PARTITIONS:   0                       ALLOCATABLE:        yes
PP SIZE:            16 megabyte(s)          LOGICAL VOLUMES:    2
TOTAL PPs:          542 (8672 megabytes)    VG DESCRIPTORS:     2
FREE PPs:           540 (8640 megabytes)    HOT SPARE:          no
USED PPs:           2 (32 megabytes)
FREE DISTRIBUTION:  109..106..108..108..109
USED DISTRIBUTION:  00..02..00..00..00
```

The `lspv` command receives a parameter (the name of the disk), and the output given by the command is the detailed information for the physical volume (hdisk3). Refer to Example 6-21.

As mentioned earlier, the size of this disk is given in physical partitions, so this command provides the map of the physical partition distribution over the five sections. In our case, we do not have stale partitions for this disk. But if you find a disk with stale partitions, you may need to synchronize the information on the volume group by using the **syncvg** command.

The **lspv** command can also list the information about the logical volumes per disk, as shown in Example 6-22.

Example 6-22   Listing the PV contents

```
# lspv -l hdisk2
hdisk2:
LV NAME             LPs   PPs   DISTRIBUTION       MOUNT POINT
ptflv               25    25    00..25..00..00..00  /ptf
hd8                 1     1     00..00..01..00..00  N/A
hd4                 4     4     00..00..04..00..00  /
hd2                 76    76    00..00..76..00..00  /usr
hd1                 1     1     00..00..01..00..00  /home
paging01            20    20    00..00..20..00..00  N/A
```

In Example 6-22, we use the **lspv -l** command on a specific PV. The output shown has the physical partition distribution of each LV across the disk (hdisk2).

Moving the contents of a PV: HP-UX 11i

In HP-UX 11i, it is possible to move the physical extent from one physical volume to another physical volume. This operation can be done with logical volumes and physical volumes.

In this example, the data from disk c2t3d0 it is moved to disk c2t3d0:

```
# pvmove  /dev/dsk/c2t4d0 /dev/dsk/c2t3d0
Physical volume "/dev/dsk/c2t4d0" has been successfully moved.
Volume Group configuration for /dev/vg_brazil has been saved in
/etc/lvmconf/vg_brazil.conf
```

In the next example, the logical volume lv_usa is moved to disk c2t4d0:

```
# pvmove -n /dev/vg_brazil/lv_usa /dev/dsk/c2t3d0 /dev/dsk/c2t4d0
Transferring logical extents of logical volume "/dev/vg_brazil/lv_usa"...
Physical volume "/dev/dsk/c2t3d0" has been successfully moved.
Volume Group configuration for /dev/vg_brazil has been saved in
/etc/lvmconf/vg_brazil.conf
```

Moving the contents of a PV: AIX 5L Version 5.x

Some reasons for moving the LVs between disks are:

► Performance. You may have unbalanced your I/O load across your disks.

► The disk is failing, so you need to move your data to a new one.

▸ You have bought a newer, faster, and bigger disk, so you want to migrate your data.

In AIX 5L, it is possible to move a logical volume from one disk to another and have this operation online. In this way, you can balance the disk workload. The command to do this is `migratepv`. The only restriction when you move the contents from a source disk to the target disk is that both disks must belong to the same volume group. Starting with AIX 5L Version 5.1, it is possible to migrate a stripe logical volume; this feature was not available in AIX Version 4.3.3. and earlier.

The following example shows the way to migrate the logical volume hd4 from hdisk0 to hdisk2:

```
# migratepv -l hd4 hdisk0 hdisk2
```

In the above example, we use the `migratepv -l` command to move only one logical volume. All the attributes for the logical volume hd4 are preserved on the target disk (hdisk2).

To move all the contents of one disk to another, we use the following syntax:

```
# migratepv hdisk0 hdisk2
```

In AIX 5L Version 5.2 and AIX 5L Version 5.3, you can also migrate logical partitions. This is possible with the `migratelp` command.

With the output of the `lvmstat` command, it is easy to identify the logical partitions with the heaviest traffic. If you have several logical partitions with heavy usage on one physical disk and want to balance these across the available disks, you can use the new `migratelp` command to move these logical partitions to other physical disks, as shown in Example 6-23.

Example 6-23   migratelp command

```
# migratelp hd3/1 hdisk1/109
migratelp: Mirror copy 1 of logical partition 1 of logical volume
        hd3 migrated to physical partition 109 of hdisk1.
```

Note: The `migratelp` command will not work with partitions of striped logical volumes.

6.3.4 Additional features

The following section provides information about LVM hot-spot management.

LVM hot-spot management: AIX 5L

Two new commands, **lvmstat** and **migratelp**, help you to identify and remedy hot-spot problems within your logical volumes. You have a hot-spot problem if some of the logical partitions on your disk have so much disk I/O that your system performance noticeably suffers. By default, no statistics for the logical volumes are gathered. The gathering of statistics has to be enabled first with the **lvmstat** command for either a logical volume or an entire volume group.

The complete command syntax for **lvmstat** is as follows:

```
# lvmstat
Usage: lvmstat { -l|-v } <name> [ -e|-d ] [-F] [-C] [-c count] [-s] [interval
[iterations]]
Reports input/output statistics for logical partitions and volumes.
```

The first use of **lvmstat**, after enabling, displays the counter values since system reboot. Each usage thereafter displays the difference from the last call:

```
# lvmstat -v rootvg -e
# lvmstat -v rootvg -C
# lvmstat -v rootvg
Logical Volume iocnt Kb_read Kb_wrtn Kbps
hd8              230    6712      16 0.00
paging01          32     150       0 0.00
lv01              11     113       0 0.00
hd1                5      89       0 0.00
hd3                0       0       0 0.00
hd9var             0       0       0 0.00
hd2                0       0       0 0.00
hd4                0       0       0 0.00
hd6                0       0       0 0.00
hd5                0       0       0 0.00
```

With the output of the **lvmstat** command described in the previous section, it is easy to identify the logical partitions with the heaviest traffic. If you have several logical partitions with heavy usage on one physical disk and want to balance these across the available disks, you can use the new **migratelp** command to move these logical partitions to other physical disks.

An example of the command **migratelp**:

```
# migratelp hd3/1 hdisk1/109
migratelp: Mirror copy 1 of logical partition 1 of logical volume
```

Multipath I/O

AIX 5L provides a feature called Multipath I/O (MPIO) that allows for a single device (disk, LUN) to have multiple paths through different adapters. These paths must reside within a single machine or logical partition of a machine. Multiple machines connected to the same device are considered as clustering and not as MPIO. In HP-UX 11i the Multipath I/O is similar to PV Links.

For a detailed explanation see 5.6, "Alternate paths/MPIO configuration" on page 131.

6.4 Quick reference

In both LVM from AIX 5L and LVM from HP-UX, the same task can be done in different ways:

AIX 5L LVM tools   smitty, Web-based System Manager (GUI), or the command line

HP-UX LVM Tools   SAM or command line.

Table 6-6 contains a quick reference for the most used tasks, using command-line tools.

Table 6-6   LVM quick reference

Task	AIX 5L	HP-UX 11i
Storage structure.	A disk is composed of physical partitions.	A disk is composed of physical extent.
	A physical volume is a physical disk; the same thing as a disk.	Physical volume is a physical disk; the same thing as a disk.
	A volume group is composed of physical volumes.	A volume group is composed of physical volumes.
	A volume group is divided into logical volumes.	A volume group is divided into logical volumes.
	A file system is placed onto a logical volume.	A file system is placed into a logical volume.
	A logical volume is extensible and can reside on more than one physical volume.	A logical volume is extensible and can reside on more than one physical volume.
	A logical volume is composed of logical partitions.	A logical volume is composed of logical extents.

Task	AIX 5L	HP-UX 11i
Run multiple tasks in a GUI environment.	► `smit lvm` ► `wsm`	`sam`
Move a logical volume to another physical volume.	`migratepv`	`pvmove`
Create a logical volume.	`mklv`	`lvcreate`
Extend a logical volume.	`extendlv`	`lvextend`
Remove a logical volume.	`rmlv`	`lvremove`
Create a volume group.	`mkvg`	`vgcreate`
Remove a disk from a volume group.	`reducevg`	`vgreduce`
Add disks to a volume group.	`extendvg`	`vgextend`
Change logical volume settings.	`chlv`	`lvchange`
Display volume group information.	`lsvg`	`vgdisplay`
Display performance statistics for storage.	`lvmstat`	
Manage volumes.	► `chlv` ► `mklv` ► `rmlv`	► `lvchange` ► `lvcreate` ► `lvremove`
Add a copy to an existing volume (mirroring).	`mklvcopy`	`lvextend`
Import/export VG.	`importvg/exportvg`	`vgimport/vgexport`

7

File system management

Administering file systems is one of the most important system administration tasks. This chapter is dedicated to the HP-UX implementation of the Veritas File System (VxFS) and AIX 5L journaled file system (JFS and JFS2).

The chapter provides some knowledge about the way the AIX 5L JFS file system works and how it is constructed. The differences between HP-UX 11i and AIX 5L Version 5.3 are also described and the important files are referenced.

The following sections are covered in this chapter:

7.1 Overview

A file system is usually an area on disk (either a *slice* or a logical volume) or sometimes memory (for example, a ramdisk). It is a construct that structures data (files, directories, and other structures) in such a way as to make that data easily accesible to authorized users or groups.

File systems maintain information and identify the location of a file or directory's data. In addition to files and directories, file systems may contain a boot block, a superblock, bitmaps, and one or more allocation groups. An allocation group contains disk i-nodes and fragments.

Both the HP-UX and AIX 5L operating environments support two types of file systems:

Disk-based   Disk-based file systems are stored on physical media, such as hard disks, CD-ROMs, and diskettes. Disk-based file systems can be written in different formats. There are both journaled (for example, VxFS) and non-journaled (for example, cdfs, cdrfs, HFS) file systems.

Network-based   Network-based file systems can be accessed over the network (for example, NFS). Typically, network-based file systems reside on one system (a server) and are accessed by other systems across the network.

The primary type on both HP-UX 11i and AIX 5L is a form of the journaled file system. For a good comparison between AIX 5Ls JFS and Veritas VxFS see section 6.2.5 of the IBM Redbook *Introducing VERITAS Foundation Suite for AIX*, SG24-6619. This book was published November 4th, 2002, and so may not contain updates relevant to VxFS disk layout Version 5.

7.1.1 HP-UX file systems types and commands

Since the introduction of HP-UX 11.x, the Veritas Journaled File System (VxFS) is the default file system in a standard install. (To modify this to some other file system type you would change /etc/defaults/fs.) Prior to 11.x, the default file system was HFS; nowadays you will normally only find /stand to be HFS.

Usually, when you administer disk-based file systems on HP-UX, you have to deal with VxFS file systems. (The standard exception to this is /stand on non-Itanium systems.)

The Veritas file system has different internal VxFS disk layout versions (which do not have a direct relationship in numbers to the VxFS software version); see Table 7-1 on page 183.

Table 7-1   Veritas file system versions versus disk layout

HP-UX OS level	Software version	VxFS disk layout version	Default disk layout
10.20	JFS 3.0	2, 3	3
11.0	JFS 3.1 JFS 3.3	2, 3 2, 3, 4	3 3
11.11	JFS 3.3 JFS 3.5	2, 3, 4	4
11.22	JFS 3.3	2, 3, 4	4
11.23	JFS 3.5	2, 3, 4, 5	5

VxFS provides the following features:

► Journaling

Journaling is the process of storing files system transactions in an intent log before the transactions are applied to the VxFS file system. Once a transaction is stored, the transaction can be applied to the file system later (in the case of VxFS, this is a circular log). This significantly speeds up fsck operations on "dirty" file systems compared to non-journaled file systems like HFS.

► Snapshots

The OnlineJFS snapshot image gives a consistent block level image of a file system at a given point in time. The snapshot will stay stable even if the file system that the snapshot was taken from continues to change. The snapshot can then be used to create a backup of the file system at the given point in time that the snapshot was taken. The snapshot also provides the capability to access files or directories as they were at the time of the snapshot.

► Large file systems

Depending on the version of VxFS, *large file systems* can mean 4 GB (VxFS V2) or 1 TB (VxFS V3 and V4).

► Large files

By default, an VxFS file system cannot have regular files larger than 2 GB (gigabytes). You must explicitly apply the largefiles option to enable a greater than 2 GB file size limit. Depending on the VxFS version, *large files* can mean either 4 GB (VxFS v2) or 1 TB (VxFS V3 and V4).

► Variable sized extent based allocation

When data is stored in the VxFS file system it is grouped in extents rather than one block at a time. This dramatically improves IO performance on large files when compared with the block-based allocation policies of HFS.

Migration

There is no LVM nor VxFS command that migrates HFS to VxFS file systems. Migration of a HFS volume can be done in two different ways:

► Back up the file system, remove it, and recreate it in the VxFS type, then restore the data to the new file system.

► If there is enough disk space available in the volume group, it is possible to create a new VxFS file system structure with the same attributes, and just copy all the files from one file system to another.

Over time the VxFS file system has updated their internal disk layout versions to provide better performance and stability. So, if you have file systems created by one version of VxFS you can use the **vxupgrade** command to move from one disk layout version to another.

For day-to-day administration of file systems in HP-UX you can either use SAM or a command line. In this chapter we primarily talk about the command line, but just remember that SAM can normally be called upon to help out.

The following list shows generic file system administrative commands in HP-UX:

clri	Clears inodes
df or bdf	Reports the number of free disk blocks and files
edquota	Edits user quotas per file system
extendfs	Extends the size of an unmounted file system
ff	Lists file names and statistics for a file system
fsadm	Manipulates advance attributes (for example, large files) and extends/defrags/reorgs file system size online (available with OnlineJFS)
fsck	Checks the integrity of a file system and repairs any damage found
fsdb	Debugs the file system
fstyp	Determines the file system type
mkfs	Makes a new file system
mount	Mounts local and remote file systems
mountall	Mounts all file systems specified in the file system table (/etc/fstab)

`ncheck`	Generates a list of path names with their i-numbers
`quot`	Summarizes file system ownership in 1024-byte blocks
`umount`	Unmounts local and remote file systems
`umountall`	Unmounts all file systems specified in the file system table (/etc/fstab)
`vxdump`	Performs full or incremental backup of a file system
`vxfsconvert`	Converts from HFS to VxFS
`vxrestore`	Restores files from a backup
`vxtunefs`	Tunes VxFS file systems
`vxupgrade`	Upgrades VxFS file systems from one disk layout version to another

7.1.2 AIX 5L file systems types and commands

AIX 5L Version 5.1 introduced the Journaled File System 2 (JFS2). JFS2 is an enhanced and updated version of the JFS on AIX Version 4.3 and previous releases. JFS2 is only recommended for systems that are running the 64-bit kernel. Under AIX 5L Version 5.3 JFS2 is the default file system created.

For a good reference on the AIX 5L file system types see the File System Types section under AIX Information → System Management Guides → System Management Concepts: Operating System and Devices from:

```
http://publib.boulder.ibm.com/infocenter/pseries/index.jsp?topic=/com.ibm.a
ix.doc/aixbman/admnconc/fs_types.htm
```

Table 7-2 on page 186 highlights the differences between the JFS and the JFS2.

JFS provides the following features:

► Journaling

Journaling is the process of storing transactions (changes that make up a complete JFS operation) in a journal log (separate jfslog/jfs2log logical volume that is the default, or JFS2 has the option of an *inline* intent log) before the transactions are applied to the JFS file system. Once a transaction is stored, the transaction can be applied to the file system later.

► Extent Based Allocation

When data is stored in a JFS2 file system it is grouped in extents rather than one block at a time.

► Snapshots

AIX 5L Version 5.2 introduced the JFS2 snapshot image. The JFS2 snapshot image gives a consistent block-level image of a file system at a given point in time. The snapshot will stay stable even if the file system that the snapshot was taken from continues to change. The snapshot can then be used to create a backup of the file system at the given point in time that the snapshot was taken. The snapshot also provides the capability to access files or directories as they were at the time of the snapshot.

► Large file systems

Both versions of JFS support file systems greater than 2 GB in size (see Table 7-2).

► Large files

Both versions of JFS support files greater than 2 GB in size (see Table 7-2).

Table 7-2   Journaled file system differences

Function	JFS	JFS2
Architectural maximum file	64 GB	1 PB[a]
Architectural maximum file system size	1 TB[b]	4 PB
Maximum file size tested	64 GB	1 TB
Number of i-nodes	Fixed, set at file system creation	Dynamic, limited by disk space
Directory organization	Linear	B-tree
Compression	Yes	No
Default ownership at creation	sys.sys	root.system
SGID of default file mode	SGID=on	SGID=off
Quotas	Yes	No

a. PB stands for Petabytes, which is equal to 1,048,576 GB.
b. TB stands for Terabytes, which is equal to 1,024 GB.

Compatibility

In some cases, there will be many servers coexisting with different versions of AIX 5L in a data center. From the JFS point of view, it is not possible to mount the JFS2 file system on AIX Version 4 machines.

Migration

There is no LVM nor JFS command that migrates JFS to JFS2 volumes automatically. Migration of a JFS volume can be done in two different ways:

▶ Back up the file system, remove it, and recreate it in the JFS2 type, then restore the data to the new file system.

▶ If there is enough disk space available in the volume group, it is possible to create a new JFS2 file system structure with the same attributes, and just copy all the files from one file system to another.

JFS2 rootvg support for 64-bit systems

AIX 5L Version 5.1 introduced a feature to set all file systems in the rootvg as JFS2 type file systems. While installing a system with the complete overwrite option, you can enable the 64-bit kernel and JFS2. If this option is enabled, the installation task will create JFS2 file systems in the rootvg.

In AIX 5L, you have the following tools for file systems management:

▶ Web-based System Manager
▶ SMIT or smitty
▶ Command line based management

Figure 7-1 on page 188 shows a Web-based System Manager menu that could be used for managing file systems. Using this menu, you can perform most of the tasks related to file systems management.

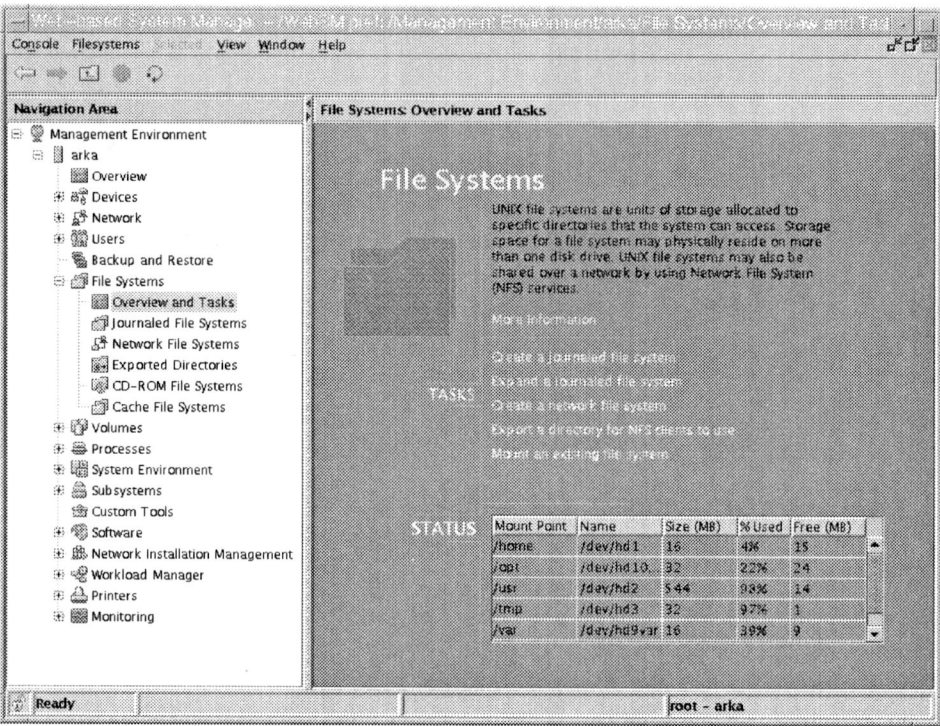

Figure 7-1   File systems management

To create user-defined JFS2 file systems in AIX 5L, use either the SMIT fast path **smitty jfs2** or the **crfs** command with the -v jfs2 flag.

The following is the list of AIX 5L file system management commands that are discussed in this chapter:

backup   Performs full or incremental backup of a file system.

chfs   Changes the characteristics of a file system.

crfs   Adds a file system.

dd   Reads the InFile parameter or standard input, does the specified conversions, then copies the converted data to the OutFile parameter or standard output; the input and output block size can be specified to take advantage of raw physical I/O.

defragfs   Increases contiguous free space in nonfragmented file systems.

df   Reports information about space on file systems.

edquota	Edits user quotas per file system.
ff	Lists file names and statistics for a file system.
fsck	Checks the integrity of a file system and repairs any damage found.
fsdb	Debugs the file system.
lsfs	Displays the characteristics of a file system (-q being a usefull flag).
mkfs	Makes a file system.
mount	Makes a file system available for use.
ncheck	Generates a list of path names with their i-numbers.
restore	Restores files from a backup.
rmfs	Removes a file system.
quot	Summarizes file system ownership in 512-byte blocks (JFS only).
umount	Unmounts a previously mounted file system, directory, or file.

VERITAS File System

The VERITAS File System is another file system type that can be purchased from Veritas. It provides an alternative to the AIX 5L LVM and there is a supported version for AIX 5L Version 5.3. The Veritas file system (VxFS) is the same one used in HP-UX.

For more information, refer to 5.1, "Overview" on page 116 and the IBM Redbook *Introducing VERITAS Foundation Suite for AIX*, SG24-6619, for a detailed examination of this topic.

7.2 Creating a file system

The following section describes how to create a file system in HP-UX and AIX 5L.

7.2.1 Creating a file system in HP-UX

In HP-UX 11i, every file system corresponds to a logical volume (or possibly a slice on a disk). In order to create a file system you could do this in one of two ways:

► Use the following SAM hierarchy: **Disks and File Systems** → **Logical Volumes**, then **Actions** → **Create** and create a new logical volume for the file system to reside in. The default from this SAM panel is to create a logical volume for File System usage (meaning by default VxFS).

▶ Create the file system from the command line as follows:

a. Create the logical volume:

```
lvcreate -L <size in Mb> -n <lv name> <vg name>
```

b. Create the file system:

```
newfs -F vxfs /dev/<vg name>/r<lv name>
```

c. If you want the file system to be mounted automatically on boot, add the appropriate line into /etc/fstab.

d. Mount the file system:

```
mount <mount point>
```

7.2.2 Creating a file system in AIX 5L

In AIX 5L, every file system corresponds to a logical volume. In order to create a journaled file system, use the following SMIT hierarchy:

1. Execute the SMIT fast path command **smitty crfs**, which will show a screen similar to Example 7-1.

Example 7-1   smitty crfs command

```
                         Add a File System

Move cursor to desired item and press Enter.

  Add an Enhanced Journaled File System
  Add a Journaled File System
  Add a CDROM File System



F1=Help          F2=Refresh       F3=Cancel       F8=Image
F9=Shell         F10=Exit         Enter=Do
```

2. Select Add an Enhanced Standard Journaled File System twice to add a new JFS2 file system.

3. Select the volume group in which you want this new file system to be created by using the arrow keys. In this case, since there is only one volume group (rootvg), only rootvg is displayed. Select rootvg as your target volume group by pressing the Enter key.

4. Once you select the target volume group, a screen similar to Example 7-2 on page 191 is displayed.

Example 7-2   Setting characteristics of the new file system

```
                     Add an Enhanced Journaled File System

Type or select values in entry fields.
Press Enter AFTER making all desired changes.

                                                      [Entry Fields]
Volume group name                                     rootvg
  SIZE of file system
          Unit Size                                   Megabytes        +
*         Number of units                             []               #
* MOUNT POINT                                          []
  Mount AUTOMATICALLY at system restart?              no               +
  PERMISSIONS                                         read/write       +
  Mount OPTIONS                                       []               +
  Block Size (bytes)                                  4096             +
  Logical Volume for Log                                               +
  Inline Log size (MBytes)                            []               #
  Extended Attribute Format                           Version 1        +
  ENABLE Quota Management?                            no               +

F1=Help            F2=Refresh          F3=Cancel           F4=List
F5=Reset           F6=Command          F7=Edit             F8=Image
F9=Shell           F10=Exit            Enter=Do
```

5. In the Size of file system parameter, enter the size of the file system you want to create. As of AIX 5L Version 5.2 you can choose the unit size to be one of Mb (default), Gb, or 512 Byte (historic). As of AIX 5L Version 5.2 you can just specify the unit size to be Megabytes and then the number of units to be 4. Prior to AIX 5L Version 5.2, if you wanted to create a file system of 4 MB size, you would multiply the number of megabytes (four in this case) with 2048 to get 512-byte blocks (you will need to create a file system this large (8192 in this case)).

6. Next, in the MOUNT POINT parameter, enter the full path where you want your file system to attach itself to in the file system hierarchy. A mount point is a directory or file at which the new file system, directory, or file is made accessible.

7. Press Enter to create the file system. The screen shown in Example 7-3 indicates the successful completion of the process.

Example 7-3   smitty crfs results

```
                          COMMAND STATUS

Command: OK          stdout: yes          stderr: no

Before command completion, additional instructions may appear below.
```

```
File system created successfully.
261932 kilobytes total disk space.
New File System size is 524288


F1=Help            F2=Refresh         F3=Cancel          F6=Command
F8=Image           F9=Shell           F10=Exit           /=Find
n=Find Next
```

Alternatively, you can achieve the same task on the command line using the **crfs** command:

```
# crfs -v jfs2 -g'rootvg' -a size='<size>' -m'/test'
```

If '<size>' has the M suffix, it is interpreted to be in Megabytes. If Value has a G suffix, it is interpreted to be in Gigabytes; if it is lacking a suffix it is interpreted as 512byte (for example, -a size='16M'). For example:

```
# crfs -v jfs2 -g'rootvg' -a size='16M' -m'/test'
```

This will create a journaled file system of 16 MB with /test as the mount point in the rootvg volume group.

> **Note:** AIX 5L Version 5.1 and later support the JFS2 file system and previous versions of AIX support only the JFS file system.

> **Tip:** Unlike HP-UX's **lvcreate/newfs**, the **crfs** command is like a combination of the two and will also update /etc/filesystems.

7.3 Mounting and unmounting a file system

Mounting is a concept that makes file systems, files, directories, devices, and special files available for use at a particular location. It is the only way a file system is made accessible. Once you have created the file system, the next task is to make it available to your users. The root (/) file system is always mounted. Any other file system can be connected or disconnected from the root (/) file system.

When you mount a file system, any files or directories in the underlying mount point directory are unavailable as long as the file system is mounted. These files are not permanently affected by the mounting process, and they become available again when the file system is unmounted. However, mount directories are typically empty, because you usually do not want to obscure existing files.

In this section, only mounting of local file systems is discussed (that is, there is no discussion of NFS mounts).

7.3.1 Mounting and unmounting in HP-UX

In HP-UX, file system information is stored in the /etc/fstab file. The typical structure of this file is shown in Example 7-4.

Example 7-4   File system information

```
# System /etc/fstab file.  Static information about the file systems
# See fstab(4) and sam(1M) for further details on configuring devices.
/dev/vg00/lvol3 /      vxfs delaylog 0 1
/dev/vg00/lvol1 /stand hfs  defaults 0 1
/dev/vg00/lvol4 /tmp   vxfs delaylog 0 2
/dev/vg00/lvol5 /home  vxfs delaylog 0 2
/dev/vg00/lvol6 /opt   vxfs delaylog 0 2
/dev/vg00/lvol7 /usr   vxfs delaylog 0 2
/dev/vg00/lvol8 /var   vxfs delaylog 0 2
/dev/vg00/lvol9 /test/dir vxfs rw,suid,nolargefiles,delaylog,datainlog 0 2
/dev/vg00/lvol9 /test  vxfs rw,suid,nolargefiles,delaylog,datainlog 0 2
```

> **Tip:** In HP-UX, both **mount -a** and **mountall** interpret the order of what is in /etc/fstab. For example, if you have the fstab above, HP-UX will actually mount /test first and then /test/dir. This is different from the AIX 5L behavior.

Commands used for mounting and unmounting file systems in HP-UX are listed below.

mount	Mounts file systems and remote resources.
mountall	Mounts all file systems specified in the /etc/fstab file. The **mountall** command is run automatically when entering run level 1 (with the /sbin/rc1.d/S100localmount link).
umount	Unmounts file systems and remote resources.
umountall	Unmounts all file systems specified in the /etc/fstab file. The **umountall** command is run automatically when exiting run level 1 (with the /sbin/rc0.d/K900localmount link).

The **mount** command will not mount a read/write file system that has known inconsistencies. If you receive an error message from the **mount** or **mountall** commands, you might need to manually check the file system with **fsck**.

The **umount** commands will not unmount a file system that is busy. A file system is considered busy if a user is accessing a file or directory in the file system, if a program has a file open in that file system, or if the file system is shared.

If there is an entry in /etc/fstab for the file system you want to mount, you can mount it by typing:

```
# mount mount-point
```

For example:

```
# mount /test
```

> **Important:** There must be a mount point on the local system to mount a file system. A mount point is a directory to which the mounted file system is attached.

In HP-UX **mount** also enables you to *remount* a filesystem to change other mount options like:

► Read-write/read-only
► Enable/disable quotas
► Log parameters (for example, log, delaylog, nolog)
► And many others

For example, to use remount /home so that the SUID bit is ignored:

```
# mount |grep home
/home on /dev/vg00/lvol5 delaylog on Thu Jun 16 09:29:09 2005
# mount -o remount,nosuid /home
# mount |grep home
/home on /dev/vg00/lvol5 nosuid,log on Thu Jun 16 09:27:42 2005
```

You can also mount all file systems that have valid entries in the /etc/fstab file by using the **mountall** command.

```
# mountall [-l | -r][-F fstype]
```

For the available options description, refer to the **mountall** man page.

If no options are specified, all file systems listed in the /etc/fstab file are attempted to be mounted. All the file systems are checked and fixed with **fsck**, if necessary, before mounting.

The following example shows how to mount all file systems listed in the /etc/fstab file using **mountall**:

```
# mountall
mountall: /dev/vg00/lvtest has to be fsck'd
mountall: diagnostics from fsck
```

```
vxfs fsck: not a valid vxfs file system
mountall: cannot fsck /dev/vg00/lvtest
mountall: diagnostics from fsck
invalid super-block
file system check failure, aborting ...
itialize aggregate
mountall: /dev/vg00/lvtest failed in fsck
mountall: /dev/vg00/lvtest cannot be mounted
mountall: /dev/vg00/lvtest has to be fsck'd
mountall: diagnostics from fsck
vxfs fsck: sanity check: /dev/vg00/lvblah needs checking
mountall: /dev/vg00/lvblah was fsck'd and fixed
```

Note: HP-UX's version of **mountall** does not display warnings when trying to re-mount already mounted file systems. This is different from the AIX 5L behavior.

You could also use **mount -a** to mount all file systems listed in the /etc/fstab file:

```
# mount -a
vxfs mount: not a valid vxfs file system
mount: /dev/vg00/lvol8 is already mounted on /var
mount: /dev/vg00/lvol7 is already mounted on /usr
mount: /dev/vg00/lvol6 is already mounted on /opt
mount: /dev/vg00/lvol5 is already mounted on /home
mount: /dev/vg00/lvol4 is already mounted on /tmp
mount: /dev/vg00/lvol1 is already mounted on /stand
vxfs mount: /dev/vg00/lvblah is corrupted. needs checking
```

Note: Unlike **mountall**, **mount -a** does not perform any **fsck**'s even if required; it will just produce an error for the corrupted file system.

If there is no specific entry in the /etc/fstab file for the file system you want to mount, you can simply use the **mount** command:

```
# mount [-o mount-options] <lv name> <mount-point>
```

For example:

```
# mount /dev/vg00/lvlocal /usr/local
```

For details about specific mount options, please refer to the **mount** man page. (Note: You need to use **man 1m mount**, otherwise you are likely to be looking at the C programing man page.)

To umount file systems in HP-UX, use the **umount** command:

```
# umount [mount-point|device]
```

For example:

```
# umount /home
```

or

```
# umount /dev/vg00/lvlocal
```

To unmount all the file systems listed in the /etc/fstab file, use the **umountall** or **umount -a** commands. For example:

```
# umountall
umountall: umount : has failed.
umountall: diagnostics from umount
umount: cannot unmount /opt : Device busy
umountall: umount : has failed.
umountall: diagnostics from umount
umount: cannot unmount /tmp : Device busy
umountall: umount : has failed.
.....
```

All systems are unmounted, except those that are busy. For the file systems that were busy and not unmounted you can try and make them available to be unmounted by using the **fuser** command and then try again to unmount them:

```
# fuser -c -k mount-point
```

For example, to send a **kill -9** to all processes accessing the /home file system, use the following command:

```
# fuser -c -k /home
/home: 4006c
```

To verify that there are no processes accessing the file system, type:

```
# fuser -c mount-point
```

For example:

```
# fuser -c /home
/home:
```

You can now re-attempt to unmount /home.

umountall also has the option of -k, which will send the KILL signal to all processes that have files open on all file systems that it is trying to unmount.

7.3.2 Mounting and unmounting in AIX 5L

In AIX 5L, the file system information is stored in the /etc/filesystems file. This file lists all file systems that can potentially be mounted and their mounting configuration. The typical structure of this file is shown in Example 7-5.

Example 7-5   File system information

```
/:
        dev     = /dev/hd4
        vol     = "root"
        mount   = automatic
        check   = false
        free    = true
        vfs     = jfs
        log     = /dev/hd8
        type    = bootfs

/home:
        dev     = /dev/hd1
        vol     = "/home"
        mount   = true
        check   = true
        free    = false
        vfs     = jfs
        log     = /dev/hd8

/usr:
        dev     = /dev/hd2
        vol     = "/usr"
        mount   = automatic
        check   = false
        free    = false
        vfs     = jfs
        log     = /dev/hd8
        type    = bootfs

/proc:
        dev     = /proc
        vol     = "/proc"
        mount   = true
        check   = false
        free    = false
        vfs     = procfs
/test:
        dev         = /dev/lv02
        vfs         = jfs2
        log         = /dev/lv00
        mount       = false
```

```
        account        = false
          type= newgroup

/test:
        dev            = /dev/lv01
        vfs            = jfs2
        log            = /dev/lv00
        mount          = false
        account        = false
        type           = newgroup
```

Tip: In AIX 5L, the order of the entries in /etc/filesystems is significant. In the example /etc/filesystems above, AIX 5L will try and mount /test/dir *before* it attempts to mount /test. This can be a surprise to someone from an HP-UX background.

In AIX 5L, to mount a file system, you may use either the command line or SMIT.

Commands used for mounting and unmounting file systems in AIX 5L are listed below:

mount   Mounts file systems and remote resources.

mount -a   Mounts all file systems specified in the /etc/filesystems file with a mount=true parameter. The **mount -a** command is run automatically during boot. (Note that there is no **mountall** command in AIX 5L.)

umount   Unmounts file systems and remote resources.

umountall   Unmounts all mounted file systems (except /, /tmp, /proc, and /usr). The **umountall** command is run automatically when shutting down.

The following command shows how to mount a file system (/mountpoint):

```
mount /mountpoint
```

For example:

```
mount /test
```

Alternatively, if you know the name of the device associated with your file system, you can use the device name to mount your newly created file system.

If you want to mount all the file systems, you can use the following command to mount all the file systems at one time:

```
mount [-a|all]
```

For example:

```
[node6][/]> mount all
mount: 0506-324 Cannot mount /dev/hd1 on /home: The requested resource is busy.
mount: 0506-324 Cannot mount /proc on /proc: The requested resource is busy.
mount: 0506-324 Cannot mount /dev/hd10opt on /opt: The requested resource is
busy.
mount: 0506-324 Cannot mount /dev/nimlv01 on /nimrepo: The requested resource
is busy.
mount: 0506-324 Cannot mount /dev/smblv00 on /samba: The requested resource is
busy.
mount: 0506-324 Cannot mount /dev/bklv00 on /mksysb: The requested resource is
busy.
```

> **Note:** Unlike HP-UX's **mountall** command, AIX 5L displays warnings when attempting to mount an already mounted file system (like those above).

> **Tip:** A useful option in AIX 5L is represented in /etc/filesystems by the "type =" parameter. You can use **mount -t <type>** to mount only those file systems with the specified *type*. Type is really just a label to group a set of file systems.

A file system can be also be mounted using the following SMIT fast path hierarchy:

1. Executing **smitty mount** will display the screen shown in Example 7-6.

Example 7-6 smitty mount command

```
                        Mount a File System

Move cursor to desired item and press Enter.

    List All Mounted File Systems
    Mount a File System
    Mount a Group of File Systems


F1=Help           F2=Refresh         F3=Cancel          F8=Image
F9=Shell          F10=Exit           Enter=Do
```

2. Use the arrow keys to move the cursor down and select Mount a File System by pressing the Enter key. A screen similar to Example 7-7 is shown.

Example 7-7 Mount a File System menu

```
                        Mount a File System

Type or select values in entry fields.
```

Press Enter AFTER making all desired changes.

```
                                                      [Entry Fields]
     FILE SYSTEM name                            []                      +
     DIRECTORY over which to mount               []                      +
     TYPE of file system                                                 +
     FORCE the mount?                            no                      +
     REMOTE NODE containing the file system      []
       to mount
     Mount as a REMOVABLE file system?           no                      +
     Mount as a READ-ONLY system?                no                      +
     Disallow DEVICE access via this mount?      no                      +
     Disallow execution of SUID and sgid programs  no                    +
       in this file system?



F1=Help            F2=Refresh         F3=Cancel          F4=List
F5=Reset           F6=Command         F7=Edit            F8=Image
F9=Shell           F10=Exit           Enter=Do
```

3. Use the arrow keys to move down to the "DIRECTORY over which to mount" field.

4. Press F4 to get a list of the mount points that you have defined for your file system. Use the arrow keys to select the file system you want to mount. Press Enter to make the selection. This will display the mount point you just selected in the "DIRECTORY over which to mount" field.

5. Press Enter again and wait for the SMIT OK prompt, which indicates the successful completion of the process.

To unmount the file system in AIX 5L, use the **umount** command:

```
# umount /<mountpoint>
```

For example:

```
# umount /home
```

To umount all mounted file systems, type **umount -a** or **umount all** or even **umountall**. There is a difference between **umountall** and **umount**; **umountall** will not attempt to unmount "/, /tmp, /proc and /usr", while **umount** will try (they will most likely be busy anyway and fail). For example:

```
# umountall
umount: 0506-349 Cannot unmount /dev/hd10opt: The requested resource is busy.
umount: 0506-349 Cannot unmount /dev/hd3: The requested resource is busy.
```

A file system can be also be unmounted using the following SMIT fast path hierarchy:

1. Executing **smitty umount** will display the screen shown in Example 7-8.

Example 7-8   smitty umount menu

```
                        Unmount a File System

Move cursor to desired item and press Enter.

   Unmount a File System
   Unmount a Group of File Systems

F1=Help              F2=Refresh          F3=Cancel           F8=Image
F9=Shell             F10=Exit            Enter=Do
```

2. You may chose to unmount all mounted file systems (except /, /tmp, /proc, and /usr), unmount a group of file systems (for example, bootfs), or unmount a single file system. Select Unmount a File System. It opens the menu shown in Example 7-9.

Example 7-9   Unmount a File System screen

```
                        Unmount a File System

Type or select values in entry fields.
Press Enter AFTER making all desired changes.

                                               [Entry Fields]
   Unmount ALL mounted file systems?            no                    +
     (except /, /tmp, /usr)
           -OR-
   Unmount all REMOTELY mounted file systems?   no                    +

   NAME of file system to unmount               []                    +
   REMOTE NODE containing the file system(s)    []
     to unmount




F1=Help              F2=Refresh          F3=Cancel           F4=List
F5=Reset             F6=Command          F7=Edit             F8=Image
F9=Shell             F10=Exit            Enter=Do
```

3. Fill in all the information according to your requirements. For example, use the arrow keys to move down to the "NAME of file system to unmount" option. Press F4, chose the file system you want to unmount, and press Enter.

4. Press Enter again and wait for the SMIT OK prompt, which indicates the successful completion of the process.

7.4 Checking file system consistency

Normally, all file systems are checked before mounting at boot time according to their entries in the /etc/fstab (HP-UX 11i) or /etc/filesystems (AIX 5L Version 5.x) files. Both of the operating systems use the **fsck** command to perform this check. The syntax of the **fsck** command is very similar for HP-UX 11i and AIX 5L Version 5.3. There are only minor differences. For a detailed description, refer to the man pages for **fsck**.

For the **fsck** program, the key entry in the /etc/fstab file is the "fsck pass" field (anything >0 will be checked), while in the /etc/filesystems, **fsck** looks for the check field. Based on these fields, **fsck** decides whether to perform a check on the file system.

7.4.1 Checking file system consistency in HP-UX 11i

In HP-UX 11i, the **fsck** command checks file system consistency and interactively repairs the file system. The general syntax of the **fsck** command is as follows:

```
fsck [-F FStype] [-V] [-m] [special...]
or  fsck [-F FStype] [-V] [-m] [-o specific_options] [special...]
```

In HP-UX 11i, during bootup, a preliminary check is run on each file system to be mounted from a hard disk using the boot script **/sbin/bcheckrc**, which checks all the file systems. **fsck** will check the file systems in the order specified by the pass number field. All file systems with the same pass number will be checked via the **fsck** parallel checking algorithm. Those without a pass number will be checked sequentially at the end.

To modify the order of file system checking at boot time, you would edit /etc/fstab entries in the fsck pass field, and save the changes. The next time the system is booted, the new values are used.

Sometimes you need to interactively check file systems:

► When they cannot be mounted
► When they develop problems while in use

When an in-use file system develops inconsistencies, error messages might be displayed in the console window or the system might crash, but you still have to use the **fsck** command to recover from this errors.

You might want to see if the file system needs checking. To do this, you should umount the file system and use the **fsck -m /dev/<vgname>/<lvname>** command. In this command, the state flag in the superblock of the file system you specify is checked to see whether the file system is clean or requires checking. If you omit the device argument, all the file systems listed in /etc/fstab with a fsck pass value greater than 0 are checked. For example:

```
# fsck -m /dev/vg00/lvtest
vxfs fsck: sanity check: /dev/vg00/lvtest OK
```

The recommended way to check file systems interactively is as follows:

1. Unmount the local file systems:

   ```
   # umountall -l
   ```

2. Check the file systems:

   ```
   # fsck
   ```

   All file systems in the /etc/fstab file with entries in the fsck pass field greater than zero are checked. You can also specify the mount point directory or /dev/<vgname>/<device-name> as arguments to **fsck**. For example:

   ```
   # fsck /dev/vg00/lvtest
   log replay in progress
   pass0 - checking structural files
   pass1 - checking inode sanity and blocks
   pass2 - checking directory linkage
   pass3 - checking reference counts
   pass4 - checking resource maps
   ```

3. If you corrected any errors, type **fsck** and press Enter.

   fsck might not be able to fix all errors in one execution. You may also need to run **fsck** in full mode with fsck -o full.

4. Rename and move any files put in the lost+found directory.

   Individual files put in the lost+found directory by **fsck** are renamed with their inode numbers. If possible, rename the files and move them where they belong. You might be able to use the **grep** command to match phrases with individual files and the **file** command to identify file types. When whole directories are dumped into lost+found, it is easier to figure out where they belong and move them back.

7.4.2 Checking file system consistency in AIX 5L Version 5.3

In AIX 5L Version 5.3, the **fsck** command checks file system consistency and interactively repairs the file system. The general syntax of the **fsck** command is as follows:

```
fsck [ --n ][ --p ] [ -y ] [ -d BlockNumber ] [ -f ] [ -ii-NodeNumber ]
```

```
[-o Options ] [ -t File ] [ -V VfsName ] [FileSystem1 -FileSystem2 ...]
```

The flags commonly used with the **fsck** command and their meanings are shown in Table 7-3.

Table 7-3 Commonly used fsck command flags

Flag	Description
-f	Performs a fast check. Under normal circumstances, the only file systems likely to be affected by halting the system without shutting down properly are those that are mounted when the system stops. The -f flag prompts the **fsck** command not to check file systems that were unmounted successfully. The **fsck** command determines this by inspecting the s_fmod flag in the file system superblock. This flag is set whenever a file system is mounted and cleared when it is unmounted successfully. If a file system is unmounted successfully, it is unlikely to have any problems. Because most file systems are unmounted successfully, not checking those file systems can reduce the checking time.
-p	Does not display messages about minor problems, but fixes them automatically. This flag does not grant the wholesale license that the -y flag does and is useful for performing automatic checks when the system is started normally. You should use this flag as part of the system startup procedures, whenever the system is being run automatically. Also allows parallel checks by group. If the primary superblock is corrupt, the secondary superblock is verified and copied to the primary superblock.
-t*File*	Specifies a file parameter as a scratch file on a file system other than the one being checked, if the **fsck** command cannot obtain enough memory to keep its tables. If you do not specify the -t flag and the **fsck** command needs a scratch file, it prompts you for the name of the scratch file. However, if you have specified the -p flag, the **fsck** command is unsuccessful. If the scratch file is not a special file, it is removed when the **fsck** command ends.
-y	Assumes a yes response to all questions asked by the **fsck** command. This flag lets the **fsck** command take any action it considers necessary. Use this flag *only* on severely damaged file systems.

The **fsck** command checks and interactively repairs inconsistent file systems. You should run this command before mounting any file system. You must be able to read the device file on which the file system resides (for example, the /dev/hd0 device).

Normally, the file system is consistent and the **fsck** command merely reports on the number of files, used blocks, and free blocks in the file system. If the file system is inconsistent, the **fsck** command displays information about the inconsistencies found and prompts you for permission to repair them. If the file system cannot be repaired, restore it from backup.

If you do not specify a file system with the FileSystem parameter, the **fsck** command will check all the file systems with the attribute check=TRUE in /etc/filesystems.

> **Note:** By default, the /, /usr, /var, and /tmp file systems have the check attribute set to false (check=false) in their /etc/filesystems stanzas. The attribute is set to false for the following reasons:
>
> ► The boot process explicitly runs the **fsck** command on the /, /usr, /var, and /tmp file systems.
>
> ► The /, /usr, /var, and /tmp file systems are mounted when the /etc/rc file is executed. The **fsck** command will not modify a mounted file system, and **fsck** results on mounted file systems are unpredictable.

7.5 Changing file system attributes

In both the HP-UX 11i and AIX 5L operating systems, you have the ability to change certain system attributes after file system creation.

HP-UX 11i

In HP-UX you use a set of commands to manipulate file systems (and logical volumes). Some of these are **fsadm**, **extendfs**, **lvextend**, and **mount**.

Please see below for some of the more common tasks performed in day-to-day administration.

AIX 5L

In AIX 5L, most file system maintenance is performed with the **chfs** command.

The syntax of the **chfs** command is as follows:

```
chfs [-n Nodename] [-m NewMountpoint] [-u Group] [-A {yes|no}]
     [-t {yes|no}] [-p {ro|rw}] [-a Attribute=Value] [-d Attribute]
     Filesystem
```

For more information about the **chfs** command options, refer to *AIX Logical Volume Manager from A to Z: Troubleshooting and Commands*, SG24-5433, or to the man page for the **chfs** command.

The **chfs** command changes the attributes of a file system. The new mount point, automatic mounts, permissions, and file system size can be set or changed. The FileSystem parameter specifies the name of the file system expressed as a mount point.

Some file system attributes are set at the time the file system is created and cannot be changed. For the Journaled File System (JFS), such attributes include the fragment size, block size, number of bytes per i-node, compression, large file support, and the minimum file system size. For the Enhanced Journaled File System (JFS2), the block size cannot be changed.

You can use the file systems application in Web-based System Manager to change file system characteristics. You could also use the System Management Interface Tool (SMIT) or **smitty chfs** fast path to run this command.

> **Note:** AIX 5L supports the JFS2 file system and previous versions of AIX support only the JFS file system.

You can see examples of using the **chfs** command below.

7.5.1 Extending a file system in HP-UX

To extend a file system in HP-UX use either **extendfs** (for unmounted HFS or VxFS file systems) or **fsadm** (for OnlineJFS online VxFS file systems).

For example, to extend the file system in /dev/vg00/lvtest to 200Mb:

1. Extend the logical volume that contains the file system:

```
# bdf /dev/vg00/lvtest
Filesystem            kbytes     used    avail %used Mounted on
/dev/vg00/lvtest 163840    1277   152403   1%      /testdir
# lvextend -L 200 /dev/vg00/lvtest
Logical volume "/dev/vg00/lvtest" has been successfully extended.
Volume Group configuration for /dev/vg00 has been saved in
/etc/lvmconf/vg00.conf
```

2. Unmount the file system and extend it:

```
# umount /testdir
# extendfs /dev/vg00/lvtest
```

3. Re-mount the file system and verify the changes:

```
# mount /testdir
# bdf /dev/vg00/lvtest
Filesystem            kbytes     used    avail %used Mounted on
/dev/vg00/lvtest 204800    1293   190788   1%      /testdir
```

To extend a file system while it is still mounted (OnlineJFS required):

1. Extend the logical volume that contains the file system:

```
# bdf /test2
Filesystem            kbytes    used    avail %used Mounted on
/dev/vg00/lvtest2     4096      3420    631   84%   /test2
# lvextend -l 2 /dev/vg00/lvtest2
Logical volume "/dev/vg00/lvtest2" has been successfully extended.
Volume Group configuration for /dev/vg00 has been saved in
/etc/lvmconf/vg00.conf
```

2. Extend the file system online and verify the changes:

```
# fsadm -b 8M /test2
fsadm: /etc/default/fs is used for determining the file system type
vxfs fsadm: /dev/vg00/rlvtest2 is currently 4096 sectors - size will be
increased
# bdf /test2
Filesystem            kbytes    used    avail %used Mounted on
/dev/vg00/lvtest2     8192      3420    4471  43%   /test2
```

7.5.2 Extending a file system in AIX 5L

To do this:

1. To change the file system size (and at the same time, the logical volume that contains it) of the /test Journaled File System, enter:

```
# chfs -a size=24576 /test
```

or

```
# chfs -a size=12M /test
```

This command changes the size of the /test Journaled File System to 24576 512-byte blocks, or 12 MB (provided it was previously no larger than this).

2. To increase the size of the /test Journaled File System, enter:

```
# hfs -a size=+8192 /test
```

or

```
# chfs -a size=+4M /test
```

This command increases the size of the /test Journaled File System by 8192 512-byte blocks, or 4 MB.

7.5.3 Reducing a file system in HP-UX

VxFS also offers the ability to reduce a file system (if there are enough free extents). It is advisable to first perform a defragmentation of the file system and then follow by using the **fsadm -b <newsize>** command specifying a smaller size (that is, you specify the end result you want to have).

This option is not available for HFS file systems.

The only way to reduce the size of an HFS file system is by performing a backup, recreate, and restore. This method can also be used for VxFS file systems.

7.5.4 Reducing a file system in AIX 5L

As of AIX 5L Version 5.3, you can use the **chfs -a size=** command to reduce the size of JFS2 file systems.

If **size** starts with a hyphen (-) or is smaller than the existing size, it will be taken as a request to shrink the file system. The **size** parameter behaves like normal, and can take suffixes of G (for GB), M (for MB), or if nothing, then 512 Byte.

There is no command to show exactly how much a file system can be shrunk since the **df** command does not show the size of the metadata. In addition, the freed space reported by the **df** command is not necessarily the space that can be truncated by a shrink request due to file system fragmentation. A fragmented file system may not be shrunk if it does not have enough free space for an object to be moved out of the region to be truncated, and a shrink does not perform file system defragmentation.

The only way to reduce the size of a JFS file system is to back up, delete/recreate, and restore.

7.5.5 Large files in HP-UX

In HP-UX you can set the *largefiles* attribute either at file system creation or after it. You can even change this attribute while the file system is mounted, though HP advises us to make the change with the file system unmounted.

When creating the file system, you can specify whether it should accept large files. For example:

```
# mkfs (or newfs) -F vxfs -o largefiles /dev/vg00/rlvtest
```

To change whether a VxFS file system will accept files greater than 2 GB, you can use **fsadm -o largefiles <mount point>**. To see whether a file system is configured for largefiles use **fsadm <mount point>**.

For example:

```
# fsadm /test
fsadm: /etc/default/fs is used for determining the file system type
```

```
nolargefiles
# fsadm -o largefiles /test
fsadm: /etc/default/fs is used for determining the file system type
# fsadm /test
fsadm: /etc/default/fs is used for determining the file system type
largefiles
```

Obviously, changing back from largefiles to nolargefiles is denied if there are any files greater than 2 GB on the file system.

7.5.6 Large files in AIX 5L

On creation, either select "Add a Large File Enabled File System" from the appropriate smitty menu or, if using the **crfs** command, supply the "-a bf=true" parameter.

To tell if a file system is large/big file enabled, use the **lsfs** command with -q, as follows:

```
# lsfs -q /blah
Name            Nodename   Mount Pt    VFS   Size    Options    Auto Accounting
/dev/lv01         --       /blah       jfs   1048576 nodev,rw   yes  no
(lv size: 1048576, fs size: 1048576, frag size: 4096, nbpi: 4096, compress: no,
bf: true, ag: 8)
```

> **Tip:** In AIX 5L the bigfiles (bf) attribute is set when the file system is created, and unlike in HP-UX, it cannot be changed afterwards.

7.5.7 Changing a file system mountpoint in HP-UX

To change where a file system is mounted in HP-UX, you directly edit /etc/fstab and supply the new mount point (or through SAM).

You would then need to umount and remount the file system for the changes to take effect.

In HP-UX it does not matter what the underlying permissions are on the mount point. In fact, it is often recommended that a mount point have permissions of 000, as this will stop any files from being created in the mount point when the file system is not mounted.

7.5.8 Changing a file system mountpoint in AIX 5L

In AIX 5L, you should use **chfs** to change the mount point, as follows:

```
# df -k /mount
Filesystem      1024-blocks       Free %Used     Iused %Iused Mounted on
```

```
/dev/lv01            524288    507780    4%        17    1% /mount
# chfs -m /newmount /mount
# df -k /mount
Filesystem      1024-blocks     Free %Used    Iused %Iused Mounted on
/dev/lv01            524288    507780    4%        17    1% /mount
# umount /mount
# mount /newmount
# df -k /mount /newmount
Filesystem      1024-blocks     Free %Used    Iused %Iused Mounted on
/dev/hd4            4194304   3888220    8%      3637    1% /
/dev/lv01            524288    507780    4%        17    1% /newmount
```

> **Important:** If you directly edit /etc/filesystems this *will* work, *but*, if you ever use exportvg/importvg, the file system will end up back on the original mount point, as this is one of the values stored in the logical volume control block (LVCB) that is modified for you via the **chfs** command. You can look at this with the (undocumented) **/usr/sbin/getlvcb -AT <lv name>**.

> **Tip:** The underlying permissions of the mountpoint are significant in AIX 5L; this can be a trap for the unwary. If you use SMIT or crfs to create the file system and mount point, it will correctly set the permissions for you. If you are creating/modifying mount points yourself, make sure you give the mount point *at least* execute access for everyone.
>
> If a user does not have execute access on the underlying mount point, then they will not be able to do anything that uses ".". For example, ../bin/runme would say it did not exist, even if it does.

7.5.9 Mirroring in HP-UX

To mirror a file system (requires MirrorDisk UX):

1. Make sure the file system has a *Strict Allocation* policy (there is not much gained from mirroring to the same disk):

```
# lvdisplay /dev/vg00/lvol3
--- Logical volumes ---
LV Name                     /dev/vg00/lvol3
VG Name                     /dev/vg00
LV Permission               read/write
LV Status                   available/syncd
Mirror copies               0
Consistency Recovery        MWC
Schedule                    parallel
LV Size (Mbytes)            140
Current LE                  35
```

```
Allocated PE                35
Stripes                     0
Stripe Size (Kbytes)        0
Bad block                   off
Allocation                  strict
IO Timeout (Seconds)        default
```

2. Next allocate an additional copy of the logical volume to it:

```
lvextend -m 1 /dev/<vg name>/<lv name>
```

3. You now have a mirrored logical volume, and *mirror copies* will be incremented. You can have up to two mirror copies.

> **Note:** Unlike the AIX 5L command **mirrorvg**, in HP-UX there is no command to mirror a full volume group. All you need to do is a simple loop in your favorite shell. For example:
>
> ```
> for LV in /dev/vg01/lv*
> do
>     lvextend -m 1 $LV
> done
> ```

To split a mirror from a mirrored logical volume:

1. Split the mirror:

```
#lvsplit /dev/vg00/lvmystuff
Logical volume "/dev/vg00/lvmystuffb" has been successfully created with
character device "/dev/vg00/lvmystuffb".
Logical volume "/dev/vg00/lvmystuff" has been successfully split.
Volume Group configuration for /dev/vg00 has been saved in
/etc/lvmconf/vg00.conf
```

2. If the file system was mounted at the time, you need to clean it up:

```
# fsck /dev/vg00/lvmystuffb
fsck: /etc/default/fs is used for determining the file system type
fsck: /etc/default/fs is used for determining the file system type
log replay in progress
replay complete - marking super-block as CLEAN
```

3. Now you can mount it just like normal:

```
# mount /dev/vg00/lvmystuffb /backup
```

4. After you have finished with it umount it:

```
# umount /backup
```

5. Then merge back with the original source:

```
# lvmerge /dev/vg00/lvmystuffb /dev/vg00/lvmystuff
Logical volume "/dev/vg00/lvmystuffb" has been successfully merged
```

```
with logical volume "/dev/vg00/lvmystuff".
Logical volume "/dev/vg00/lvmystuffb" has been successfully removed.
Volume Group configuration for /dev/vg00 has been saved in
/etc/lvmconf/vg00.conf
```

From the man page of lvmerge:

```
Whenever a mirrored logical volume is split into two logical volumes, a bit
map is stored that keeps track of all writes to either logical volume in
the split pair.  When the two logical volumes are subsequently merged using
lvmerge, the bit map is used to decide which areas of the logical volumes
need to be resynchronized.
```

7.5.10 Mirroring in AIX 5L

To mirror a logical volume in AIX 5L use either the **mklvcopy** or the smitty
mklvcopy fastpath. For example, from the command line:

```
# lslv fslv00|grep COPIES
COPIES:              1              SCHED POLICY:   parallel
# mklvcopy -s y -k fslv00 2
COPIES:              2              SCHED POLICY:   parallel
```

The -s y option specifies that we want each PP copy on a different hdisk. The -k
option specifies that we want the mirrors synchronized on completion.

For more information, see the man page for **mklvcopy**.

To split a mirror from a mirrored logical volume:

1. Just like in HP-UX, it is not advisable to split a logical volume while it is in use,
   so for this example we will first unmount the file system:

   ```
   # umount /test
   ```

2. Now we can split the logical volume copy:

   ```
   # splitlvcopy fslv00 1
   fslv01
   ```

3. You can now mount the file system just like normal (note that it has not been
   added into /etc/filesystems, so you need to specify the log device):

   ```
   # mount -o log=/dev/loglv01 /dev/fslv01 /mnt
   ```

4. After you have finished, unmount it.

   ```
   # umount /mnt
   ```

5. There is no way to merge a split logical volume back, so we just delete the
   created logical volume:

   ```
   # rmlv fslv01
   Warning, all data contained on logical volume fslv01 will be destroyed.
   ```

```
rmlv: Do you wish to continue? y(es) n(o)? y
rmlv: Logical volume fslv01 is removed.
```

6. Then re-mirror it again:

```
# mklvcopy -k fslv01 2
```

An alternative way of splitting a mirrored JFS (not JFS2) file system is with the splitcopy option of the **chfs** command.

1. To split off a copy of a mirrored file system and mount it as read-only for use as an online backup, enter:

```
# chfs -a splitcopy=/backup /fredrick
lv01copy00
backup requested(0x100000)...
log redo processing for /dev/lv01copy00
syncpt record at 3028
end of log 3248
syncpt record at 3028
syncpt address 3028
number of log records  = 6
number of do blocks = 0
number of nodo blocks = 0
# df -k /backup /fredrick
Filesystem    1024-blocks    Free %Used    Iused %Iused Mounted on
/dev/lv01copy00     262144    253876   4%       17    1% /backup
/dev/lv01          262144    253876   4%       17    1% /fredrick
# lsvg -l rootvg|grep -E "LV NAME|fredrick|backup"
LV NAME            TYPE        LPs   PPs   PVs  LV STATE      MOUNT POINT
lv01              jfs         1     2     1    open/stale    /fredrick
lv01copy00        jfs         0     0     0    open/syncd    /backup
```

This mounts a read-only copy of /testfs at /backup.

In order to make an online backup of a mounted file system, the logical volume that the file system resides on must be mirrored. The JFS log logical volume for the file system must also be mirrored. The number of copies of the JFS log must be equal to the number of copies of the file system's logical volume.

To re-integrate the source file system so that it is fully mirrored and all PPs are synchronized, just unmount the /backup file system and then remove it.

For example:

```
# umount /backup
# rmfs -r /backup
# ps -ef|grep [s]ync
root 20700 24422   1 13:40:56  pts/2   0:00 lresynclv -l
000197aa00004c00000001047d7b8dd8
```

```
    root 24422     1    0 13:40:56  pts/2  0:00 /bin/ksh /usr/sbin/syncvg -l
lv01
# lsvg -l rootvg|grep fredrick
lv01              jfs          1     2     1      open/syncd     /fredrick
```

For a closer look at using the splitcopy option see *AIX Logical Volume Manager from A to Z: Introduction and Concepts*, SG24-5432.

7.5.11 JFS snapshots in HP-UX

A snapshot is a point-in-time read-only copy of a VxFS file system, which can be mounted just like a normal file system. One way to make use of JFS snapshots is for creating point-in-time backups, thereby reducing downtime for an application.

To create a VxFS snapshot when you have OnlineJFS installed, you would perform the following steps.

1. Use **lvcreate** to create a logical volume large enough to hold all the changes that may happen in the source file system during the time the snapshot is mounted, for example:

   ```
   #lvcreate -l 10 -n lvsnap vg01
   ```

2. Mount a snapshot of a source file system. This is a point in time copy of a single file system, for example:

   ```
   # mount -F vxfs -o snapof=/dev/vg00/lvmystuff /dev/vg00/lvsnap /snap
   ```

   Note that the file system needs to be mounted.

3. On /snap (in this example), you now effectively have a copy of whatever VxFS file system is contained in /dev/vg00/lvmystuff mounted on /snap.

4. After you have finished using /snap, use **umount /snap** to unmount it and possibly **lvremove /dev/vg00/lvsnap** to remove the logical volume.

7.5.12 JFS snapshots in AIX 5L

A snapshot is a point-in-time read-only copy of a JFS2 file system, which can be mounted just like a normal file system. One way to make use of JFS2 snaphosts is for creating point-in-time backups, thereby reducing downtime for an application.

> **Note:** JFS2 snapshots are only available for JFS2 file systems (not JFS).

1. Use the snapshot command to create a snapshot of the /work filesystem:

   ```
   # snapshot -o snapfrom=/work -o size=16M
   Snapshot for file system /work created on /dev/fslv03
   ```

2. Mount the snapshot:

```
# mount -V jfs2 -o snapshot /dev/fslv03 /tmp_mnt
# df -k /tmp_mnt /work
Filesystem   1024-blocks      Free %Used    Iused %Iused Mounted on
/dev/fslv03       262144    261760   1%        -      - /tmp_mnt
/dev/fslv01       262144    217124  18%      837     2% /work
```

3. Query what snapshots have been created for /work:

```
# snapshot -q /work
Snapshots for /work
Current  Location    512-blocks  Free      Time
         /dev/fslv02  524288     523520    Mon Jun 13 14:21:56 CDT 2005
*        /dev/fslv03  524288     523520    Mon Jun 13 14:23:28 CDT 2005
```

4. Delete the older snapshot:

```
# snapshot -d /dev/fslv02
rmlv: Logical volume fslv02 is removed.
```

> **Note:** The **snapshot** command provides an easy interface for managing JFS2 snapshots. You could also create a snapshot with the **mount -o snapto=** command, similar to HP-UX. Please see the examples at the end of the **mount** man page for further details.

7.6 Removing a file system

This section provides information about how to remove a file system in HP-UX and AIX 5L.

7.6.1 Removing a file system in HP-UX

To remove a file system in HP-UX:

1. Make sure you have the file system unmounted:

```
# bdf /filesystem
Filesystem      kbytes    used   avail %used Mounted on
/dev/vg00/lvfile 204800    4606  187682   2% /filesystem
# umount /filesystem
```

2. Remove the logical volume that contains the file system:

```
# lvremove /dev/vg00/lvfile
The logical volume "/dev/vg00/lvfile" is not empty;
do you really want to delete the logical volume (y/n) : y
Logical volume "/dev/vg00/lvfile" has been successfully removed.
Volume Group configuration for /dev/vg00 has been saved in
/etc/lvmconf/vg00.conf
```

3. Remove the line in /etc/fstab.

7.6.2 Removing a file system in AIX 5L

In AIX 5L Version 5.1, you can use the `smitty rmfs` fast path or the `rmfs` command to remove a file system.

The following example shows the steps involved to remove a file system:

1. Using the **mount** command to check the file systems that are currently mounted will display the following screen:

```
# mount
  node       mounted        mounted over     vfs       date        options
-------- ---------------  ---------------  ------  ------------ ---------------
          /dev/hd4        /                jfs     Apr 18 17:27 rw,log=/dev/hd8
          /dev/hd2        /usr             jfs     Apr 18 17:27 rw,log=/dev/hd8
          /dev/hd9var     /var             jfs     Apr 18 17:27 rw,log=/dev/hd8
          /dev/hd3        /tmp             jfs     Apr 18 17:27 rw,log=/dev/hd8
          /dev/hd1        /home            jfs     Apr 18 17:28 rw,log=/dev/hd8
          /proc           /proc            procfs  Apr 18 17:28 rw
          /dev/hd10opt    /opt             jfs     Apr 18 17:28 rw,log=/dev/hd8
          /dev/lv01       /test            jfs2    Apr 25 18:03 rw,log=/dev/lv00
```

2. See if the file system you want to remove is shown in the list:

    – Yes: Continue with step 3.
    – No: Go to step 5.

3. Unmount the file system by using the **umount** command:

    umount *filesystem_name*

4. Repeat step 1 to check whether the file system has successfully been unmounted.

5. Using the SMIT fast path command `smitty rmfs` to remove the file system will display a screen similar to the one shown in Example 7-10.

Example 7-10   smitty rmfs screen

```
                        Remove a File System

Move cursor to desired item and press Enter.

   Remove a Journaled File System
   Remove an Enhanced Journaled File System
   Remove a CDROM File System


F1=Help           F2=Refresh          F3=Cancel          F8=Image
```

6. Choose the Remove a Journaled File System option or the Remove an Enhanced Journaled File System option, depending on the type of the file system you want to remove, and press Enter.

7. Then you have to chose which file system you want to remove. Press F4 to get a list of all the file systems that are defined on the system. Select the file system to be removed using the arrow keys and press Enter.

8. The name of the file system you just selected will be shown in the FILE SYSTEM name parameter.

9. If you want to keep the directory name that was used to mount this file system, press Enter to complete the command; otherwise, change the Remove Mount Point field to YES and press Enter to complete the process.

Alternatively, you could replace steps 5 through 9 with the **rmfs** command:

```
# rmfs filesystem_name
```

This command will remove the appropriate entry out of /etc/filesystems, as well as delete the logical volume that holds the file system.

To remove the mount point when the file system is removed, add the -r flag.

7.7 Displaying file system information

This section describes how to list basic information about file systems, such as listing defined file systems, displaying the mount table, or getting information about available file system space.

7.7.1 Displaying defined file systems in HP-UX

In HP-UX, you can simply view the contents of the /etc/fstab file to list all the defined file systems. For example:

```
# cat /etc/fstab
# System /etc/fstab file.  Static information about the file systems
# See fstab(4) and sam(1M) for further details on configuring devices.
/dev/vg00/lvol3 / vxfs delaylog 0 1
/dev/vg00/lvol1 /stand hfs defaults 0 1
/dev/vg00/lvol4 /tmp vxfs delaylog 0 2
/dev/vg00/lvol5 /home vxfs delaylog 0 2
```

This will only tell you about file systems that someone thought were interesting enough to actually mount. To see all the logical volumes in a volume group that may or may not have a file system on them, you can do either of the following:

▶ Look at the logical volumes defined to a volume group with **vgdisplay**:

```
vgdisplay -v|grep "LV Name"
   LV Name                    /dev/vg00/lvol1
   LV Name                    /dev/vg00/lvol2
   LV Name                    /dev/vg00/lvol3
   LV Name                    /dev/vg00/lvol4
   LV Name                    /dev/vg00/lvol5
```

▶ Look at the logical volume special files in the VG directory:

```
# ls /dev/vg00/lv*
/dev/vg00/lvol3    /dev/vg00/lvol4    /dev/vg00/lvol8
/dev/vg00/lvol1    /dev/vg00/lvol5    /dev/vg00/lvol2
```

To display detailed information about a specific file system, use **fstyp** and **fsadm**. For example:

```
# fsadm /harrison
fsadm: /etc/default/fs is used for determining the file system type
nolargefiles
# fstyp -v /dev/vg_brazil/lvol444
vxfs
version: 4
f_bsize: 8192
f_frsize: 1024
f_blocks: 28672
f_bfree: 27563
f_bavail: 25841
f_files: 6920
f_ffree: 6888
f_favail: 6888
f_fsid: 1074069506
f_basetype: vxfs
f_namemax: 254
f_magic: a501fcf5
f_featurebits: 0
f_flag: 0
f_fsindex: 7
f_size: 28672
```

7.7.2 Displaying defined file systems in AIX 5L Version 5.3

In AIX 5L Version 5.3, you can list the contents of the /etc/filesystems file or use the **lsfs** command. For example:

```
# lsfs
```

```
Name              Nodename    Mount Pt    VFS     Size   Options   Auto Accounting
/dev/hd4          --          /           jfs2    --     --        yes  no
/dev/hd1          --          /home       jfs2    --     --        yes  no
/dev/hd2          --          /usr        jfs2    --     --        yes  no
/dev/hd9var       --          /var        jfs2    --     --        yes  no
/dev/hd3          --          /tmp        jfs2    --     --        yes  no
/proc             --          /proc       procfs  --     --        yes  no
/dev/hd10opt      --          /opt        jfs2    --     --        yes  no
```

There is also a command called **lsvgfs**.

```
#lsvgfs rootvg
/
/usr
/var
/tmp
/home
/opt
```

These commands only show those file systems that were considered interesting enough to be included in /etc/filesystems.

If someone has created a file system and then removed it from /etc/filesystems, you might be able to find it by looking at the logical volumes within the volume group. For example:

```
lsvg -l rootvg
rootvg:
LV NAME             TYPE      LPs    PPs    PVs  LV STATE       MOUNT POINT
hd5                 boot      1      1      1    closed/syncd   N/A
hd6                 paging    2      2      1    open/syncd     N/A
hd8                 jfs2log   1      2      1    open/syncd     N/A
hd4                 jfs2      1      1      1    open/syncd     /
hd2                 jfs2      6      6      1    open/syncd     /usr
hd9var              jfs2      1      1      1    open/syncd     /var
```

To display detailed information about a specific file system, use **lsfs -q**. For example:

```
lsfs -q /home
Name              Nodename    Mount Pt    VFS     Size   Options   Auto Accounting
/dev/hd1          --          /home       jfs2    --     --        yes  no
   (lv size: 524288, fs size: 524288, block size: 4096, sparse files: yes,
inline log: no, inline log size: 0, EAformat: v1, Quota: no, DMAPI: no)
```

Due to the different structure of the LVM, by just performing a **df -kP** in AIX 5L, you cannot see what volume groups the file systems belong to. In HP-UX, you can do a:

```
# bdf | grep vg00
```

```
/dev/vg00/lvol3      143360    87928    55048    61% /
/dev/vg00/lvol1      295024    59176   206344    22% /stand
etc....
```

In AIX 5L, the closest you get to this is:

```
# df -kP $(lsvgfs rootvg)
Filesystem     1024-blocks       Used Available Capacity Mounted on
/dev/hd4             65536      22252     43284     34% /
/dev/hd2           1114112    1087732     26380     98% /usr
/dev/hd9var          65536       6088     59448     10% /var
/dev/hd3            196608     101200     95408     52% /tmp
/dev/hd1             65536        356     65180      1% /home
/dev/hd10opt         65536      21184     44352     33% /opt
```

7.7.3 Displaying the file system mount table

To list all the currently mounted file systems with their mount options, you can use the **mount** command in both HP-UX and AIX 5L operating systems.

7.7.4 Display the file system mount table in HP-UX

The example for HP-UX looks like the following lines:

```
# mount
/ on /dev/vg00/lvol3 log on Thu Jun  9 16:52:10 2005
/var on /dev/vg00/lvol8 delaylog on Thu Jun  9 16:52:24 2005
/usr on /dev/vg00/lvol7 delaylog on Thu Jun  9 16:52:25 2005
/tmp on /dev/vg00/lvol4 delaylog on Thu Jun  9 16:52:25 2005
/opt on /dev/vg00/lvol6 delaylog on Thu Jun  9 16:52:26 2005
/home on /dev/vg00/lvol5 delaylog on Fri Jun 10 14:06:39 2005
/stand on /dev/vg00/lvol1 defaults on Fri Jun 10 14:06:39 2005
/blah/dir on /dev/vg00/lvcopy delaylog,nolargefiles on Mon Jun 13 13:46:00 2005
/mnt on /dev/vg00/lvgwm ro,snapof=/dev/vg00/lvcopy,snapsize=20480 on Mon Jun 13
13:46:02 2005
```

In HP-UX, you can also list the contents of the /etc/mnttab file to perform this task (though you do not edit this file directly). For example:

```
# cat /etc/mnttab
/dev/vg00/lvol3 / vxfs log 0 1 1118350330
/dev/vg00/lvol8 /var vxfs delaylog 0 0 1118350344
/dev/vg00/lvol7 /usr vxfs delaylog 0 0 1118350345
/dev/vg00/lvol4 /tmp vxfs delaylog 0 0 1118350345
/dev/vg00/lvol6 /opt vxfs delaylog 0 0 1118350346
coffee:(pid966) /net ignore ro,intr,port=717,map=-hosts,indirect,dev=0000 0 0
1118353783
/dev/vg00/lvol5 /home vxfs delaylog 0 0 1118426799
/dev/vg00/lvol1 /stand hfs defaults 0 0 1118426799
```

```
/dev/vg00/lvcopy /blah/dir vxfs delaylog,nolargefiles 0 0 1118684760
/dev/vg00/lvgwm /mnt vxfs ro,snapof=/dev/vg00/lvcopy,snapsize=20480 0 0
1118684762
```

7.7.5 Displaying the file systems mount table in AIX 5L

In AIX 5L, use the **mount** command. For example:

```
# mount
     node        mounted        mounted over   vfs      date          options
  --------   ---------------   -------------  -----  ------------  ----------------
           /dev/hd4          /                jfs2   May 04 02:08  rw,log=/dev/hd8
           /dev/hd2          /usr             jfs2   May 04 02:08  rw,log=/dev/hd8
           /dev/hd9var       /var             jfs2   May 04 02:08  rw,log=/dev/hd8
           /dev/hd3          /tmp             jfs2   May 04 02:08  rw,log=/dev/hd8
           /dev/hd1          /home            jfs2   May 04 02:09  rw,log=/dev/hd8
           /proc             /proc            procfs May 04 02:09  rw
           /dev/hd10opt      /opt             jfs2   May 04 02:09  rw,log=/dev/hd8
           /dev/fslv03       /tmp_mnt         jfs2   Jun 13 14:23  ro,snapshot
```

7.7.6 Displaying the available file system space

In both systems, HP-UX and AIX 5L, use the **df** command to list the available space in a file system. A sample output for AIX 5L Version 5.3 looks like the following:

```
# df -k
Filesystem    1024-blocks      Free %Used    Iused %Iused Mounted on
/dev/hd4          262144    245200   7%       2105    4% /
/dev/hd2         1572864    244944  85%      37741   35% /usr
/dev/hd9var       262144    249012   6%        489    1% /var
/dev/hd3          262144    260320   1%         84    1% /tmp
/dev/hd1          262144    261680   1%         14    1% /home
/proc                  -         -   -           -    - /proc
/dev/hd10opt      262144    149408  44%       3600   10% /opt
```

The HP-UX output is:

```
/stand          (/dev/vg00/lvol1    ):    471552 blocks    32208 i-nodes
/home           (/dev/vg00/lvol5    ):     36144 blocks      540 i-nodes
/opt            (/dev/vg00/lvol6    ):    646400 blocks    10169 i-nodes
/tmp            (/dev/vg00/lvol4    ):    125392 blocks     1962 i-nodes
/usr            (/dev/vg00/lvol7    ):    702736 blocks    11065 i-nodes
/var            (/dev/vg00/lvol8    ):    683184 blocks    10750 i-nodes
/               (/dev/vg00/lvol3    ):     93472 blocks     1451 i-nodes
```

So you normally use the **bdf** command:

```
# bdf
Filesystem         kbytes     used    avail %used Mounted on
```

```
/dev/vg00/lvol3    143360    96312    46736   67% /
/dev/vg00/lvol8    512000   167944   341592   33% /var
/dev/vg00/lvol7   1257472   903392   351368   72% /usr
/dev/vg00/lvol4     65536     2416    62696    4% /tmp
/dev/vg00/lvol6   1740800  1415064   323200   81% /opt
/dev/vg00/lvol5     20480     2280    18072   11% /home
/dev/vg00/lvol1    295024    29744   235776   11% /stand
```

Tip: In AIX 5L, the most similar command to the HP-UX **bdf** is **df -kP**.

```
# df -kP
Filesystem     1024-blocks      Used Available Capacity Mounted on
/dev/hd4            262144     86044    176100     33% /
/dev/hd2           2097152   2002480     94672     96% /usr
/dev/hd9var         262144     68368    193776     27% /var
/dev/hd3            262144     30316    231828     12% /tmp
/dev/hd1            262144      9304    252840      4% /home
/proc                    -         -         -      - /proc
/dev/hd10opt        262144    115792    146352     45% /opt
/dev/lv00         10485760   2078308   8407452     20% /work
```

7.8 Back up and restore file systems

In HP-UX, the **fbackup** and **frecover** commands are the recommended commands for scheduled backups of complete file systems. Though if you are using VxFS file systems you can also use the **vxdump** and **vxrestore** commands.

Similarly, in AIX 5L Version 5.x, you should use the **backup** and **restore** commands for preforming backups of complete file systems.

For more information about performing system backups and restoring, refer to Chapter 8, "Backup and restore" on page 243.

7.9 File system logging

A file system log is a formatted list of file system transaction records. The general concept of the logging process is similar in the HP-UX and AIX 5L operating systems. The only differences are in the implementation of this process.

7.9.1 File system logging in HP-UX

In HP-UX only VxFS has the concept of *logging*, as HFS is not a transaction-oriented file system.

HP-UX uses the Veritas file system and the transaction logs for VxFS are INLINE logs, that is, there is no separate logical volume holding the transaction log.

There is no separate formatting for transaction logs in HP-UX, though you can specify the log size on creation of the file system with "-o logsize=" in file system blocks. See the `mkfs_vxfs` man page for more information.

7.9.2 File system logging in AIX 5L

In AIX 5L, there are two different methods for handling the JFS log:

- ► External JFS or JFS2 log (outline log)
- ► Internal JFS2 log (inline log)

The outline log is the more common variety of JFS logging on an AIX 5L system. This enables multiple journaled file systems to use a common log, called a JFS log.

For example, after initial installation, all file systems within the root volume group use logical volume hd8 as a common JFS log. The default log size is one partition (PP); if the PP size for the rootvg was 64 Mb, the root volume group would normally contain a 64 MB JFS log called /dev/hd8.

One advantage of an external JFS log is that it can be placed on a separate disk to the JFS file system that it provides logging for, thereby reducing I/O contention.

> **Tip:** A rule of thumb for sizing JFS logs is to allocate 2 MB of JFS or JFS2 log for every 1 GB of data or 1 partition for every 512 partitions of file system space used.

With JFS2 you have the option of creating an INLINE log, that is, the JFS2 log is part of the file system and there is no external or separate jfs2log defined. This is what an HP-UX administrator would be used to. To create a file system with an inline log rather than the default outline log, you could use the **crfs** parameter "-a log=INLINE".

The **logform** command initializes a logical volume for use as a JFS or JFS2 log device. This stores transactional information about file system metadata changes and can be used to roll back incomplete operations if the machine crashes. When you create a JFS2 file system with an inline log, you do not need to use the **logform** command.

The general syntax of the **logform** command is:

```
# logform LogName
```

Note:

► The **logform** command is destructive; it wipes out all data in the logical volume.

► You generally only need to format the JFS or JFS2 log after creation. When creating another file system that will make use of an already formatted log, there is nothing to do.

► If you run **logform** on a JFS2 file system that has an INLINE log, then only the transactions in the INLINE log are destroyed; the file system data will not be affected.

► If you attempt to run **logform** on a JFS2 file system that does not have an INLINE log, then the command will exit without doing anything.

► Accidentally running this on a logical volume containing a file system completely destroys the file system's data. The **logform** command should only be run on CLOSED logical volumes. If a log device is open due to its use by a mounted file system, the file system should be unmounted prior to running **logform** against the log device. The **logform** command destroys all log records on existing log devices, which may result in file system data loss. You can check to ensure that the log device is closed by running the following:

```
# lsvg -l VGname
```

The external JFS or JFS2 log reside in separate logical volumes. You can also add additional JFS logs if you need to, but a detailed description of the process is beyond the scope of this book. For more information about adding additional JFS logs, refer to the *IBM @server Certification Study Guide - pSeries AIX System Support*, SG24-6199, or to the *IBM @server Certification Study Guide - pSeries AIX System Administration*, SG24-6191.

7.10 Compressed file systems

This section describes how compressed file systems are handled in HP-UX and AIX 5L.

7.10.1 Compressed file systems in HP-UX

There is no native support for compressed file systems in HP-UX.

7.10.2 Compressed file system in AIX 5L

If you have limited disk space, compressed JFS file systems can help you to save disk space. If you want to use compressed JFS file systems, you have to define that at the time of file system creation. Once the file system is created, there is no way to enable this feature.

Note: JFS2 does not support the compressed file system type.

To create a JFS compressed file system:

1. Use the `smitty crjfs` fast path. It opens the screen shown in Example 7-11.

Example 7-11 smitty crjfs screen

```
                    Add a Journaled File System

Move cursor to desired item and press Enter.

  Add a Standard Journaled File System
  Add a Compressed Journaled File System
  Add a Large File Enabled Journaled File System



F1=Help          F2=Refresh        F3=Cancel         F8=Image
F9=Shell         F10=Exit          Enter=Do
```

2. Chose the Create a Compressed Journaled File System option.

3. When asked for the volume group in which to create the file system, use the arrow keys to make your selection. If there is only one volume group defined in the system (rootvg), there will be no other choice. When you select the volume group, press Enter. A screen similar to Example 7-12 appears.

Example 7-12 Adding compressed Journaled File System

```
                 Add a Compressed Journaled File System

Type or select values in entry fields.
Press Enter AFTER making all desired changes.

                                                  [Entry Fields]
    Volume group name                             rootvg
  * SIZE of file system (in 512-byte blocks)      []
  * MOUNT POINT                                    []
    Mount AUTOMATICALLY at system restart?         no                    +
    PERMISSIONS                                   read/write             +
    Mount OPTIONS                                 []                     +
    Start Disk Accounting?                         no                    +
```

```
Fragment Size (bytes)                        512              +
Number of bytes per inode                    512              +
Allocation Group Size (MBytes)               8                +


F1=Help          F2=Refresh        F3=Cancel         F4=List
F5=Reset         F6=Command        F7=Edit           F8=Image
F9=Shell         F10=Exit          Enter=Do
```

4. Fill in all the required information and press Enter. Wait for the OK result, which indicates the successful completion of the process.

7.11 File system defragmentation

The following section contains file system defragmentation.

7.11.1 File system defragmentation in HP-UX

HP-UX OnlineJFS supports defragmentation of VxFS file systems. There is no need to defragment HFS.

If you do not have OnlineJFS, then the only way to defragment the file system is to perform a backup and a restore.

You can defragment an OnlineJFS file system while it is mounted by using **fsadm**:

```
# fsadm -EeDd -t 3600 /mountpoint
```

When performing a defragmentation on HP-UX one nice feature is -t. This specifies how many seconds the defragmentation will run for.

See the online man page for **fsadm_vxfs** for more detailed information.

7.11.2 File system defragmentation in AIX 5L

JFS and JFS2 support the defragmentation of free space in a mounted and actively accessed file system. Once a file system's free space has become fragmented, defragmenting the file system allows it to provide more I/O-efficient disk allocations and to avoid some out of space conditions.

If you want to defragment an existing JFS or JFS2 file system, use the relevant **smitty jfs** or **smitty jfs2** fast path and then chose the Defragment a Journaled File System or Defragment an Enhanced Journaled File System option. The following example shows the defragmenting of a JFS2-based file system:

1. Type **smitty jfs2** and press Enter.

2. Chose Defragment an Enhanced Journaled File System.

3. Make your selection of the file system using the arrow keys and press Enter. The screen shown in Example 7-13 opens.

Example 7-13   Defragment and Enhanced Journaled File System

```
            Defragment an Enhanced Journaled File System

Type or select values in entry fields.
Press Enter AFTER making all desired changes.


                                                   [Entry Fields]
     File System Name                              /test
     Perform, Query, or Report ?                   perform              +



F1=Help          F2=Refresh        F3=Cancel          F4=List
F5=Reset         F6=Command        F7=Edit            F8=Image
F9=Shell         F10=Exit          Enter=Do
```

4. Chose the perform option (which is the default) and press Enter. A screen similar to Example 7-14 indicates successful completion of the process.

Example 7-14   Result of file system defragmentation in smitty

```
                         COMMAND STATUS

Command: OK            stdout: yes            stderr: no

Before command completion, additional instructions may appear below.

Defragmenting device /dev/lv01.  Please wait.
Total allocation groups: 1.
1 allocation groups defragmented.
defragfs completed successfully.
Total allocation groups: 1.
1 allocation groups are candidates for defragmenting.
Average number of free runs in candidate allocation groups: 1.



F1=Help          F2=Refresh        F3=Cancel          F6=Command
F8=Image         F9=Shell          F10=Exit           /=Find
n=Find Next
```

Alternatively, you can use the **defragfs** command.

The syntax of the **defragfs** command is as follows:

```
# defragfs [ -q | -r ] { Device | FileSystem }
```

For information about specific options, refer to the **defragfs** man page.

The **defragfs** command increases a file system's contiguous free space by reorganizing allocations to be contiguous rather than scattered across the disk. You can specify the file system to be defragmented with the Device variable and the path name of the logical volume (for example, /dev/hd4). You can also specify it with the FileSystem variable, which is the mount point in the /etc/filesystems file.

The **defragfs** command is intended for fragmented and compressed file systems. However, you can use the **defragfs** command to increase contiguous free space in nonfragmented file systems.

You must mount the file system read-write for this command to run successfully. Using the -q flag or the -r flag generates a fragmentation report. These flags do not alter the file system.

The following examples show you how to use this command to perform specific tasks:

1. To defragment the /data1 file system located on the /dev/lv00 logical volume, enter the following command:

   ```
   # defragfs /data1
   ```

2. To defragment the /data1 file system by specifying its mount point, enter the following command:

   ```
   # defragfs /data1
   ```

3. To generate a report on the /data1 file system that indicates its current status as well as its status after being defragmented, enter the following command:

   ```
   # defragfs -r /data1
   ```

7.12 Miscellaneous file system commands

The following section contains miscellaneous file system commands.

7.12.1 HP-UX specific

vxtunefs allows the tuning or display of VxFS file systems at run time. For example:

```
# vxtunefs
vxfs vxtunefs: Usage:
    vxtunefs [-p] [-s [ -f tunefstab ] [ -o options ]]
        [mount point | special ] ...
```

where options is a comma separated list of one or more of the following:

```
[read_pref_io=value],
[read_nstream=value],
[read_unit_io=value],
[write_pref_io=value],
[write_nstream=value],
[write_unit_io=value],
[pref_strength=value],
[buf_breakup_sz=value],
[discovered_direct_iosz=value],
[max_direct_iosz=value],
[qio_cache_enable=value],
[max_diskq=value],
[initial_extent_size=value],
[max_seqio_extent_size=value],
[default_indir_size=value],
[max_buf_data_size=value]
```

```
    -o and -f options are mutually exclusive
    The default tunefstab is /etc/vx/tunefstab
# vxtunefs /goddard
Filesystem i/o parameters for /goddard
read_pref_io = 65536
read_nstream = 1
read_unit_io = 65536
write_pref_io = 65536
write_nstream = 1
write_unit_io = 65536
pref_strength = 10
buf_breakup_size = 131072
discovered_direct_iosz = 262144
max_direct_iosz = 785408
default_indir_size = 8192
qio_cache_enable = 0
max_diskq = 1048576
initial_extent_size = 8
max_seqio_extent_size = 2048
max_buf_data_size = 8192
```

7.12.2 AIX 5L Version 5.3 specific

To delete the accounting attribute from a file system, enter # **chfs -d account /home**. This command removes the accounting attribute from the /home file system. The accounting attribute is deleted from the /home: stanza of the /etc/filesystems file.

To list information about the file system:

```
#lsfs -q /mydir
Name            Nodename    Mount Pt VFS   Size     Options   Auto Accounting
/dev/fslv01     --          /mydir   jfs2  524288   rw        yes  no
   (lv size: 524288, fs size: 524288, block size: 4096, sparse files: yes,
inline log: no, inline log size: 0, EAformat: v1, Quota: no, DMAPI: no)
```

7.12.3 Generic commands

To list i-node and path names for a file system use **ncheck** (the **ff** command does something similar but has more options):

```
# ncheck /work
  /work:
  16       /lost+found/.
  17       /gcc-3.3.2.0.exe
  16384    /rajeev/.
```

7.13 Paging/swap space management

Usually, paging space is added and configured at the time of system installation. Typically, after the first boot of the system, you have to perform basic system customization, such as setting the root's password, configuring a network interface, setting time and date and, among others, also setting a paging space. For more information about basic system customization at the time of installation, refer to Chapter 3, "Installing and upgrading tasks" on page 29.

Paging space is also often referred to as swap space.

7.13.1 Paging/swap space management in HP-UX

During the HP-UX installation, there is at least one swap space created; by default this is created on /dev/vg00/lvol2. During installation, you have the option of changing the size of this swap space.

In HP-UX, paging space is more commonly referred to as swap space.

HP-UX has three different types of swap:

File system swap Uses a *swap file* on an existing file system. This is bad from a performance point of view, but can get you out of trouble short term.

Pseudo swap This enables large memory systems (anything over 2 Gb) to *pretend* that up to seven-eights of its physical memory can be used as swap space. This topic is beyond the scope of this paper; there are many documents detailing the performance benefit of pseudo swap on the Internet. The following link is a good place for a search:

http://www.itrc.hp.com

Device swap   This is what everyone is more used to. It is the main type of swap that is used (equivalent to the AIX 5L paging space).

A device swap is the only type of swap that we will focus on in this paper.

The following commands are used to manage swap space:

swapon   Activates a paging space

swapinfo   Provides usage statistics of currently active swap space

The *primary* swap space (defined with lvlnboot -s /dev/...) is activated by the kernel very early on in the piece. On entering run level 1 the **swapon** command is used to activate additional swap spaces so that paging activity occurs across several devices. HP-UX has the ability to prioritize swap spaces by specifying the priority in the /etc/fstab file. Lower numbers have a higher priority and will be used first. If two swap devices have the same priority, then HP-UX will stripe across those devices. For performance reasons you should never have more than one swap device on a single disk.

Active swap spaces cannot be removed. To remove an active swap space, it must first be made inactive. To accomplish this in HP-UX you must comment the swap space out of /etc/fstab and reboot. You can then perform whatever action you have planned.

7.13.2 Paging/swap space management in AIX 5L

In AIX 5L, the installation creates a default paging logical volume (hd6) on drive hdisk0, also referred to as the primary paging space.

The default paging space size is determined during the system customizing phase of the AIX 5L installation according to the following standards:

► Paging space can use no less than 16 MB, except for hd6. In AIX Version 4.2.1, hd6 can use no less than 32 MB, and in AIX Version 4.3 and later, no less than 64 MB.

► Paging space can use no more than 20 percent of the total disk space.

► If real memory is less than 256 MB, paging space is two times real memory.

► If real memory is greater than or equal to 256 MB, paging space is 512 MB.

For detailed information about AIX 5L paging space considerations, refer to the *IBM @server Certification Study Guide - pSeries AIX System Administration*, SG24-6191.

Avoid adding paging space to the volume groups on portable disks in systems prior to AIX 5L Version 5.1. Removing a disk that is online with an active paging space will require a reboot to deactivate the paging space and, therefore, cause user disruption.

> **Note:** AIX versions up to AIX Version 4.3: A volume group that has a paging space volume on it cannot be varied off or exported while the paging space is active. Before deactivating a volume group having an active paging space volume, ensure that the paging space is not activated automatically at system initialization and then reboot the system.
>
> AIX 5L Version 5.1 (and up): The paging space can be dynamically deactivated using the `swapoff` command.

The following commands are used to manage paging space:

`chps`	Changes the attributes of a paging space (including increasing the size).
`lsps`	Displays the characteristics of a paging space.
`mkps`	Creates an additional paging space.
`rmps`	Removes an inactive paging space.
`swapon`	Activates a paging space.
`swapoff`	Deactivates one or more paging spaces.

The `swapon` command is used during early system initialization (/sbin/rc.boot) to activate the initial paging-space device. During a later phase of initialization, when other devices become available, the `swapon` command is used to activate additional paging spaces so that paging activity occurs across several devices.

Active paging spaces cannot be removed. To remove an active paging space, it must first be made inactive. To accomplish this in AIX versions up to AIX Version 4.3, use the `chps` command so the paging space is not used on the next system restart. Then, after restarting the system, the paging space is inactive and can be removed using the `rmps` command. In AIX 5L Version 5.1 (and up), use the `swapoff` command to dynamically deactivate the paging space, then proceed with the `rmps` command.

Note: In AIX versions up to AIX Version 4.3, paging space cannot be dynamically deactivated. It requires a system reboot. So, any maintenance task that requires removal of paging space will have to be scheduled at an appropriate time to minimize user disruption.

7.13.3 Activating paging space in HP-UX

Swap spaces other than *primary swap* are specified with type of *swap* in /etc/fstab. They are activated at boot with a **swapon -a** command.

If you just need to activate a particular swap device after boot, you use the **swapon** command to enable it.

```
# swapon /dev/vg00/lvswap2
```

The primary paging space (defined by **lvlnboot -v**) is activated at priority 1 by the kernel on boot.

7.13.4 Activating paging space in AIX 5L

The paging space devices that are activated by the **swapon -a** command are listed in the /etc/swapspaces file, as shown in the following example. A paging space is added to this file when it is created by the **mkps -a** command, removed from the file when it is deleted by the **rmps** command, and added or removed by the **chps -a** command. For example:

```
# cat /etc/swapspaces
* /etc/swapspaces
*
* This file lists all the paging spaces that are automatically put into
* service on each system restart (the 'swapon -a' command executed from
* /etc/rc swaps on every device listed here).
*
* WARNING: Only paging space devices should be listed here.
*
* This file is modified by the chps, mkps and rmps commands and referenced
* by the lsps and swapon commands.
hd6:
        dev = /dev/hd6
paging00:
        dev = /dev/paging00
paging01:
        dev = /dev/paging01
```

7.13.5 Monitoring paging space resources in HP-UX

To display information about active swap devices, use the **swapinfo** command. For example:

```
# swapinfo -taw
               Kb       Kb       Kb  PCT START/      Kb
TYPE        AVAIL     USED     FREE USED LIMIT RESERVE  PRI  NAME
dev       1048576        0  1048576   0%     0       -    1  /dev/vg00/lvol2
reserve         -   207428  -207428
memory    1157876   385648   772228  33%
total     2206452   593076  1613376  27%     -       0    -
```

7.13.6 Monitoring paging space resources in AIX 5L

In AIX 5L, the **lsps** command displays the characteristics of paging spaces, such as the paging space name, physical volume name, volume group name, size, percentage of the paging space used, whether the space is active or inactive, and whether the paging space is set to automatic. The paging space parameter specifies the paging space whose characteristics are to be shown.

The following examples show the use of the **lsps** command with various flags to obtain the paging space information. The -c flag will display the information in colon format and paging space size in physical partitions:

```
# lsps -a -c
#Psname:Pvname:Vgname:Size:Used:Active:Auto:Type
paging01:hdisk0:rootvg:20:1:y:y:lv
paging00:hdisk2:rootvg:20:1:y:y:lv
hd6:hdisk1:rootvg:24:1:y:y:lv
# lsps -a
Page Space   Physical Volume  Volume Group   Size    %Used  Active  Auto  Type
paging01     hdisk0           rootvg         320MB      1    yes     yes   lv
paging00     hdisk2           rootvg         320MB      1    yes     yes   lv
hd6          hdisk1           rootvg         384MB      1    yes     yes   lv
# lsps -s
Total Paging Space    Percent Used
        1024MB              1%
```

7.13.7 Adding and activating a paging space in HP-UX

To create a device swap space in HP-UX you just define a logical volume with **lvcreate**, then update /etc/fstab appropriately; for example:

```
/dev/vg00/lvswap2 - swap 1  0
```

You then activate it with the **swapon** command.

7.13.8 Adding and activating a paging space in AIX 5L

In AIX 5L, to make a paging space available to the operating system, you must add the paging space and then activate it. The total space available to the system for paging is the sum of the sizes of all active paging-space logical volumes.

> **Note:** You should not add paging space to volume groups on portable disks because removing a disk with an active paging space will cause the system to crash.

The following example shows the steps to create a new 256 MB paging space logical volume.

You can perform this action from the command line; for example, to create a 16 PP paging space, activate it now and on subsequent reboots just type:

```
# mkps -a -n -s 16 vgazgard
```

Or you can use SMIT to perform the same task.

1. Run the SMIT fast path **smitty mkps** to obtain a screen, as shown in Example 7-15.

Example 7-15 smitty mkps command

```
                        VOLUME GROUP name

Move cursor to desired item and press Enter.

   rootvg
   vgazgard

F1=Help              F2=Refresh            F3=Cancel
F8=Image             F10=Exit              Enter=Do
/=Find               n=Find Next
```

2. Use the arrow keys to highlight the rootvg volume group name, and then press the Enter key to obtain a screen, as shown in Example 7-16.

Example 7-16 Add Another Paging Space attributes

```
                      Add Another Paging Space

Type or select values in entry fields.
Press Enter AFTER making all desired changes.

                                           [Entry Fields]
    Volume group name                      vgazgard
```

```
     SIZE of paging space (in logical partitions)        []
 #
     PHYSICAL VOLUME name                                                           +
     Start using this paging space NOW?               no                            +
     Use this paging space each time the system is    no                            +
         RESTARTED?


     F1=Help          F2=Refresh         F3=Cancel        F4=List
     F5=Reset         F6=Command         F7=Edit          F8=Image
     F9=Shell         F10=Exit           Enter=Do
```

3. Type 16 in the "SIZE of paging space (in logical partitions)" field; 16 times 16 MB results in a 256 MB paging logical volume (we assume, at this point, that the logical partition size for your system is 16 MB).

4. Use the Tab key to toggle the "Start using this paging space NOW?" field from no to yes, or use the F4 key to select it.

5. Use the Tab key to toggle the "Use this paging space each time the system is RESTARTED?" field from no to yes.

6. Press the Enter key to create the paging logical volume.

7. SMIT returns the new device name, paging01, with an OK prompt. Press the F10 key to return to the command line.

8. You can now use the **lsps -a** command to check that the new device (paging02) is added and active.

```
# lsps -a
Page Space   Physical Volume   Volume Group   Size   %Used Active Auto Type
paging02     hdisk0            rootvg         256MB      1    yes   yes lv
paging01     hdisk0            rootvg         320MB      1    yes   yes lv
paging00     hdisk2            rootvg         320MB      1    yes   yes lv
hd6          hdisk1            rootvg         384MB      1    yes   yes lv
```

7.13.9 Changing attributes of a paging space in HP-UX

To change anything (for example, increase or decrease size or remove) to do with existing active swap devices in HP-UX, you need to:

1. Comment or remove the entry from /etc/fstab.
2. Reboot the system to deactivate the swap.
3. Perform whatever change you wanted to do.
4. Uncomment or add the entry back in to /etc/fstab.
5. Either reboot the system or use the **swapon** command to activate the device.

7.13.10 Changing attributes of a paging space in AIX 5L

You can change only the following two attributes for a paging space logical volume:

► Deactivate or activate a paging space for the next reboot.
► Increase the size of an already existing paging space.

AIX 5L Version 5.1 added the abilities to deactivate a paging space and to decrease the size of a paging space without having to reboot.

Deactivating paging spaces

The following example shows how to deactivate a paging logical volume, paging02:

1. Run the SMIT fast path command **smitty chps** to get to the PAGING SPACE name screen, as shown in Example 7-17.

Example 7-17   smitty chps command

```
                          PAGING SPACE name

Move cursor to desired item and press Enter.

    paging02
    paging01
    paging00
    hd6


F1=Help                 F2=Refresh              F3=Cancel
F8=Image                F10=Exit                Enter=Do
/=Find                  n=Find Next
```

2. Use the arrow keys to highlight the paging02 paging space name and then press the Enter key.

3. Use the Tab key to toggle the "Use this paging space each time the system is RESTARTED?" field from yes to no, as shown in Example 7-18.

Example 7-18   Changing attributes of paging space in AIX Version 4.3

```
            Change / Show Characteristics of a Paging Space

Type or select values in entry fields.
Press Enter AFTER making all desired changes.

                                                    [Entry Fields]
    Paging space name                           paging02
    Volume group name                           rootvg
    Physical volume name                        hdisk0
```

```
NUMBER of additional logical partitions              []
Or NUMBER of logical partitions to remove            []                      #
     Use this paging space each time the system is    yes                     +
          RESTARTED?


F1=Help            F2=Refresh          F3=Cancel          F4=List
F5=Reset           F6=Command          F7=Edit            F8=Image
F9=Shell           F10=Exit            Enter=Do
```

4. Press Enter to change the paging02 paging logical volume.

5. When SMIT returns an OK prompt, you can press the F10 key to return to the command line.

6. Reboot the system and run the **lsps -a** command to confirm that the status of paging02 has changed to inactive.

Dynamically deactivating a paging space in AIX 5L

The **swapoff** command deactivates paging spaces without requiring a reboot.

The **swapoff** command syntax is as follows:

```
# swapoff DeviceName {DeviceName ...}
```

Use the **swapoff /dev/paging02** command to deactivate paging space paging02, or use the SMIT fast path **smitty swapoff** as shown in Example 7-19.

Example 7-19   smitty swapoff command

```
                        Deactivate a Paging Space

Type or select values in entry fields.
Press Enter AFTER making all desired changes.

                                               [Entry Fields]
     PAGING SPACE name                        paging02               +



F1=Help            F2=Refresh          F3=Cancel          F4=List
F5=Reset           F6=Command          F7=Edit            F8=Image
F9=Shell           F10=Exit            Enter=Do
```

> **Note:** It is necessary to move all pages in use on the paging space being deactivated to other paging spaces; therefore, there must be enough space available in the other active paging spaces.

Increasing the size of a paging space

The following example shows how to increase the size of an already existing paging space, paging02, by 64 MB.

1. Run the SMIT fast path command `smitty chps` to get to a PAGING SPACE name prompt screen, as shown in Example 7-17 on page 237.

2. Use the arrow keys to highlight the paging02 paging space name, and then press the Enter key.

3. Type 4 for the "NUMBER of additional logical partitions" field, as 4 times 16 MB will result in a 64 MB increase in paging space.

4. Press the Enter key to change the paging02 paging logical volume.

5. When SMIT returns an OK prompt, you can press the F10 key to return to the command line.

6. Run the `lsps -a` command to confirm that the size of paging02 has increased.

Decreasing the size of a paging space

AIX 5L Version 5.1 introduced the `chps -d` command. This allows the size of a paging space to be decreased without having to deactivate it, then reboot, then remove the paging space, then recreate it with a smaller size, and then reactivate it.

Use the `chps -d` command to decrease the size of paging02 by two logical partitions, as shown in the following example:

```
# chps -d 2 paging02
shrinkps: Temporary paging space paging03 created.
shrinkps: Paging space paging02 removed.
shrinkps: Paging space paging02 recreated with new size.
```

Removing a paging space in AIX 5L Version 5.3

The following example shows how you would remove paging space paging02 in AIX 5L Version 5.3:

```
# swapoff /dev/paging02
# rmps paging02
rmlv: Logical volume paging02 is removed.
```

In AIX 5L, you also have other possibilities for managing your paging space, such as:

► Reducing the size of the hd6 default paging space.
► Moving the hd6 paging space to another volume group.
► Moving the hd6 paging space within the same VG.

Describing these topics is beyond the scope of this book. For an explanation on these topics, refer to the *IBM @server Certification Study Guide - pSeries AIX System Administration*, SG24-6191.

7.14 Quick reference

Table 7-4 displays the tasks, commands, and location of files or information that is needed to perform file system management in HP-UX 11i and AIX 5L.

Table 7-4   Quick reference for file system management

Task/location	AIX 5L	HP-UX 11i
Running multiple tasks in a GUI environment	Chose one of the following: ► Web-based System Manager ► smitty ► `smitty fs`	SAM
Creating a file system	`crfs`	`newfs` or `mkfs`
Mounting a file system	`mount`	`mount`
Unmounting a file system	`umount`	`umount`
Checking a file system	`fsck`	`fsck`
Changing a file system	`chfs`	`fsadm, extendfs, lvextend, mount`
Removing a file system	`rmfs`	N/A
Displaying defined file systems	`lsfs,` `cat /etc/filesystems`	`cat /etc/fstab`
Displaying current mount table	`mount`	`mount,` `cat /etc/mnttab`
Displaying available file system space	`df -kP`	`bdf`
Back up file system/files/directories	`backup`	`fbackup, vxdump`
Restore file system/files/directories	`restore`	`frecover, vxrestore`
Monitoring paging space	`lsps`	`swapinfo -tawm`
Adding paging space	`mkps`	`lvcreate` and `swapon`

Task/location	AIX 5L	HP-UX 11i
Changing paging space	`chps`	N/A
Removing paging space	`rmps`	/etc/fstab

Backup and restore

8

In this chapter we discuss the important topic of backups. We discuss the different available backup methods. Also, this chapter explains the different commands and options available in AIX 5L and HP-UX for performing backups and doing restores.

This chapter contains the following:

8.1 Overview

Creating backups is one of the most important tasks for a system administrator. All companies and organizations place a high importance on disaster recovery. Thus, it is critical that there is a strategy in place for performing successful backups.

The *primary* reason for backups is so that data can be recovered in the event of a disk failing or some other catastrophic event occurring. That said, we can also often recover files for users if they accidentally delete something.

The data on a computer is usually far more important and expensive to replace than the machine itself. Many companies have gone out of business because they did not plan for disaster recovery. Backup to tape is the cheapest alternative, but a duplicate disk or complete system would also provide protection and faster recovery from disaster.

If the administrators take a careful and methodical approach to backing up the file systems, they are always able to restore recent versions of files or file systems with little difficulty.

Backups should be taken:

- ► Daily, frequently, and regularly of user data
- ► Before an OS upgrade or installation
- ► Before any software installation/upgrade
- ► Before adding any hardware
- ► While reorganizing the file systems

Backups are not only for disaster recovery. One way to transfer a number of files from one system to another is to back up those files on tape, CD-ROM, or diskette, and transfer them to the other system.

There are three types of backups.

Full backups	These are the full system backups. Normally, full backups contain entire user and system data backup. Usually, full backups are performed once weekly or monthly.
Incremental backups	Back up only those files that have changed since the last lower level backup. There are two methods we can use to take incremental backups. The first method is to take a full backup, and then take the backup of those files that have changed since the previous day. For example, if you perform the full backup on Sunday, for the remaining days in the week, take the backup of the

changes that occurred since the previous day. This requires more tapes, but takes less time. But if you miss any one of the tapes, you cannot restore the entire data.

In the other method, you also need to make a full backup first. Then take the backup of all the files that have changed since the last full backup for the rest of the week. For example, make a full backup on Sunday, and for the remaining days in the week make the backup of all the files that have changed since Sunday. This method of backup takes longer, but you will not need the previous day's tape when restoring.

System backup
This is the image backup of the operating system. If you have a system image backup, it will be easy to recover the system in case your operating system or root file system crashes.

In the following sections we discuss the different backup commands and system utilities that are commonly used. These are used to perform the different types of backups listed above.

8.2 Backing up files and file systems

In this section we discuss the different commands used to perform file and file system backups. We also explain the backup methodologies for these backups.

8.2.1 The fbackup and backup commands

In HP-UX, there are a number of backup commands and utilities used for performing backups. The **fbackup** utility is flexible and has some good features, and it is also used by the System Administration Manager (SAM). It is used to back up files and file systems, and it allows full and incremental backups of the file systems. You can also back up individual files with an easy-to-use file selection option, and you can create an online index file.

The following are the generally used options of the **fbackup** command:

f
This specifies the name of the device file. The local tape drive device is usually specified. This can also be a file to be used for the archive. A tape device on a remote device can also be specified.

[-0-9]	This specifies the level of the backup. A single digit is used to specify the level. Level 0 is used for a full backup. The higher levels are used for incremental backups.
[-i path]	The path is used to specify the complete directory tree to be included in the backup. You can specify multiple paths.
[-e path]	The path is used to specify the directory tree that is to be excluded from the backup. You can specify multiple paths.
[-u]	Used to update a database of past backups. The update includes the backup level, the backup start and end times, and the name of the graph file that is used. The -g option must be used in order to use this option.
[-g]	Used to specify a graph file. The graph file includes the directory trees to be included or excluded from the backup. Used instead of specifying the -i and -e options.
[-v]	Specifies that backup run in verbose mode. Displays messages as the backup is running.

Refer to the *fbackup (1M) manual page* for the other options used in fbackup and further details of the command.

In AIX 5L, three procedures can be used to back up the files and file systems: The Web-based System Manager, `smit` or `smitty`, and the **backup** command.

Let us discuss the options and arguments that can be passed to the **backup** command. The copies created by this command are in one of two formats:

► The individual files are backed up using the -i flag.

► The entire file system is backed up by i-node using the level and file system parameters.

The following options are the some of the ones we use in the **backup** command:

-Level	Specifies the backup level (0 to 9). The default level is 9. Level 0 is the full backup.
[f]	Specifies the output device. The default device is /dev/rfd0.
i	Specifies that files be read from standard input and archived by file name.
[u]	Updates the /etc/dumpdates file with the raw device name of the file system and the time, date, and level of the backup. You must specify the -u flag if you are making

incremental backups. The -u flag applies only to backups by i-node.

[v] Causes the **backup** command to display additional information about the backup. It displays the size of the files.

8.2.2 Backing up files and directories

We now see some examples of the use of the specified commands in this topic. We discuss using Web-based System Manager and **smitty** tools to perform the backup in AIX 5L.

Example 8-1 shows the use of the **fbackup** command in HP-UX to make a full backup of the directory /var/tmp to the tape device /dev/rmt/0m. This will back up all the files and directories that are under /var/tmp.

Example 8-1   fbackup command

```
# fbackup -vf /dev/rmt/0m -i /var/tmp
fbackup(1004): session begins on Thu Jun 23 10:05:40 2005
fbackup(3203): volume 1 has been used 2 time(s)
fbackup(3024): writing volume 1 to the output file /dev/rmt/0m
     1: / 16
     2: /var 16
     3: /var/tmp 16
     4: /var/tmp/envd.action2 1
     5: /var/tmp/envd.action5 1
     6: /var/tmp/ntp 1
     7: /var/tmp/swagent.log 5
fbackup(1005): run time: 13 seconds
fbackup(3055): total file blocks read for backup: 56
fbackup(3056): total blocks written to output file /dev/rmt/0m: 99
#
```

In HP-UX, the same backup as performed above can also be done using SAM. This is done as follows. From the SAM main menu select **Backup and Recovery** → **Interactive Backup and Recovery** → **Select Tape Device to use for backup** → **Action** → **Back Up Files Interactively...** → **Select Backup Scope**.

Type in the files and directory to be backed up and add to the Included Files list.

As you move to the next screens, a message is displayed. Select Yes to proceed. The backup will start and you will see the same messages as were seen with the backup, which was run from the command line in Example 8-1.

Example 8-2 shows how to back up all the directories and files under the /tmp/bos directory in AIX 5L.

Example 8-2   backup command

```
[p650n04]> find /tmp/bos -print | backup -qivf /dev/rmt0
Backing up to /dev/rmt0.
Cluster 51200 bytes (100 blocks).
Volume 1 on /msmount/backupfile1
a               0 /tmp/bos
a            5968 /tmp/bos/bos.rte.cfgfiles
a           32251 /tmp/bos/bos.rte.post_i
a           75934 /tmp/bos/bos.rte.pre_i
a             398 /tmp/bos/incompat.pkgs
a               0 /tmp/bos/old.html
a          253403 /tmp/bos/bos.rte.inventory
a           40686 /tmp/bos/bos.rte.al
a            4061 /tmp/bos/bos.rte.size
a           72261 /tmp/bos/bos.rte.tcb
a               0 /tmp/bos/etc
a             880 /tmp/bos/etc/motd
a               0 /tmp/bos/etc/objrepos
a           20480 /tmp/bos/etc/objrepos/CuAt
a            4096 /tmp/bos/etc/objrepos/CuAt.vc
a            4096 /tmp/bos/etc/objrepos/CuDep
a           16384 /tmp/bos/etc/objrepos/CuDv
a           36864 /tmp/bos/etc/objrepos/CuDvDr
a            4096 /tmp/bos/etc/objrepos/CuPath
a            4096 /tmp/bos/etc/objrepos/CuPath.vc
a            4096 /tmp/bos/etc/objrepos/CuPathAt
a            4096 /tmp/bos/etc/objrepos/CuPathAt.vc
a           24576 /tmp/bos/etc/objrepos/CuVPD
a            3572 /tmp/bos/etc/rc
a            2344 /tmp/bos/etc/tsh_profile
a           10257 /tmp/bos/files_added
a              67 /tmp/bos/cfgfiles.moved
a               0 /tmp/bos/sbin
a           26101 /tmp/bos/sbin/rc.boot
a               0 /tmp/bos/usr
a               0 /tmp/bos/usr/lib
a               0 /tmp/bos/usr/lib/objrepos
a            4096 /tmp/bos/usr/lib/objrepos/vendor
a            4096 /tmp/bos/usr/lib/objrepos/vendor.vc
a               0 /tmp/bos/usr/sbin
a            4493 /tmp/bos/usr/sbin/skulker
The total size is 663748 bytes.
Backup finished on Thu Jun 23 10:13:15 CDT 2005; there are 1400 blocks on 1
volumes.
```

In AIX 5L, you can back up the files and directories using the `smitty backfile` fast path command (see Example 8-3). The same screen can be reached from the smitty main menu as follows: **smitty** → **System Storage Management (Physical & Logical Storage)** → **Files & Directories** → **Backup a File or Directory**.

Example 8-3   smitty backfile

```
                         Backup a File or Directory

Type or select values in entry fields.
Press Enter AFTER making all desired changes.

                                                      [Entry Fields]
This option will perform a backup by name.
* Backup DEVICE                                      [/dev/rmt0]            +/
* FILE or DIRECTORY to backup                        [/tmp/bos]
  Current working DIRECTORY                          []                      /
  Backup LOCAL files only?                           yes                    +
  VERBOSE output?                                    yes                    +
  PACK files?                                        no                     +


F1=Help           F2=Refresh        F3=Cancel        F4=List
F5=Reset          F6=Command        F7=Edit          F8=Image
F9=Shell          F0=Exit           Enter=Do
```

In Example 8-3, the fields are as follows:

► FILE or DIRECTORY to backup: The parameter for the **find** command, which will run in the background. Here we need to specify the path name that we need to back up. In our example, we have specified that the /tmp/bos directory is to be backed up. If the full path name is used here, then the names would be stored with the full path names.

► Current working DIRECTORY: Performs a **cd** to that directory before starting the backup. If you want a backup from the current directory, and you want to make sure you are in the right directory, you can put the name of the directory here.

► Backup LOCAL files only?: Ignores any network file systems. Files backed up will be from the local system only.

8.2.3 Backing up file systems

We have seen how to back up individual files and directories in the previous topic. Now we explain how file systems can be backed up in HP-UX and AIX 5L.

File system backups should be performed when the system activity is very low. You need to do the following steps before performing the full file system backup.

In HP-UX:

▶ Bring the system down to single user mode if absolute consistency is required when doing a full backup. If this is not possible, it is a good idea to unmount the file system. However, as detailed in the fbackup (1M) man page, fbackup provides the capability to retry an active file should it be in use when being backed up.

▶ Run the full backup of the file system.

In AIX 5L Version 5.1:

▶ Unmount the file system before backing up. This is recommended for user-created logical volumes (other than /); otherwise, errors in mapping on restore may occur.

Example 8-4 shows backing up the file system /tmp and directory /var/tmp to tape device /dev/rmt/0m. Option 0 specifies a full backup, level 0. The I option creates an index file that lists all the backed up items. The -i option specifies the paths to the file systems and directories to be included in the backup and the -e option is used to exclude the file systems and directories from the backup.

Example 8-4   fbackup command

```
# fbackup -0I /bckfiles/bckindex -f /dev/rmt/0m -i /tmp -i /var/tmp -e
/var/tmp/ntp
fbackup(1004): session begins on Thu Jun 23 17:23:14 2005
fbackup(3203): volume 1 has been used 14 time(s)
fbackup(3024): writing volume 1 to the output file /dev/rmt/0m
fbackup(3055): total file blocks read for backup: 232
fbackup(3056): total blocks written to output file /dev/rmt/0m: 373
#
```

The same backup could have been performed using a graph file instead of using the include and exclude options on the command line (Example 8-5). You specify the name and location of the graph file with the -I option. The graph file would then consist of the file systems and directories for backup inclusion and exclusion. The graph file that was used is shown in Example 8-6 on page 251.

The -u option updates the /var/adm/fbackupfiles/dates database file with the following information (Example 8-5).

Example 8-5   fbackup command using graph file

```
# fbackup -0uI /bckfiles/bckindex -f /dev/rmt/0m -g /bckfiles/mngraph
fbackup(1004): session begins on Thu Jun 23 17:09:03 2005
```

```
fbackup(3203): volume 1 has been used 7 time(s)
fbackup(3024): writing volume 1 to the output file /dev/rmt/0m
fbackup(3055): total file blocks read for backup: 232
fbackup(3056): total blocks written to output file /dev/rmt/0m: 373
#
```

Back up the level, start and end time of the backup, and the graph file used. The database file is used mainly for incremental backups.

Example 8-6   Graph file

```
# more mngraph
i /tmp
i /var/tmp
e /var/tmp/ntp

#
```

The above backup can also be done using SAM. It can be done interactively or scheduled automatically from SAM. A tape device on a remote server can be used for the backups.

Other backup commands in HP-UX

There are a number of other commands that can be used in HP-UX for backups. The generic commands available in most flavors of UNIX are discussed in "Other UNIX backup commands" on page 274.

Here we briefly describe some of the other commands that are available in HP-UX. These commands are similar to the **fbackup** and **frestore** commands.

dump	Used for incremental and full file system backups. Uses the /var/adm/dumpdates and /etc/fstab for changes for incremental backup details. Only used for *HFS* file systems.
rdump	Used as for the **dump** command but this does the backup to a remote system device. Only used for *HFS* file systems.
restore	Restores incremental file system backups previously saved by the **dump** command. Only used for *HFS* file systems.
rrestore	Restores incremental file system backups previously saved by the **rdump** command. Done from a remote server tape device. Only used for *HFS* file systems.

vxdump	Used for incremental and full file system backups. Uses the /var/adm/dumpdates and /etc/fstab for changes for incremental backup details. Used for *VxFS* file systems.
rvxdump	Used as the **vxdump** above is used, but used to back up to a tape device on a remote system. Used for *VxFS* file systems.
vxrestore	Used to restore file system backups incrementally from backups performed with the **vxdump** command. Used for *VxFS* file systems.
rvxrestore	Used to restore file system backups from tapes on a remote system. These are incremental backups previously performed with the **rvxdump** command. Used for *VxFS* file systems.

In AIX 5L

The command we show in Example 8-7 will make a full backup of the file system /home. The 0 option specifies that it is a level 0 backup, so it should make a full backup of the file system. If you specify 1 instead of 0, it will make a backup of all the files that have changed since the last level 0 backup. Option u updates the backup record in the /etc/dumpdates file.

Example 8-7   backup command

```
[p650n04][/]> backup -0uf /dev/rmt0 /home
backup: The date of this level 0 backup is Thu Jun 23 18:15:01 CDT 2005.
backup: The date of the last level 0 backup is the epoch.
backup: Backing up /dev/rhd1 (/home) to /dev/rmt0.
backup: Mapping regular files. This is Pass 1.
backup: Mapping directories. This is Pass 2.
backup: There are an estimated 86 1k blocks.
backup: Backing up directories. This is Pass 3.
backup: Backing up regular files. This is Pass 4.
backup: There are 106 1k blocks on 1 volumes.
backup: There is a level 0 backup on Thu Jun 23 18:15:01 CDT 2005.
backup: The backup is complete.
```

If you do not specify a file system name, the root (/) file system is backed up.

Note: If you do not specify the -i option, the **backup** command will perform a file system backup by i-node.

Using the **smitty backfilesys** command, you can perform the file system backup. Type **smitty backfilesys** at the command prompt, and you will see a menu similar to Example 8-8. Specify the required options and press the Enter key to start the backup.

Example 8-8   smitty backfilesys

```
                        Backup a File System
Type or select values in entry fields.
Press Enter AFTER making all desired changes.

                                                    [Entry Fields]
    This option will perform a backup by inode.
* FILESYSTEM to backup                          []                      +/
* Backup DEVICE                                 [/dev/fd0]              +/
  Backup LEVEL (0 for a full backup)            [0]                      #
  RECORD backup in /etc/dumpdates?              no                       +


F1=Help          F2=Refresh        F3=Cancel        F4=List
F5=Reset         F6=Command        F7=Edit          F8=Image
F9=Shell         F10=Exit          Enter=Do
```

8.3 Restoring files and file systems

Quite often, users request that the system administrators restore files that the user has accidentally deleted. Also, we have to restore entire file systems in case of a disaster, or if we plan to reduce the file system size.

In HP-UX

In HP-UX, the **frecover** command is used to restore the data backed up with the **fbackup** command.

Let us see some of the examples using the **frecover** commands.

To display the contents of the backup tape, run the following command:

```
# frecover -Nrv -f /dev/rmt/0m
```

To selectively restore data from the backup tape, use the following command:

```
# frecover -x -i /var -i /tmp -f /dev/rmt/0m
```

The above example restores the /var and /tmp file systems.

To restore the entire backup from the tape, use the following command:

```
# frecover -rvf /dev/rmt/0m
```

To restore a file relative to the current working directory, use the following command:

```
# frecover -xFv -i /var/tmp/backfile1 -f /dev/rmt/0m
```

The above example restores the file backfile1 to the current directory.

The above recoveries can also be done using SAM, using the **Backup and Recovery** → **Interactive Backup and Recovery** menus.

A graph file can also be used to list the file systems to be recovered. This would be used instead of specifying the file systems on the command line. A tape device on a remote server can be used for the backups.

For other options and use of the `frecover` command, see the frecover (1M) manual page.

In AIX 5L

You can use `smitty`, `restore`, and `restvg` commands to restore the data.

8.3.1 Using smitty

Using smitty, we can restore the individual files, entire file system, and volume group backups.

To restore the individual files

To do this:

1. Enter the following smitty fast path command:

   ```
   # smitty restfile
   ```

2. You will see a screen similar to Example 8-9.

Example 8-9   smitty restfile

```
                        Restore a File or Directory

Type or select values in entry fields.
Press Enter AFTER making all desired changes.
                                                [Entry Fields]
* Restore DEVICE                                [/dev/fd0]              +/
* Target DIRECTORY                              [.]                     /
  FILE or DIRECTORY to restore                  []
  (Leave blank to restore entire archive.)
```

```
VERBOSE output?                                        no              +
Number of BLOCKS to read in a single input             []              #
   operation
```

```
F1=Help              F2=Refresh            F3=Cancel           F4=List
F5=Reset             F6=Command            F7=Edit             F8=Image
F9=Shell             F10=Exit              Enter=Do
```

3. If you are restoring from the tape, select /dev/rmt0 or the device applicable to your system as the restore device. Select the directory (the default is the current directory). If you wish, you can enable the verbose option (the default is no). Press Enter after making your selections to start the restoration.

To restore file systems

To do this:

1. Type the following command at the shell prompt:

   # smitty restfilesys

2. You will see the screen shown in Example 8-10.

Example 8-10   smitty restfilesys

```
                    Restore a File System

Type or select values in entry fields.
Press Enter AFTER making all desired changes.

                                              [Entry Fields]
* Restore DEVICE                              [/dev/fd0]          +/
* Target DIRECTORY                            [.]                 /
  VERBOSE output?                             yes                 +
  Number of BLOCKS to read in a single input  []                 #
     operation

F1=Help              F2=Refresh            F3=Cancel           F4=List
F5=Reset             F6=Command            F7=Edit             F8=Image
F9=Shell             F10=Exit              Enter=Do
```

3. Select the restore device "target DIRECTORY" (where you want to restore the data) and press Enter to start restoring the data.

Note: You must be at the top of the file system you are restoring; for example, if you are restoring /home, you must be in /home.

8.3.2 restore command

The **restore** command is used to restore the files and directories backed up with the **backup** command. The path names on the backup will be preserved on the restore. If the backup was created with the relative path name, the data will be restored relative to the current directory.

To display the contents of the media (tape drive /dev/rmt0), use the following command:

```
# restore -Tvf /dev/rmt0
```

To restore individual files or directories from the tape device /dev/rmt0, use the following command:

```
# restore -xvf /dev/rmt0 /home/user1/dir1
```

The above command will restore the directory contents /home/user1/dir1.

To restore the entire contents of the /dev/rmt0 tape, use the **restore -r** command. This command works with the backups taken by i-node. It will also make sure that the restore sequence is correct when you are restoring incremental backups. It creates the restoresymtable file under the root directory. It will make sure that the level of the backup you are restoring is in order. You should always restore the level 0 backup and follow the ascending order from them. Once you recover the entire file system, make sure that you remove the restoremytable file in order to be ready for future recoveries. Otherwise, you will not be able to restore the level 0 backup the next time. The following command restores the entire file system from the device /dev/rmt0:

```
# restore -rqvf /dev/rmt0
```

To perform an interactive restore, use the -i option.

8.4 Backing up JFS snapshot file systems

The following section explains how to back up JFS snapshot file systems.

8.4.1 On HP-UX

On HP-UX, you can use any backup utility, except the **dump** command, to back up the mounted snapshot file system. In the following example, the command used to mount the snapshot file system is shown. A snapshot is taken of the *bmslv* logical volume, which is contained in the *lvol9* logical volume ad mounted on the */tmp/tms* mount point.

```
mount -F vxfs -o snapof=/dev/vg00/bmslv /dev/vgabc/lvol9 /tmp/tms
```

The command used in our example below to perform the backup is the **fbackup** command. Other backup utilities (except dump) could also be used.

```
fbackup -vf /dev/rmt/0m -i /tmp/tms
```

8.4.2 On AIX 5L Version 5.3

This section describes how to make and back up a snapshot of a JFS2 file system.

Make and back up a snapshot of a JFS2

With JFS enhancements in AIX 5L Version 5.2, some new commands were introduced to support snapshot images. One of these is the **backsnap** command. This allows the creation of a snapshot and backing up this snapshot to tape without unmounting or quiescing the file system, all with one command.

The use of the **backsnap** command is shown below:

```
backsnap -m /tmp/snapshot -s size=20M -i f/dev/rmt0 /home/tms
```

A snapshot of the /home/tms file system is created. A new 20-megabyte logical volume for the snapshot is created and is mounted on /tmp/snapshot, which is then backed up by name to the tape device /dev/rmt0. After the backup completes, the snapshot remains mounted:

```
    backsnap -R -m /tmp/snapshot -s size=20M -O -f /dev/rmt0 /home/tms
```

A snapshot of the /home/tms file system is created. A new 20-megabyte logical volume for the snapshot is created and is mounted on /tmp/snapshot. The data is then backed up by inode to the tape device /dev/rmt0. The -R option deletes the snapshot after the backup completes.

You can do the various snapshot procedures using Web-based System Management, SMIT, or use the **backsnap** and **snapshot** commands. For more details on snapshots refer to the *AIX 5L 5.3 Commands Reference*, Volume 1, SC23-4888-02, AIX 5L 5.3 Commands Reference, Volume 5, SC23-4892-02, and *AIX 5L Version 5.3 System Management Guide: Operating System and Devices,* SC23-4910-01.

Make an online backup of a JFS

To make an online backup of a mounted JFS, the logical volume that the file system resides on and the logical volume that its log resides on must be mirrored.

The command below splits off a mirrored copy of the /home/tms file system to a new mount point named /splitcopy:

```
chfs -a splitcopy=/tmscopy /home/tms
```

After this, a read-only copy of the file system is available in /tmscopy. A backup of the /tmscopy can be performed to a tape device.

This section briefly described how to back up snapshots of the JFS file systems. For more information about creating JFS snapshot file systems, refer to 7.5.12, "JFS snapshots in AIX 5L" on page 214.

8.5 Backing up volume groups

In AIX 5L, you can make a backup of an entire volume group with the **savevg** command. The **savevg** command finds and backs up all files belonging to a specified volume group. To run the **savevg** command:

▶ The volume group must be varied on.
▶ The file systems must be mounted.

The **savevg** command uses the data file created by the **mkvgdata** command. This data file can be one of the following:

▶ /image.data

Contains information about the root volume group (rootvg). The **savevg** command uses this file to create a backup image that can be used by Network Installation Management (NIM) to reinstall the volume group to the current system or to a new system.

▶ /tmp/vgdata/vgname/vgname.data

Contains information about a user volume group. The VGName variable reflects the name of the volume group. The **savevg** command uses this file to create a backup image that can be used by the **restvg** command to remake the user volume group.

The following are some of the options used with the **savevg** command:

-e	Excludes files specified in the /etc/exclude.vgname file from being backed up by this command.
-f	Specifies the device or file name on which the image is to be stored. The default is the /dev/rmt0 device.
-i	Creates the data file by calling the **mkvgdata** command.
-v	Verbose mode. Lists files as they are backed up.
VGName	Volume group name that you need to back up.

Here are some examples of using the **savevg** command.

To back up a volume group, do the following:

1. Check which volume group you want to back up. List the volume groups with the following command:

```
# lsvg
rootvg
datavg
```

2. To make a backup of the rootvg (root volume group) to a tape (/dev/rmt0), run the command in Example 8-11.

Example 8-11   savevg command

```
# savevg -if/dev/rmt0 rootvg
Creating information file (/image.data) for rootvg..
Creating pseudo tape boot image..
Creating list of files to back up.
Backing up 22549 files...................
22549 of 22549 files (100%)
0512-038 savevg: Backup Completed Successfully.
```

You can make a backup of datavg in the same manner by passing the volume group parameter to datavg. As the default device for the **savevg** command is the /dev/rmt0 tape device, there is no need to specify the -f flag. So, the following command works the same way as the one shown in Example 8-11:

```
savevg -i rootvg
```

Though the **savevg** command backs up the rootvg, it is not bootable. To create a bootable image, we have to use the **mksysb** command. We discuss this command in 8.6, "Creating a bootable system image" on page 262.

You can use the smitty tool to back up the volume group. To run the backup through smitty, do the following:

1. At the command prompt, run the **smitty savevg** fast path.

2. The system will pop-up the screen shown in Example 8-12.

Example 8-12   smitty savevg

```
                    Back Up a Volume Group to Tape/File

Type or select values in entry fields.
Press Enter AFTER making all desired changes.

                                                      [Entry Fields]
        WARNING:  Execution of the savevg command will
                  result in the loss of all material
                  previously stored on the selected
```

```
      output medium.

 * Backup DEVICE or FILE                                []                    +\
 * VOLUME GROUP to back up                               []                    +
   List files as they are backed up?                     no                    +
   Generate new vg.data file?                            yes                   +
   Create MAP files?                                     no                    +
   EXCLUDE files?                                        no                    +
   EXPAND /tmp if needed?                                no                    +
   Disable software packing of backup?                   no                    +
   Number of BLOCKS to write in a single output          []  #
 (Leave blank to use a system default)

 F1=Help            F2=Refresh         F3=Cancel          F4=List
 F5=Reset           F6=Command         F7=Edit            F8=Image
 F9=Shell           F10=Exit           Enter=Do
```

Fill in the required fields "Backup DEVICE or FILE" and "VOLUME GROUP to backup" and press Enter.

Snapshot support for mirrored volume groups

An LVM enhancement in AIX 5L Version 5.2 provides snapshot support for mirrored volume groups. A fully mirrored volume group can be split into a snapshot volume group.

To split a volume group, all logical volumes in the volume group must have a mirror copy, and the mirror must exist on a disk or set of disks that contains only this set of mirrors. The original volume group will stop using the disks that are now part of the snapshot volume group. New logical volumes and mount points will be created in the snapshot VG.

Both volume groups will keep track of changes in physical partitions (PPs) within the volume group so that when the snapshot volume group is rejoined with the original volume group, consistent data is maintained across the rejoined mirror copies.

In the following example, the file system /data is a file system in the volume group datavg mirrored from hdisk2 to hdisk3. The **splitvg** command is run to split the mirror in the snapshot volume group, snapvg. Then an online backup is taken of the data:

```
splitvg -y snapvg datavg
```

1. The volume group, datavg, is split and the volume group, snapvg, is created. Also, the mount point /fs/data is created.

   ```
   backup -f /dev/rmt0 /fs/data
   ```

2. An inode-based backup of the unmounted file system /fs/data is created on tape.

```
joinvg datavg
```

3. The snapshot VG snapvg is rejoined with the original VG datavg and synchronized in the background.

Refer to the *AIX 5.3 Commands Reference* and *AIX 5L Differences Guide Version 5.2 Edition*, SG24-5765, for more about the restrictions and details of snapshot support for mirrored volume groups.

8.5.1 Restoring volume groups

The **restvg** command is used in AIX 5L to recover user volume groups. It restores the volume group and all its files and containers. The smitty option is shown below:

1. Enter the **smitty** command at the command prompt:

```
# smitty restvg
```

2. The smitty menu Example 8-13 appears on the screen.

Example 8-13   smitty restvg

```
                          Remake a Volume Group

Type or select values in entry fields.
Press Enter AFTER making all desired changes.

                                                      [Entry Fields]
* Restore DEVICE or FILE                              []                  +/
  SHRINK the filesystems?                             no                  +
  Recreate logical volumes and filesystems only?      no                  +
  PHYSICAL VOLUME names                               []                  +
      (Leave blank to use the PHYSICAL VOLUMES listed
       in the vgname.data file in the backup image)
  Use existing MAP files?                             yes                 +
  Physical partition SIZE in megabytes                []                  +#
      (Leave blank to have the SIZE determined
       based on disk size)
  Number of BLOCKS to read in a single input          []                  #
      (Leave blank to use a system default)
  Alternate vg.data file                              []                  /
      (Leave blank to use vg.data stored in
       backup image)

F1=Help            F2=Refresh         F3=Cancel         F4=List
F5=Reset           F6=Command         F7=Edit           F8=Image
```

3. Select the device Restore device, from which you are doing the restore operation.

4. Select the physical volume names, if you want to restore to specific hard disks; otherwise, leave it blank to use the volume list in the vgname.data file, which is in the backup image.

Select other options according to your requirements, and then press the Enter key to start the restoration.

Here are some command-line examples of restvg:

```
restvg -f /dev/rmt0
```

The above command restores the volume group image from the /dev/rmt0 tape device onto the original disks.

```
restvg -f /dev/rmt1 hdisk2 hdisk3
```

The above command restores the volume group image from the /dev/rmt1 tape device onto the hdisk2 and hdisk3 disks.

```
restvg -r -f /dev/rmt0
```

The above example recreates the volume group logical volume structure without restoring any files using the vgname.data file inside of the volume group backup located on the tape in /dev/rmt0.

```
restvg -l -f /dev/rmt0
```

The above displays volume group information about the volume group backed up on the tape in /dev/rmt0.

> **Note:** With the -r option, only the volume group structure is created. The volume group, logical volumes, and file systems are created from the backup, without restoring any files or data. This is useful for users who use third-party software for restoring data and just need all the AIX 5L logical volume structure in place.

8.6 Creating a bootable system image

The following sections review how to create a bootable system image.

8.6.1 In HP-UX

A utility on HP-UX allows a quick recovery of a system that has become unbootable. This could be because of a bad root disk or problems with the root volume group. The utility is part of the Ignite-UX package, which is supplied with the operating system media.

The utility includes two commands for creating bootable recovery archives that are used for system recovery. The archives contain the systems configuration information and root volume group files.

make_tape_recovery Creates a bootable tape that is self-contained and that is used to restore the system from the local system tape device. The archive can span multiple volumes.

make_net_recovery Creates and stores the archive on another system in the network. The archive can be initiated from either the system designated as the Ignite server or run from the client system. The archive created is specific for the system it was created for and contains its hostname, IP address, and networking details. The recovery from this archive is dependent on the Ignite-UX server being available.

With both of the commands you can decide to include or exclude specific files in the archive. The archive includes, by default, a list of essential files. They are considered essential because they are required to bring up a functional system. This list is contained in file /opt/igite/recovery/mnr_essentials. Below we list some of the commonly used options and a few examples of the `make_tape_recovery` command:

a This specifies the tape device to be used for the backup. The default is /dev/rmt/0mn unless the /var/opt/ignite/recovery/default file exists.

A This is based on files that are to be included in the archive. It will include all the files for the disks and volume groups necessary for the included file list.

i Runs in interactive mode, which allows the selections of files and directories to be included in the backup.

p Previews the backup creation process but does not actually create the archive on tape. Can later be resumed with the -r option.

v Runs the process in verbose mode.

x include= Specifies the files and directories to include in the backup.

x inc_entire	Specifies the disk device name or volume group name to include in the backup. Will include all the file systems for the specified volume group or disk.
x exclude=	Specifys the files and directories to exclude from the backup.
r include=	Resumes the backup to the tape device after the preview was done with the -p option.

Some examples of creating an archive from the command line follow.

The following makes a system backup that includes all of the vg00 and vg01 volume groups:

```
make_tape_recovery -x inc_entire=vg00 -x inc_entire=vg01
```

The following previews a system backup in verbose mode, which will include all the essential files as listed in /opt/ignite/recovery/mnr_essentials or the user defined file, if it exists.

```
make_tape_recovery -A -v -p
```

The following resumes the system backup, which was previewed above. This will display the volume groups and disks being included in the backup.

```
make_tape_recovery -A -v -r
```

Refer to the make_tape_recovery (1M) manual page for details of the other options and use of the command. For the use and options of the **make_net_recovery** command, refer to the make_recovery (1M) manual page and also to the Ignite-UX Administration Guide and other documentation related to Ignite-UX, which can be found at:

```
http://www.docs.hp.com/
```

8.6.2 In AIX 5L

In AIX 5L, one of the important features is that we can make a backup of the operating system image. The **mksysb** command is used for this. The **mksysb** command creates a backup of the operating system (that is, the root volume group). You can use this backup to reinstall a system to its original state if it becomes corrupted. If you create the backup on tape, the tape is bootable and includes the installation programs needed to install from the backup. The tape format includes a boot image, a bosinstall image, and an empty table of contents followed by the system backup image.

However, if the intent of the backup is to provide a customized system for use on another machine, the mksysb is considered a clone. Cloning means preserving either all or some of a system's customized information for use on a different machine. The target systems might not contain the same hardware devices or adapters, require the same kernel (uniprocessor or microprocessor), or be the same hardware platform (rs6k, rspc, or chrp) as the source system.

There are three options available for making a system backup. You can make a system backup (bootable image) with the Web-based System Manager, smit, or smitty and the `mksysb` command.

Using Web-based System Manager

To make a system backup using the Web-based System Manager, follow these steps:

1. Enter the `wsm &` command.

2. Double-click the Backup and Restore icon. You will see a menu similar to Figure 8-1.

3. Double-click the **Backup the System** option. Select the appropriate options and start the backup.

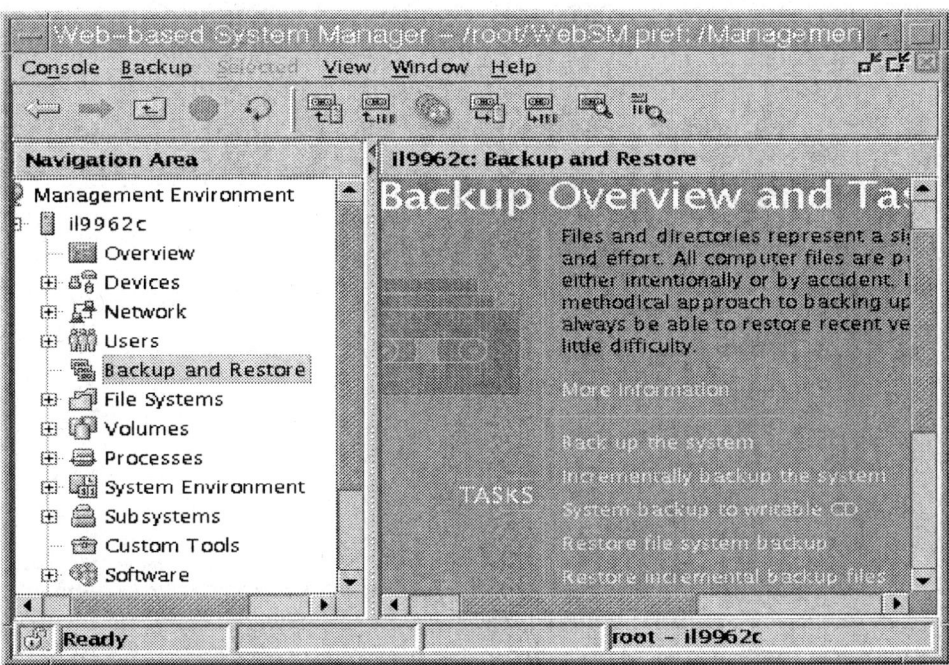

Figure 8-1 Backup menu

Using smitty

You can make a system image backup using the **smitty mksysb** fast path. As the root user, at the command prompt, type:

```
# smitty mksysb
```

It will pop up a window titled Back Up the System. This is shown in Example 8-14.

Example 8-14   Backup of system image

```
                          Back Up the System

Type or select values in entry fields.
Press Enter AFTER making all desired changes.

                                                    [Entry Fields]
      WARNING:   Execution of the mksysb command will
                 result in the loss of all material
                 previously stored on the selected
                 output medium. This command backs
                 up only rootvg volume group.

*  Backup DEVICE or FILE                  []              +\
   Create MAP files?                                no           +
   EXCLUDE files?                                   no           +
   List files as they are backed up?               no           +
   Verify readability if tape device?              no           +
   Generate new /image.data file?                  yes          +
   EXPAND /tmp if needed?                           no           +
   Disable software packing of backup?             no           +
   Backup extended attributes?                      yes          +
   Number of BLOCKS to write in a single output    []           #
(Leave blank to use a system default)

F1=Help            F2=Refresh         F3=Cancel         F4=List
F5=Reset           F6=Command         F7=Edit           F8=Image
F9=Shell           F10=Exit           Enter=Do
```

Let us discuss some of the options in the above menu:

► Creation of a MAP File

This option generates a layout mapping of the logical-to-physical partitions for each logical volume in the volume group. This mapping is used to allocate the same logical-to-physical partition mapping when the image is restored.

► EXCLUDE Files?

This option excludes the files and directories listed in the /etc/exclude.rootvg file from the system image backup.

► List files as they are backed up?

Changes the default to see each file listed as it is backed up. Otherwise, you will see a percentage-completed progress while the backup is created.

► Verify readability if tape device?

Attempts to read the backup image from the tape and report any read errors if they occur.

► Generate new /image.data file?

If you have already generated a new /image.data file and do not want a new file to be created, change the default to no.

► EXPAND /tmp if needed?

Choose yes if the /tmp file system can automatically expand (if necessary) during the backup.

If you chose a file as the backup medium, press Enter. If you chose a tape as the backup medium, insert the first blank backup tape into the drive and press Enter.

The COMMAND STATUS screen displays, showing the status messages while the system makes the backup image.

If you chose a tape as the backup medium, the system might prompt you to insert the next tape during the backup by displaying a message similar to the following:

```
Mount next Volume on /dev/rmt0 and press Enter.
```

If this message displays, remove the tape and label it, including the BOS version number. Then insert another tape and press Enter.

When the backup process finishes, the COMMAND: field changes to OK.

Press F10 to exit smitty when the backup completes.

If you chose a tape as the backup medium, remove the last tape and label it. Write-protect the backup tapes.

Record any backed-up root and user passwords. Remember that these passwords become active if you use the backup to either restore this system or install another system.

mksysb command

Apart from the above two options, you can make a backup of the system image with the **mksysb** command. The following are some examples of using the **mksysb** command:

► To generate a system backup and create an /image.data file to a tape device named /dev/rmt0, enter:

```
# mksysb -i /dev/rmt0
```

► To generate a system backup with a new /image.data file, but exclude certain files, create a /etc/exclude.rootvg file containing the file names to exclude and enter:

```
# mksysb -i -e /dev/rmt0
```

This command will back up the /home/user1/tmp directory, but not the files it contains.

► To generate a system backup file named /mksysb_images/node1 and a new /image.data file for that image, enter:

```
# mksysb -i /mksysb_images/node1
```

The -i flag calls the **mkszfile** command, which generates the /image.data file. The /image.data file contains information about volume groups, logical volumes, file systems, paging space, and physical volumes. This information is included in the backup for future use by the installation process.

8.6.3 Creating system image backups on CD and DVD

In AIX 5L Version 5.3, you can create the bootable system image on CD or DVD. There are two types of bootable system image backups.

Personal CDs

These are the system backup CDs that are bootable only on the source system. So, a personal backup CD can only boot and install the machine on which it was created.

Generic CDs

Generic backup CDs are bootable on any target system. Generic backups CDs are more suitable for an environment that has a large number of machines, and needs to install the same operating system image, but all the machines might not have the same hardware configuration. A generic backup CD created on POWER-based machine can boot any other POWER-based machine.

There are three options available to create the backup on CD. You can create the CD by using the **wsm**, **smitty**, or **mkcd** commands.

Option 1

In the Web-based System Manager GUI, use the Backup and Restore application, and select the option System backup wizard method. This will let you create the bootable or non-bootable backups on CD-R, DVD-R, or DVD-RAM.

Option 2

Using smitty, you can back up the system images to the CD. To use smitty, follow the procedure given below:

1. Type the **smitty mkcd** command at the shell prompt. It asks whether you would like to use an existing system image or create new one. Select the no option if you want to create new one, and press Enter. You will see a screen similar to Example 8-15 on page 270.

```
                        Back Up This System to CD

Type or select values in entry fields.
Press Enter AFTER making all desired changes.

                                                        [Entry Fields]
CD-R Device                                             [ ]                    +

mksysb creation options:
  Create map files?                                    no                     +
  Exclude files?                                       no                     +
Disable software packing of backup?                    no                     +
Backup extended attributes?                            yes                    +

File system to store mksysb image                      []                     /
   (If blank, the file system
    will be created for you.)

File system to store CD file structure                 []                     /
   (If blank, the file system
    will be created for you.)

File system to store final CD images                   []                     /
   (If blank, the file system
    will be created for you.)

If file systems are being created:
   Volume Group for created file systems               [rootvg]               +

Advanced Customization Options:
Do you want the CD to be bootable?                     yes                    +
Remove final images after creating CD?                 yes                    +
Create the CD now?                                     yes                    +
Install bundle file                                    []                     /
File with list of packages to copy to CD               []                     /
Location of packages to copy to CD                     []                     +/
Customization script                                   []                     /
User supplied bosinst.data file                        []                     /
Debug output?                                          no                     +
User supplied image.data file                          []                     /



F1=Help              F2=Refresh         F3=Cancel          F4=List
F5=Reset             F6=Command         F7=Edit            F8=Image
F9=Shell             F10=Exit           Enter=Do
```

Example 8-15   smitty mkcd

A few of the above options are:

1. Enter the name of the CD-R device. This can be left blank if the Create CD
   now? field is set to no.

2. Specify the File system to store mksysb image. You can specify any file
   system that is mounted on the system. Otherwise, you can leave it blank, and
   the **mkcd** command creates the fie systems and removes them once the
   backup is over. For the next two options, the same applies.

3. If you set "Create the CD now" as no, the CD will not be created, and the file systems we specified in the above fields will remain the same.

4. After setting the appropriate options, press Enter to start the backup.

For a complete description and explanations of the other options in Smitty mkcd, refer to the chapter "Creating System Backups" in *AIX 5L Version 5.3 Installation Guide and Reference*, SG23-4887. This manual also has the procedure to create a backup to DVD.

Option 3

The third option to create the system image backup on CD is to use the mkcd command.

To create a bootable system image on a CD-ROM device /dev/cd1, use the following command:

```
# mkcd -d /dev/cd1
```

To create a backup on DVD-R or DVD-RAM, use the following command:

```
# mkcd -d /dev/cd1 -L
```

> **Note:** The mkcd command creates the following file systems if they are not created already or if alternative file systems are not specified:
>
> ► /mkcd/mksysb_images
> ► /mkcd/cd_fs
> ► /mkcd/cd_images
>
> The total file system size required for CD-R is around 1.5 GB and for DVD-R is around 9 GB.

8.6.4 Restoring the system image

The following sections contain information about restoring system images.

On HP-UX

To restore the system from the tape archive created with make_tape_recovery, the following steps are performed. These would usually be done after a disk or other problem has been resolved:

1. Insert the tape in the tape device.

2. Power up or boot the system.

3. Interrupt the boot sequence to interact with the PDC within the ten-second time-out period.

4. Select the tape device to boot from.

5. Do not choose the option to interact with the ISL.

6. The restore of the system will be done automatically.

7. If necessary, restore other user files and file systems from backups done with the user data backups such as fbackup.

On AIX 5L

To restore the system image, boot the system as though you are doing the installation. You have to boot the system in install/maintenance mode. Follow the steps given below to restore the system backup:

1. Check whether the tape device is in the boot list before the hard disk. To check this, use the `# bootlist -m normal -o` command.

2. Insert the tape into the tape drive.

3. Shut down the system by entering `shutdown -F`.

4. Power on the machine. The machine will boot from the tape and prompt you to define the console and the language settings. After answering those questions, the Installation and Maintenance menu is displayed.

> **Note:** You can also boot from the Installation CD instead of the tape to restore the system image. The CD will also present the same screens.

5. In Installation and Maintenance menu, select option 3, Start Maintenance Mode for System Recovery (see Example 8-16).

Example 8-16   Installation and Maintenance menu

```
                 Welcome to Base Operating System
                   Installation and Maintenance
        1 Start Install Now with Default Settings
        2 Change/show Installation Settings and Install
     >> 3 Start Maintenance Mode for System Recovery
```

6. The Maintenance menu is displayed. Select 4, Install from a System Backup Option, as in Example 8-17.

Example 8-17   Maintenance menu

```
                        Maintenance
        1 Access A Root Volume Group
        2 Copy a System Dump to Removable media
        3 Access Advanced Maintenance Functions
     >> 4 Install from a System Backup
```

7. Once you get the Choose Tape Drive menu, select the tape device where your mksysb backup tape is inserted (Example 8-18).

Example 8-18   Restoration of system backup

```
                        Choose Tape Drive
Tape Drive                Path Name
>>> 1 tape/scsi/4mm/2GB /dev/rmt0
```

8. After selecting the tape drive, the Installation and Maintenance menu will appear. Now choose option 2, Change/Show Installation Settings and Install (Example 8-19).

Example 8-19   Restoration of system backup

```
              Welcome to Base Operating System
                 Installation and Maintenance

Type the number of your choice and press Enter. Choice is indicated by >>.
    1 Start Install Now With Default Settings
>> 2 Change/ Show Installation Settings and Install
    3 Start maintenance Mode for System Recovery
```

9. The System Backup and Installation and Settings menu now appears. From this menu, select option 1 to specify disks where you want to install the backup image (Example 8-20).

Example 8-20   Restoration of system dump

```
        System Backup Installation and Settings

Type the number of your choice and press Enter.

    1 Disk(s) where you want to install hdisk0
    2 use maps
    3 Shrink File Systems
    0 Install with the settings listed above
```

10. In Example 8-20 you can enable the two other options. Enable the Use maps option if you took the backup using the map file option. The default is no. If you enable Shrink File Systems the backup will be restored using the minimum space. The default is no. If Yes, all the file systems in rootvg are shrunk.

11. Finally, select option 0 (Install with the settings listed above). The mksysb image will be restored.

8.6.5 Cloning a system backup

Use this procedure to install a `mksysb` backup on a target system that it was not created on. Be sure to boot from the product media appropriate for your system and at the same maintenance level of BOS as the installed source system that the `mksysb` backup was made on. For example, you can use the BOS Version 5.3 product media with a `mksysb` backup from a BOS Version 5.3 system. This procedure is to be used when installing a backup tape to a different system. After booting from the product media, complete the following steps when the Welcome to the Base Operating System Installation and Maintenance screen is displayed:

1. Select the Start Maintenance Mode for System Recovery option.

2. Select the Install from a System Backup option.

3. Select the drive containing the backup tape and insert the media for that device. The system reads the media and begins the installation.

4. You will be prompted again for the BOS install language, and the Welcome screen is displayed. Continue with the Prompted Installation process, as cloning is not supported for nonprompted installations. The mksysb files are system specific.

After the `mksysb` backup installation completes, the installation program automatically installs additional devices and the kernel (uniprocessor or microprocessor) on your system using the original product media you booted from. Information is saved in BOS installation log files. To view BOS installation log files, enter the `cd /var/adm/ras` command and view the devinst.log file in this directory.

For further information about installing from system backups, refer the *AIX 5L Version 5.3 Installation Guide and Reference*, SC23-4887.

8.7 Other UNIX backup commands

Each UNIX platform provides its native backup tools or commands, but there are some generic backup commands, which can be used in almost every UNIX platform. With these commands, it is easy to transfer the data across the different UNIX platforms. The following are some such commands, which are most commonly used by system administrators:

- ► `tar`
- ► `cpio`
- ► `dd`

8.7.1 tar command

tar stands for *tape archive*. This is one of the most commonly used commands by system administrators.

The following are the commonly used options of the tar command:

-c	Creates the backup.
-x	Extracts files from tar backup.
-t	Reads the contents of the tar backup.
-v	Verbose option. Displays all the files and directories while they are getting restored or backed up.
-f	Device or file name of the tar archive to which you are writing into or reading/restoring from.

Here are some of the examples using the tar command.

The following command copies the contents of the /home/tms directory into the tape device /dev/rmt0:

```
# tar -cvf /dev/rmt0 /home/tms
```

The following command copies the contents of the /home/tms directory into the archive file hometms.tar:

```
# tar -cvf hometms.tar /home/tms
```

The following command displays the contents of the tar archive existing in /dev/rmt0:

```
# tar -tvf /dev/rmt0
```

The following command extracts the contents of the entire tar archive from /dev/rmt0:

```
# tar -xvf /dev/rmt0
```

To extract only one directory called /home/tms/applications from the archive file hometms.tar, enter the following command:

```
# tar -xvf hometms.tar /home/tms/applications
```

8.7.2 cpio command

cpio stands for *copy input/output*. This is another generic UNIX tool.

These are the generally used options of cpio:

-o	Creates cpio image.

-i	Reads/restores from cpio image.
-t	Displays the contents of the cpio image.
-v	Verbose option. Displays the files during backup and restore.
-d	Creates the necessary directories while restoring the image.

To copy all the contents of the current directory into the tape device, enter the following command:

```
# find . -print | cpio -ov > /dev/rmt0
```

To restore from the cpio image, use the following command:

```
# cpio -idv </dev/rmt0
```

To list contents of the cpio image, run:

```
# cpio -itv < /dev/rmt0
```

8.7.3 dd command

The **dd** command reads the input file parameter or standard input, converts it, and writes it to output file parameter or standard output.

The following options are some of the commonly used **dd** options:

if	Specifies the input file.
of	Specifies the output file.
conv	Specifies the conversion to be done. You can convert one form of the data to another with this option, for example, lower case to upper case, ascii to ebcdic, and so on.

The following example copies the /home/user1/data file to the floppy disk:

```
# dd if=/home/user1/data of=/dev/rfd0
```

The following example converts the text.asci file from ASCII characters to EBCDIC and stores them in the text.ebc file:

```
# dd if=text.asci of=text.ebc conv=ebcdic
```

The **dd** command is useful when you need to copy specific blocks of data. For example, if a file system's super block in the first block is corrupt, and the copy of the superblock is kept in the 256th block, the **dd** command can copy the 256th block to the first block to repair the file system. You can use the following command:

```
dd count=1 bs=4k skip=256 seek=1 if=/dev/hd5 of=/dev/hd5
```

Other backup tools

If you have a large number of machines, making a backup of each machine individually is not an easy task for system administrators. To address this problem, there are many products available from different vendors for enterprise wide backup. Here is a list of some products:

► Tivoli Storage Manager from IBM

    http://www.tivoli.com/products/index/storage-mgr/

► HP OpenView Storage Data Protector

    http://www.openview.hp.com/products/oms/index.asp

► VERITAS Net Backup

    http://www.veritas.com

8.8 Quick reference

Table 8-1 shows a comparison between HP-UX and AIX 5L for backup and restore commands.

Table 8-1   Quick reference for backup and restore

Tasks	AIX 5L command	HP-UX commands
GUI interfaces to perform the backup and restoration	**smitty fs** fast path, smitty, and the Web-based System Manager	SAM Backup and recovery
Backing up files/file systems	**backup**	**fbackup**
Restoring files/file systems	**restore**	**frecover**
Backing up volume groups	**savevg**	make_tape_recovery make_net_recovery
Restoring volume groups	**restvg**	Ignite-UX recovery

Tasks	AIX 5L command	HP-UX commands
Backup of system image	`mksysb`	make_tape_recovery make_net_recovery
Create a CD with mksysb and savevg images	`mkcd`	N/A

Network management

This chapter contains the following:

► Overview
► IPV6 introduction
► Configuring network interfaces
► Configuring TCP/IP
► TCP/IP daemons
► Network File System (NFS)
► Configuration of DNS
► Quick reference

9.1 Overview

In this chapter we discuss the TCP/IP configuration in HP-UX 11i and AIX 5L. We will not discus in detail TCP/IP protocols, IP addressing, and so on. We provide a brief introduction to IPv6, but aside from this, the rest of this chapter will generally be IPv4/IPv6 neutral.

We discuss the following topics:

► Brief introduction to IPv6
► Configuration of network interface
► Different TCP/IP daemons
► Basic configuration of DNS
► Basic configuration NFS

9.1.1 ITCP/IP V6

IP next generation (IPng) is a new version of the Internet Protocol designed as a successor to IP Version 4. IPng is assigned IP version number 6 and is formally called IPv6. The next version of TCP/IP is also called IPng (Next Generation) and will be fully supported on AIX 5L. For more information, see RFC 1883 and RFC 1885 at:

    http://www.ietf.org/rfc.html

Both AIX 5L Version 5.3 and HP-UX 11i have support for IPv6. In the case of AIX 5L, that support is built into the operating system, just waiting to be used. In the case of HP-UX 11i Version 1 (for example, PA-RISC installations) you need to download and install an additional product called TOUR (Transport Optional Upgrade Release) to enable IPv6 (and a couple of other) enhancements. For those IPF (Itanium) folks out there running HP-UX 11i Version 2, IPv6 comes as part of the base operating system.

IPV6 introduction

IPng was designed to take an evolutionary step beyond IPv4. It was not a design goal to take a radical step away from IPv4. Functions that work in IPv4 were kept in IPng. Functions that did not work were removed. The changes from IPv4 to IPng fall primarily into the following categories:

► Header Format Simplification

   Some IPv4 header fields have been dropped or made optional to reduce the common-case processing cost of packet handling and to keep the bandwidth cost of the IPng header as low as possible despite the increased size of the addresses. Even though the IPng addresses are four times longer than the IPv4 addresses, the IPng header is only twice the size of the IPv4 header.

- ► Improved Support for Options

  Changes in the way IP header options are encoded allows for more efficient forwarding, less stringent limits on the length of options, and greater flexibility for introducing new options in the future.

- ► Authentication and Privacy Capabilities

  IPng includes the definition of extensions that provide support for authentication, data integrity, and confidentiality. This is included as a basic element of IPng and will be included in all implementations.

IPng solves the Internet scaling problem, provides a flexible transition mechanism for the current Internet, and was designed to meet the needs of new markets, such as nomadic personal computing devices, networked entertainment, and device control. It does this in an evolutionary way that reduces the risk of architectural problems.

IPng supports large hierarchical addresses that will allow the Internet to continue to grow and provide new routing capabilities not built into IPv4. It has anycast addresses that can be used for policy route selection and scoped multicast addresses that provide improved scalability over IPv4 multicast. It also has local use address mechanisms that provide capability for plug and play installation.

Internet Protocol Version 6 (IPv6) was first introduced in AIX Version 4.3.0, with support of the host function only. This means that no gateway support was included, so IPv6 packets could not be forwarded from one interface to another on the same RS/6000. In AIX Version 4.3.2, IPV6 routing is supported.

IPV6 128-bit addressing

Here we provide a brief introduction to the IPV6 addressing mechanism.

As shown in the following example, an IPv6 address is represented by hexadecimal digits separated by colons, where IPv4 addresses are represented by decimal digits separated by dots or full-stops. IPv6 is, therefore, also known as colon-hex addressing, compared to IPv4's dotted-decimal notation.

IPv6 addresses are 128-bit identifiers for interfaces and sets of interfaces.

Note that IPv6 refers to interfaces and not to hosts, as with IPv4.

There are three conventional forms for representing IPv6 addresses as text strings:

▶ The preferred form is x:x:x:x:x:x:x:x:, where the x's are the hexadecimal values of the eight 16-bit pieces of the address, each separated by a colon. Examples are:

```
FEDC:BA98:7654:3210:FEDC:BA98:7654:3210
1080:0:0:0:8:800:200C:417A
```

Note that it is not necessary to write the leading zeros in an individual field, but there must be at least one numeral in every field (except for the case described next).

▶ Due to the method used to allocate certain styles of IPv6 addresses, it will be common for addresses to contain long strings of zero bits. To make writing addresses containing zero bits easier, a special syntax is available to compress the zeros. The use of :: (two colons) indicates multiple groups of 16-bits of zeros. Note that the :: can only appear once in an address.

The :: can also be used to compress the leading and/or trailing zeros in an address. For example, the following addresses:

```
1080:0:0:0:8:800:200C:417A a unicast address
FF01:0:0:0:0:0:0:43 a multicast address
0:0:0:0:0:0:0:1 the loopback address
0:0:0:0:0:0:0:0 the unspecified addresses
```

may be represented as:

```
1080::8:800:200C:417A a unicast address
FF01::43 a multicast address
::1 the loopback address
:: the unspecified addresses
```

▶ An alternative form that is sometimes more convenient when dealing with a mixed environment of IPv4 and IPv6 nodes is x:x:x:x:x:x:d.d.d.d, where x is the hexadecimal values of the six high-order 16-bit pieces of the address, and d is the decimal values of the four low-order 8-bit pieces of the address (standard IPv4 representation). Examples:

```
0:0:0:0:0:0:13.1.68.3
0:0:0:0:0:FFFF:129.144.52.38
```

or in compressed form:

```
::13.1.68.3.380
::FFFF:129.144.52.38
```

FFFF is used to represent addresses of IPv4-only nodes (those that do not support IPv6).

Types of IPV6 address

In IPv6, there are three types of addresses, as discussed below.

Unicast

This is an identifier for a single interface. A packet sent to a unicast address is delivered to the interface identified by that address. A unicast address has a particular scope, as shown in the following lists:

► link-local

- Valid only on the local link (that is, only one hop away)
- Prefix is fe80::/16

► site-local

- Valid only at the local site (for example, inside IBM Austin)
- Prefix is fec0::/16

► global

- Valid anywhere on the Internet
- Prefix may be allocated from unassigned unicast space

There are also two special unicast addresses:

► ::/128 (unspecified address)

► ::1/128 (loopback address: Note that, in IPv6, this is only one address, not an entire network.)

Multicast

This is an identifier for a set of interfaces (typically belonging to different nodes). A packet sent to a multicast address is delivered to all interfaces identified by that address. A multicast address is identified by the prefix ff::/8. As with unicast addresses, multicast addresses have a similar scope. This is shown in the following lists:

► Node-local

- Valid only on the source node (for example, multiple processes listening on a port)
- Prefix is ff01::/16 or ff11::/16

► Link-local

- Valid only on hosts sharing a link with the source node (for example, Neighbor Discovery Protocol [NDP] data)
- Prefix is ff02::/16 or ff12::/16

► Site-local

- Valid only on hosts sharing a site with the source node (for example, multicasts within IBM Austin)

- Prefix is ff05::/16 or ff15::/16

► Organization-local

- Valid only on hosts sharing organization with the source node (for example, multicasts to all of IBM)

- Prefix is ff08::/16 or ff18::/16

The 0 or 1 part in these prefixes indicates whether the address is permanently assigned (1) or temporarily assigned (0).

Anycast

This is an identifier for a set of interfaces (typically belonging to different nodes). An anycast address is an address that has a single sender, multiple listeners, and only one responder (normally, the nearest one, according to the routing protocols' measure of distance). An example may be several Web servers listening on an anycast address. When a request is sent to the anycast address, only one responds.

Anycast addresses are indistinguishable from unicast addresses. A unicast address becomes an anycast address when more than one interface is configured with that address.

Additional protocols and functions related to IPV6

There are some additional features that are strictly related to IPng and that are available with AIX 5L; we now introduce only the most important of these features:

► Internet Control Message Protocol (ICMPv6)

While IP V4 uses ICMP V4, ICMPv6 is used by IPv6 nodes to report errors encountered in processing packets and to perform other Internet-layer functions, such as diagnostics (ICMPv6 ping) and multicast membership reporting.

► Neighbor Discovery

The Neighbor Discovery (ND) protocol for IPv6 is used by nodes (hosts and routers) to determine the link-layer addresses for neighbors known to reside on attached links and maintain per-destination routing tables for active connections. Hosts also use Neighbor Discovery to find neighboring routers that forward packets on their behalf and detect changed link-layer addresses. Neighbor Discovery protocol (NDP) uses the ICMPv6 protocol with a unique message type to achieve the above function. In general terms, the IPv6

Neighbor Discovery protocol corresponds to a combination of the IPv4 protocols Address Resolution Protocol (ARP), ICMP Router Discovery (RDISC), and ICMP Redirect (ICMPv4), but with many improvements over these IPv4 protocols.

► Stateless Address Auto configuration

IPv6 defines both a stateful and stateless address auto configuration mechanism. Stateless auto configuration requires no manual configuration of hosts, minimal (if any) configuration of routers, and no additional servers. The stateless mechanism allows a host to generate its own addresses using a combination of locally available information and information advertised by routers. Routers advertise prefixes that identify the subnet(s) associated with a link, while hosts generate an interface-token that uniquely identifies an interface on a subnet. An address is formed by combining the two. In the absence of routers, a host can only generate link-local addresses. However, link-local addresses are sufficient to allow communication among nodes attached to the same link.

► Tunneling over IP

The key to a successful IPv6 transition is compatibility with the existing installed base of IPv4 hosts and routers. Maintaining compatibility with IPv4 while deploying IPv6 streamlines the task of transitioning the Internet to IPv6. In most deployment scenarios, the IPv6 routing infrastructure will be built up over time. While the IPv6 infrastructure is being deployed, the existing IPv4 routing infrastructure can remain functional and can be used to carry IPv6 traffic. Tunneling provides a way to use an existing IPv4 routing infrastructure to carry IPv6 traffic.

9.1.2 Quality of Service support

From AIX Version 4.3.3 IBM introduced *Quality of Service* (QoS) support and has continually been providing enhancements for it. The demand for QoS arises from such applications as digital audio/video applications or real-time applications.

At this point HP-UX does not have any built-in support for QoS.

AIX 5L implementation of QoS

AIX 5L QoS implementation is based on the Internet Engineering Task Force (IETF) standards, Integrated Services (IntServ), and Differentiated Services (DiffServ). IntServ utilizes the Resource ReSerVation Protocol (RSVP) available to applications via the RSVP API (RAPI). DiffServ support includes IP packet marking for IP packets selected via filtering. The AIX 5L QoS also offers bandwidth management functions, such as Traffic Shaping and Policing. The AIX 5L QoS scope covers both QoS and policy-based networking.

This enhancement to AIX 5L provides system administrators with the benefits of both QoS support and policy-based networking in meeting the challenges of QoS offerings across complex networks.

QoS enhancements in AIX 5L

AIX 5L further enhances the QoS implementation to support overlapping policies in the QoS manager. And for the manageability of a QoS configuration, AIX 5L also offers four new commands. These are described in the following section.

QoS manager command-line support in AIX 5L

Beginning with AIX 5L, four new command line programs will be available to add, modify, delete, and list Quality of Service policies. These AIX 5L commands operate on the /etc/policyd.conf policy agent configuration file. Once you perform one of these commands, the change takes effect immediately, and the local configuration file of the policy agent gets updated to permanently keep the change.

Tho QoS command-line interface consists of the commands provided in the following list with their given syntax and usage:

► The `qosadd` command adds the specified Service Category or Policy Rule entry in the policyd.conf file and installs the changes in the QoS manager.

► The `qosmod` command modifies the specified Service Category or Policy Rule entry in the policyd.conf file and installs the changes in the QoS manager.

► The `qoslist` command lists the specified Service Category or Policy Rule.

► The `qosremove` command removes the specified Service Category or Policy Rule entry in the policyd.conf file and the associated policy or service in the QoS Manager.

9.2 Configuring network interfaces

The following sections contain information about configuring network interfaces.

9.2.1 Interface naming conventions

The following section describes the interface naming convention in HP-UX.

Naming convention in HP-UX

When you install HP-UX, it automatically detects each adapter card and installs the corresponding interface software. HP-UX creates appropriate network interfaces called *lanX*, which is independent of the network type (for example, token-ring and Ethernet will both be called lanX). See Example 9-1.

Example 9-1   ioscan -funC lan

```
Class    I  H/W Path  Driver      S/W State H/W Type  Description
=================================================================
lan      1  0/0/0     lan2        CLAIMED   INTERFACE Built-in LAN
                      /dev/diag/lan1  /dev/ether1    /dev/lan1
lan      8  0/10/0/0  lan8        CLAIMED   INTERFACE HP PCI Token Ring
                      /dev/lan8
```

Naming convention in AIX 5L

When you install AIX 5L, it automatically detects each adapter card and installs the corresponding interface software. AIX 5L uses the naming convention shown in Table 9-1 for network devices and interfaces.

Table 9-1   Interface naming conventions

Device type	Device name	Interface name
Asynchronous Transfer Mode (ATM)	atm#	at#
Ethernet (IEEE 802.3)	ent#	et#
Ethernet (Standard, Version 2)	ent#	en#
Fiber Distributed Data Interface (FDDI)	fddi#	fi#
Loopback	N/A	lo#
Token-Ring	tok#	tr#

The # sign represents the number of the device or interface you intend to use.

9.2.2 Network interface identification

Before you can configure an interface it may be nice to know its name.

Network interface identification in HP-UX

In HP-UX, you can use SAM. Otherwise, there are at least two ways of finding out what network interfaces you have installed:

`ioscan -funC lan`   Displays all the LAN interfaces and devices the kernel knows about on your system

| lanscan | | Displays network interfaces, states, and MAC addresses, as shown in Example 9-2 |

Example 9-2 HP-UX lanscan

```
# lanscan
Hardware Station       Crd Hdw   Net-Interface  NM   MAC     HP-DLPI   DLPI
Path     Address       In# State NamePPA         ID   Type    Support   Mjr#
0/0/0/0  0x00306E27ECC2   0  UP    lan0 snap0     1   ETHER      Yes     119
0/12/0/0/4/0 0x00306E254798 2 UP   lan2 snap2     2   ETHER      Yes     119
0/12/0/0/5/0 0x00306E254799 3 UP   lan3 snap3     3   ETHER      Yes     119
0/12/0/0/6/0 0x00306E25479A 4 UP   lan4 snap4     4   ETHER      Yes     119
0/12/0/0/7/0 0x00306E25479B 5 UP   lan5 snap5     5   ETHER      Yes     119
0/10/0/0 0x00306E278EBE 1  UP     lan1 snap1     6   ETHER    Yes      119
```

To display all the network interfaces that have an IP address configured (HP-UX does not have an **ifconfig -a** option), use **netstat -ni**. You can then use **ifconfig <lanX>** for more detailed information about a particular interface, as shown in Example 9-3.

Example 9-3 HP-UX ifconfig lan2

```
# ifconfig lan2
lan2: flags=843<UP,BROADCAST,RUNNING,MULTICAST>
        inet 192.168.76.12 netmask fffff00 broadcast 192.168.76.255
```

Network interface identification in AIX 5L

There are at least two ways to identify network interfaces on your AIX 5L server. The first command that you can run is:

```
# lsdev -Cc if
```

This will produce a simple list of all interfaces on the system, whether they are being actively used by the system or not. Refer to Example 9-4.

Example 9-4 AIX 5L lsdev -Cc if

```
# lsdev -Cc if
en0 Defined    17-08 Standard Ethernet Network Interface
en1 Available  21-08 Standard Ethernet Network Interface
en2 Defined    3A-08 Standard Ethernet Network Interface
et0 Defined    17-08 IEEE 802.3 Ethernet Network Interface
et1 Defined    21-08 IEEE 802.3 Ethernet Network Interface
et2 Defined    3A-08 IEEE 802.3 Ethernet Network Interface
lo0 Available        Loopback Network Interface
tr0 Available  1A-08 Token Ring Network Interface
```

The second command that you can run is:

```
# ifconfig -a
```

This will produce a list of all network interfaces on the system that have IP addresses already assigned and are actively being used by the system. Refer to Example 9-5.

Example 9-5   AIX 5L ifconfig -a

```
# ifconfig -a
en1:
flags=4e080863<UP,BROADCAST,NOTRAILERS,RUNNING,SIMPLEX,MULTICAST,GROUPRT,64BIT,
PSEG>
        inet 192.168.1.3 netmask 0xffffff00 broadcast 192.168.1.255
tr0: flags=e0a0043<UP,BROADCAST,RUNNING,ALLCAST,MULTICAST,GROUPRT,64BIT>
        inet 9.3.240.52 netmask 0xffffff00 broadcast 9.3.240.255
lo0:
flags=e08084b<UP,BROADCAST,LOOPBACK,RUNNING,SIMPLEX,MULTICAST,GROUPRT,64BIT>
        inet 127.0.0.1 netmask 0xff000000 broadcast 127.255.255.255
        inet6 ::1/0
```

To get information about one specific network interface, including state, IP address, and netmask, run the command:

```
# ifconfig Interface
```

To get information about tr0, for example, run the command:

```
# ifconfig tr0
tr0: flags=e0a0043<UP,BROADCAST,RUNNING,ALLCAST,MULTICAST,GROUPRT,64BIT>
        inet 9.3.240.52 netmask 0xffffff00 broadcast 9.3.240.255
```

9.2.3 Network interface configuration

In this section we discuss the network interface configuration.

Configuration of network interfaces for HP-UX

During the installation process of HP-UX, you can optionally configure the network interfaces, either during the selection of the installation parameters or on first boot.

As usual, you can either use SAM to configure the interfaces or the command line (and configuration files).

Configuration with SAM

To configure a network interface via SAM, select **Networking and Communications** → **Network Interface Cards**. This gives you a single point of configuration for the IP address and supported speed settings (for example, 100 Half/Full, etc.) for all the defined network adapters in your system.

Configuration without SAM

To configure an interface without SAM, there are two steps:

1. Configure the hardware (adapter speed and adapter settings).

   To configure the adapter speed (and other card options) use the `lanadmin` command (but this will not be maintained across reboots).

   To configure the speed (and other card options) to be maintained across reboots, you must edit the appropriate configuration file that lives in /etc/rc.config.d. The name and options this file has depend on the type of hardware you have installed. For example, the 100-M interfaces above are a 4-port card using the *btlan* driver. This means we would need to edit the /etc/rc.config.d/hpbtlanconf file and fill in the appropriate fields.

2. Configure the IP address of the adapter.

   As like most (if not all) *nix's, HP-UX has the `ifconfig` command for direct configuration of an IP interface. Any configuration performed with `ifconfig` will not be maintained across system reboots.

   To have the IP address configured for each reboot, HP-UX uses a file called /etc/rc.config.d/netconf, which contains a line for each interface for which you want an IP address directly assigned. For example:

```
INTERFACE_NAME[0]=lan0
IP_ADDRESS[0]=9.12.18.30
SUBNET_MASK[0]=255.255.255.0
BROADCAST_ADDRESS[0]=9.12.18.255
INTERFACE_STATE[0]=up
DHCP_ENABLE[0]=0
```

To quickly display all configured IP addresses in HP-UX, use `netstat -ni`.

Configuration of network interfaces for AIX 5L

In AIX 5L, you can configure the network interface using the Web-based System Manager, smitty, or the `ifconfig` command.

There are two components to configuring an interface on AIX 5L. Similar to HP-UX, you have the physical *card* options (like speed and duplicity), as well as the logical interface options (like IP address).

Configuration of the device settings

The underlying device must be configured while it is not in use (for example, you cannot change the speed or duplicity of the interface while it is in the interface list [shows up in netstat -ni]).

As usual, you can perform this task via WebSM, **smitty chgenet**, or a command line.

For an Ethernet card, when you are changing adapter settings, you are actually modifying the ODM entries for the logical device of *entX* (for example, ent0). The IP address information lives on the logical device of *en0*.

To list adapter settings use **lsattr -El <adapter>**, as shown in Example 9-6.

Example 9-6   AIX 5L lsattr -El ent0

```
[p650n04][/]> lsattr -HEl ent0
attribute        value             description                        user_settable

alt_addr         0x000000000000    Alternate Ethernet Address           True
busintr          101               Bus interrupt level                  False
busmem           0xe4030000        Bus memory address                   False
chksum_offload   yes             Enable hardware transmit and receive checksum True
intr_priority    3                 Interrupt priority                   False
ipsec_offload    no                IPsec Offload                        True
large_send       yes               Enable TCP Large Send Offload        True
media_speed      100_Full_Duplex Media Speed                            True
poll_link        no                Enable Link Polling                  True
poll_link_timer 500                Time interval for Link Polling       True
rom_mem          0xe4000000        ROM memory address                   False
rx_hog           1000              RX Descriptors per RX Interrupt      True
rxbuf_pool_sz    1024              Receive Buffer Pool Size             True
rxdesc_que_sz    512               RX Descriptor Queue Size             True
slih_hog         10                Interrupt Events per Interrupt       True
tx_preload       1520              TX Preload Value                     True
tx_que_sz        8192              Software TX Queue Size               True
txdesc_que_sz    512               TX Descriptor Queue Size             True
use_alt_addr     no                Enable Alternate Ethernet Address    True
```

To modify use:

```
chdev -l ent0 -a <attribute>=<value>
```

Example 9-7   AIX 5L modify a network interface

```
# chdev -l ent0 -a media_speed=100_Half_Duplex
ent0 changed
```

To change the speed of a network adapter in AIX 5L, you must first *detach* the interface.

Configuring using smitty

The smitty fast path command used to configure TCP/IP is `smitty tcpip`. You can configure a network interface using the `smitty inet` fast path. For these examples, we use an Ethernet interface, en0:

1. Check whether the en0 interface exists by selecting List All Network Interfaces by entering the following command:

   ```
   # smitty inet
   ```

2. If en0 does not exist, select the Add a Network Interface option, and then select Add a Standard Ethernet Network Interface. You should see a panel similar to Example 9-8.

Example 9-8   Adding a network interface

```
                        Add a Network Interface

Move cursor to desired item and press Enter.

   Add a Standard Ethernet Network Interface
   Add an IEEE 802.3 Network Interface
   Add a Token-Ring Network Interface
   Add a Serial Line INTERNET Network Interface
   Add a Serial Optical Network Interface
   Add a 370 Channel Attach Network Interface
   Add a FDDI Network Interface
   Add a Virtual IP Address Interface

F1=Help            F2=Refresh         F3=Cancel         F8=Image
F9=Shell           F10=Exit           Enter=Do
```

3. Press Enter to select en0 and fill in the Internet address and network mask information. On completion of adding the standard Ethernet network interface, you should see the message en0 Available.

4. If en0 already exists, select Change/Show Characteristics of a Network Interface. The smitty fast path is `smitty chinet`. A sample screen is shown in Example 9-9.

Example 9-9   Changing network interface configuration

```
                 Change / Show a Standard Ethernet Interface

Type or select values in entry fields.
Press Enter AFTER making all desired changes.

                                                    [Entry Fields]
   Network Interface Name                           en0
   INTERNET ADDRESS (dotted decimal)                [9.3.240.52]
```

```
Network MASK (hexadecimal or dotted decimal)        [255.255.255.0]
Current STATE                                       up                    +
Use Address Resolution Protocol (ARP)?              yes                   +
BROADCAST ADDRESS (dotted decimal)                  []

F1=Help            F2=Refresh          F3=Cancel          F4=List
F5=Reset           F6=Command          F7=Edit            F8=Image
F9=Shell           F10=Exit            Enter=Do
```

5. On completion of changing the standard Ethernet interface, you should see a
   message that the en0 interface has been changed.

The ifconfig command

In AIX 5L, the **ifconfig** command allows you to configure and modify properties
of network interfaces directly without the use of smitty. Often administrators find
this easier than using the smitty panels for network administration—though
changes done via the **ifconfig** command do not persist over reboots.

The syntax of the **ifconfig** command for configuring and modifying network
interfaces is given below:

```
ifconfig Interface [AddressFamily [Address [DestinationAddress ]] [Parameters
..] ]
```

There are three address families that can be used with the **ifconfig** command:

inet   The default dotted decimal notation for a system that is
                      part of the DARPA-Internet. This is the address family that
                      ifconfig uses by default.

inet6   The default dotted decimal notation for a system that is
                      part of the DARPA-Internet running IPv6.

ns   The default dotted hexadecimal notation for a system that
                      is part of a Xerox Network Systems family.

The common command parameters and their functions for the **ifconfig**
command are listed in the Table 9-2.

Table 9-2   ifconfig functions

Parameter	Function
alias	Establishes an additional network address for the interface.
delete	Removes the specified network address from the interface.
detach	Removes an interface from the network interface list.

Parameter	Function
down	Makes an interface inactive (down).
mtu *value*	Sets the maximum IP packet size to value bytes (maximum transmission unit), ranging from 60 to 65535.
netmask *mask*	Specifies how much of the address to reserve for subdividing networks into subnetworks.
up	Marks an interface as active (up).

Configuration of an interface via the command line

To configure an interface from the command line you would use **the chdev** command as shown in Example 9-10.

Example 9-10   AIX 5L configuring an IP address

```
# chdev -l 'en0' -a netaddr='292.168.100.54' -a state='up'
# ifconfig en0
en0:
flags=5e080863,c0<UP,BROADCAST,NOTRAILERS,RUNNING,SIMPLEX,MULTICAST,GROUPRT,64B
IT,CHECKSUM_OFFLOAD,PSEG,CHAIN>
        inet 292.168.100.54 netmask 0xffffff00 broadcast 292.168.100.255
```

9.2.4 Activation and deactivation of interfaces

Activation and deactivation of an interface from the command line can be performed in the same way by both HP-UX and AIX 5L.

Activation of an interface

Before messages can be transmitted through a network interface, the interface must be placed in the up or active state. To activate an interface, run the command:

```
# ifconfig Interface [address ][netmask Netmask] up
```

To activate a network interface using ifconfig, such as tr0, run the command:

```
# ifconfig tr0 up
```

To activate a network interface, such as the loopback interface (lo0), and assign it an IP address, run the command:

```
# ifconfig lo0 127.0.0.1 up
```

To activate a network interface, such as a token ring interface (tr0), and assign it an IP address and netmask, run the command:

```
# ifconfig tr0 10.1.2.3 netmask 255.255.255.0 up
```

Deactivating a network interface

To stop messages from being transmitted through an interface, the interface must be placed in the down or inactive state. To deactivate an interface using **ifconfig**, run the command:

```
# ifconfig Interface down
```

For example, to deactivate the network interface tr0, run the command:

```
# ifconfig tr0 down
```

This command does not remove any IP addresses assigned to the interface from the system, nor does it remove the interface from the network interface list.

Making the interface state persist across reboots in AIX 5L

Neither of the commands above will be maintained across a system reboot in AIX 5L. For this to occur, you can use the **chdev** command, which will modify the existing system as well as maintain the state across reboots.

Example 9-11   AIX 5L configuring and interface down, persistently

```
# chdev -l en0 -a state=down
en0 changed
OR
# chdev -l en0 -a state=up
en0 changed
```

9.2.5 Deletion of an IP address from an interface

The following section describes how to delete an IP address from an interface in HP-UX.

Deletion of an IP address from an interface for HP-UX

HP-UX does not have a **ifconfig delete** command. It relies on both **ifconfig down** and **ifconfig unplumb** to provide a similar result.

To delete an IP address and have that deletion persist across reboots, you need to use SAM, or you can manually modify /etc/rc.config.d/netconf to remove the references to the interface in question.

Deletion of an IP address from an interface for AIX 5L

To delete the address of 192.168.22.44 from en0 on an AIX 5L machine:

```
# ifconfig en0 delete 192.168.22.44
```

In AIX 5L if you do not specify the IP address, **ifconfig** will delete the IP address that was added to the interface first and any alias that may be there will become the base address.

This command does not place the interface in the down state, nor does it remove the interface from the network interface list.

Once again, the use of the **ifconfig en0 delete** command is only good for the currently running system. To have the IP address deletion persist through machine reboots, you need to have the entries in the ODM modified.

You can do this via WebSM, **smitty rminet**, or **rmdev -l <name> -d**.

Example 9-12   AIX 5L smitty rminet

```
# smitty rminet
+-----------------------------------------------------------------------------+
|                         Available Network Interfaces                        |
| Move cursor to desired item and press Enter.                                |
|                                                                             |
|     en0    1c-08    Standard Ethernet Network Interface                     |
|     en1    1j-08    Standard Ethernet Network Interface                     |
|     et0    1c-08    IEEE 802.3 Ethernet Network Interface                   |
|     et1    1j-08    IEEE 802.3 Ethernet Network Interface                   |
|                                                                             |
|                                                                             |
| F1=Help                  F2=Refresh                  F3=Cancel              |
| Esc+8=Image              Esc+0=Exit                  Enter=Do               |
| /=Find                   n=Find Next                                        |
+-----------------------------------------------------------------------------+
en0 deleted
```

9.2.6 Detaching/unplumbing a network interface

To remove an interface from the network interface list, the interface must be detached from the system. Performing this step temporarily (it will not persist across reboots) removes the network interface from the interface list, that is, the interface will no longer carry any traffic (not even any arp traffic).

In AIX 5L, this command is useful if you need to change any of the underlying card characteristics, like network speed, as you cannot modify the card characteristics in AIX 5L while the device is in use.

Detaching a network interface in HP-UX

Detaching a network interface in HP-UX is called *unplumbing*. In fact, when you perform an **ifconfig lan0 <ip address>**, you are also actually *plumbing* the interface, as shown in Example 9-13.

Example 9-13   HP-UX unplumbing an interface

```
# netstat -ni
Name         Mtu Network         Address              Ipkts      Opkts
lan1         1500 10.1.1.0        10.1.1.198           1138078    948005
# ifconfig lan1 unplumb
# netstat -ni
Name         Mtu Network         Address              Ipkts      Opkts
#
```

Detaching a network interface in AIX 5L

To detach a network interface from the system using **ifconfig**, run the command:

```
# ifconfig Interface detach
```

For example, to remove the interface tr0 from the network interface list, run the command:

```
# ifconfig tr0 detach
```

This command immediately removes all network addresses assigned to the interface and removes the interface from the output of the **ifconfig -a** command. To add an interface back to the system, or to add a new interface to the network interface list, run the command:

```
# ifconfig Interface
```

Where *Interface* is the network interface you want to add.

You can also use **chdev** to perform this change as shown in Example 9-14.

Example 9-14   AIX 5L, demonstration of using chdev -a state=detach

```
# netstat -if inet -I en0
Name Mtu   Network     Address          Ipkts Ierrs   Opkts Oerrs  Coll
en0  1500  link#2      0.6.29.dc.59.4     182     0      14     0     0
en0  1500  192.168.100 rocky              182     0      14     0     0
# ifconfig en0
```

```
en0:
flags=4e080863,80<UP,BROADCAST,NOTRAILERS,RUNNING,SIMPLEX,MULTICAST,GROUPRT,64B
IT,PSEG,CHAIN>
        inet 192.168.100.224 netmask 0xffffff00 broadcast 192.168.100.255
# chdev -l en0 -a state=detach
en0 changed
# netstat -if inet -I en0
Name Mtu  Network    Address             Ipkts Ierrs    Opkts Oerrs  Coll
# ifconfig en0
en0:
flags=4e080822,80<BROADCAST,NOTRAILERS,SIMPLEX,MULTICAST,GROUPRT,64BIT,PSEG,CHA
IN>
# chdev -l en0 -a state=up
en0 changed
# ifconfig en0
en0:
flags=4e080863,80<UP,BROADCAST,NOTRAILERS,RUNNING,SIMPLEX,MULTICAST,GROUPRT,64B
IT,PSEG,CHAIN>
        inet 192.168.100.224 netmask 0xffffff00 broadcast 192.168.100.255
# netstat -if inet -I en0
Name Mtu  Network    Address             Ipkts Ierrs    Opkts Oerrs  Coll
en0  1500 link#2     0.6.29.dc.59.4          0     0        2     0     0
en0  1500 192.168.100 rocky                  0     0        2     0     0
```

9.2.7 IP address aliases

Both HP-UX and AIX 5L provide ways of assigning multiple IP addresses to a single interface card. In AIX 5L this is called *IP address aliasing*. This is a useful tool for such activities as providing two different initial home pages through a Web server application.

The concept is implemented slightly differently on the two platforms.

IP address aliasing and HP-UX

In the HP-UX world, to create an IP alias you actually create a logical Interface of the form lanX:[number].

You can do this via the Networking and Communication panel in SAM, Just select the interface you would like to have the alias on and then choose Add IP Logical Interface. Or you can modify /etc/rc.config.d/netconf with the appropriate entries.

To create an alias use the **ifconfig** command as shown in Example 9-15.

Example 9-15   HP-UX creation of a logical interface

```
# netstat -ni
```

```
Name            Mtu Network          Address            Ipkts      Opkts
lan1           1500 10.1.1.0         10.1.1.198       1144835     954218
lo0            4136 127.0.0.0        127.0.0.1         250349     250349
# ifconfig lan1:1 10.1.1.196 netmask 255.255.255.0
Name            Mtu Network          Address            Ipkts      Opkts
lan1:1         1500 10.1.1.0         10.1.1.196            13          0
lan1           1500 10.1.1.0         10.1.1.198       1145134     954484
lo0            4136 127.0.0.0        127.0.0.1         250416     250416
```

All the normal networking commands can now be used on the logical interface.
For example:

```
# ifconfig lan1:1
lan1:1: flags=843<UP,BROADCAST,RUNNING,MULTICAST>
        inet 2.2.2.2 netmask ffffff00 broadcast 2.2.2.255
```

IP address aliasing and AIX 5L

Through the **ifconfig** command, you can bind multiple network addresses to a
single network interface by defining an alias. To bind an alias to a network
interface, run the command:

```
# ifconfig Interface Address [netmask Netmask] alias
```

For example, to bind the IP address of 9.3.240.52 to tr0 with a netmask of
255.255.255.0, see Example 9-16.

Example 9-16 AIX 5L creation of an IP alias

```
# ifconfig en0 1.1.1.1 netmask 255.255.255.0 alias
# ifconfig en0
en0:
flags=5e080863,c0<UP,BROADCAST,NOTRAILERS,RUNNING,SIMPLEX,MULTICAST,GROUPRT,64B
IT,CHECKSUM_OFFLOAD,PSEG,CHAIN>
        inet 192.168.100.54 netmask 0xffffff00 broadcast 192.168.100.255
        inet 1.1.1.1 netmask 0xffffff00 broadcast 1.1.1.255
# netstat -niI en0
en0   1500  link#2        0.2.55.3a.7.db       5157    0     759    0    0
en0   1500  192.168.100   192.168.100.54       5157    0     759    0    0
en0   1500  1.1.1         1.1.1.1              5157    0     759    0    0
```

To make this alias persist across reboots, use one of the standard tools of
WebSM, **smitty mkinet4al** (or mkinet6al if you want an IPv6 alias), or a **chdev
-l <enx> -a alias4=<address>**.

When this alias is no longer required, you can remove it using the command:

```
# ifconfig en0 1.1.1.1 netmask 255.255.255.0 delete
```

If you do not specify which alias is to be removed from a network interface, the system will default and remove the primary network address from the interface. After this occurs, the first alias in the list of network addresses for the interface will become the primary network address for the interface. To remove all aliases from an interface, you must delete each alias individually.

To have this persist across reboots, you would use one of the WebSM, `smitty rminet4al`, or `chdev` commands.

9.3 Basic TCP/IP configuration

The following section describes basic TCP/IP configuration in HP-UX and AIX 5L.

9.3.1 Configuring TCP/IP in HP-UX

To configure a basic TCP/IP environment for HP-UX, the configuration screens allow you to pre-set most of the environment, or leave it until first boot.

If you want to modify any of the parameters that can be set during installation, you can also use the `/sbin/set_parms` command. (For more information see the man page.)

You can also configure the basics of TCP/IP from within SAM.

Both these methods allow you to configure your network interface cards with IP addresses, hostname, name resolution, and default gateway.

9.3.2 Configuring TCP/IP in AIX 5L

This topic explains how to configure the TCP/IP in AIX 5L. You can do the basic configuration of TCP/IP, such as assigning IP address, domain name, or gateway with the Web-based System Manager or smitty tools.

Prerequisites
If you want to configure your system to communicate with the other hosts in the network, the following conditions should be met:

► The TCP/IP software must be installed.
► You should have root authority.

Configuring with smitty

To do this:

1. Type **smitty tcpip** fast path. You will see the menu shown in Example 9-17.

Example 9-17   TCP/IP configuration

```
                             TCP/IP

Move cursor to desired item and press Enter.

   Minimum Configuration & Startup
   Further Configuration
   Use DHCP for TCPIP Configuration & Startup
   IPV6 Configuration
   Quality of Service Configuration & Startup



F1=Help              F2=Refresh           F3=Cancel            F8=Image
F9=Shell             F10=Exit             Enter=Do
```

2. Select the Minimum Configuration & Startup option and press Enter. All the available network interfaces are displayed. Select the network interface and press Enter. In our case, we are using interface en0 for our example (Example 9-18).

Example 9-18   Minimum TCP/IP configuration

```
                  Minimum Configuration & Startup

 To Delete existing configuration data, please use Further Configuration menus
Type or select values in entry fields.
Press Enter AFTER making all desired changes.

[TOP]                                                 [Entry Fields]
* HOSTNAME                                            []
* Internet ADDRESS (dotted decimal)                  []
  Network MASK (dotted decimal)                       []
* Network INTERFACE                                  en0
  NAMESERVER
          Internet ADDRESS (dotted decimal)           []
          DOMAIN Name                                 []
  Default Gateway
      Address (dotted decimal or symbolic name)       []
      Cost                                           [0]                      #
      Do Active Dead Gateway Detection?               no                      +
[MORE...2]

F1=Help              F2=Refresh           F3=Cancel            F4=List
```

```
F5=Reset            F6=Command          F7=Edit             F8=Image
F9=Shell            F10=Exit            Enter=Do
```

3. Fill in the details of hostname, Internet address, network mask, and so on. Press Enter to start the configuration. Once the configuration is complete, you will see the menu shown in Example 9-19.

Example 9-19   TCP/IP configuration

```
COMMAND STATUS

Command: OK           stdout: yes             stderr: no

Before command completion, additional instructions may appear below.

en0
siva
inet0 changed
en0 changed
inet0 changed

F1=Help             F2=Refresh          F3=Cancel           F6=Command
F8=Image            F9=Shell            F10=Exit            /=Find
n=Find Next
```

mktcpip command

If you prefer the command-line option, you can configure the TCP/IP with the `mktcpip` command. The man page has good information about `mktcpip`.

You can specify all the required parameters with a single command, like the example shown below:

```
# mktcpip -h siva -a 19.3.240.52 -m 255.255.0.0 -i en0 \
-n 9.3.240.2 -d itsc.austin.ibm.com -g 9.3.240.1 -s -C 0 -A no
```

9.4 Some IP networking troubleshooting commands

So you have a TCP/IP network up and running, but there are some problems. Where would you start to look?

The basic building block of networking is the routing, that is, how do you get from X to Y? You can see the routing table on UNIX by using the `netstat` command, as shown in Example 9-20 on page 303.

Example 9-20   netstat -nr

```
myHP-UX # netstat -nr
Routing tables
Destination         Gateway          Flags  Refs Interface  Pmtu
127.0.0.1           127.0.0.1        UH       0  lo0        4136
10.1.1.198          10.1.1.198       UH       0  lan1       4136
10.1.1.0            10.1.1.198       U        2  lan1       1500
127.0.0.0           127.0.0.1        U        0  lo0           0
default             10.1.1.1         UG       0  lan1          0


myAIX5.3# netstat -nr
Routing tables
Destination      Gateway         Flags   Refs      Use  If   PMTU Exp Groups

Route tree for Protocol Family 2 (Internet):
default          192.168.100.60  UG         0       24  en0   -   -       -
127/8            127.0.0.1       U          6      502  lo0   -   -   -
192.168.100.0    192.168.100.224 UHSb       0        0  en0   -   -   -    =>
192.168.100/24   192.168.100.224 U          1    14069  en0   -   -   -
192.168.100.224  127.0.0.1       UGHS       0        0  lo0   -   -   -
192.168.100.255  192.168.100.224 UHSb       0        0  en0   -   -   -

Route tree for Protocol Family 24 (Internet v6):
::1              ::1             UH         0        0  lo0   -   -   -
```

Of course, there is also the **traceroute** command, which can often prove useful.

Example 9-21   AIX 5L tracroute example

```
myAIX5.3# trying to get source for 10.1.1.2
source should be 192.168.100.224
traceroute to 10.1.1.2 (10.1.1.2) from 192.168.100.224 (192.168.100.224), 30
hops max
outgoing MTU = 1500
 1  192.168.100.60 (192.168.100.60)  1 ms  1 ms  1 ms
 2  10.1.1.2 (10.1.1.2)  1 ms  1 ms  1 ms
```

A really useful command available in AIX 5L Version 5.3 is **route get**, which tells
you which way AIX 5L will send the packets.

Example 9-22   AIX 5L route get example

```
myAIX5.3# # route get 10.1.1.2
   route to: 10.1.1.2
destination: default
       mask: default
    gateway: 192.168.100.60
  interface: en0
```

```
interf addr: itsomaster.itso.com
       flags: <UP,GATEWAY,DONE>
   recvpipe  sendpipe  ssthresh  rtt,msec   rttvar  hopcount    mtu    expire
       0        0         0         0         0        0         0       -39
```

9.5 Further TCP/IP configuration

Both HP-UX and AIX 5L have many other options regarding TCP/IP, which can be configured from either their command lines or their menu-based configuration tools.

For AIX 5L, customizing your TCP/IP configuration beyond the minimal configuration is easily done through SMIT, the command line, or the Web-based System Manager. SMIT menus guide you through such tasks as:

► Managing static routes
► Flushing the routing table
► Setting or showing hostnames
► Managing network interfaces or drivers
► Managing domain names or the hosts table (/etc/hosts file)
► Managing network services for the client or server
► Starting or stopping TCP/IP daemons

To perform all the above tasks, you can use the Web-based System Manager or the `smitty configtcp` fast path.

9.6 TCP/IP daemons

Daemons are the processes that run continuously in the background and perform the functions required by other processes. Transmission Control Protocol/Internet Protocol (TCP/IP) provides daemons for implementing certain functions in the operating system. These daemons are background processes that run without interrupting other processes (unless that is part of the daemon function).

Many of these daemons start at the system startup time, but in some cases it is more efficient to only start the daemons on demand. In both HP-UX and AIX 5L, this is done via the daemon called *inetd*.

We can start and stop TCP/IP daemons through either the commands or by editing the configuration files, depending on the operating systems.

9.6.1 TCP/IP daemons in HP-UX

HP-UX has a traditional approach to system daemons. In effect, there are two types—those not started by `inetd` and those that are.

Some TCP/IP daemons started directly include:

gated   Provides gateway routing functions.

inetd   Invokes and schedules other daemons when requests for the daemons' services are received. This daemon can also start other daemons. The inetd daemon is also known as the super daemon.

mrouted   Forwards a multicast datagram along a shortest tree.

named   Provides the naming function for the Domain Name Server Protocol (DOMAIN).

rwhod   Sends broadcasts to all other hosts every three minutes and stores information about logged-in users and network status.

snmpd   Handles the Simple Network Management Protocol.

To a great extent, the daemons that are run from `inetd` in HP-UX are also those run in AIX 5L, so for some examples, please see "TCP/IP daemons in AIX 5L" on page 305.

9.6.2 TCP/IP daemons in AIX 5L

AIX 5L has an additional concept in relation to daemons. It has the (default) option of using something called the *System Resource Controller (SRC)* to help manage and control daemons it knows about.

In SRC terms a *subsystem* is a daemon that is controlled by SRC and a *subserver* is a daemon that in turn is controlled by a *subsystem*. What this effectively means is that `inetd` is a subsystem and everything that it spawns is a subserver.

At IPL time, the /init process will run /etc/rc.tcpip after starting the System Resource Control. The /etc/rc.tcpip file is a shell script that, when executed, uses SRC commands to initialize selected daemons. It can also be executed at any time from the command line.

Subsystems and subservers

The categories of subsystem and subserver are mutually exclusive. That is, daemons are not listed as both a subsystem and as a subserver. The only TCP/IP subsystem that controls other daemons is the inetd daemon. Thus, all TCP/IP subservers are also inetd subservers.

Daemon commands and daemon names are usually (though not always) denoted by a d at the end of the name.

Some TCP/IP daemons controlled by the SRC are the following:

gated	Provides gateway routing functions. And in addition it supports the Simple Network Management Protocol (SNMP).
inetd	Invokes and schedules other daemons when requests for the daemons' services are received. This daemon can also start other daemons. The inetd daemon is also known as the super daemon.
iptrace	Provides an interface-level packet-tracing function for Internet protocols.
named	Provides the naming function for the Domain Name Server Protocol (DOMAIN).
routed	Manages the network routing tables and supports the Routing Information Protocol (RIP).
rwhod	Sends broadcasts to all other hosts every three minutes and stores information about logged-in users and network status.
timed	Provides the timeserver function.

Some TCP/IP daemons controlled by the inetd subsystem are the following:

comsat	Notifies users of incoming mail.
fingerd	Provides a status report on all logged-in users and network status at the specified remote host. This daemon uses the Finger protocol.
ftpd	Provides the file transfer function for a client process using the File Transfer Protocol (FTP).
rexecd	Provides the foreign host server function for the `rexec` command.
rlogind	Provides the remote login facility function for the `rlogin` command.

rshd	Provides the remote command execution server function for the **rcp** and **rsh** commands.
talkd	Provides the conversation function for the **talk** command.
syslogd	Reads and logs system messages. This daemon is in the RAS group of subsystems.
telnetd	Provides the server function for the TELNET protocol.
tftpd	Provides the server function for the Trivial File Transfer Protocol (TFTP).

9.6.3 Stopping and restarting TCP/IP daemons

The following sections describe how to stop and start TCP/IP daemons.

Stopping and restarting TCP/IP daemons in HP-UX

The following section explains how to stop and start TCP/IP daemons in HP-UX.

Non-inetd daemons

In HP-UX, daemons that start up outside of *inetd's* control are generally started during the standard rc boot sequence (that is, they have start and stop scripts located in /sbin/rcX.d directories). For more information, see 4.2.1, "Startup process in HP-UX" on page 94.

To enable a particular non-inetd daemon to start on boot, say *samba*, you would need to edit its configuration environment in /etc/rc.config.d/samba, and in this case change the RUN_SAMBA=0 to equal 1.

You can then use **/sbin/init.d/samba start** and **stop** to start and stop samba. Most daemons in HP-UX are configured in this way.

inetd daemons

In HP-UX you configure TCP/IP that are only required to start on demand, via the *inetd* daemon in th**e /etc/inetd.conf** configuration file.

After updating the file (as per the man page), you then need to let inetd know about the change. You can do this in one of two ways:

► **/usr/sbin/inetd -c**
► **kill -HUP <inetd PID>**

Both of these make inetd re-read its configuration file.

In HP-UX, you also have the option of configuring a inetd.sec file, which provides an additional layer of security by not even starting the daemon requested unless the source address is coming from an valid host as defined by inetd.sec. For example, to turn on verbose logging for **ftpd** (which is started via **inetd**) you would modify /etc/inetd.conf to contain:

```
ftp            stream tcp nowait root /usr/lbin/ftpd        ftpd -lv
```

and then refresh the **inetd** daemon like so:

```
# inetd -c
```

To stop an inetd daemon, you just comment out the daemon you wish to stop and then get the daemon to re-read the configuration file.

Stopping and restarting TCP/IP daemons in AIX 5L

The subsystems can be stopped using the Web-based System Manager, SMIT, or by using the **stopsrc** and **startsrc** commands.

Using Web-based System Manager

You can stop/start the subsystems and subservers using the Web-based System Manager. If you want to use the Web-based System Manager GUI interface, follow these steps:

1. Enter the **wsm** command. In the GUI window, select **Network → TCP/IP (IPv4 and IPv6) → Subsystems**.

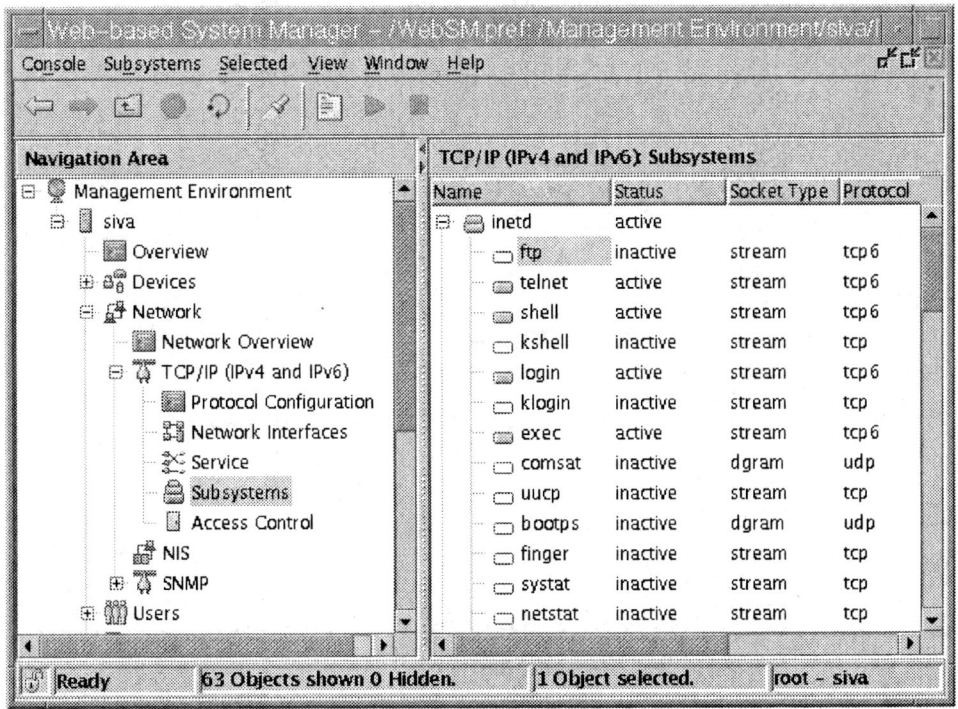

Figure 9-1   TCP/IP

2. You can view the window like the one in Figure 9-1. Right-click the service that you want to stop or start. Select **Activate** to start the subsystem. If it is already active, you can stop the subsystem by selecting the **Deactivate** option.

Using smitty

To use this:

1. Type the `smitty` command. Select the Processes & Subsystems option and press Enter.

2. You will see a screen similar to Example 9-23.

Example 9-23   Processes & Subsystems

```
                        Processes & Subsystems

Move cursor to desired item and press Enter.

    Processes
    Subsystems
    Subservers
```

```
F1=Help          F2=Refresh       F3=Cancel       F8=Image
F9=Shell         F10=Exit         Enter=Do
```

3. Select the subsystems or subservers option, depending on your requirements.

4. You can list, start, or stop the subsystems.

The subsystems started from the rc.tcpip can be stopped using the **stopsrc** command. These subsystems can be restarted using the **startsrc** command.

The stopsrc, startsrc, and refresh commands

You can stop/start the subsystems using the **stopsrc** and **startsrc** commands.

The following command stops the named subsystem:

```
# stopsrc -s named
```

To restart the named subsystem, enter the following command:

```
# startsrc -s named
```

Using the **startsrc** and **stopsrc** commands only affects the currently running system; the changes will not persist across reboots.

To *refresh* a non-signal communication subsystem, you can use the intuitive command of **refresh**. In most cases, what this does is to send a SIGHUP to the process ID.

```
# refresh -s inetd
```

The /etc/tcp.clean script can be used to stop TCP/IP daemons. It will stop the following daemons and remove the /etc/locks/lpd TCP/IP lock files. You can use this command if you wish to stop all:

► ndpd-host
► lpd
► routed
► gated
► sendmail
► inetd
► named
► timed
► rwhod
► iptrace
► snmpd
► rshd
► rlogind

- telnetd
- syslogd

The /etc/tcp.clean script does not stop the portmap and nfsd daemons. If you want to stop the portmap and the nfsd daemons, use the `stopsrc -s portmap` and the `stopsrc -s nfsd` commands.

Restarting TCP/IP daemons

The /etc/rc.tcpip script can be used to restart all the stopped TCP/IP daemons that would normally be started on IPL. Alternatively, you can use the `startsrc -s` command to start individual TCP/IP daemons.

Where all these TCP/IP daemons are started from

To enable the startup on boot of a particular TCP/IP daemon, you would usually either use Web-based System Manager or SMIT to have the change persist across reboots.

If you wanted to perform the step yourself, all you need to do is to edit the /etc/rc.tcpip script and update the appropriate start line.

The inetd daemon

The /usr/sbin/inetd daemon provides Internet service management for a network. This daemon reduces system load by invoking other daemons only when they are needed and by providing several simple Internet services internally without invoking other daemons.

Starting and refreshing inetd

When the daemon starts, it reads its configuration information from the file specified in the Configuration File parameter. If the parameter is not specified, the inetd daemon reads its configuration information from the /etc/inetd.conf file.

Once started, the inetd daemon listens for connections on certain Internet sockets in the /etc/inetd.conf and either handles the service request itself or invokes the appropriate server once a request on one of these sockets is received.

The /etc/inetd.conf file can be updated by using the System Management Interface Tool (SMIT), the System Resource Controller (SRC), or by editing the /etc/inetd.conf.

If you change the /etc/inetd.conf using SMIT, then the inetd daemon will be refreshed automatically and will read the new /etc/inetd.conf file. If you change the file using an editor, run the `refresh -s inetd` or `kill -1 InetdPID` commands to inform the inetd daemon of the changes to its configuration file.

To start any one of the subservers controlled by the inetd daemon, remove the pound (#) sign in column one of the respective entry in the /etc/inetd.conf file. You can check the details of subservers started in inetd by using the `lssrc -ls` command.

Stopping inetd

Use the `stopsrc -s inetd` command to stop the inetd daemon, as shown in Example 9-24.

Example 9-24   Stopping inetd

```
# stopsrc -s inetd
0513-044 The /usr/sbin/inetd Subsystem was requested to stop.
```

When the inetd daemon is stopped, the previously started subserver processes are not affected. However, new service requests for the subservers can no longer be satisfied. In other words, existing sessions are not affected when the inetd daemon is stopped, but (for example) no new telnet and ftp sessions can be established without first restarting the inetd daemon.

9.7 Network File System (NFS)

Network File System is a facility for sharing files in heterogeneous environment machines, operating systems, and networks. NFS is supported over TCP/IP via both UDP (NFS V2 and 3) and TCP (NFS V2, V3, and V4).

NFS is a distributed file system that allows users to access files and directories located on remote systems, and treats those files and directories as though they were local. NFS provides its services through the client/server model.

NFS was developed by Sun™ Micro Systems in 1984, and has become the *de facto* standard. It has become so popular not only for its efficiency in file sharing, but also because it runs on over 100 different hardware platforms.

At this point in time, there are three active versions of NFS:

Version 2	Introduced in 1985. It is still around, but has effectively been replaced by Version 3.
Version 3	Widely available across multiple vendors; around since 1996.
Version 4	Defined by RFC3010 in 2000 and updated by RFC3530 in 2003. NFS V4 can be configured to provide a much more secure way of sharing files than previous versions of NFS.

It is currently not supported by the same breadth of vendors as Version 3.

In this topic, we explain how to configure NFS in HP-UX as well as in AIX 5L. As HP-UX currently does not have built-in support for NFS V4. This chapter concentrates on NFS V3.

For how to configure NFS V4 in AIX 5L, please see *Securing NFS in AIX An Introduction to NFS v4 in AIX 5L Version 5.3*, SG24-7204.

NFS terminology

The following terms are used quite often in this topic:

NFS server   A computer system that shares its local file systems to be accessed by other systems in the network.

NFS client   A computer system that mounts the file systems that are shared in the network locally.

Common daemons used for NFS

For NFS V3, both HP-UX and AIX 5L have a common core of daemons that perform the same tasks on both.

NFS client daemons consist of biod, rpc.statd, and rpc.lockd.

NFS server daemons consist of rpc.mountd, nfsd, rpc.statd, and rpc.lockd.

And, when an RPC server program initializes, it registers its services with the portmap/rpcbind daemon. These daemons are as follows:

rpc.lockd   Processes lock requests through the RPC package.

rpc.statd   Provides crash-and-recovery functions for the locking services on NFS.

biod   Sends the client's read and write requests to the server.

rpc.mountd   Answers requests from clients for file system mounts.

nfsd   Starts the daemons that handle a client's request for file system operations.

portmap   Maps RPC program numbers to Internet port numbers. This is the AIX 5L name for rpcbind.

rpcbind   This is HP-UX's name for portmap.

9.7.1 Configuring an NFS server

If the appropriate product (NFS in HP-UX) or filesets (bos.net.nfs in AIX 5L) are installed (which they are on a default base installation), then both HP-UX and AIX 5L are set to go as either NFS clients or NFS servers, depending on your need.

Configuring an NFS server to start on HP-UX

To turn on or off an HP-UX machine as an NFS server, you can use SAM (Networking and Communications → Networked File Systems → Exported Local File Systems → menu Actions → Disable NFS Server), but all this really does is edit /etc/rc.config.d/nfsconf and change the variable NFS_SERVER, where 1 is on, and 0 is off.

In this nfsconf, you can also tune the number of the NFS daemons that are started during NFS server startup.

Configuring an NFS server to start on AIX 5L

To configure the NFS server, use the following instructions:

1. Start the portmap daemon if it is not running already.

2. Start the NFS daemons using SRC, if it is not already started. The NFS daemons can be started individually or all at once. To start NFS daemons individually, run:

   `# startsrc -s daemon`

   where *daemon* is any one of the daemons listed above. For example, to start the nfsd daemon:

   `# startsrc -s nfsd`

   To start all of the NFS daemons:

   `# startsrc -g nfs`

   Not all the daemons in the SRC group of NFS are required to be running for NFS V3. nfsrgyd and gssd are only used for NFS V4.

3. Create the exports in the /etc/exports file.

If the /etc/exports file does not exist, the nfsd and the rpc.mountd daemons will *not* be started, thereby prohibiting you from acting as an NFS server. You can create an empty /etc/exports file by running the **touch /etc/exports** command. This will allow the nfsd and the rpc.mountd daemons to start, although no file systems will be exported. Please be careful with the permissions on this file, as anyone who can update it could then use NFS to gain access to any file on the local system. The recommended permissions are root:sys and 500.

9.7.2 Exporting a directory via NFS

In the previous section, we started up the NFS server, but we have yet to get it to do anything.

An NFS server *exports* a directory to one or more NFS clients. Both HP-UX and AIX 5L do this in the same way (at least at the file/command line level).

Exporting a directory temporarily

To temporarily export a directory (non-persistent across reboots), you can use **exportfs -i**. For example, to export /software read-only to the hosts heckle and jeckle see Example 9-25.

Example 9-25   Using exportfs to temporarily export a directory in NFS

```
# exportfs -i -o access=heckle:jeckle /software
```

Using the command line to export a directory permanently

Both HP-UX and AIX 5L store the file systems they wish to export on NFS server start up in the /etc/exports file. For detailed information see the man page for *exports*.

In order to export file systems using a text editor, follow this procedure:

1. Edit the file /etc/exports with your favorite text editor. Create an entry for each directory to be exported using the full path name of the directory, as shown in Example 9-26.

Example 9-26   /etc/exports file

```
/software -access=heckle:jeckle /software
/usr
```

2. List each directory to be exported starting in the left margin. No directory should include any other directory that is already exported. Save and close the /etc/exports file.

3. Now we need to export those directories:

   ```
   # exportfs -av
   ```

   Or on AIX 5L (though the **share** commands are included for HP-UX compatibility):

   ```
   # shareall
   ```

4. To verify what you have just exported:

   ```
   # showmount -e
   /software heckle:jeckle
   ```

/usr (everyone)

Export an NFS using SAM

In SAM head to **Networking and Communications** → **Networked File Systems** → **Exported Local File Systems** → menu, **Actions** → **Add Exported File System**, and fill in the blanks. This will update /etc/exports and also issue the `exportfs -a` command for you.

Export an NFS using SMIT

To export file systems using SMIT, follow this procedure:

1. Verify that NFS is already running on the NFS server with the following command. If the daemons are not running, start the NFS as in Example 9-27.

Example 9-27   AIX 5L displaying the NFS SRC group

```
# lssrc -g nfs
Subsystem          Group          PID      Status
  biod             nfs            540806   active
  rpc.statd        nfs            442518   active
  rpc.lockd        nfs            549000   active
  nfsd             nfs            1056946  active
  rpc.mountd       nfs            843856   active
```

2. Run `smitty mknfsexp` to export the directory. You will see the smitty screen shown in Example 9-28.

Example 9-28   Exporting NFS

```
                        Add a Directory to Exports List
Add a Directory to Exports List

Type or select values in entry fields.
Press Enter AFTER making all desired changes.

 [TOP]                                             [Entry Fields]
* Pathname of directory to export                 []                          /
  Anonymous UID                                   [-2]
  Public filesystem?                              no                       +
* Export directory now, system restart or both    both                     +
  Pathname of alternate exports file              []
  Allow access by NFS versions                    []                       +
  External name of directory (NFS V4 access only) []
* Security method                                 [sys,krb5p,krb5i,krb5,dh,none] +
*     Mode to export directory                    read-write               +
      Hostname list. If exported read-mostly      []
      Hosts & netgroups allowed client access     []
      Hosts allowed root access                   []
```

3. Specify the directory in the "Pathname of directory to export" field. if you want to export the /home directory, specify that in the field. Set the "MODE to export directory" field to read-write, and the "EXPORT directory now, system restart, or both" field to both.

4. Specify any other optional characteristics you want or accept the default values by leaving the remaining fields as they are.

5. After specifying your options, SMITTY updates the /etc/exports file. If NFS is currently running on the servers, and you specified both in the "Export directory now, system restart or both" field, SMITTY will execute:

```
/usr/sbin/exportfs -a
```

The -a option tells the **exportfs** command to send all information in the /etc/exports file to the kernel. If NFS is not running, start NFS.

6. Verify that all file systems have been exported properly as follows; if the server name is siva, run the following command:

```
# showmount -e siva
export list for siva:
/home (everyone)
/usr  (everyone)
```

9.7.3 NFS client configuration

As we have seen, both HP-UX and AIX 5L use the same sets of clients for their implementation of NFS V3.

Enabling an NFS client in HP-UX

You can use SAM to configure a server to be an NFS client on boot, but all this really does is to edit /etc/rc.config.d/nfsconf and change the variable NFS_CLIENT, where 1 is on, and 0 is off.

Enabling an NFS client in AIX 5L

To configure an NFS client, you need to start the NFS client daemons. The daemons that must be started are portmap, biod, rpc.statd, and rpc.lockd.

9.7.4 Mounting an NFS file system

To configure either a manual/explicit or boot-time mount requires, at a minimum, the following three attributes:

▶ The server's hostname
▶ The absolute path name of the remote directory
▶ The path name of the local directory mount point

Mounting an NFS file system explicitly

When you mount a NFS file system explicitly, it is only available until the next system reboot.

To mount an NFS directory explicitly, use the following procedure for both HP-UX and AIX 5L:

1. Verify that the NFS server has exported the directory that you want to mount:

   ```
   # showmount -e Servername
   ```

   where *ServerName* is the name of the NFS server. This command displays the names of the directories currently exported from the NFS server.

2. If necessary create the local mount point using the `mkdir` command.

3. The following command shows the mounting of the /home directory shared in the server siva:

   ```
   # mount siva:/home /home1
   ```

   where siva is the name of the NFS server, /home is the directory on the NFS server you want to mount, and /home1 is the mount point on the NFS client.

Mounting an NFS file system via SMITTY

To do this:

1. On the client machine, enter the following SMITTY fast path:

   ```
   smitty mknfsmnt
   ```

   You will see a window similar to Example 9-29.

Example 9-29   Add a File System for Mounting

```
Add a File System for Mounting

Type or select values in entry fields.
Press Enter AFTER making all desired changes.

[TOP]                                                    [Entry Fields]
* Pathname of mount point                       []                         /
* Pathname of remote directory                  []
```

```
* Host where remote directory resides              []
  Mount type name                                   []
* Security method                                   []                  +
* Mount now, add entry to /etc/filesystems or both?  now                +
* /etc/filesystems entry will mount the directory    no                 +
  on system restart.
* Mode for this NFS file system                      read-write         +
* Attempt mount in background or foreground          background         +
  Number of times to attempt mount                   []                       #
  Buffer size for read                               []                       #
  Buffer size for writes                             []                       #
  NFS timeout. In tenths of a second                 []                       #
  NFS version for this NFS file system               any                +
  Transport protocol to use                          any                +
  Internet port number for server                    []                       #
* Allow execution of setuid and setgid programs      yes                +
  in this file system?
* Allow device access via this mount?                yes                +
* Server supports long device numbers?               yes                +
* Mount file system soft or hard                     hard               +
[MORE...17]


F1=Help           F2=Refresh         F3=Cancel          F4=List
F5=Reset          F6=Command         F7=Edit            F8=Image
F9=Shell          F10=Exit           Enter=Do
```

2. Though there are many options in the screen, you are not required to change all the options. Usually you select:

   – PATHNAME of mount point.

   – PATHNAME of remote directory.

   – HOST where remote directory resides.

   – MOUNT now, add entry to /etc/filesystems or both?

   – The /etc/filesystems entry will mount the directory on system RESTART.MODE for this NFS file system.

3. Change or use the default values for the remaining entries, depending on your NFS configuration.

4. When you finish making all the changes on this screen, SMIT mounts the NFS file system.

5. When the Command: field shows the OK status, exit SMIT.

9.7.5 Disabling NFS services

This section provides information about how to disable NFS services in HP-UX and AIX 5L.

Disabling NFS services in HP-UX

To disable NFS in HP-UX you can either do this via SAM, or change the appropriate NFS_CLIENT or NFS_SERVER variable in /etc/rc.config.d/nfsconf.

Disabling NFS services in AIX 5L

AIX 5L has a nice set of commands to simply enable and disable NFS on startup (or immediately).

Example 9-30   AIX 5L man page extract for rmnfs

```
The rmnfs command changes the current configuration of the system so that the
/etc/rc.nfs file is not executed on system restart. In addition, you can direct
the command to stop NFS daemons that are currently running.
```

The default execution of **rmnfs** is to both stop all the NFS daemons currently running, as well as to remove the **/etc/rc.nfs** command from inittab, thereby disabling on boot.

The **mknfs** command does exactly the opposite of **rmnfs**.

9.7.6 NFS performance

Both HP-UX and AIX 5L provide the **nfsstat** command, which can be used as the start of performance tuning NFS.

AIX 5L also provides the **nfso** command, which allows you to modify NFS tunable options (also see **smitty tuning**).

For more detailed information about tuning NFS in AIX 5L, please head to the AIX Information Center → **AIX Information** → **System Management Guides** → **Performance Management Guide** → **NFS Performance** from the following Web site:

```
http://publib.boulder.ibm.com/infocenter/pseries/index.jsp
```

9.8 DNS

The Domain Naming System (DNS) is a method for distributing of a large database of IP addresses, hostnames, and other record data across administrative areas. The end result is a distributed database maintained in sections by authorized administrators per domain. There are different programs out in the world that are used to implement DNS. BIND is what is shipped with both HP-UX and AIX 5L for performing DNS on these systems, so this is what we discuss in this section.

BIND versions

There are three current versions of BIND: BIND4, BIND8, and BIND9.

BIND 4 has been around for a long time. It has many security issues and has been depreciated by the Internet Systems Consortium (ISC) in favour of BIND 8.

BIND 8 and BIND 9 are both stable releases and should be used instead of BIND 4. If you are implementing an IPv6 network, then BIND 9 is the only way to go, as it provides support for IPv6 name resolution. For more differences between the different BIND versions, see:

    http://www.isc.org/products/BIND

The examples we give below are based on BIND8. BIND8 uses the configuration file /etc/named.conf. One other good reference for an example for either HP-UX or AIX 5L can be found at:

    http://publib.boulder.ibm.com/infocenter/pseries/topic/com.ibm.aix.doc/aixb
    man/commadmn/HT_commadmn_dns.htm#commadmn_dns

To convert previous versions of the BIND configuration file (that is, /etc/named.boot) to the BIND 8.x.x configuration file /etc/named.conf, you can use the scripts provided by HP-UX and AIX 5L Version 5.3.

To convert /etc/named.boot (BIND 4) to /etc/named.conf (BIND 8/9):

► In HP-UX 11i, see the /usr/share/doc/11iRelNotes.txt. There is a script called /usr/bin/named-bootconf.pl, which gets run after a couple of steps.

► In AIX 5L Version 5.1, run the /usr/samples/tcpip/named-bootconf.pl script. You need Perl Version 5.0 or later to run this script.

AIX 5L Version 5.3 will run BIND8 by default (check to see what /usr/sbin/named is linked to), though it can be configured to run BIND4 or BIND9 as well. The default OE for HP-UX 11i comes with BIND8 installed, though you can go to http://software.hp.com and search for BIND9 to download and install it as a separate free package.

Domain structure

A hostname is the name of a machine. The hostname is usually attached to the left of the domain name. The result is a host's domain name. Domain names reflect the domain hierarchy. Domain names are written from the most specific (a hostname) to the least specific (a top-level domain), from left to right, with each part of the domain name separated by a dot. A fully qualified domain name (FQDN) starts with a specific host and ends with a top-level domain followed by the root domain (the dot, "."). www.ibm.com is the FQDN of workstation www in the ibm domain of the com top-level domain. A domain is part of the name space, and it may cover several zones.

Types of domain name servers

There are several types of name servers:

Master name server Loads its data from a file or disk and can delegate authority to other servers in its domain.

Slave name server Slave name server acts as a backup to the master server. It maintains the copy of the databases that the master has. The database is refreshed after a specified time, which is defined as refresh variable.

Stub name server Although its method of database replication is similar to that of the slave name server, the stub name server only replicates the name server records of the master database rather than the whole database.

Hint server Indicates a name server that relies only on the hints that it has built from previous queries to other name servers. The hint name server responds to queries by asking other servers that have the authority to provide the information needed if a hint name server does not have a name-to-address mapping in its cache.

9.8.1 Configuration of DNS

There are several files involved in configuring name servers:

named.conf This file is read when the named daemon starts. The records in the conf file tell the named daemon which type of server it is, which domains it has authority over (its zones of authority), and where to get the data for initially setting up its database. The default name of this file is /etc/named.conf. However, you can change the name of this file by specifying the name and path of the file on the command line when the named daemon is started. If you intend to use the /etc/named.conf as the conf file and it does not exist, a message is generated in the syslog file and named terminates. However, if an alternative conf file is specified, and the alternative file does not exist, an error message is not generated and named continues.

cache   Contains information about the local cache. The local cache file contains the names and addresses of the highest authority name servers in the network. The cache file uses the Standard Resource Record Format. The name of the cache file is set in the conf file.

domain data   There are three typical domain data files, also referred to as the named data files. The named local file contains the address resolution information for local loopback. The named data file contains the address resolution data for all machines in the name server zone of authority. The named reverse data file contains the reverse address resolution information for all machines in the name server zone of authority. The domain data files use the Standard Resource Record Format. Their file names are user definable and are set in the conf file. By convention, the names of these files generally include the name of the daemon (named), and the type of file and name of the domain is given in the extension. For example, the name server for the domain itso might have the following files:

```
named.itso.data
named.itso.rev
named.itso.local
```

When modifying the named data files, the serial number in the Start Of Authority (SOA) Resource Record must be incremented for slave name servers to properly realize the new zone changes.

resolv.conf   The presence of this file indicates to a host to go to a name server to resolve a name first. If the resolv.conf file does not exist, the host looks in the /etc/hosts file for name resolution. On a name server, the resolv.conf file must exist and can contain the local host address, the loopback address (127.0.0.1), or be empty.

We discuss setting up the DNS master, slave servers, and clients. The configuration process is similar in both HP-UX and AIX 5L Version 5.3.

9.8.2 Configuring master server

There are many easily found articles on the Internet regarding configuration and best practices of management for DNS. This section is just meant as a lightweight guide in configuring a simple DNS master.

HP-UX comes with the **host_to_named**, which quickly and simply converts a hosts file to a straightforward configuration that can be used for BIND4, 8, and 9. These files can actually be copied across to an AIX 5L box with success.

The following steps are used to configure the master name server:

1. Change the domain name of the server to the domain for which you are configuring the name server.
2. Create the name server configuration file (/etc/named.conf).
3. Create the name data file. This file contains hostnames to IP address resolution information.
4. Create the IP file. This contains reverse address resolution information.
5. Create the local IP zone file.
6. Create the /etc/resolv.conf file. This file identifies this host as primary server.
7. Start the named daemon.

We use the following information to set up the DNS:

Domain name	itso.com
Network ID	10.1.2
Master server	Hostname: itsomaster; IP address 10.1.2.1
Slave server	Hostname: itsoslave; IP address 10.1.2.2

The rest of the hosts are clients in the network.

Now let us start configuring the master DNS server:

1. Create the file /etc/named.conf; it looks like the one in Example 9-31.

Example 9-31   /etc/named.conf file

```
# cat /etc/named.conf
options {
        directory "/etc/named";
        datasize 2098;
};

//Names of the configuration files
```

```
//Host to IP resolution file.
zone "itso.com" in {
        type master;
        file "db.itso";
};

//Reverse address Resolution
zone "2.1.10.in-addr.arpa" in {
        type master;
        file "db.10.1.2";
};

//Local resolution
zone "0.0.127.in-addr.arpa" in {
        type master;
        file "local_resol";
};
```

In Example 9-31 on page 324:

- The definition *options* contains the entire server configuration options.

- The *directory* entry tells the named daemon that all files listed in this file are stored in the /etc/named directory.

- The entry *type master* specifies that this host is the primary DNS server.

- The entry file *filename* specifies that the zone information is stored in the file name specified in this field. In our case, the zone files are db.itso, db.10.1.2, and local_resol. All these files are stored in the /etc/named directory (remember that we have the specified directory name as /etc/named in the directory field).

2. Create the zone file that contains the name to address resolution. Create the /etc/named/db.itso file. In our example, the file looks like Example 9-32.

Example 9-32   Domain information file: /etc/named/db.itso

```
;
; SOA rec
@ IN SOA itsomaster.itso.com. root.itsomaster.itso.com. (
        01 ; Serial Number
        10800 ; Refresh time
        10800 ; Retry time every 3 hrs
        604800 ; expire after a week
        86400  ; TTL 1 day
)
;Name Servers
                IN NS itsomaster
;Addresses
localhost       IN A 127.0.0.1
```

```
itsomaster      IN A 10.1.2.1
itsoslave       IN A 10.1.2.2
itsocl1         IN A 10.1.2.55
itsocl2         IN A 10.1.2.69
```

If you look at Example 9-32 on page 325, the line that starts with the @ symbol is called SOA (Start Of Authority Record). It is mandatory for the zone information file. In that record:

- The @ sign specifies the domain name. In our case, it is itso.com.

- itsomaster.itso.com specifies the name of the primary server's fully qualified domain name (FQDN).

- root.itsomaster.itso.com specifies the e-mail ID of the user who administers this domain.

- The *serial number* is the version number of this data file. The number should be incremented each time you update the data. Slave servers check for the serial number, to see if they want to download the from the primary master server.

- The *Refresh time* is the time interval in seconds that the slave server checks for the change of data.

- The *Retry time* is the time interval that the slave server waits after the failure of the primary master server.

- The *Expire time* is the upper time limit used by the slave server to flush the data after the continued failure to contact the master server.

- The *Minimum* is the minimum time to live used as the default. This overrides individual entries if those entries are lower.

The NS record must be defined for each name server in the domain.

If you see the other lines, each line contains the hostname and IP address of the machines in this domain.

The following are some of the terms you should know:

NS   Name Server

IN   Internet

A   Address

TTL   Time to live

CNAME   Canonical name

In all the configuration files, lines beginning with the characters ; , #, /*, or // are comments.

3. Our next step is to create the reverse address resolution data file (/etc/named/ip_to_host). It should look like Example 9-33 on page 327.

```
;
; SOA rec
@ IN SOA itsomaster.itso.com. root.itsomaster.itso.com. (
        01 ; Serial Number
        10800 ; Refresh time
        10800 ; Retry time every 3 hrs
        604800 ; expire after a week
        86400  ; TTL 1 day
)

;Name Servers
        IN NS itsomaster.itso.com.
;Host names
1       IN PTR itsomaster.itso.com.
2       IN PTR itsoslave.itso.com.
55      IN PTR itsocl1.itso.com.
69      IN PTR itsocl2.itso.com.
```

It uses the same format as the host to IP address resolution data file, which we explained in step 3. But this file uses the PTR (domain name pointer) type records to map the IP address to hostnames.

4. Create the local / loopback IP zone file (/etc/named/local_resol). It looks like Example 9-34. This file contains the local loopback address for the network 127.0.0.1.

Example 9-34   Local IP zone file: /etc/named/local_resol

```
;
; SOA rec
@ IN SOA itsomaster.itso.com. root.itsomaster.itso.com. (
        01 ; Serial Number
        10800 ; Refresh time
        10800 ; Retry time every 3 hrs
        604800 ; expire after a week
        86400  ; TTL 1 day
)

;Name Servers
        IN NS itsomaster.itso.com.

;Host names
1       IN PTR localhost.
```

5. Create the /etc/resolv.conf file. It looks like Example 9-35 on page 328.

Example 9-35   /etc/resolv.conf file for master server

```
domain itso.com
nameserver 127.0.0.1
```

6. In HP-UX 11i, you need to edit the /etc/nsswitch.conf and modify the line containing the hosts entry. After modifying it, the line should look similar to:

   ```
   hosts: files dns
   ```

   In AIX 5L, the equivalent file is /etc/netsvc.conf.

   More details are in 9.8.6, "Name resolution order" on page 333.

   In HP-UX the resolution order is set by /etc/nsswitch.conf; it defaults to "NIS, FILES". In AIX 5L the resolution order is set by /etc/netsvc.conf; it defaults to "DNS,NIS,HOSTS".

7. Start the named daemons to start the functioning of the DNS master server. To start the daemon in AIX 5L, use the SRC command **startsrc -s named**.

   To start the daemon in HP-UX, modify /etc/rc.config.d/namesrvs and change NAMED=0 to NAMED=1 and then run "**/sbin/init.d/named start**".

9.8.3 Configuring the slave name server

The steps for configuring the slave name server are:

1. Create the name server configuration file (/etc/named.conf).

2. Create the local IP zone file.

3. Create the /etc/resolv.conf file.

4. Start the named daemon.

Let us now start configuring the slave DNS Server:

1. Create the /etc/named.conf file. It looks similar to Example 9-36. The file looks the same as the one we have defined for the master server. The type of the server in this case is slave. You need to specify the master name server address in the masters record.

Example 9-36   /etc/named.conf for slave server

```
options {
        directory "/etc/named";
        datasize 2098;
};

//Names of the configuration files

//Host to IP resolution file.
```

```
zone "itso.com" in {
        type slave;
        file "db.itso.bak";
        masters {
                10.1.2.1;
        };
};

//Reverse address Resolution
zone "2.1.10.in-addr.arpa" in {
        type slave;
        file "db.10.1.2.bak";
        masters {
                10.1.2.1;
        };
};

//Local resolution
zone "0.0.127.in-addr.arpa" in {
        type master;
        file "local_resol";
};
```

2. Create the local /loop back IP zone file. It will be the same as the one we have created the for slave server, except for the name of the server in the NS record. See the Example 9-37 for details.

Example 9-37   Loopback IP zone file

```
;
; SOA rec
@ IN SOA itsomaster.itso.com. root.itsomaster.itso.com. (
        01 ; Serial Number
        10800 ; Refresh time
        10800 ; Retry time every 3 hrs
        604800 ; expire after a week
        86400  ; TTL 1 day
)

;Name Servers
        IN NS itsoslave.itso.com.

;Host names
1       IN PTR localhost.
```

3. In HP-UX 11i, you need to edit the /etc/nsswitch.conf and modify the line containing the hosts entry. After modifying it, the line should look similar to:

```
hosts: files dns
```

In AIX 5L, the equivalent file is /etc/netsvc.conf.

More detail are in 9.8.6, "Name resolution order" on page 333.

4. Create the /etc/resolv.conf file, as specified in step 5 in 9.8.2, "Configuring master server" on page 324.

5. Start the named daemons as specified in step 7 in 9.8.2, "Configuring master server" on page 324.

You now have a DNS slave.

9.8.4 Configuring DNS clients

Now that we have done the hard part of configuring a master DNS, 99 percent of your machines will only be DNS *clients*. These take much less to set up, but be aware that even though your machine may be a client, unless you have made sure that it is properly configured via the *Name Resolution Order*, you may never actually get around to asking the DNS any questions. To configure name resolution, see 9.8.6, "Name resolution order" on page 333.

You need to follow the steps given below to configure the DNS client:

1. Create /etc/resolv.conf. This file looks like the Example 9-38. You need to specify the names server and the domain name in this file.

Example 9-38   /etc/resolv.conf for DNS client

```
nameserver      10.1.2.1
domain  itso.com
```

nameserver	This is the name/IP address that this client will contact for DNS services. There can be three of these lines. The first nameserver will be attempted if it has a time out, then the others will be attempted in the same manner.
domain	This is the default domain that will be added to any unqualified query.
Other Options	There are more options possible in resolv.conf. Please see the resolv.conf man page.

2. In HP-UX 11i, you need to edit/create the /etc/nsswitch.conf and modify the line containing the hosts entry. After modifying it, the line should look similar to:

```
hosts: files dns
```

In AIX 5L, the equivalent file is /etc/netsvc.conf.

More details are in 9.8.6, "Name resolution order" on page 333.

Make sure that resolv.conf is readable, as only the people who can read it will be able to query the DNS.

For those who like SMITTY, it also has the ability to configure the resolv.conf file; just type **smitty resolv.conf**.

9.8.5 Querying and debugging DNS clients

There are many useful tools for performing DNS queries; a couple are mentioned below.

The nslookup command

nslookup is a DNS program that can be used as a debugging tool. **nslookup** directly queries the name server. It is helpful in:

► Determining if a name server is running
► Determining if it is properly configured
► Querying the IP address or name of a host

You can run the **nslookup** command in interactive or non-interactive mode.

Let us see some examples of the **nslookup** command. Please note that there are differences between the HP-UX and AIX 5L **nslookup** command-line options, but for simple queries you will not notice any difference.

Example 9-39 shows the non-interactive way of running the **nslookup** command.

Example 9-39   nslookup in a non-interactive way

```
#nslookup itsocl1
Server:  itsomaster.itso.com
Address:  10.1.2.1

Name:    itsocl1.itso.com
Address:  10.1.2.3
```

To run **nslookup** in an interactive way, just type **nslookup** on the command line and press Enter. At the > prompt, you can query the hostname or IP address.

Example 9-40 shows the interactive way of running the **nslookup** command.

Example 9-40 nslookup in an interactive way

```
#nslookup
Default Server: itsomaster.itso.com
Address:  10.1.2.1

> itsocl1
Server:  itsomaster.itso.com
Address:  10.1.2.1

Name:    itsocl1.itso.com
Address:  10.1.2.3

> 10.1.2.2
Server:  itsomaster.itso.com
Address:  10.1.2.1

Name:    itsoslave.itso.com
Address:  10.1.2.2
```

The dig command

The **dig** command is the *Domain Information Groper* (according to the man page). By default, HP-UX does not have **dig** installed, though it comes with the BIND9 installation. AIX 5L, on the other hand, already comes with **dig**.

The description in Example 9-41 is straight from the HP-UX **dig** man page.

Example 9-41 HP-UX dig man page extract

```
        dig (domain information groper) is a flexible tool for interrogating
        Domain Name System (DNS) servers.  It performs DNS lookups and
        displays the answers that are returned from the name server(s) that
        were queried.  Most DNS administrators use dig to troubleshoot DNS
        problems because of its flexibility, ease of use, and clarity of
        output.  The dig command has two modes: simple command-line mode for
        single or multiple queries and batch mode for reading lookup requests
        from a file.
```

A very simple example of using **dig** is shown in Example 9-42.

Example 9-42 dig example

```
 dig  itsomaster.itso.com
; <<>> DiG 9.2.0 <<>> itsomaster.itso.com
;; global options:  printcmd
;; Got answer:
```

```
;; ->>HEADER<<- opcode: QUERY, status: NOERROR, id: 43363
;; flags: qr aa rd ra; QUERY: 1, ANSWER: 1, AUTHORITY: 1, ADDITIONAL: 1
;; QUESTION SECTION:
;itsomaster.itso.com.           IN      A

;; ANSWER SECTION:
itsomaster.itso.com.    86400   IN      A       10.1.2.1

;; AUTHORITY SECTION:
itso.com.               86400   IN      NS      itsomaster.itso.com.

;; ADDITIONAL SECTION:
itsomaster.itso.com.    86400   IN      A       10.1.2.1

;; Query time: 1 msec
;; SERVER: 127.0.0.1#53(127.0.0.1)
;; WHEN: Wed Jun 29 18:02:30 2005
;; MSG SIZE  rcvd: 91
```

The nsquery command - HP-UX only

HP-UX comes with a useful command called **nsquery**. This command allows you to override the name resolution order as specified by /etc/nsswitch.conf and try different resolution schemes.

The equivalent sort of functionality is available in AIX 5L by setting the NSORDER environment variable.

9.8.6 Name resolution order

HP-UX and AIX 5L both handle the name resolution order in slightly different ways. HP-UX uses a file called /etc/nsswitch.conf, while AIX 5L uses a file called /etc/netsvc.conf (*or* an NSORDER variable can override this).

The default search order for HP-UX and AIX 5L (if the configuration files do not exist) are also different.

Table 9-3 Default name resolution order

HP-UX	AIX 5L
nis [NOTFOUND=return] files	bind,nis,hosts

As you can see from Table 9-3, on HP-UX, if you just created a /etc/resolv.conf, by default, it would never be used. If you did the same on AIX 5L, it will be the first method used.

It is often useful, from a general administration point of view, to change the default resolution order, such that the hosts file can override the enterprise name resolution. This allows a system administrator a bit more flexibility for possibly choosing particular local interfaces to hosts and can help during troubleshooting connectivity issues.

Name resolution order in HP-UX

In HP-UX, the default name resolution order can be overridden by creating the /etc/nsswitch.conf configuration file and specifying the desired order.

Example 9-43   HP-UX example of /etc/nsswitch.conf

```
hosts:        dns [NOTFOUND=return] nis [NOTFOUND=return] files
```

In the above example, the DNS (as specified by /etc/resolv.conf) will first be queried. If it is unavailable, then NIS will get a go. If it is unavailable, then lastly we will check the local /etc/hosts file.

Name resolution order in AIX 5L

In AIX 5L Version 5.x, the default name resolution order can be overridden by creating the /etc/netsvc.conf configuration file and specifying the desired order. Here is an example:

```
hosts=bind,local
```

The above example shows that the local network is a domain network using a name server for name resolution and an /etc/hosts file for backup.

If the NSORDER environment variable set, it will override the /etc/netsvc.conf file and the default name resolution order. Here is the example of the NSORDER variable:

```
NSORDER=nis=auth,bind,local
```

The above example shows NIS as authoritative will be queried first. The other services will not be queried even if NIS cannot resolve the name. The DNS or /etc/hosts file will be queried only if NIS is not available.

9.9 Quick reference

Table 9-4 on page 335 shows a comparison between AIX 5L and HP-UX for network commands.

Table 9-4   Quick reference for network management

Tasks	AIX 5L	HP-UX 11i
Run multiple tasks in a GUI environment.	Choose one of the following: ► The `smitty tcpip` fast path ► smitty ► `wsm`	SAM
Configure TCP/IP.	`mktcpip`	Editing all of the following: ► /etc/hosts ► /etc/rc.config.d/netconf ► /etc/rc.cofig.d/<appropriate hw config file>
Display interface settings.	`ifconfig`	`ifconfig`
Configure interface.	`ifconfig, chdev`	`ifconfig`
Change name service.	`chnamsv`	Edit /etc/nsswitch.conf
Unconfigure name service.	`rmnamsv`	Edit /etc/nsswitch.conf

Display name service.	`lsnamsv`
	or
	`cat /etc/resolv.conf`
		`cat /etc/nsswitch.conf`

Configure hostname resolution order.	`vi /etc/netsvc.conf` or NSORDER environment variable	`vi /etc/nsswitch.conf`

Tune network parameters.	`smitty TunNo`
	or
	`/usr/sbin/no`
		`ndd` (run time only)
		and
		`/etc/rc.config.d/nddconf`

Hostname lookups.	`nslookup, dig, host`	`nslookup`
		`dig` (if BIND9 installed)
		`nsquery`

Exporting/unexporting a file system via NFS.	`exportfs, share, shareall, unshare, unshareall`	`exportfs`
Enabling NFS.	`mknfs`	`edit` `/etc/rc.config.d/nfsconf`

Tasks	AIX 5L	HP-UX 11i
Disabling NFS.	**rmnfs**	edit /etc/rc.config.d/nfsconf
Mounting an NFS file system.	**mount** /etc/filesystems	**mount** /etc/fstab
Configure host entries.	**hostent** *or* modify /etc/hosts	**/etc/hosts**
Convert config from BIND 4.	**/usr/samples/tcpip/named-bootconf.pl**	**/usr/bin/named-bootconf.pl**

User management

This chapter provides guidelines and planning information for managing user accounts and groups. It includes information about the files used to store user account and group information and about customizing the user's work environment. Basic differences between HP-UX and AIX 5L are described and the important files are referenced.

The following topics are covered:

10.1 Overview

One of the basic system administration tasks is to set up a user account for each user. A typical user account includes the information a user needs to log in and use a system. User account information consists of five main components:

User name

A unique name that an user needs to log in to a system. It is also known as a login name.

Password

A secret combination of characters that a user must enter along with his user name to gain access to a system.

Home directory

Every user must have a directory designated especially to him. This is typically the user's current directory at login. The user should have full permissions to access that directory and the files it may contain.

Initialization files

These are typically shell scripts that control how the user's working environment is set up when a user logs in to a system. There are system-wide environment files as well as a user's own files, usually located in the user's home directory.

Group

User groups should be made for people who need to share files on the system, such as people who work in the same department or people who are working on the same project. In general, create as few user groups as possible. Usually, there are some system-defined and system administrator groups, but it is always a good idea to create your own groups for managing user accounts.

User accounts, their passwords, and groups are fundamentals of system security, so it is very important to have them set properly. User management policy is also considered a part of system security policy. When we think about user management, we usually mean the following tasks and issues:

- Adding users
- Removing users
- Listing users
- Changing users' passwords and other attributes
- User and system-wide environment files
- Password files
- Profile template
- Defining system resource limits for users
- Configuration information for user authentication
- Working with groups

All of these points are described below. Also, a comparison between HP-UX and AIX 5L regarding these topics is made and a quick reference is given.

You have a variety of tools for managing user accounts and groups in both HP-UX and AIX 5L operating systems.

In HP-UX, you can use the following options for user and group management:

► System Administration Manager SAM (GUI)
► Command-line based management

The following list includes the commands used for user administration in HP-UX:

`useradd`	Creates a new user login on the system
`passwd`	Changes the user login password and attributes
`usermod`	Changes the user login attributes
`logins`	Displays system and user login data
`listusers`	Lists users login details
`userdel`	Removes a user login from its home directory
`who`	Identifies the users currently logged in
`groupadd`	Creates a new group on the system
`groupmod`	Modifies a group on the system
`groupdel`	Removes a group from the system

In AIX 5L, you have the following tools:

► Web-based System Manager
► SMIT
► Command-line based management

Figure 10-1 on page 340 shows the Web-based System Manager menu that should be used for managing users and groups. Using this menu, you can perform most of the tasks related to user management.

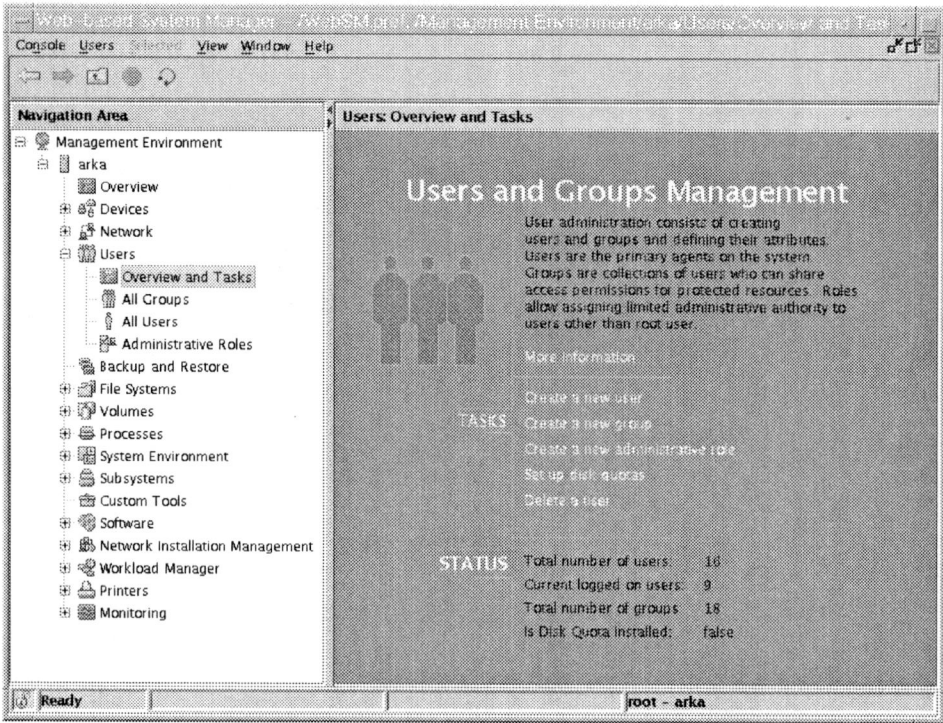

Figure 10-1   Web-based System Manager users and groups management

The following list includes the most important commands used for user administration in AIX 5L:

mkuser	Creates a new user account
passwd	Creates or changes the password of a user
chuser	Changes user attributes (except password)
lsuser	Lists user attributes
rmuser	Removes a user and its attributes
chsec	Changes security attributes in the configuration files
login	Initiates a user session
who	Identifies the users currently logged in
dtconfig	Enables or disables the desktop autostart feature

The differences are the tools and commands available in both systems to perform these tasks. The basic functionality of the commands is similar.

10.2 Adding users

This section describes how to manage users in HP-UX and AIX 5L.

In HP-UX

To add a new user login in HP-UX, you do following:

1. Start the SAM application.

2. Go into Accounts for Users and Groups.

3. Go into Users. Select **Add**.

4. Fill in all the new user login details.

5. Select **OK**.

6. Select the option to force the change of the password at the next login.

7. Choose a password for the new login.

SAM can be configured to allow specific non-root users to do user management. This is done by assigning the Accounts for Users and Groups function using *Restricted SAM*. These users would then only have access to this function in SAM, allowing them to perform all the user and group management tasks. Refer to the *sam (1M) manual page* for further details.

The HP-UX **useradd** and **groupadd** commands can also be used to create user logins and groups on the system. The example below shows how to create a new user login from the command line:

```
useradd -g resgroup -s /usr/bin/ksh -c "Hess Waltman Tel-241498" -m hessw
```

The **useradd** command with only the -D option displays the default values that will be used when creating a new user login. The values displayed are group, home directory, shell, skeleton directory, inactive, and expire. These values can be modified with the **useradd** command so that new logins will be created with the changed values. Below are some examples:

```
# useradd -D
GROUPID  20
BASEDIR  /home
SKEL     /etc/skel
SHELL    /sbin/sh
INACTIVE -1
EXPIRE
```

The above displays the current default values used when creating a new user login, if not specified on the command line.

```
# useradd -D -b /prod/home
```

The above command changes the default value for the home directory to /prod/home. This will apply to new user logins created. The file that is updated and stores the default values is /etc/default/useradd.

In AIX 5L

In AIX 5L, the **mkuser** command creates a new user account. The name parameter, by default, must be a unique 8-byte or less string. However, from AIX 5L Version 5.3, its length is configurable with the **chdev** command. By default, the **mkuser** command creates a standard user account. To create an administrative user account, specify the -a flag. The **mkuser** command does not create password information for a user; therefore, the new accounts are disabled until the **passwd** command is used to add authentication information to the /etc/security/passwd file. The **mkuser** command only initializes the Password attribute of /etc/passwd file with an asterisk (*).

Here are some possible options:

▶ To create the smith account with smith as an administrator, enter:

```
mkuser -a annie
```

You must be the root user to create smith as an administrative user.

▶ To create the smith user account and set the su attribute to a value of false, enter:

```
mkuser su=false annie
```

▶ To create a user account, smith, with the default values in the /usr/lib/security/mkuser.default file, enter:

```
mkuser smith
```

> **Tip:** In AIX 5L, you can also use the **useradd** command to add a new user account. The syntax of the command is exactly the same as in HP-UX.

Alternatively, you can use SMIT:

a. Run **smitty mkuser** to access the menu, as shown in Example 10-1.

b. Type annie for the field User NAME.

c. Press the Enter key to create the user.

d. When SMIT returns an OK prompt, press the F10 key to return to the command prompt.

Example 10-1   Adding a user

```
                             Add a User

Type or select values in entry fields.
```

Press Enter AFTER making all desired changes.

```
[TOP]                                            [Entry Fields]
* User NAME                                      [annie]
  User ID                                        []
  ADMINISTRATIVE USER?                           false              +
  Primary GROUP                                  []                 +
  Group SET                                      []                 +
  ADMINISTRATIVE GROUPS                          []                 +
  ROLES                                          []                 +
  Another user can SU TO USER?                   true               +
  SU GROUPS                                      [ALL]              +
  HOME directory                                 []
  Initial PROGRAM                                []
  User INFORMATION                               []
  EXPIRATION date (MMDDhhmmyy)                    [0]
[MORE...37]


F1=Help          F2=Refresh        F3=Cancel          F4=List
F5=Reset         F6=Command        F7=Edit            F8=Image
F9=Shell         F10=Exit          Enter=Do
```

10.3 Removing users

This section discusses how to remove users in HP-UX and AIX 5L.

In HP-UX

To delete a user login in HP-UX, do the following:

1. Start the SAM application.

2. Go into Accounts for Users and Groups.

3. Go into Users and select the specific user login.

4. From the Actions menu, select **Remove** and press Enter.

5. Choose an option to delete, leave, or transfer the user files and directories.

6. Select **OK** and **Yes** to continue.

You can also use the **userdel** command to remove the user login. The -r option removes the home directory of the user. An example of using the **userdel** command to delete existing user account follows:

```
userdel -r annie
```

In AIX 5L

In AIX 5L, the **rmuser** command removes the user account identified by the Name parameter. This command removes a user's attributes without removing the user's home directory and files. The user name must already exist as a string of eight bytes or less. If the -p flag is specified, the **rmuser** command also removes passwords and other user authentication information from the /etc/security/passwd file.

Only the root user can remove administrative users.

The following example shows the use of the **rmuser** command to remove a user account smith and its attributes from the local system:

```
rmuser annie
```

To remove the user smith account and all its attributes, including passwords and other user authentication information in the /etc/security/passwd file, use the following command:

```
rmuser -p annie
```

> **Tip:** In AIX 5L, you can also use the **userdel** command to remove the user's account. The syntax is exactly the same as in HP-UX.

Alternatively, you can go through the SMIT hierarchy by performing these steps:

1. Running **smitty rmuser** will open a menu, as shown in Example 10-2.
2. Type annie for the field User NAME.
3. Press the Enter key.
4. When SMIT returns an OK prompt, press the F10 key to return to the command prompt.

Example 10-2   Removing a user

```
                       Remove a User from the System

Type or select values in entry fields.
Press Enter AFTER making all desired changes.

                                                     [Entry Fields]
* User NAME                                          [annie]               +
  Remove AUTHENTICATION information?                 yes                   +


F1=Help              F2=Refresh           F3=Cancel            F4=List
F5=Reset             F6=Command           F7=Edit              F8=Image
```

10.4 Displaying currently logged in users

To achieve this task in HP-UX, you can simply use the **who** or **w** commands.

Example 10-3   who command

```
# who
root        pts/ta      Jun 30 09:36
root        pts/tc      Jun 29 12:07
root        pts/td      Jun 27 11:57
maryanne    pts/te      Jun 29 16:15
tommy       pts/tf      Jun 29 17:13
annie       pts/tg      Jun 29 17:15
```

These two commands produce output similar to Example 10-3 and Example 10-4.

Example 10-4   w command

```
# w
  9:42am  up 9 days, 17:26,  6 users,  load average: 0.27, 0.26, 0.26
User      tty           login@  idle  JCPU  PCPU  what
root      pts/ta        9:36am    2                more -s
root      pts/tc        12:07pm  14                more 11iRelNotes.txt
root      pts/td        11:57am   1                w
maryanne  pts/te        4:15pm  17:26              sh
tommy     pts/tf        5:13pm  16:29              -ksh
annie     pts/tg        5:15pm  16:20              -ksh
```

From the output, you can get information about:

► The user name of the logged-in user
► The terminal line of the logged-in user
► The date and time the user logged in
► The hostname if a user is logged in from a remote system (optional)

In AIX 5L, they are exactly the same commands. Their functionality is also the same. The **who** command displays information about all users currently on the local system. The following information is displayed:

► Login name
► tty
► The date and time of login

Entering **who am i** or **who am I** displays your login name, tty, and the date and time you logged in. If the user is logged in from a remote machine, then the hostname of that machine is displayed as well. The **who** command can also display the elapsed time since the line activity occurred; the process ID of the command interpreter (shell), logins, logoffs, restarts; and changes to the system clock, as well as other processes generated by the initialization process.

> **Note:** The /etc/utmp file contains a record of users logged into the system. The **who -a** command processes the /etc/utmp file, and if this file is corrupted or missing, no output is generated from the **who** command.

The following examples show the usage of the **who** command with various flags:

▶ The following example shows the command used to display information about all the users who are logged on to the system:

```
[p650n04][/]> who
root        pts/0       Jun 28 13:06        (tot198.itso.ibm.com)
root        pts/1       Jun 29 12:26        (frl14p.itso.ibm.com)
root        pts/2       Jun 28 14:18        (tot198.itso.ibm.com)
root        pts/3       Jun 28 16:30        (frl14p.itso.ibm.com)
annie       pts/4       Jun 29 12:53        (frl14p.itso.ibm.com)
```

▶ The following example shows the command used to display your user name:

```
# who am I
root        pts/3       Jun 28 16:30        (frl14p.itso.ibm.com)
```

▶ The following example shows how to display the run-level of the local system:

```
# who -r
    .           run-level 2 Jun 28 13:05        2    0    S
```

10.5 Changing users, passwords, and other attributes

In HP-UX, the following are some of the tasks for changing user login attributes:

▶ Change the user's password.
▶ Disable a user's account.
▶ Change password aging for a user account.
▶ Change a user's login shell.
▶ Change a user's primary or secondary group.

In AIX 5L, you have a variety of options to choose from when changing a user's attributes. You may choose any of the above plus the following options:

▶ Make a user an administrative user by setting the admin attribute to true.
▶ Change any attributes of an administrative user.

> ► Add a user to an administrative group.

10.5.1 Changing a user's password

This section describes how to change a user's password in HP-UX and AIX 5L.

In HP-UX

In HP-UX, this goal may be achieved in two ways. The first way is using SAM.

1. Start the SAM application.

2. Go into Accounts for Users and Groups.

3. Go into Users and select the specific user login.

4. From the Actions menu, select **Modify User's Password** and press Enter.

5. Type the new password twice when prompted.

The second way of changing a user's password in HP-UX is using the **passwd** command, as shown in the following example:

```
# passwd annie
Changing password for annie
New password:
Re-enter new password:
Passwd successfully changed
#
```

In AIX 5L

In AIX 5L, the **passwd** command will create an encrypted passwd entry in /etc/security/passwd and change the password attribute of /etc/passwd from an asterisk (*) to an exclamation point (!). Some examples are:

► To change your full name in the /etc/passwd file, enter:

```
# passwd -f smith
```

The **passwd** command displays the name stored for your user ID. For example, for login name smith, the **passwd** command could display the message shown in the following example:

```
# passwd -f annie
 annie's current gecos:
            " "
 Change (yes) or (no)? > n
 Gecos information not changed.
```

If you enter a Y for yes, the **passwd** command prompts you for the new name. The **passwd** command records the name you enter in the /etc/passwd file.

► To change your password, enter passwd.

The **passwd** command prompts you for your old password, if it exists and if you are not the root user. After you enter the old password, the command prompts you twice for the new password.

▶ You can also use **pwdadm**. The **pwdadm** command administers users' passwords. The root user or a member of the security group can supply or change the password of the user specified by the User parameter. The invoker of the command must provide a password when queried before being allowed to change the other user's password. When the command executes, it sets the ADMCHG attribute. This forces the user to change the password the next time a **login** command or an **su** command is given for the user. Only the root user, a member of the security group, or a user with PasswdAdmin authorization can supply or change the password of the user specified by the User parameter. When this command is executed, the password field for the user in the /etc/passwd file is set to an exclamation point (!), indicating that an encrypted version of the password is in the /etc/security/passwd file. The ADMCHG attribute is set when the root user or a member of the security group changes a user's password with the **pwdadm** command. The following example shows how to set a password for user harrison, a member of the security group:

```
pwdadm harrison
```

When prompted, the user who invoked the command is prompted for a password before smith's password can be changed.

▶ Alternatively, you can use SMIT:

a. Running **smitty passwd** will open a menu, as shown in Example 10-5.

Example 10-5 Changing a user password

```
                        Change a User's Password

Type or select values in entry fields.
Press Enter AFTER making all desired changes.

                                                    [Entry Fields]
    User NAME                                       [harrison]
+



F1=Help            F2=Refresh         F3=Cancel         F4=List
F5=Reset           F6=Command         F7=Edit           F8=Image
F9=Shell           F10=Exit           Enter=Do
```

b. Type harrison for the field User NAME.

c. Press Enter, and you will be prompted to enter the new password (twice), as shown in Example 10-6.

Example 10-6   Entering a user password

```
Changing password for "harrison"
harrison's New password:
Enter the new password again:
```

d. Enter the new password and press the Enter key.

e. When SMIT returns an OK prompt, press the F10 key to return to the command prompt.

10.5.2 Disabling a user account

The following section describes how to disable a user account in HP-UX and AIX 5L.

In HP-UX

In HP-UX, disabling a user account may be achieved in the following way:

1. Start the SAM application.

2. Go into Accounts for Users and Groups.

3. Go into Users and select the specific user login.

4. From the Actions menu, select **Deactivate** and press Enter.

5. Choose an option to delete, leave, or transfer the user files and directories.

6. Select **OK** and **Yes** to continue.

7. Verify that you have disabled the user account by attempting to log in with the disabled user account.

You can enable the user account by performing the above steps and selecting **Reactivate** in step 4 above and typing a new password when prompted.

You can also disable a user account by using the `passwd -1` *user_name* command.

In AIX 5L

In AIX 5L, you can lock or unlock a user account using one simple smitty menu. At the command prompt, type `smitty users`, then select Lock/Unlock a User's Account, select user name, and set "Is this user ACCOUNT LOCKED?" to true, as shown in Example 10-7 on page 350.

Example 10-7   Disabling a user's account

```
                  Lock / Unlock a User's Account

Type or select values in entry fields.
Press Enter AFTER making all desired changes.

                                              [Entry Fields]
  * User NAME                                 adm
    Is this user ACCOUNT LOCKED?              true                    +




F1=Help           F2=Refresh        F3=Cancel         F4=List
F5=Reset          F6=Command        F7=Edit           F8=Image
F9=Shell          F10=Exit          Enter=Do
```

10.5.3 Modifying a user account

This section describes how to modify a user account in HP-UX and AIX 5L.

In HP-UX

In HP-UX, modifying existing user logins can be done from the SAM Accounts for Users and Groups menu.

All the following can be done from this menu:

- ► Change the user's login name.
- ► Change the user ID for the user login.
- ► List current user attributes.
- ► Change the user's password.
- ► Disable a user's account.
- ► Change a user's description (comment).
- ► Change the password aging for a user account.
- ► Change a user's login shell.
- ► Change a user's home directory.
- ► Change a user's primary or secondary group.
- ► Change the password aging for the account.

Using the command line, you can also list and modify the user's attributes. For listing users and their attributes, you can use two commands, the **logins** and **listusers** commands, which displays user login information. The syntax of the commands and an example follow:

```
logins [-admopstux] [-g groups] [-l logins]
```

Example 10-8   logins command

```
# logins
nobody        -2     nogroup     -2
root          0      sys         3
daemon        1      daemon      5
bin           2      bin         2
sys           3      sys         3
adm           4      adm         4
uucp          5      sys         3
lp            9      lp          7
nuucp         11     nuucp       11
hpdb          27     other       1      ALLBASE
www           30     other       1
webadmin      40     other       1
mysql         102    mysql       102
maryanne      103    users       20     Test Mary,Brazil,1817,2094
tommy         104    resgroup    103    Tom Da,Pok,897,890
hessw         106    resgroup    103    Hess Waltman Building C
annieh        987    resgroup    103    annie,,,
```

The **logins** command displays some useful user and system login details. The command is executed without flags. In Example 10-8, the login command executed without any flags, displays the user login, UID, group name, group ID, and the user login information. Some of the options for the command are briefly described:

a   Displays the user expiration information

p   Displays logins with no passwords

u   Displays only user logins

s   Displays only system logins

x   Displays extended user login details

d   Displays logins with duplicate user IDs

For the use of the other options and further details on the logins command, refer the *logins (1M) manual page.*

```
listusers [ -g groups ]   [ -l logins ]
```

Example 10-9   listusers command

```
# listusers
annieh         annie,,,
hessw          Hess Waltman Building C Tel-241498
maryanne       Test Mary,Brazil,1817,2094
mysql
```

Executed without any options (Example 10-9 on page 351), the **listusers** command lists all user logins sorted by login. For a detailed description of available options, please refer to the *listusers man page* for this command.

You can use the **usermod** command to modify an existing user account. The usermod utility modifies a user's login definition on the system. It changes the definition of the specified login and makes the appropriate login-related system file and file system changes. The syntax of the **usermod** command looks like the following lines:

```
usermod [-u uid [-o] ] [-g group] [-G group [, group...]]
        [-d dir [-m] ] [-s shell] [-c comment] [-f inactive]
        [-l new_logname] [-e expire]  login
```

For example:

► To change the home directory of user annie to /export/home/annie_new and move the contents of the original directory, type:

```
usermod -d /export/home/annie_new -m annie
```

► To change user annie shell to /bin/ksh, type:

```
usermod -s /bin/ksh annie
```

In AIX 5L

In AIX 5L, there are two separate menus for displaying and changing users' attributes. They are shown later in this section.

The **lsuser** command displays the user account attributes. This is similar to the **logins** command in HP-UX. You can use this command to list all attributes of all of the users or all the attributes of specific users except their passwords. Since there is no default parameter, you must enter the ALL keywords to see the attributes of all the users. By default, the **lsuser** command displays all user attributes. To view selected attributes, use the -a List flag. If one or more attributes cannot be read, the **lsuser** command lists as much information as possible.

> **Note:** If you have a Network Information Service (NIS) database installed on your system, some user information may not appear when you use the **lsuser** command.

By default, the `lsuser` command lists each user's attributes on one line. It displays attribute information as Attribute=Value definitions, each separated by a blank space. To list the user attributes in stanza format, use the -f flag. To list the information as colon-separated records, use the -c flag.

The following examples show the use of the `lsuser` command with various flags:

► To display the user ID and group-related information for the root account in stanza form, enter:

```
# lsuser -f -a id pgrp home root
root:
        id=0
        pgrp=system
        home=/
```

► To display the user ID, groups, and home directory of user annie in colon format, enter:

```
# lsuser -c -a id home groups annie
```

► To display all the attributes of user annie in the default format, enter:

```
# lsuser annie
```

All the attribute information appears with each attribute separated by a blank space.

► To display all the attributes of all the users, enter:

```
# lsuser ALL
```

All the attribute information appears with each attribute separated by a blank space.

► Alternatively, you can use SMIT:

a. Run `smitty lsuser`, which will produce the menu shown in Example 10-10.

b. When SMIT returns an OK prompt, press the F10 key to return to the command prompt.

Example 10-10   Listing users attributes

```
                        COMMAND STATUS

Command: OK          stdout: yes          stderr: no

Before command completion, additional instructions may appear below.

[TOP]
root     0       /
daemon   1       /etc
bin      2       /bin
```

```
sys       3        /usr/sys
adm       4        /var/adm
uucp      5        /usr/lib/uucp
guest     100      /home/guest
nobody    -2       /
lpd       9        /
lp        11       /var/spool/lp
invscout           200      /var/adm/invscout
snapp     201      /usr/sbin/snapp
nuucp     6        /var/spool/uucppublic
ipsec     202      /etc/ipsec
sshd      204      /var/empty
rootgwm   0        /home/rootgwm
annie     207      /home/annie
harrison           7        /home/harrison
```

```
F1=Help        F2=Refresh      F3=Cancel      F6=Command
F8=Image       F9=Shell        F10=Exit       /=Find
n=Find Next
```

The **chuser** command changes attributes for the user identified by the Name parameter. The user name must already exist as an alphanumeric string of eight bytes or less.

> **Note:** Do not use the **chuser** command if you have a Network Information Service database installed on your system.

Only the root user can use the **chuser** command to perform the following tasks:

► Make a user an administrative user by setting the admin attribute to true.
► Change any attributes of an administrative user.
► Add a user to an administrative group.

The following examples show the use of the **chuser** command with various flags:

► To allow user smith to access this system remotely, enter:

    # chuser rlogin=true annie

► To change the date that user annie will expire to 5 p.m., 31 July, 2005, enter:

    # chuser expires=0731170005 annie

► To add annie to the group programmers, enter:

    # chuser groups=programmers annie

> **Tip:** In AIX 5L, you can also use the **usermod** command to modify a user's account. The syntax of the command is exactly the same as in HP-UX.

Alternatively, you can go through the SMIT hierarchy by:

a. Running **smitty chuser**, which will display the menu shown in Example 10-11.

b. Type annie for the User NAME field.

c. Use the arrow keys to highlight the Primary GROUP field and type programmers in it.

d. Press Enter.

e. When SMIT returns an OK prompt, press the F10 key to return to the command prompt.

Example 10-11   Changing user characteristics

```
                  Change / Show Characteristics of a User

Type or select values in entry fields.
Press Enter AFTER making all desired changes.

[TOP]                                              [Entry Fields]
* User NAME                                        annie
  User ID                                          [207]
#
  ADMINISTRATIVE USER?                             false                 +
  Primary GROUP                                    [staff]               +
  Group SET                                        [staff]               +
  ADMINISTRATIVE GROUPS                            []                    +
  ROLES                                            []                    +
  Another user can SU TO USER?                     true                  +
  SU GROUPS                                        [ALL]                 +
  HOME directory                                   [/home/annie]
  Initial PROGRAM                                  [/usr/bin/ksh]
  User INFORMATION                                 []
  EXPIRATION date (MMDDhhmmyy)                      [0]
[MORE...37]


F1=Help             F2=Refresh          F3=Cancel          F4=List
F5=Reset            F6=Command          F7=Edit            F8=Image
F9=Shell            F10=Exit            Enter=Do
```

10.6 Customizing a user's work environment

Providing user initialization files for the user's login shell is a part of a user's administration tasks. A user initialization file is usually a shell script that sets up a work environment for a user after the user logs in to a system. Basically, you can perform any task in a user initialization file that you can do in a shell script, but its primary job is to define the characteristics of a user's work environment, such as a user's search path, environment variables, and windowing environment. Depending on a login shell, different initialization file (or files) are used when a user logs into a system.

In HP-UX

In HP-UX, there are the following initialization files for different shells:

- ► For the POSIX shell: $HOME/.profile
- ► For the Bourne shell: $HOME/.profile
- ► For the C shell: $HOME/.cshrc and $HOME/.login
- ► For the Korn shell: $HOME/.profile and $HOME/$ENV

The HP-UX environment also provides default user initialization files for each shell in the /etc/skel directory on each system, as shown below:

- ► For the C shell: /etc/skel/login and /etc/skel/cshrc
- ► For the Bourne and Korn shells: /etc/skel/.profile

The user initialization files can be customized by both the administrator and the user. This feature can be accomplished with centrally located and globally distributed environment initialization files, called site initialization files. Site initialization files give you the ability to introduce new functionality to the user's work environment whenever you want to do so. However, the user is still able to customize his own initialization file located in the user's home directory.

When you reference a site initialization file in a user initialization file, all updates to the site initialization file are automatically reflected when the user logs in to the system or when a user starts a new shell.

Any customization that can be done in a user initialization file can also be done in a site initialization file. These files typically reside on a server (or set of servers), and appear as the first statement in a user initialization file. Also, each site initialization file must be the same type of shell script as the user initialization file that references it.

> **Tip:** It is always a good practice to reference site initialization files or files in a user initialization file.

In AIX 5L

The default shell is Korn shell on AIX 5L. In AIX 5L, the purpose of providing and using initialization files is exactly the same as in HP-UX. The only difference is in names and locations of the files. Most of the important initialization files in AIX 5L are listed below:

/etc/security/environ   Contains the environment attributes for users

/etc/environment	Specifies the basic environment for all processes
/etc/profile	Specifies additional environment settings for all users
$HOME/.profile	Specifies environment settings for specific user needs

10.6.1 /etc/security/environ

The /etc/security/environ file is an ASCII file that contains stanzas with the environment attributes for users. Each stanza is identified by a user name and contains attributes in the Attribute=Value form with a comma separating the attributes. Each line is ended by a new-line character, and each stanza is ended by an additional new-line character. If the environment attributes are not defined, the system uses the default values.

The `mkuser` command creates a user stanza in this file. The initialization of the attributes depends upon their values in the /usr/lib/security/mkuser.default file. The `chuser` command can change these attributes, and the `lsuser` command can display them. The `rmuser` command removes the entire record for a user.

A basic /etc/security/environ file is shown in the following example, which has no environment attributes defined; therefore, the system is using default values:

```
# pg /etc/security/environ
default:
root:
daemon:
bin:
sys:
adm:
uucp:
guest:
```

10.6.2 /etc/environment

The /etc/environment file contains variables specifying the basic environment for all processes. When a new process begins, the exec subroutine makes an array of strings available that have the form Name=Value. This array of strings is called the environment. Each name defined by one of the strings is called an environment variable or shell variable. Environment variables are examined when a command starts running.

The /etc/environment file is not a shell script. It should only contain data in Name=Value format, and should not contain shell commands. Trying to run commands from this file may cause failure of the initialization process.

When you log in, the system sets environment variables from the environment file before reading your login profile, .profile. The following variables are a few of the ones that make up part of the basic environment:

HOME
The full path name of the user login or HOME directory. The login program sets this to the directory specified in the /etc/passwd file.

LANG
The locale name currently in effect. The LANG variable is set in the /etc/environment file at installation time.

NLSPATH
The full path name for message catalogs.

PATH
The sequence of directories that commands (such as **sh**, **time**, **nice**, and **nohup**) search when looking for a command whose path name is incomplete. The directory names are separated by colons.

TZ
The time zone information. The TZ environment variable is set by the /etc/environment file.

> **Note:** Changing the time zone only affects processes that begin after the change is made. The init process only reads /etc/environment at startup; therefore, init and its child processes will not be aware of a change to TZ until the system is rebooted.

10.6.3 /etc/profile and $HOME/.profile

The /etc/profile file contains further environment variables, as well as any commands to run that apply to all users. Use the /etc/profile file to control variables such as:

► Export variables
► File creation mask (umask)
► Terminal types
► Mail messages to indicate when new mail has arrived

Commands to be included in /etc/profile should be appropriate for all users of the system. An example of a command that you may want all users to run when they log in is the **news** command.

The $HOME/.profile file allows you to customize your individual working environment. The .profile file also overrides commands and variables set in the /etc/profile file. Use the .profile file to control personal settings such as:

► Shells to open
► Default editor
► Default printer

- ► Prompt appearance
- ► Keyboard sound

10.7 Password files

In both HP-UX and AIX 5L, the purpose and location of password files is very similar. The files are located in the /etc directory. In HP-UX, the file is /etc/passwd. For AIX 5L, the basic two files are /etc/passwd and /etc/security/passwd.

In HP-UX

In HP-UX, if the default standard system security is used, then the /etc/passwd file is used to authenticate users when logging in.

The fields in the passwd file are separated by colons and the structure of every single line in the file appears as:

```
username:password:uid:gid:comment:home-directory:login-shell
```

For example:

```
hessw:*:106:103:Hess Waltman Building C Tel-241498:/home/hessw/tmp:/usr/bin/csh
```

Trusted system

HP-UX also has an optional trusted system, which provides additional security features. The system can be converted to a trusted system at any time and it is highly recommended that you use this among the other security features. It results in a more strict password and authentication system.

After conversion to a trusted system, a new protected database is created. The encrypted passwords from /etc/passwd are moved to the new protected database, replacing the password field with an asterisk (*).

The trusted system uses two password files for user logins and authentication. It uses /etc/passwd and /tcb/files/auth/, which is the protected database. Passwords are encrypted and stored in the users's protected database. The file format of a user protected database file is as follows:

```
/tcb/files/auth/user first char/user name
```

Shadow passwords

HP-UX also has a password security feature to increase system security, called HP-UX Shadow passwords. This comes shipped with HP-UX 11i v2 or can be downloaded for earlier versions from:

```
http://software.hp.com
```

This allows the encrypted passwords stored in /etc/passwd to be now be hidden and stored in the shadow file, /etc/shadow. This file is only accessible by privileged users.

In AIX 5L

In AIX 5L, the /etc/passwd file contains basic user attributes. This is an ASCII file that contains an entry for each user. Each entry defines the basic attributes applied to a user.

When you use the `mkuser` command to add a user to your system, the command updates the /etc/passwd file.

An entry in the /etc/passwd file has the following form with all the attributes separated by a colon (:):

```
Name:Password:UserID:PrincipleGroup:Gecos:HomeDirectory:Shell
```

Password attributes can contain an asterisk (*), indicating an incorrect password or an exclamation point (!), indicating that the password is in the /etc/security/passwd file. Under normal conditions, the field contains an exclamation point (!). If the field has an asterisk (*), and a password is required for user authentication, the user cannot log in.

The shell attribute specifies the initial program or shell (login shell) that is started after a user invokes the `login` command or **su** command. The Korn shell is the standard operating system login shell and is backwardly compatible with the Bourne shell. If a user does not have a defined shell (/usr/bin/sh), the system default shell (Bourne shell) is used. The Bourne shell is a subset of the Korn shell.

The `mkuser` command adds new entries to the /etc/passwd file and fills in the attribute values as defined in the /usr/lib/security/mkuser.default file. The Password attribute is always initialized to an asterisk (*), which is an invalid password. You can set the password with the **passwd** or **pwdadm** commands. When the password is changed, an exclamation point (!) is added to the /etc/passwd file, indicating that the encrypted password is in the /etc/security/passwd file.

Use the **chuser** command to change all user attributes except the password. The **chfn** command and the **chsh** command change the Gecos attribute and Shell attribute, respectively. To display all the attributes in this file, use the **lsuser** command. To remove a user and all the user's attributes, use the **rmuser** command.

Example 10-12 shows a sample listing of the /etc/passwd file.

Example 10-12   Contents of /etc/passwd file

```
# cat /etc/passwd
root:!:0:0::/:/usr/bin/ksh
daemon:!:1:1::/etc:
bin:!:2:2::/bin:
sys:!:3:3::/usr/sys:
adm:!:4:4::/var/adm:
uucp:!:5:5::/usr/lib/uucp:
guest:!:100:100::/home/guest:
nobody:!:4294967294:4294967294::/:
lpd:!:9:4294967294::/:
lp:*:11:11::/var/spool/lp:/bin/false
invscout:*:200:1::/var/adm/invscout:/usr/bin/ksh
snapp:*:201:12:snapp login user:/usr/sbin/snapp:/usr/sbin/snappd
nuucp:*:6:5:uucp login user:/var/spool/uucppublic:/usr/sbin/uucp/uucico
ipsec:*:202:1::/etc/ipsec:/usr/bin/ksh
sshd:*:204:202::/var/empty:/usr/bin/ksh
rootgwm:!:0:0:Geoffs root:/home/rootgwm:/usr/bin/ksh
annie:!:207:1::/home/annie:/usr/bin/ksh
harrison:!:7:7::/home/harrison:/usr/bin/ksh
```

The /etc/security/passwd file is an ASCII file that contains stanzas with password information. Each stanza is identified by a user name followed by a colon (:) and contains attributes in the form Attribute=Value. Each attribute is ended with a new line character, and each stanza is ended with an additional new line character.

Although each user name must be in the /etc/passwd file, it is not necessary to have each user name listed in the /etc/security/passwd file. A typical file would have contents similar to the one shown in Example 10-13.

Example 10-13   Contents of /etc/security/passwd file

```
# cat /etc/security/passwd
root:
        password = tnYdhjq5G2h.2
        lastupdate = 1109024627
        flags =
```

```
daemon:
        password = *

bin:
        password = *

sys:
        password = *

adm:
        password = *

uucp:
        password = *

guest:
        password = *

nobody:
        password = *

lpd:
        password = *

rootgwm:
        password = wPjXpBf37o4ug
        lastupdate = 1118773810

annie:
        password = umnq7ZK2LqfcQ
        lastupdate = 1120069466
        flags = ADMCHG

harrison:
        password = 2FZQSTgsnTP5g
        lastupdate = 1120069844
        flags = ADMCHG
```

10.8 Administering groups

A group is a collection of users who can share access permissions for protected resources. A group is usually known as a UNIX group.

Each group must have a name, a group identification (GID) number, and a list of user names that belong to the group. A GID identifies the group internally to the system.

The two types of groups that a user can belong to are:

Primary group   Specifies a group that the operating system assigns to files created by the user. Each user must belong to a primary group.

Secondary groups   Specifies one or more groups to which a user also belongs.

In AIX 5L, there are three types of groups:

User group   User groups should be made for people who need to share files on the system, such as people who work in the same department or people who are working on the same project. In general, create as few user groups as possible.

System administrator groups   System administrator groups correspond to the SYSTEM group. SYSTEM group membership allows an administrator to perform some system maintenance tasks without having to operate with root authority.

System-defined groups   There are several system-defined groups. The STAFF group is the default group for all non-administrative users created in the system. You can change the default group by using the **chsec** command to edit the /usr/lib/security/mkuser.default file. The SECURITY group is a system-defined group having limited privileges for performing security administration.

In both HP-UX and AIX 5L systems, the **groups** command lists the groups that a user belongs to. A user can have only one primary group at a time. However, the user can temporarily change the user's primary group with the **newgrp** command to any other group in which the user is a member.

When adding a user account, you must assign a primary group for a user or accept the default, which is the staff group. The primary group should already exist (if it does not exist, specify the group by a GID number). Group information can be managed through local files or name service table and maps. In the case of local files, they are usually located in the /etc directory.

In HP-UX, it is the /etc/group file. The fields in each line of the group file are separated by colons, so the structure of each line looks like following:

```
group-name:group-password:gid:user-list
```

For example:

```
adm::4:root,adm,adm
```

Generally, you use SAM or the command line for groups administration related tasks in HP-UX.

In AIX 5L, you can use the **smitty groups** fast path. It opens the screen shown in Example 10-14.

Example 10-14   Smitty groups menu

```
                              Groups

Move cursor to desired item and press Enter.

  List All Groups
  Add a Group
  Change / Show Characteristics of a Group
  Remove a Group



F1=Help              F2=Refresh           F3=Cancel            F8=Image
F9=Shell             F10=Exit             Enter=Do
```

In AIX 5L, there are two files related to groups administration: /etc/group and /etc/security/group.

10.8.1 Adding a group

The following section introduces how to add a group in HP-UX and AIX 5L.

In HP-UX

In HP-UX, you can use SAM to add a new group definition. Follow these steps:

1. Start the SAM application.

2. Go into Accounts for Users and Groups.

3. Go into Groups.

4. From the Actions menu, select **Add** and press Enter.

5. Type the new group name and group ID.

6. Type a group ID or keep the system-assigned ID.

7. Select the users to add to the new group.

8. Select **OK**.

The list of groups displayed in the Groups window is updated to include the new group.

Alternatively, you can use the **groupadd** command. The **groupadd** command creates a new group definition on the system by adding the appropriate entry to the /etc/group file. The syntax is very simple:

```
groupadd [ -g gid [ -o ] ] group
```

For example:

```
groupadd -g 150 res_users
```

In AIX 5L

In AIX 5L, type `smitty mkgroup` at the command prompt to add a new group. The menu shown in Example 10-15 should appear on your screen.

Example 10-15   Creating a new group

```
                              Add a Group

Type or select values in entry fields.
Press Enter AFTER making all desired changes.

                                               [Entry Fields]
* Group NAME                                   [res_users]
  ADMINISTRATIVE group?                         false                  +
  Group ID                                     [150]                   #
  USER list                                    [annie]                 +
  ADMINISTRATOR list                           [annie,harrison]        +
  Projects                                     []                      +

F1=Help            F2=Refresh         F3=Cancel         F4=List
F5=Reset           F6=Command         F7=Edit           F8=Image
F9=Shell           F10=Exit           Enter=Do
```

Fill in all the necessary information and then press Enter.

Alternatively, you can use the **mkgroup** command. Examples of using this command follow:

▶ To create a new group account called finance, type:

```
# mkgroup finance
```

► To create a new administrative group account called payroll, type:

```
# mkgroup -a payroll
```

Only the root user can issue this command.

► To create a new group account called managers and set yourself as the administrator, type:

```
# mkgroup -A managers
```

► To create a new group account called managers and set the list of administrators to steve and mike, type:

```
# mkgroup adms=steve,mike managers
```

10.8.2 Modifying an existing group

In this section we describe how to modify an existing group in HP-UX or AIX 5L.

In HP-UX

In HP-UX, you can use SAM to modify an existing group. Follow these steps:

1. Start the SAM application.
2. Go into Accounts for Users and Groups.
3. Go into Groups.
4. From the Actions menu, select **Modify** and press Enter.
5. Change the group name or ID.
6. Use the Add and Remove options to add or remove users.
7. Select **OK**.

   The group information displayed in the Groups window is updated.

Alternatively, you can use the **groupmod** command. The **groupmod** command modifies the definition of the specified group by modifying the appropriate entry in the /etc/group file. The syntax is also very simple for this command:

```
groupmod [ -g gid [ -o ] ] [ -n name ] group
```

For example:

```
groupmod -g 271 -o res_users1
```

In AIX 5L

In AIX 5L, you can use the **smitty chgroup** menu to modify an existing group. Then you choose the name of the group you want to modify. You should get a menu similar to Example 10-16 on page 367.

Example 10-16   Modifying group attributes

```
                         Change Group Attributes

Type or select values in entry fields.
Press Enter AFTER making all desired changes.

                                             [Entry Fields]
Group NAME                                   [staff]
  Group ID                                   [1]                    #
  ADMINISTRATIVE group?                       false                 +
  USER list                                  [invscout,ipsec,sshd,r> +
  ADMINISTRATOR list                         []                     +
  Projects                                   []                     +


F1=Help            F2=Refresh        F3=Cancel          F4=List
F5=Reset           F6=Command        F7=Edit            F8=Image
F9=Shell           F10=Exit          Enter=Do
```

You can also use the **chgroup** command. A few examples of using this command are:

► To add sam and carol to the finance group, which currently only has frank as a member, type:

```
chgroup users=sam,carol,frank  finance
```

► To remove frank from the finance group, but retain sam and carol, and to remove the administrators of the finance group, type:

```
chgroup users=sam,carol adms= finance
```

In this example, two attribute values were changed. The name frank was omitted from the list of members, and the value for the adms attribute was left blank.

10.8.3 Deleting a group

This section describes how to delete a group in HP-UX or AIX 5L.

In HP-UX

In HP-UX, you can use SAM to delete a group. Follow these steps:

1. Start the SAM application.

2. Go into Accounts for Users and Groups.

3. Go into Groups.

4. Select a group from the list.

5. From the Actions menu, select **Remove** and press Enter.

6. The list of users belonging to the group is displayed in the top window. From the second window, select from one of the three options for the group;s files. The options are: leave the files where they are, reassign to the user's primary group or to reassign to another group.

7. Select **OK** and **Yes** to continue.

   The group entry is deleted from the Groups window.

You can also use the **groupdel** command. The **groupdel** utility deletes a group definition from the system. It deletes the appropriate entry from the /etc/group file. The synopsis of this command looks like the following lines:

```
groupdel group
```

In AIX 5L

In AIX 5L, you can use the **smitty rmgroup** menu to delete a group. Then chose the name of the group you want to remove and press Enter.

Alternatively, you can use the **rmgroup** command. An example of using the command may look like this:

```
rmgroup users
```

10.9 Checking passwords and group definition consistency

In both the HP-UX and AIX 5L operating systems, there are tools that may be used to check the password file for any inconsistencies and to verify all entries in the group file. The commands are **pwck** and **grpck**.

The **pwck** command scans the password file and notes any inconsistencies. The checks include validation of the number of fields, login name, user ID, group ID, and whether the login directory and the program-to-use-as-shell exist.

In HP-UX

The default password file checked by HP-UX is /etc/passwd. If the -s option is used, the protected password database is checked. The syntax for this command is:

```
/usr/sbin/pwck [-s] [-l] [file]
```

In AIX 5L, it also scans the /etc/security/passwd file. The syntax for this command is:

```
/usr/sbin/pwck
```

A sample output of the **pwck** command in AIX 5L is shown in Example 10-17.

Example 10-17 pwck command

```
# pwck
3001-402  The user "imnadm" has an invalid password field in /etc/passwd.
3001-414  The stanza for "imnadm" was not found in /etc/security/passwd.
3001-402  The user "invscout" has an invalid password field in /etc/passwd.
3001-414  The stanza for "invscout" was not found in /etc/security/passwd.
3001-402  The user "lp" has an invalid password field in /etc/passwd.
3001-414  The stanza for "lp" was not found in /etc/security/passwd.
3001-421  The user "lp" does not have a stanza in /etc/security/user.
3001-402  The user "nuucp" has an invalid password field in /etc/passwd.
3001-414  The stanza for "nuucp" was not found in /etc/security/passwd.
3001-402  The user "smith" has an invalid password field in /etc/passwd.
3001-414  The stanza for "smith" was not found in /etc/security/passwd.
3001-402  The user "snapp" has an invalid password field in /etc/passwd.
3001-414  The stanza for "snapp" was not found in /etc/security/passwd.
3001-402  The user "test" has an invalid password field in /etc/passwd.
3001-414  The stanza for "test" was not found in /etc/security/passwd.
```

The **grpck** command differs in HP-UX and AIX 5L, but the general purpose is almost the same. In HP-UX, **grpck** verifies all entries in the group file. This verification includes a check of the number of fields, group name, group ID, whether any login names belong to more than NGROUPS_MAX groups, and that all the login names appear in the password file. The default group file is /etc/group.

The syntax of this command in HP-UX is:

```
/usr/sbin/grpck [ file ]
```

A sample output of the grpck command follows:

```
# grpck
```

```
rsgrp::103:annieh
        Duplicate group ID
```

In AIX 5L, the **grpck** command verifies the correctness of the group definitions in the user database files by checking the definitions for ALL the groups or for the groups specified by the Group parameter. If more than one group is specified, there must be a space between the groups.

The syntax of the **grpck** command in AIX 5L is:

```
grpck { -n | -p | -t | -y } { ALL | Group ... }
```

Here are some examples of using **grpck** command in AIX 5L:

▶ To verify that all the group members and administrators exist in the user database, and have any errors reported (but not fixed), enter:

```
# grpck -n ALL
```

▶ To verify that all the group members and administrators exist in the user database and to have errors fixed, but not reported, enter:

```
# grpck -p ALL
```

▶ To verify the uniqueness of the group name and group ID defined for the install group, enter:

```
# grpck -n install
```

or

```
# grpck -t install
```

or

```
# grpck -y install
```

The **grpck** command does not correct the group names and IDs. Therefore, the -n, -t, and -y flags report problems with group names and group IDs, but do not correct them.

10.10 Defining system resource limits for users

In both the HP-UX and AIX 5L operating systems, you may use the **ulimit** command or built-in shell functions. Basically, the syntax is the same (see **man ulimit** for the command syntax). The general purpose of using this command is to set or get limitations on the system resources available to the current shell and its descendents. In HP-UX, some system-wide kernel parameters may also need to be changed, depending on the required user process resources.

In AIX 5L, the limits are defined in the /etc/security/limits file. The /etc/security/limits file is an ASCII file that contains stanzas that specify the process resource limits for each user. These limits are set by individual attributes within a stanza.

Each stanza is identified by a user name followed by a colon and contains attributes in the Attribute=Value form. Each attribute is ended by a new-line character, and each stanza is ended by an additional new-line character. If you do not define an attribute for a user, the system applies default values.

When you create a user with the **mkuser** command, the system adds a stanza for the user to the /etc/security/limits file. Once the stanza exists, you can use the **chuser** command to change the user's limits. To display the current limits for a user, use the **lsuser** command. To remove users and their stanzas, use the **rmuser** command.

This /etc/security/limits file contains these default limits:

```
fsize = 2097151
core = 2097151
cpu = -1
data = 262144
rss = 65536
stack = 65536
nofiles = 2000
```

These values are used as default settings when a new user is added to the system. The values are set with the **mkuser** command when the user is added to the system, or changed with the **chuser** command. Limits are categorized as either soft or hard. With the **ulimit** command, you can change your soft limits, up to the maximum set by the hard limits. You must have root user authority to change resource hard limits.

Many systems do not contain one or more of these limits. The limit for a specified resource is set when the Limit parameter is specified. The value of the Limit parameter can be a number in the unit specified with each resource, or the value can be unlimited. To set the specific ulimit to unlimited, use the value *unlimited*.

> **Note:** Setting the default limits in the /etc/security/limits file sets system-wide limits, not just limits taken on by a user when that user is created.

The current resource limit is printed when you omit the Limit parameter. The soft limit is printed unless you specify the -H flag. When you specify more than one resource, the limit name and unit is printed before the value. If no option is given, the -f flag is assumed.

In the following example, **ulimit** was used to set the file size limit to 51,200 bytes:

```
ulimit -f 100
```

10.11 Quick reference

Table 10-1 on page 372 displays tasks, commands, and the location of files or information that is needed to perform user management in HP-UX and AIX 5L.

Table 10-1   Quick reference for user management

Task/locations	AIX 5L	HP-UX
Running multiple tasks in a GUI environment	Chose one of the following: ► **wsm** ► smitty ► The **smitty users** fast path	SAM
Adding users	**mkuser**	**useradd**
Removing users	**rmuser**	**userdel**
Displaying currently logged users	**who** or **w**	**who** or **w**
Displaying users and their attributes	**lsuser**	**listusers** **logins**
Password files	/etc/passwd and /etc/security/passwd	/etc/passwd If trusted: /tcb/files/auth /etc/shadow if installed
Administering users' passwords	**passwd** or **pwdadm**	**passwd**
Modifying user account	**chuser**	**usermod**
System-wide environment file	/etc/profile and /etc/environment	/etc/profile
Profile template	/etc/security/.profile	/etc/skel/.profile
Adding a group	**mkgroup**	**groupadd**
Group files	/etc/group and /etc/security/group	/etc/group
Modifying a group	**chgroup**	**groupmod**
Deleting a group	**rmgroup**	**groupdel**
Checking passwords and group definitions consistency	**pwck** and **grpck**	**pwck** and **grpck**

Task/locations	AIX 5L	HP-UX
Defining system resources limits for user	/etc/security/limits or `ulimit`	`ulimit` kernel parameters

11

Printing management

In AIX 5L, IBM includes both the traditional AIX 5L print subsystem, as well as the System V print subsystem, which has been a printing standard for many years in the UNIX environment. For more complex printing environments, IBM also offers a print management product called Infoprint® Manager. In this chapter, we discuss the following topics:

11.1 Printing overview

This section introduces printing on HP-UX and AIX 5L.

HP-UX 11i

In HP-UX 11i you have two subareas for printers, LP Spooler and HP Distributed Printer Service. HP Distributed Printer Service (HPDPS) is used with Distributed Computing Environment (DCE). HPDPS is not supported on releases after HP-UX 11i Version 1.

For more information about HP Distributed Printer Service, go to the HP documents Web site at:

`http://docs.hp.com`

The HP-UX 11i operating system uses the LP Spooler, which is the System V interface, and uses the System V and/or the BSD printing protocol. The BSD and System V printing protocol is widely used and provides compatibility between the different types of systems from various manufacturers.

The following commands are used to create and manage the LP Spooler:

`lp`	Submit and queue print jobs.
`cancel`	Cancel jobs.
`lpstat`	Gives status of the print queue.
`accept`	Enable queuing.
`reject`	Disable queuing.
`enable`	Start printing to a device.
`disable`	Stop printing to a device.
`lpsched`	Printing daemon.
`lpshut`	Stop the printing daemon.

For more information about LP Spooler configuration, go to the man pages or HP documents Web site at:

`http://docs.hp.com`

AIX 5L

In AIX 5L, IBM includes both the traditional AIX 5L print subsystem, which is the BSD printing protocol, as well as the System V print subsystem, which has been a printing standard for many years in the UNIX environment. For more complex printing environments, IBM also offers a print management product called *Infoprint Manager*.

Some of the features of the Infoprint Manager include:

► Secure, scalable enterprise printing support

► Reliability for mission-critical applications such as SAP/R3

► The ability to manage, print, store, and reprint to printer, fax machines, and more

► Multiple printer support (up to 1000+ pages per minute)

► Includes printing in your Tivoli system management solution

For more information about Infoprint Manager, refer to the following Web page:

`http://www.printers.ibm.com/R5PSC.NSF/Web/ipmgraixhome`

11.2 AIX 5L print subsystem versus System V print subsystem

This section compares the AIX 5L print subsystem to the System V print subsystem.

AIX 5L print subsystem characteristics

This section provides information about the AIX 5L print subsystem characteristics.

► Flexible printer drivers. AIX 5L printer drivers provide many printing options that can be easily controlled using the command-line options to the **qprt** command. Printer defaults can be easily managed using SMIT or the command line.

► System management tools. The AIX 5L print subsystem includes mature and powerful system management, using either the Web-based System Manager or SMIT, as well as the command line. System management tools for the System V print subsystem are less mature in this initial release. Some specific system management advantages using the AIX 5L print subsystem are:

  – Limits fields and options validation
  – Easy printer customization
  – Single-step print device and queue creation
  – Support for dial-in administration

► Customizable spooling subsystem. The AIX 5L print subsystem is specifically designed so that it can be used to serialize other types of jobs beyond just printing.

In the AIX 5L printing environment, files to be printed are sent to the AIX 5L print spooler daemon (qdaemon) using any of the AIX 5L print commands (**enq**, **qprt**, **lp**, or **lpr**). The spooler daemon serializes the jobs. The spooler sends jobs, one at a time, to back-end programs that may filter the data before sending it to the local printer driver or network printing application.

In summary, the main advantages of AIX 5L printing have to do with flexibility and ease of use. AIX 5L printing is tightly integrated into SMIT and the Web-based System Manager. Also, System V is not yet mature on AIX 5L, although system management features will be enhanced in future releases of AIX 5L.

System V print subsystem characteristics

This section describes System V print subsystem characteristics.

▶ Long-term strategy. The IBM long-term printing strategy for AIX 5L is to maintain compatibility with other UNIX systems.

▶ Standard PostScript filters. The System V print subsystem includes a number of filters for converting a number of different file formats to PostScript.

▶ Support for forms. The System V print subsystem provides a mechanism for mounting forms on printers and allowing or denying user access based on the form that is mounted. To provide this capability under AIX 5L printing, you must create multiple queues and manage which queues are enabled while a form is mounted.

▶ Security. System V printing includes built-in capabilities for restricting user access to certain printers. Using the AIX 5L print subsystem, the back-end program must be customized to restrict user access.

In the System V printing environment, files to be printed are sent to the System V print service daemon (lpsched) using the **lp** or **lpr** commands. The print service daemon serializes the jobs so they will be printed in the order in which they were submitted. The print service may filter the file to format the data so that it matches the types of data acceptable to the printer. The print service then sends files, one at a time, to the interface program, which may do additional filtering before sending the file to the local printer driver or network printing application.

11.2.1 Switching between AIX 5L and System V print subsystems

The default print subsystem in AIX 5L is the current AIX 5L print subsystem; the System V print subsystem is an alternate method of printing. At install time, the AIX 5L subsystem is always set as the active one, and System V is always inactive. They cannot both be set to the active state at the same time using the normal procedures. However, there is nothing to prevent an administrator from overriding this manually for some print operations.

There are three ways to switch between print subsystems: 1) from Web-based System Manager, 2) using SMIT, and 3) using the command line.

In Example 11-1 we show how this is accomplished by using SMIT and using the command line.

The option to Change/Show Current Print Subsystem has been added to the top-level Print Spooling menu in SMIT, as shown in Example 11-1.

Example 11-1 Changing print subsystem

```
                        Print Spooling

Move cursor to desired item and press Enter.

  AIX Print Mode Only:

  Start a Print Job
  Manage Print Jobs
  List All Print Queues
  Manage Print Queues
  Add a Print Queue
  Add an Additional Printer to an Existing Print Queue
  Change / Show Print Queue Characteristics
  Change / Show Printer Connection Characteristics
  Remove a Print Queue
  Manage Print Server
  Programming Tools

  AIX and System V Print Mode:

  Change / Show Current Print Subsystem



F1=Help              F2=Refresh          F3=Cancel           F8=Image
F9=Shell             F10=Exit            Enter=Do
```

By Choosing Change/Show Current Print Subsystem, the next panel will display the line to select the print subsystem, as shown here:

```
  Change / Show Current Print Subsystem [AIX]
```

The current subsystem will show up in the box on the right, and the field will toggle between two choices, AIX 5L and System V. Executing the panel will run the **/usr/aix/bin/switch.prt** command, which will in turn run the /usr/aix/bin/switch.prt.subsystem script, which will take the value displayed as input. Running the command with the current system as input will result in an error. Running the command with the alternate subsystem will switch the system from the current one to the alternate one. The more queues that are defined in the subsystem that you are exiting, the longer it will take for the command to switch.

Using the command line

The `switch.prt` command can be used to switch between printer subsystems or to display the currently active printer subsystem. The syntax of the command is:

```
# switch.prt [-s print_subsystem] [-d]
```

The valid values for print_subsystem are AIX 5L and System V. Running the command with the -d flag will display the current print subsystem. For example:

```
# switch.prt -s SystemV
# switch.prt -s AIX
```

For security reasons, this command is a front-end to the /usr/aix/bin/switch.prt.subsystem script, which will do the real work. This command is also called by the Web-based System Manager and SMIT interfaces.

System files associated with printing

The following are characteristics of system files associated with printing:

► The /etc/qconfig file describes the queues and devices available for use by the printing commands.

► The /var/spool directory contains the files and directories used by the printing programs and daemons.

► The /var/spool/lpd/qdir directory contains information about files queued to print.

► The /var/spool/qdaemon directory contains copies of the files that are spooled to print.

► The /var/spool/lpd/stat directory is where the information about the status of jobs is stored. It is used by the qdaemon and backend programs.

► The /var/spool/lpd/pio/@local directory holds virtual printer definitions. This is where the attributes of printers are paired with the attributes of corresponding data stream types.

It is recommended that SMIT be used to update these device-related files. In most cases, updating standard system files is not recommended.

11.3 Print queue administration

Local printing to serial and parallel attached printers for both the System V and AIX 5L print subsystems is done through standard AIX 5L device drivers. Before using either print subsystem, you should be aware of how these device drivers work and some of the commands that you can use to look at the devices.

Print devices can be added from the command line, from SMIT, and from the Web-based System Manager. The device created in all three methods will be the same, and can be used by either of the base print subsystems. The printer type that you add when creating a device determines the buffer size and some timing parameters for the serial or parallel device driver that is ultimately used. It is not important that the device printer type and the print subsystem printer type match exactly, only that they are similar in type. If you are adding a laser printer, then you should choose any laser printer that is similar in speed to the actual print model you will be using.

When a print device is added, the device is represented by a special character device file in /dev with a name starting with lp, and a number of the printer that is given in sequential order as the devices are added. A list of all the printers currently on a system can be listed with **lsdev**, as shown here:

```
# lsdev -Cc printer
lp0 Available 00-00-0P-00 Lexmark Optra laser printer
lp1 Available 00-00-S2-00 IBM Network Printer 12
lp2 Available 00-00-S1-00 Hewlett-Packard Color LaserJet 4500
```

This not only gives you the models of all printers that have been added, but also tells you whether they are available, and the adapter and port number where they have been installed.

To list all the available printer types, use the following command:

```
# lsdev -Pc printer
```

Individual device files can be listed with the **ls -l** command:

```
# ls -l /dev/lp0
crw-rw-rw- 1 root system 26, 0 Oct 19 13:52 /dev/lp0
```

Device files for local serial and parallel devices should always have a listing starting with *cr* for character devices that are readable.

11.3.1 Adding a local print queue

Follow these steps to add a local print queue using SMIT. In this example we show the text-based SMIT screens, but the same functionality is available from the GUI-based SMIT on X Windows displays.

1. Enter the following command:

```
# smitty mkpq
```

After entering this command, the menu shown in Example 11-2 will be displayed.

Example 11-2   smitty mkpq screen

```
                         Add a Print Queue

Move cursor to desired item and press Enter. Use arrow keys to scroll.

      # ATTACHMENT TYPE        DESCRIPTION
       local                   Printer Attached to Local Host
       remote                  Printer Attached to Remote Host
       xstation                Printer Attached to Xstation
       ascii                   Printer Attached to ASCII Terminal
       hpJetDirect             Network Printer (HP JetDirect)
       file                    File (in /dev directory)
       ibmNetPrinter           IBM Network Printer
       ibmNetColor             IBM Network Color Printer
       other                   User Defined Backend

F1=Help                 F2=Refresh              F3=Cancel
F8=Image                F10=Exit                Enter=Do
/=Find                  n=Find Next
```

2. In Example 11-2, a list of options is displayed. Move the cursor to the desired item and press Enter. In this example, select the local option and press Enter. Use the arrow keys to scroll. The menu shown in Example 11-3 will be displayed.

Example 11-3   Printer Type menu

```
                         Printer Type

Move cursor to desired item and press Enter.

      Bull
      Canon
      Dataproducts
      Hewlett-Packard
      IBM
      Lexmark
      OKI
      Printronix
      QMS
      Texas Instruments
      Other (Select this if your printer type is not listed above)
```

```
F1=Help           F2=Refresh        F3=Cancel
F8=Image          F10=Exit          Enter=Do
/=Find            n=Find Next
```

3. Example 11-3 on page 382 shows the available printer drivers. If your printer model is not listed, select Other, which is at the bottom of the list. To get there, use the down arrow or page down key. If you select a printer model that has its device driver installed (available) on your system, the screen shown in Example 11-4 will be displayed.

> **Note:** If your printer model is not listed, you can install the printer driver from the AIX 5L CD-ROMs. To do this, issue a `smitty pdp command` and select Install Additional Printer/Plotter software.

Example 11-4   Printer interface

```
                        Printer Interface

        Move cursor to desired item and press Enter.

            parallel
            rs232

F1=Help           F2=Refresh        F3=Cancel
F8=Image          F10=Exit          Enter=Do
/=Find            n=Find Next
```

4. In Example 11-4, we select the parallel option, and the following parent adapter selection list is displayed. In this example, there is only one adapter to choose (see Example 11-5). If there were more than one adapter, they would also be listed. Select the parent adapter that corresponds to the communications port you have connected your printer.

Example 11-5   Parent adapter menu

```
                        Parent Adapter

        Move cursor to desired item and press Enter.

            ppa0 Available 01-R1 CHRP IEEE1284 (ECP) Parallel Port Adapter

F1=Help           F2=Refresh        F3=Cancel
F8=Image          F10=Exit          Enter=Do
/=Find            n=Find Next
```

5. In Example 11-6, you are prompted to choose a name for each queue created for each type of mode your printer can emulate. Each name that you enter will create a separate queue and virtual printer. Choose names so that it is easy to remember the name of each queue. In our example, we have chosen the name PCL-mv200 for the PCL Emulation queue and PS-mv200 for the PostScript queue. After choosing the queue names, press Enter.

Example 11-6   Add a Print Queue menu

```
                         Add a Print Queue

Type or select values in entry fields.
Press Enter AFTER making all desired changes.


                                            [Entry Fields]
   Description                              IBM 4079 Color Jetprin>
   Names of NEW print queues to add
      GL Emulation                          [PCL-mv200]
      PostScript                            [PS-mv200]

   Printer connection characteristics
*     PORT number                           [p]                      +
      Type of PARALLEL INTERFACE            [standard]               +
      Printer TIME OUT period (seconds)     [600] +#
      STATE to be configured at boot time   available                +




F1=Help            F2=Refresh         F3=Cancel         F4=List
F5=Reset           F6=Command         F7=Edit           F8=Image
F9=Shell           F10=Exit           Enter=Do
```

6. If you see a screen like Example 11-7, you have successfully configured a printer into the print spooling subsystem.

Example 11-7   Output

```
                         COMMAND STATUS

Command: OK          stdout: yes          stderr: no

Before command completion, additional instructions may appear below.

Added printer 'lp0'.

Added print queue 'PCL-mv200'.
Added print queue 'PS-mv200'.
```

You can also add a print queue through the command line, but using the Web-based System Manager or SMIT to add a print queue avoids dealing with a queue, a queue device, and a virtual printer. If you are going to add a virtual printer queue, then the steps to add the printer become quite complicated, and, unless you are going to create shell scripts to add your queues, should be avoided. The steps shown below show how to add a remote queue that does not use a virtual printer. This procedure could also be used to add a queue with a custom backend:

1. Add a queue using the **mkque** command. For example, the following command will configure a remote queue. It configures just the queue and not the queue device:

   ```
   # mkque -qlp -a "host=puttifar" -a "rq=solar"
   ```

   - The -q flag specifies the name of the queue to be added (lp).

   - The -a flag specifies a line to be added to the queue stanza in the qconfig file (host=puttifar and rq=solar). These flags must be entered last when entering the **mkque** command on the command line.

2. Add a queue device associated with the queue you have added, using the **mkquedev** command. For the queue we added in the previous example, the following command will add a device named lpdev that has /usr/lib/lpd/rembak as its backend:

   ```
   # mkquedev -qlp -dlpdev -a "backend=usr/lib/lpd/rembak"
   ```

   - The -q flag specifies the name of the queue (this name must already exist) to which the queue device is added. The **mkquedev** command automatically adds the device=attribute to the specified queue stanza.

   - The -a flag specifies the attribute to be added to the device stanza in the /etc/qconfig file (backend=usr/lib/lpd/rembak).

11.3.2 Displaying a queue configuration information

Once printers have been established, you may wish to review their configuration. This section will describe how this can be accomplished using SMIT and the command line.

To display the names of all the configured queues, enter the following command:

```
# smitty lsallq
```

This SMIT command lists the names of all configured queues, as shown in Example 11-8.

Example 11-8   smitty lsallq command

```
                            COMMAND STATUS

Command: OK              stdout: yes              stderr: no

Before command completion, additional instructions may appear below.

# PRINT QUEUE          PRINTER               DESCRIPTION
  PCL-mv200            lp0                   ibm4079 (GL Emulation)
  PS-mv200             lp0                   ibm4079 (PostScript)


F1=Help               F2=Refresh            F3=Cancel            F6=Command
F8=Image              F9=Shell              F10=Exit             /=Find
n=Find Next
```

To list installed printer queues from command line, type:

```
# lsallq -c
```

11.3.3 Deleting a queue

You may need to remove a print queue from time to time. To delete a queue or queue device, you must have root authority. You can do this by using one of the interfaces (Web-based System Manager, SMIT, or the command line). Using the Web-based System Manager or SMIT is a lot easier than using the command line, because you only deal with the print queue itself. If the print queue has any device associated with it, the Web-based System Manager or SMIT automatically removes it for you. If you have many print queues associated with the same device, and you want to remove all the queues, the Web-based System Manager or SMIT removes all the queues for you without removing the queue device, except for the last print queue, when the Web-based System Manager or SMIT removes the queue and its associated device. In the following example we describe how to delete a print queue using SMIT and the command line.

To delete a queue, enter the following command in the command prompt:

```
# smitty rmpq
```

Example 11-9   Remove a Print Queue

```
                        Remove a Print Queue
```

```
Type or select a value for the entry field.
Press Enter AFTER making all desired changes.

                                                        [Entry Fields]
* PRINT QUEUE name                                      []                        +


F1=Help              F2=Refresh           F3=Cancel            F4=List
F5=Reset             F6=Command           F7=Edit              F8=Image
F9=Shell             F10=Exit             Enter=Do
```

The Remove a Print Queue screen will be displayed (Example 11-9 on page 386). Press the F4 key to select a queue you want to remove. The screen in Example 11-10 will be displayed.

Example 11-10 Print Queue name

```
                            PRINT QUEUE name

     Move cursor to desired item and press Enter. Use arrow keys to scroll.

        # PRINT QUEUE              DESCRIPTION
          GL-mv200                 ibm4079 (GL Emulation)
          PS-mv200                 ibm4079 (PostScript)

F1=Help              F2=Refresh           F3=Cancel
F8=Image             F10=Exit             Enter=Do
F5 /=Find            n=Find Next
```

When you select a queue you want to remove, the confirmation screen will be displayed. You can simply press Enter to finish the deletion process. Press Enter to confirm the deletion of this queue. If you succeed, the command on the next screen will show OK status.

When removing the queue using the command line, you should first make sure that there are no jobs queued. If there are jobs, cancel them before removing the queues. If there is a virtual printer, it should be removed first using the **rmvirprt** command. Check to see that the queues still exist, and then remove the queue device with the **rmquedev** command, and then the queue with the **rmque** command. If there are multiple queue devices on the queue, all queue devices must be deleted using the **rmquedev** command before using the **rmque** command.

To remove print queue lp0, enter the following command:

```
# cancel 4312psg
# rmvirprt -d lp0 -q PCL-mv200
# rmquedev -q PCL-mv200 -d lp0
# rmque -q PCL-mv200
```

If you remove the queue device and do not remove the queue, a dummy queue device will be created, and the qdaemon will have problems processing the queue.

11.3.4 Enabling and disabling a queue

When a printer is not functioning properly, you may wish to take that printer offline. The terminology for this varies. Some documents talk about starting and stopping a queue, while others use the terms enabling and disabling the queue. You also have a choice for the interface to start or stop a queue. In the following example we show you how to enable and disable a print queue using SMIT and the command line.

To disable a queue, enter the following command:

```
# smitty qstop
```

Press the F4 key to select a queue to stop. The following screen will be similar to Example 11-10 on page 387.

By selecting a queue, this queue will be stopped. To start a queue, enter the following command:

```
# smitty qstart
```

You will see the screen shown in Example 11-10 on page 387 and can start again by selecting a queue.

The **qadm** command brings printers, queues, and the spooling system up or down (makes printers available or unavailable) and cancels jobs. The **qadm** command can only affect local print jobs. You must also have root user authority, or belong to either the system group or printq group, to run this command.

Examples

To bring down the PCL-mv200 queue, enter one of the following commands:

```
# qadm -D PCL-mv200
# disable PCL-mv200
```

When you check the queue status by using the **qchk** or **lpstat** command, the status of this queue will be READY.

The other options of the **qadm** command are -G and -K. The -G option gracefully brings down the queuing system. This flag temporarily interrupts the daemon process after all currently running jobs on all queues are finished. Use of this flag is the only way to bring the system down without causing problems such as jobs hanging up in the queue. The -K option brings down the printer you name, ending all current jobs immediately. Jobs remain in the queue and run again when the printer is brought back up.

11.3.5 Cancelling print jobs

To cancel all of *your* jobs on printer lp0 (or all jobs on printer lp0, if you have root user authority), enter one of the following commands:

```
# qadm -X 535pcl
# cancel 535pcl
# qcan -X 535pcl
```

The -X flag cancels the printing of the user's jobs on the specified queue (PS-mv200). If you have root user privileges, all jobs on that queue are deleted.

You can also cancel individual jobs by using the job ID. Use the following commands:

```
# qcan -x 435
# cancel 435
```

You can also use SMIT and the Web-based System Manager to do this task. The SMIT fast path is **smitty qcan**.

11.4 Remote printing

Network or remote printing can use a number of different protocols, including NetWare, AppleTalk, Banyan Vines, DECnet, TCP/IP socket applications, the Common Internet File System/Server Message Block (CIFS/SMB) protocol (used by Microsoft Windows, Samba, and IBM Fast Connect), the Internet Printing Protocol (IPP), and the most common in the TCP/IP environment: the Line Printer Daemon Protocol (LPD).

There are different techniques to set up remote printing. Here we show how to take a system with a local printer and turn it into a print server. There are other ways to set up remote printing. For example, HP Jet Direct cards are very common. If we set up the system using these, then your system is a client rather than host.

Once your system has the local queue set up, any user on that system can print. If the machine is networked, it can also provide printing for client machines by becoming a print server.

To set up a print server, you need to define the client machine names or IP addresses in /etc/hosts.lpd and then start the lpd daemon. Both of these tasks can be done through SMIT. To use SMIT, the fast path to identify the client system is **smitty mkhostslpd**.

The lpd daemon is controlled by SRC. You should use SMIT to start it, however, because SMIT will also add entries to /etc/inittab to ensure that it is started on reboot. The fast path for this screen is **smitty mkitab_lpd**.

11.4.1 Setting the system up as a print server

To do this:

1. Use this command to perform print client authorization. The screen will look like Example 11-11:

```
# smitty mkhostslpd
```

Example 11-11   Adding printer access to a client

```
                        Add Print Access for a Remote Client

Type or select values in entry fields.
Press Enter AFTER making all desired changes.


                                                        [Entry Fields]
* Name of REMOTE CLIENT                                 []
  (Hostname or dotted decimal address)


F1=Help          F2=Refresh          F3=Cancel          F4=List
F5=Reset         F6=Command          F7=Edit            F8=Image
F9=Shell         F10=Exit            Enter=Do
```

This step is done on the print server. On this screen, enter the client machine's name or IP address. A plus sign (+) is also valid. It indicates that this system will be a print server to all machines. The entries will be added to the /etc/hosts.lpd file.

2. Start the Print Server subsystem. The screen will look like Example 11-12.

Example 11-12   Start the Print Server Subsystem menu

```
                        Start the Print Server Subsystem

Type or select values in entry fields.
Press Enter AFTER making all desired changes.


                                                        [Entry Fields]
    Start subsystem now, on system restart, or both    [both]              +
```

```
TRACE lpd daemon activity to syslog?          [no]                    +
EXPORT directory containing print attributes?  [no]                    +

Note:
Exporting this print server's directory
containing its print attributes will allow
print clients to mount the directory.  The
clients can use this server's print attributes
to display and validate print job attributes
when starting print jobs destined for this
print server.  Note that the Network File
System (NFS) program product must be installed
and running.

F1=Help          F2=Refresh        F3=Cancel        F4=List
F5=Reset         F6=Command        F7=Edit          F8=Image
F9=Shell         F10=Exit          Enter=Do
```

This step is done on the print server. The lpd daemon is controlled by the system resource controller (SRC). The commands `startsrc` and `stopsrc` can be used to control lpd. By using SMIT, an entry is placed in the /etc/inittab file to ensure that lpd is started each time the machine is booted.

11.4.2 Adding a remote host-attached printer

When printing to a remote server, the administrator of that remote server must have performed several tasks to enable remote printing.

In this section we show how to configure remote printers by using SMIT.

1. You can use the `smitty mkpq` fast path, or work through the SMIT menus by typing # smitty and selecting **Print Spooling** → **Add a Print Queue**.

   The screen will look like Example 11-2 on page 382.

2. For our example, we were defining an IBM 3130 attached to a remote RS/6000, so we select remote and press Enter. The menu in Example 11-13 appears.

Example 11-13 Type of Remote Printing menu

```
                    Type of Remote Printing

           Move cursor to desired item and press Enter.

        Standard processing
        Standard with NFS access to server print queue attributes
        Local filtering before sending to print server
```

```
F1=Help              F2=Refresh           F3=Cancel
F8=Image             F10=Exit             Enter=Do
/=Find               n=Find Next
```

3. We select Standard processing in Example 11-13 on page 391. The panel in Example 11-4 on page 383 is displayed.

Example 11-14   Standard remote queue

```
              Add a Standard Remote Print Queue

Type or select values in entry fields.
Press Enter AFTER making all desired changes.

                                            [Entry Fields]
* Name of QUEUE to add                      []
* HOSTNAME of remote server                 []
* Name of QUEUE on remote server            []
  Type of print spooler on remote server    AIX Version 3 or 4    +
  Backend TIME OUT period (minutes)         [] #
  Send control file first?                  no                    +
  To turn on debugging, specify output      []
      file pathname
  DESCRIPTION of printer on remote server   []
```

```
F1=Help          F2=Refresh       F3=Cancel        F4=List
F5=Reset         F6=Command       F7=Edit          F8=Image
F9=Shell         F10=Exit         Enter=Do
```

4. Example 11-14 shows the standard remote print queue screen. We enter the hostname of the remote server (although we could have also entered the dotted decimal address), the name of the print queue that was already defined on that remote server, and the type of spooler used by the remote server; since the remote server was running AIX 5L, we selected AIX 5L Version 3 or 4. We do not set a time-out value for backend but let it default to 90 seconds. We chose not to send the control file before the data file. After entering all these values, press Enter.

11.5 Printing job management

Now that we have a printer configured, we will probably want to use it. This section reviews the several ways available to request that a job be printed and then manage the progress of that job through the print spooling subsystem. It is important that a systems administrator develops a good understanding of these commands, as users will often seek assistance on how to meet their more complex printing requirements or to get that special rush job printed. HP-UX 11i uses System V printing system. AIX 5L Version 5.x also can use the System V and BSD printing system. Table 11-1 shows an example of different printing commands.

Table 11-1   System V, BSD, and AIX 5L print commands

System V	BSD	AIX 5L
lp	lpr	qprt

11.5.1 Submitting printing jobs

There are three sets of commands for submitting, listing, and cancelling print jobs. They come from either System V, BSD, or IBM versions of UNIX and are all available in AIX 5L. The commands have slightly different options.

To submit a print job to a queue, use either **lp**, **lpr**, or **qprt**. All jobs will go to the system default queue unless the PRINTER or LPDEST variables are set. You can also specify, on the command line, which queue to use. Use -d with **lp** or use -P with **qprt** and **lpr**.

The commands **lp** and **qprt** both queue without spooling by default. Specify the -c option if spooling is desired. The command **lpr** spools and queues by default. The -c option will turn off spooling with **lpr**.

To print multiple copies, use the **qprt -N** # or **lp -n** # command; for **lpr** use just a dash followed by the number of copies (- #).

The **lp**, **lpr**, and **qprt** commands create a queue entry in /var/spool/lpd/qdir and (depending upon the options specified) copy the file to be printed to the /var/spool/qdaemon directory.

All the print commands, **lp**, **lpr**, and **qprt**, actually call the **enq** command, which places the print request in a queue. The **enq** command can be used instead of the other commands to submit jobs, view job status, and so forth. To submit a job using **enq**, run:

```
# enq -Pqueuename filename
```

The qprt command

The **qprt** command is the IBM AIX 5L printing tool. The first step in the process of printing using **qprt** is to place a print job or request into the print spooling subsystem. AIX 5L features a number of commands and facilities to perform this task. There is one prerequisite to initiating a print request, though: before you can print a file, you must have read access to it.

SMIT also would only be used when the user wants to set specific settings and does not know the **qprt** command.

To start a printing job, enter the following command:

```
# smitty qprt
```

To print the desired file, fill in, with the print queue name, where you want to print your file or press the F4 key to see a list of available queues. Press Enter after selecting the queue. If no printer is specified, the default is used.

Like Example 11-10 on page 387, the available print queues are listed by pressing the F4 key.

Select to which queue you will send your print request. In our example, we have chosen the GL-mv200 queue. The screen in Example 11-15 is displayed.

Example 11-15   Select type of text file

```
                    Print File Type

        Move cursor to desired item and press Enter.

        a ASCII
        p PCL
        n troff (ditroff) intermedia outout
        p pass-through
        s PostScript


F1=Help              F2=Refresh           F3=Cancel
F8=Image             F10=Exit             Enter=Do
F5 /=Find            n=Find Next
```

Select a print file type that you want to start. In Example 11-16, like Example 11-15, you can specify the details for your job to start, including:

► Text print options
► Job processing options
► Text formatting options
► Paper/page options
► Header/trailer page options
► Messages/diagnostics

From this point you can do various tasks.

Example 11-16   Start a print job

```
                    Start a Print Job
```

```
Type or select values in entry fields.
Press Enter AFTER making all desired changes.

                                                      [Entry Fields]
    Print queue name                                  test2
  * Name of FILE to print                             []


    -------------- Text Print Options -------------
    Print QUALITY                                     quality               +


    ----------- Job Processing Options -----------
    Number of COPIES                                  [1] +#
    Place job in 'HELD' state when queued?            no                    +
    COPY FILE and print from copy?                    no                    +
    REMOVE FILE after print job completes?            no                    +
    Print job PRIORITY                                [15] +#
    Pre-processing FILTER NAME                        []                    +
    INITIALIZE printer?                               yes                   +
    RESTORE printer?                                  yes                   +


    ----------- Text Formatting Options -----------


    ------------- Paper/Page Options --------------


    --------- Header/Trailer Page Options ---------
    SEPARATOR PAGES                                   none                  +
    Job TITLE                                         []
    'DELIVER TO' TEXT                                 []
    HOSTNAME for "PRINTED AT:" on HEADER PAGE         []


    ------------- Messages/Diagnostics ------------
    MAIL MESSAGES instead of displaying them?         no                    +
    NOTIFY when job finished?                         no                    +
    TEXT to display on console before printing job    []
    FILE to display on console before printing job    [] /
    DIAGNOSTIC LEVEL                                   (normal) - print job; > +

    F1=Help          F2=Refresh          F3=Cancel          F4=List
    F5=Reset         F6=Command          F7=Edit            F8=Image
    F9=Shell         F10=Exit            Enter=Do
```

Fill in the "Name of FILE to print" field with the name of the file you want to print, make all necessary modifications, and press Enter to print your file.

You can also do the previous task from the command line. The **qprt** command creates and queues a print job. The **qprt** command was designed to work with the virtual printer subsystem, and there are qprt print flags for most print customization. The **qprt** command has a large variety of parameters that can be used. Some of the most useful are shown here as examples:

► Use **qprt -p** to select the printer pitch. Normally values of 10 and 12 will be accepted, but sometimes a value of 17 will be accepted:

```
# qprt -p12 -P queue-name /tmp/testfile
```

► Use **qprt -z+** to print landscape, as shown here:

```
# qprt -z+ -P puttifar /tmp/testfile
```

► Use **qprt -Y+** to print duplex, as shown here:

```
# qprt -Y+ -P andrea /tmp/testfile
```

► To indent the page on the left margin, use the **qprt -i** command:

```
# qprt -i 5 -P veronica /tmp/testfile
```

► To print formatted files in pass-through mode, use the **qprt -dp** command. Note that in this example we can still specify landscape orientation:

```
# qprt -dp -z+ -P fischer /tmp/testfile
```

► To print text files to a PostScript queue, use the qprt -da flag. This can be combined with the -p flag to designate the character size the virtual printer uses (enscript) to convert the text to postscript:

```
# qprt -da -p 14 -P ps /tmp/testfile
```

Note that the flags can be combined. To print landscape, 17 characters per inch with a line printer font, try:

```
# qprt -z+ -p17 -slineprinter -P funjet /tmp/testfile
```

In addition to **qprt**, the **enq**, **lp**, and **lpr** commands can be used from the command line. Printing from CDE is done through a command called **dtprint**.

When using **lp** or **enq**, the **qprt** flags can be set with the -o options. For example, to set the pitch to 12 with lp and enq, use the following commands:

```
# lp -o -p12 -d pcl /tmp/testfile
# enq -o -p17 -P pcl /tmp/testfile
```

The **lpr** command does not use the -o flag, and so cannot be used for most virtual printer settings. By default, lpr spools all files and overrides the queue header page setting to always generate a header, unless you use the -h flag to turn off headers, as shown here:

```
# lpr -h -P pcl /home/toenntr/adress.doc
```

11.5.2 Checking status

Once a print job has been submitted to the queuing system, you may wish to see the status of the job on the print spooling subsystem. You can do this through the Web-based System Manager, SMIT, or the command line. This section describes how to use SMIT and command line to list queue information. In all ways, you can review the contents of one or more print queues to check the current status of the queues and the jobs you have submitted. They also show the status of printers and queues. In AIX 5L, there are two commands that are available: **qchk** and **qstatus**. To only check the status of the queues, enter the following command:

```
# smitty qstatus
```

The screen in Example 11-17 will be displayed.

Example 11-17   Show Status of Print Queues

```
                       Show Status of Print Queues

Type or select values in entry fields.
Press Enter AFTER making all desired changes.

                                                   [Entry Fields]
      Include status of print queues remote servers?   [yes]                +


F1=Help            F2=Refresh        F3=Cancel         F4=List
F5=Reset           F6=Command        F7=Edit           F8=Image
F9=Shell           F10=Exit          Enter=Do
```

If you want to see the status of remote server queues, select yes and press Enter. The screen shown in Example 11-18 is the output for the status of the queues.

Example 11-18   Command status

```
                         COMMAND STATUS

Command: OK            stdout: yes          stderr: no

Before command completion, additional instructions may appear below.

Queue   Dev   Status
------- ----- ---------
tdipcl lp0   DEV_BUSY
tdipsq lp0   READY


F1=Help              F2=Refresh          F3=Cancel          F6=Command
```

```
F8=Image          F9=Shell          F10=Exit          /=Find
n=Find Next
```

If you want to see the status of the print jobs in a specific queue, enter the following command:

```
# smitty qchk
```

The screen in Example 11-19 will be displayed. In this screen, you can choose to list information about all print jobs sent to a specific queue by filling the "PRINT QUEUE name (* for all queues)" field with the queue name.

Example 11-19   Show status of print jobs

```
                  Show the Status of Print Jobs

Type or select values in entry fields.
Press Enter AFTER making all desired changes.

                                                  [Entry Fields]
* PRINT QUEUE name (* for all queues)             [*]                    +
  Print JOB NUMBER                                [] +#
  Print JOB OWNER                                 []


F1=Help           F2=Refresh        F3=Cancel         F4=List
F5=Reset          F6=Command        F7=Edit           F8=Image
F9=Shell          F10=Exit          Enter=Do
```

Select a queue by pressing the F4 key to see the list of the queues. You can specify a print job number or a print job owner name. If you want to list information about a specific job number in the specified queue, fill in the job number in the Print JOB NUMBER field with the correct job number. If you want to list information about a specific print job owner in the specified queue, fill in the Print JOB OWNER field with the print job owner's user ID. To list information about all print requests on all queues, fill in the "PRINT QUEUE name (* for all queues)" field with an asterisk (*) and leave all the other fields blank.

Press Enter to see the results. Example 11-20 shows the status of the queue and jobs in the tdipclq queue.

Example 11-20   Command status

```
                       COMMAND STATUS

Command: OK           stdout: yes           stderr: no

Before command completion, additional instructions may appear below.
```

```
Queue    Dev   Status      Job Files              User        PP %  Blks  Cp Rnk
-------  ----- ---------   --- ------------------ ----------   ---- -- ----- --- ---
 tdipcl  lp0   DEV_WAIT
               QUEUED        7 /etc/motd           root              1     1   1
               QUEUED        8 /etc/hosts          root              1     1   1
               QUEUED        9 /.profile           root              1     1   1
               QUEUED       10 /.cshrc             root              1     1   1


F1=Help          F2=Refresh         F3=Cancel         F6=Command
F8=Image         F9=Shell           F10=Exit          /=Find
n=Find Next
```

Table 11-2 shows how to list jobs in a printer queue using the three different commands.

Table 11-2   List jobs in a printer queue

System V	BSD	AIX 5L
lpstat	lpq	qchk

The **qchk** command displays the current status information regarding specified print jobs, print queues, or users. Use the appropriate flag followed by the requested name or number to indicate specific status information.

The **qchk** command with no flags specifies the default print queue. Flags used in this example are explained as follows:

► The -A flag specifies all queues.

► The -L flag specifies long form mode.

► The -w delay flag specifies that print status will be displayed, until all print jobs are done. The status will be displayed by updating the screen every five seconds (delay seconds).

To display the status for the tdipsq queue, we have used the -P flag, which specifies the queue (tdipsq). To display the status for job number 12, enter the following command:

```
# qchk -#12
```

Table 11-3 on page 400 illustrates the key attributes reported via the queue status commands and what they refer to.

Table 11-3   qchk attributes

Attribute	Description
Queue	The queue name used in the qconfig file.
Dev	The queue device name used in the qconfig file.
Status	The current status of the job.
Job	The job number of this print job, which is used by many of the print spooling subsystem control commands, such as **qcan**.
Files	The name of the files being printed.
User	The user ID of the user that owns the job.
PP	Pages in the requested print job.
%	Percentage of the job completed so far.
Blks	The number of blocks the print job has been broken into.
Cp	The number of copies of the requested print job that will be printed.
Rnk	The job's rank in the print queue; the job ranked 1 should be printing.

11.5.3 Print queue status

Table 11-4 shows the different queue status modes.

Table 11-4   Queue status modes

Status	Description
READY	Indicates that the printer is up and ready to accept jobs.
DEV_WAIT	Indicates that the printer is not online, out of paper, has a paper jam, or any similar problem that will prevent the job from printing normally. The problem that causes this state has also caused a message to be sent to the job owner or the operator.
RUNNING	Indicates that a job is either enrolled to be printed or is printing.
HELD	Indicates that the job is held and will not be put on the queue until it is released using the **qhld** or **enq** command.
DOWN	Indicates that the printer is not online; it probably has been taken offline by the operator for maintenance.

Status	Description
UNKNOWN	Indicates that the **status** command cannot determine the status of the printer. This state is often an indicator of problems with printers or the print spooling subsystem.
OPR_WAIT	Indicates that the job is suspended, waiting on an operator response to a message.

Examples

The **enq -A** and **lpstat** commands can also be used. To display the queue status for a queue every five seconds, use the following command:

```
# enq -P wsmq -A -w 2
```

To get the status of only local queues, so you do not have to wait for the remote queues to time-out on unavailable or slow servers, use the following command:

```
# enq -P remque -isA
```

To display the queue with long queue names, use the following command:

```
# lpstat -vnet17a -W
```

11.5.4 Cancelling a printing job

The **qcan** command cancels either a particular job number or all jobs in a print queue. Normal users can only cancel their own jobs, while root or a member of the printq group can cancel any job from any queue.

To cancel a job, you can use the **smitty qcan** fast path, the Web-based System Manager, or use one of the commands in Table 11-5.

Table 11-5   Cancel a print job

System V	BSD	AIX 5L
cancel	lprm	qcan

Examples

To cancel Job Number 127 on whatever queue the job is on, run:

```
# qcan -x 127 or # cancel 127
```

To cancel all jobs queued on printer lp0, enter:

```
# qcan -X -Plp0 or # cancel lp0
```

11.5.5 Prioritizing a printing job

The discipline line in the /etc/qconfig file determines the order in which the printer serves the requests in the queue. In the queue stanza, the discipline field can either be set to fcfs (first-come-first-serve) or sjn (shortest-job-next). If there is no discipline in the queue stanza, requests are serviced in fcfs order.

Each print job also has a priority that can be changed via SMIT or with the `qpri` command.

Print jobs with higher-priority numbers are handled before requests with lower-priority numbers. Only a user who has root authority or who belongs to the printq group can change the priority of a local print request.

> **Note:** You can only set priorities on local print jobs. Remote print jobs are not supported.

The `qprt -R` command can also be used to set job priority. Use the `qchk -L` command to show the new job priorities.

The `qpri` command prioritizes a job in a print queue by specifying the job number and giving it a priority number. The `qpri` command works only on local print jobs. Remote print jobs are not supported. After a job has been sent to a remote host, that host can change the job's priority, but the sender cannot. You must have root user authority, or belong to either the system group or printq group to run this command.

Look at Example 11-21 for an example of how to change priorities on a printjob.

Example 11-21   The qpri command

```
# qchk -A
5132pc1  1p0    DEV_WAIT
                QUEUED     7    /etc/motd  root           1     1     1
                QUEUED     8    /etc/hosts root           2     1     2
                QUEUED     17   /.profile  root           2     1     3
                QUEUED     27   /.puttifar root           2     1     4
5132psq 1p0    DEV_WAIT
# qpri -#27 -a 20
# qchk -A
5132pc1  1p0    DEV_WAIT
                QUEUED     27   /.puttifar root           2     1     1
                QUEUED     7    /etc/motd  root           1     1     2
                QUEUED     8    /etc/hosts root           2     1     3
                QUEUED     17   /.profile  root           2     1     4
5132psq 1p0    DEV_WAIT
```

In this example, we changed the priority of job number 27 and then verified that the priority and the rank had been changed.

In the previous **qpri** command:

▶ The -#flag specifies the Job Number (14) whose priority should be changed.
▶ The -a flag specifies the Priority Number to be assigned (20).

SMIT and Web-based System Manager can also be used to change print job priorities. The SMIT fast path is **smitty qpri**.

11.5.6 Holding and releasing a printing job

The **qhld** command is used to put a temporary hold on a job that is waiting in the queue. The **qhld** command is also the command that is used to release a job back into the queue.

The **qhld** command holds and releases a spooled print job that is not being printed. The **qhld** command works on local queues only (remote queues are not supported). You must have root authority, be a member of the printq group, or be the print job owner to use this command. You can hold/release a spooled job through SMIT (**smitty qhld**) or the command line, as well as Web-based System Manager.

In Example 11-22, the -# flag specifies the job number (27) to be put in HELD state. To release job number 27, we have used the -r flag. Notice that releasing job number 27 has changed its state from HELD to QUEUED.

In the **qhld** command:

▶ The -r flag specifies the job to be released.
▶ The -# flag specifies the job number to be released.

Example 11-22   The qhld command

```
# qchk -A
Queue     Dev     Status      Job    Files     User    PP   %   Blks   Cp   Rnk
-----------------------------------------------------------------------------
5132pcl   lp0     DEV_WAIT
                  QUEUED      7      /etc/motd  root             1      1    1
                  QUEUED      8      /etc/hosts root             2      1    2
                  QUEUED      17     /.profile  root             2      1    3
                  QUEUED      27     /.puttifar root             2      1    4
5132psq  lp0     DEV_WAIT
# qhld -#27
# qchk -A
Queue     Dev     Status      Job    Files     User    PP   %   Blks   Cp   Rnk
-----------------------------------------------------------------------------
```

```
5132pcl  lp0    DEV_WAIT
                QUEUED    7   /etc/motd   root            1    1    1
                QUEUED    8   /etc/hosts  root            2    1    2
                QUEUED    17  /.profile   root            2    1    3
                HELD      27  /.puttifar  root            2    1    4
5132psq  lp0    DEV_WAIT
# qhld -r -#14
# qchk -A
Queue    Dev    Status   Job  Files       User   PP   %   Blks  Cp   Rnk
--------------------------------------------------------------------------
5132pcl  lp0    DEV_WAIT
                QUEUED    7   /etc/motd   root            1    1    1
                QUEUED    8   /etc/hosts  root            2    1    2
                QUEUED    17  /.profile   root            2    1    3
                QUEUED    27  /.puttifar  root            2    1    4
5132psq  lp0    DEV_WAIT
```

11.5.7 Moving a job between queues

Imagine a situation when you have two queues that have the same printing capabilities. The first queue has many print jobs enqueued; the second one is idle, without any print requests. In a situation like this, it would be nice to move some print jobs from the first queue to the second one.

The **qmov** command moves jobs between queues by specifying the destination queue and:

▶ The job number
▶ The queue name containing all the jobs you want to move
▶ The user whose jobs you want to move

As you can see in Example 11-23, we have four jobs in the 5132pclq queue. Since the last one is a PostScript file, let us move this print job (job ID 27) to the 8213psq queue.

Example 11-23   The qmov command

```
# qchk -A
Queue    Dev    Status   Job  Files       User   PP   %   Blks  Cp   Rnk
--------------------------------------------------------------------------
5132pcl  lp0    DEV_WAIT
                QUEUED    7   /etc/motd   root            1    1    1
                QUEUED    8   /etc/hosts  root            2    1    2
                QUEUED    17  /.profile   root            2    1    3
                QUEUED    27  /.puttifar  root            2    1    4
8213psq  lp0    DEV_WAIT
# qmov -m 8213psq -#27
# qchk -A
```

Queue	Dev	Status	Job	Files	User	PP	%	Blks	Cp	Rnk
5132pclq	lp0	DEV_WAIT								
		QUEUED	7	/etc/motd	root			1	1	1
		QUEUED	8	/etc/hosts	root			2	1	2
		QUEUED	17	/.profile	root			2	1	3
8213psq	lp0	DEV_WAIT								
		QUEUED	27	/.puttifar	root			2	1	1

In the **qmov** command in Example 11-23 on page 404:

▶ The -m flag specifies the destination queue.
▶ The -# flag specifies the job number to be moved.

What about moving all print jobs from the 5132pclq queue to the 8213psq queue? You can use the following command to move all jobs (except a job in rank position 1 if the status is running) from the 5132pclq queue to the 8213psq queue:

```
# qmov -m 5132psq -P 8213pclq
```

In this command:

▶ The -m flag specifies the destination queue.
▶ The -P flag specifies the origin queue of the jobs to be moved.

11.6 Printer pooling

Print queues can be serviced by more than one printer through printer pooling. This means that a user can submit the job to a queue, and the print service will select the first available printer assigned to that queue. Multiple printers are assigned to a single queue through the use of multiple queue devices for the same queue.

The first virtual printer is created in the normal way, as described in 11.3.1, "Adding a local print queue" on page 381. To add additional queue devices, use the SMIT option Add an Additional Printer to an Existing Print Queue through the **smitty spooler** fast path and follow the normal steps for adding a local printer. The last screen will allow you to enter the name of existing print queue. Add the queue name that you added in the first step.

When printer pooling is in effect, all jobs will print to the printer defined in the first queue device listed in /etc/qconfig, unless that printer is busy. If that printer is busy, then the job will be printed to the printer defined in the next queue device, assuming it is not busy. This is similar to printer classes in System V printing.

11.7 Quick reference

Table 11-6 shows a comparison between AIX 5L and HP-UX 11i for print management.

Table 11-6   Quick reference for printer management

Tasks	AIX 5L	HP-UX 11i
Run multiple tasks in a GUI environment.	Choose one of the following: ► The `smitty print` fast path ► smitty ► The Web-based System Manager	`sam`
Add a printer.	`mkdev`	`lpadmin`

Start a print queue.	`qadm` (AIX 5L printing subsystem)
	or
	`lpc` (System V)
		`accept`
		and
		`enable`

Stop a print queue.	`qadm` (AIX 5L printing subsystem)
	or
	`lpc` (System V)
		`disable`
		and
		`reject`

Display print queue status.	`lpstat`	`lpstat`
Cancel a printing job.	`qcan`	`cancel`

Add a print queue.	Choose one of the following:
	► AIX 5L printing subsystem:
	  − `mkque`
	  − `mkquedev`
	  − `mkvirprt`
	► System V:
	  − `lpadmin -p`
		`lpadmin`

Tasks	AIX 5L	HP-UX 11i

Change a print queue.	Choose one of the following:
	▶ AIX 5L printing subsystem:
	  — **chque**
	  — **chquedev**
	  — **chvirprt**
	▶ System V:
	  — **lpadmin -p**
		lpadmin

Remove a print queue.	Choose one of the following:
	▶ AIX 5L printing subsystem:
	  — **rmque**
	  — **rmquedev**
	  — **rmvirprt**
	▶ System V:
	  — **lpadmin -x**
		lpadmin

Display settings of a print queue.	Choose one of the following:
	▶ AIX 5L printing subsystem:
	  — **lsque**
	  — **lsquedev**
	  — **lsvirprt**
	▶ System V:
	  — **lpstat**
		lpadmin

## 12

Process management

In this chapter, the following topics are covered:

The scope of this chapter concentrates on the day-to-day tasks related to process management, such as manipulating the process priority with the **nice** and **renice** commands, sending signals to processes with the **kill** command, and running jobs in the background or foreground. The **ps** and **bindprocessor** commands are also reviewed. Some of these commands are specific only to the AIX 5L operating system. The general concept of process management is similar in HP-UX 11i and AIX 5L, but the differences are also described in this chapter.

12.1 Overview of process management related commands and tools

This section provides an overview of process management related to commands and tools for HP-UX and AIX 5L.

HP-UX 11i

In HP-UX 11i, you have the following commands available for managing the processes:

ps	Displays the status of processes.
top	Reports system activities and also lists processes.
nice	Runs a command at higher or lower than normal priority.
renice	Changes the priority of one or more processes.
kill	Send signals to a process or to a group of processes.
time, timex	Prints the elapsed execution time and the user and system processing time attributed to a command.
jobs, fg, bg, stop	Controls process execution.

By SAM, use the following SAM hierarchy: Process Management → Process Control, then mark a process and select Actions.

For more information, see the man pages of these commands.

AIX 5L

In AIX 5L, you have the following options available to perform process management related tasks:

► Web-based System Manager
► SMIT, smitty, or the smitty process fast path
► Command-line based tools

Figure 12-1 on page 411 shows the main menu in Web-based System Manager for managing processes.

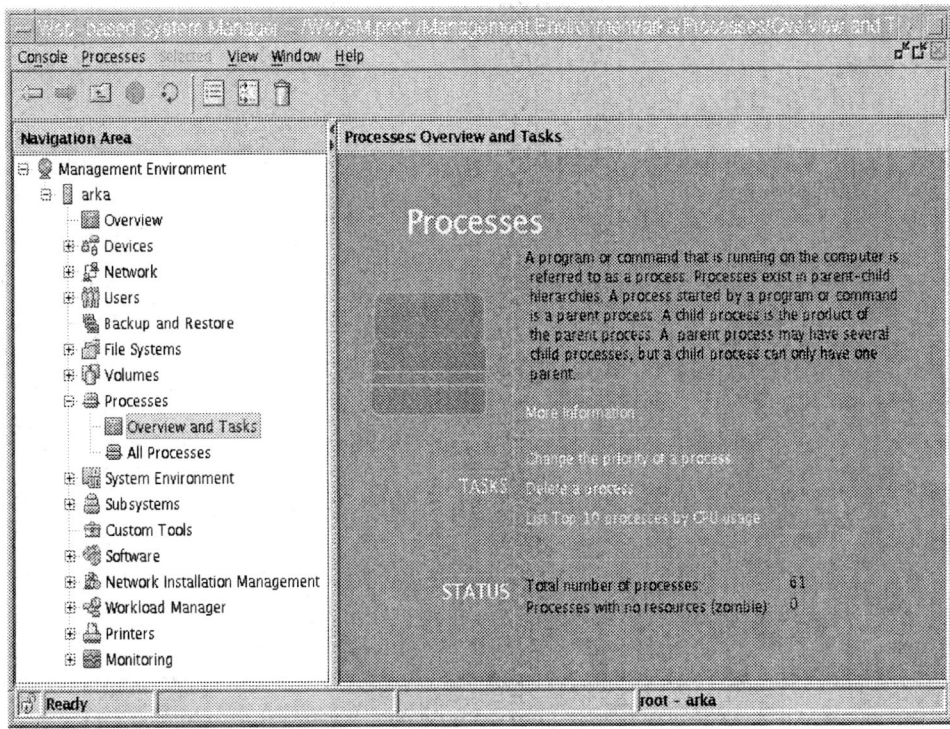

Figure 12-1   Web-based System Manager processes main window

The corresponding smitty process menu is shown in Example 12-1.

Example 12-1   smitty process menu

```
                        Processes

Move cursor to desired item and press Enter.

  Show All Current Processes
  Remove a Process
  Bind a Process to a Processor
  Unbind a Process



F1=Help              F2=Refresh          F3=Cancel          F8=Image
F9=Shell             F10=Exit            Enter=Do
```

The following list shows the commands available in AIX 5L for managing the
processes:

ps   Displays the status of processes

topas	Reports system activities and also lists processes
nice	Runs a command at higher or lower than normal priority
renice	Changes the priority of one or more processes
kill	Send signals to a process or to a group of processes
time	Prints the elapsed execution time and the user and system processing time attributed to a command
tprof	Reports CPU usage for individual programs and the whole system
jobs, fg, bg, stop	Controls process execution
bindprocessor	Binds or unbinds the kernel threads of a process to a processor
emstat	Shows emulation exception statistics

12.2 Listing information about processes

Basically, in both HP-UX 11i and AIX 5L, you should use the **ps** command to list information about processes. The **ps** command enables you to check the status of active processes on a system, as well as display technical information about the processes. This data is useful for such administrative tasks as determining how to set process priorities.

Depending on which options you use, **ps** reports the following information:

- ▶ Current status of the process
- ▶ Process ID
- ▶ Parent process ID
- ▶ User ID
- ▶ Scheduling class
- ▶ Priority
- ▶ Address of the process
- ▶ Memory used
- ▶ CPU time used

You can use the **ps** command in two cases:

- ▶ Use of the **ps** command in CPU usage study
- ▶ Use of the **ps** command in memory usage study

Depending on what options you use along with the **ps** command, you get different outputs. Also, the syntax and available options differ slightly in HP-UX 11i and AIX 5L. For more information about the options and the output of the **ps** command, refer to the man pages for this command.

HP-UX 11i

In HP-UX 11i, to list all the processes being executed on a system, use the **ps** command in the following way:

```
# ps [-ef]
```

ps   Displays only the processes associated with your login session.

ps -ef   Displays full information about all the processes being executed on the system.

The following example shows the output from the **ps** command when no options are used:

```
# ps
   PID TTY       TIME COMMAND
 19745 pts/tb    0:00 telnetd
 19746 pts/tb    0:00 sh
 21683 pts/tb    0:00 ps
```

The next example shows output from **ps -ef**. This shows that the first process executed when the system boots is sched (the swapper) followed by the init process, pageout, and so on. Refer to Example 12-2.

Example 12-2   ps -ef command

```
# ps -ef
     UID   PID  PPID  C   STIME TTY      TIME COMMAND
    root     0     0  0  Jun 20 ?       0:08 swapper
    root     8     0  0  Jun 20 ?       0:00 supsched
    root     9     0  0  Jun 20 ?       0:00 strmem
    root    10     0  0  Jun 20 ?       0:00 strweld
    root    11     0  0  Jun 20 ?       0:00 strfreebd
    root     2     0  0  Jun 20 ?       0:02 vhand
    root     3     0  0  Jun 20 ?      16:09 statdaemon
    root     4     0  0  Jun 20 ?       0:47 unhashdaemon
    root    12     0 15  Jun 20 ?      20:06 ttisr
    root    13     0  0  Jun 20 ?       0:00 ioconfigd
    root     1     0  0  Jun 20 ?       0:00 init
    root    19     0  0  Jun 20 ?       0:00 lvmkd
    root    20     0  0  Jun 20 ?       0:00 lvmkd
    root    21     0  0  Jun 20 ?       0:00 lvmkd
    root    22     0  0  Jun 20 ?       0:00 lvmkd
    root    23     0  0  Jun 20 ?       0:00 lvmkd
    root    24     0  0  Jun 20 ?       0:00 lvmkd
    root    25     0  0  Jun 20 ?       0:00 lvmschedd
    root    26     0  0  Jun 20 ?       0:00 smpsched
    root    27     0  0  Jun 20 ?       0:00 smpsched
    root    28     0  0  Jun 20 ?       0:00 smpsched
```

```
root     29   0 0 Jun 20  ?              0:00 smpsched
root     30   0 0 Jun 20  ?              0:00 sblksched
root     31   0 0 Jun 20  ?              0:00 sblksched
root   2691   1 0 Jun 20  console        0:00 /usr/sbin/getty console console
root  20450   1 0 12:25:45 ?             0:00 /usr/sbin/biod 16
root    365   1 0 Jun 20  ?              0:29 /usr/sbin/syncer
root     37   0 0 Jun 20  ?             29:11 vxfsd
root    457   1 0 Jun 20  ?              0:00 /usr/sbin/ptydaemon
```

The **top** command can also be used to show the process and performance information. Refer to Example 12-3.

Example 12-3 The top command

```
System: brazil                              Wed Jun 29 16:51:55 2005
Load averages: 0.27, 0.26, 0.27
136 processes: 121 sleeping, 15 running
Cpu states:
CPU    LOAD    USER    NICE    SYS    IDLE   BLOCK   SWAIT   INTR   SSYS
 0     0.00    0.0%    0.0%    0.0%  100.0%   0.0%    0.0%    0.0%   0.0%
 1     1.00    0.4%    0.0%    5.5%   94.1%   0.0%    0.0%    0.0%   0.0%
 2     0.00    1.0%    0.0%    1.8%   97.2%   0.0%    0.0%    0.0%   0.0%
 3     0.08    5.9%    0.0%    0.6%   93.5%   0.0%    0.0%    0.0%   0.0%
---    ----   -----   -----   -----  -----   -----   -----   -----  -----
avg    0.27    1.8%    0.0%    2.0%   96.2%   0.0%    0.0%    0.0%   0.0%

Memory: 184072K (141452K) real, 617628K (536124K) virtual, 933404K free   Page#

CPU TTY       PID USERNAME PRI NI   SIZE    RES STATE    TIME %WCPU  %CPU COMMAND
 3  ?        8186 root     152 20 15992K 38628K run     90:18  2.36  2.36 mxagent
 0  ?        1233 root     152 20 16544K 22664K run    100:09  0.86  0.86 prm3d
 3  pts/tb  21705 root     178 20   580K   512K run      0:00  0.97  0.81 top
 0  ?          37 root     152 20    0K   1888K run     29:12  0.53  0.53 vxfsd
 2  ?        1195 root     -16 20 11116K 10612K run     23:22  0.19  0.19 mid
 2  ?        2298 root     152 20  1808K  1760K run      1:03  0.16  0.16 agdb
 1  ?        2132 root     152 20  2584K  2364K run      1:33  0.16  0.16 rep
 1  ?          12 root     -32 20    0K     32K sleep   20:07  0.15  0.15 ttisr
 1  ?        2317 root     152 20  2852K  1900K run      2:30  0.12  0.12 alarm
 1  ?           3 root     128 20    0K     32K sleep   16:10  0.12  0.12 stat
 2  ?        1342 root     154 10   680K   844K sleep   19:05  0.12  0.12 psmctd
 0  ?        1013 root     152 20  2044K  3064K run     11:51  0.11  0.11 cims
 3  ?        1441 root     152 20  3920K  5036K run      1:09  0.10  0.10 vxsvc
 0  ?        1527 root     152 20  1076K  2356K run      0:18  0.10  0.10 samd
```

AIX 5L

In AIX 5L, you can use the Web-based System Manager to list information about the processes. You can chose one of two options:

► List the top 10 processes by CPU usage, as shown in Figure 12-2.

Command	Owner n...	Process ID	Parent ID	Started	Current CPU	Total CPU	TTY
syncd	root	7760	1	Apr 18	0	00:09:03	–
X	root	6024	6722	Apr 18	11	00:05:06	–
dtsession	root	14094	18438	Apr 19	0	00:01:52	–
java	root	22848	14878	10:29:15	13	00:01:50	pts/1
rmcd	root	10136	8026	Apr 18	0	00:01:35	–
dtwm	root	17624	14094	Apr 19	0	00:00:53	–
ttsession	root	13894	1	Apr 19	0	00:00:47	–
init	root	1	0	Apr 18	0	00:00:38	–
IBM.CSMAgentR...	root	17292	8026	Apr 24	0	00:00:27	–
snmpd	root	7498	8026	Apr 18	0	00:00:21	–

Figure 12-2   The top 10 processes list in Web-based System Manager

► List all processes, as shown in Figure 12-3 on page 416.

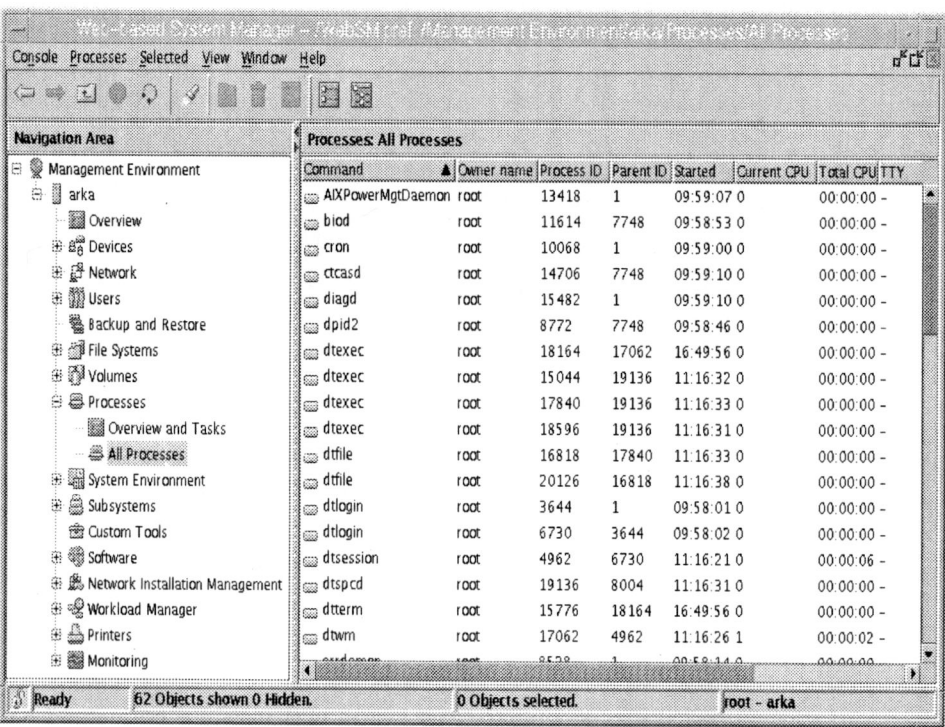

Figure 12-3   Listing all processes using Web-based System Manager

When you have all processes displayed, you can select one or more of them and then you can use the Selected menu to perform certain tasks on the selected processes. The selected menu is shown in Figure 12-4 on page 417.

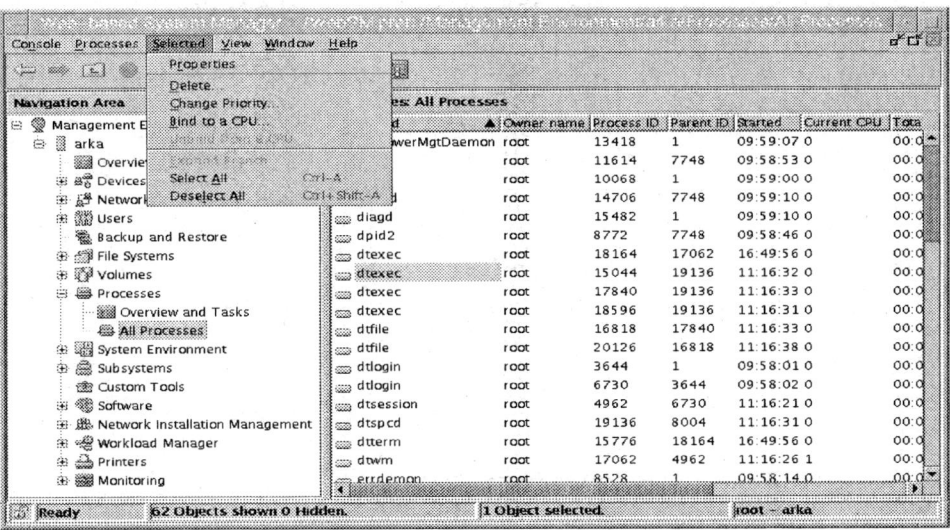

Figure 12-4   Using the Selected menu in Web-based System Manager

Alternatively, you can go through the SMIT hierarchy by doing the following steps:

1. Run **smitty process**, which will open the menu shown in Example 12-1 on page 411.

2. Chose the "Show All Current Processes" option and press Enter. It will open the menu shown in Example 12-4.

Example 12-4   "Show THREADS information?" question

```
                        Show THREADS information

Move cursor to desired item and press Enter.

    1 no
    2 yes

F1=Help                 F2=Refresh              F3=Cancel
F8=Image                F10=Exit                Enter=Do
/=Find                  n=Find Next
```

3. Use the arrow keys to make your choice and press Enter.

4. A screen similar to Example 12-5 should appear along with an OK prompt.

Example 12-5   Processes list output from smitty

```
                        COMMAND STATUS
```

```
Command: OK              stdout: yes              stderr: no

Before command completion, additional instructions may appear below.

[TOP]
     UID    PID  PPID   C    STIME    TTY  TIME CMD
     root     1     0   0 09:57:06     -  0:00 /etc/init
     root  3644     1   0 09:58:01     -  0:00 /usr/dt/bin/dtlogin -daemon
     root  4206     1   0 09:59:20     -  0:00 /usr/bin/itesmdem itesrv.ini
/etc
/IMNSearch/search/
     root  4464     1   0 09:57:14     -  0:00 /usr/lib/methods/ssa_daemon -1
ss
a0
     root  4958  6730   0 09:59:11     -  0:07 dtgreet
     root  5244     1   0 09:58:14     -  0:01 /usr/sbin/syncd 60
     root  5714  7748   0 09:58:37     -  0:00 /usr/sbin/portmap
     root  6136  9290   3 10:43:51  pts/0  0:00 smitty process
     root  6226  7748   0 09:59:20     -  0:00
/usr/sbin/rsct/bin/IBM.ServiceRMd
[MORE...34]


F1=Help              F2=Refresh          F3=Cancel          F6=Command
F8=Image             F9=Shell            F10=Exit           /=Find
n=Find Next
```

There is one more tool in AIX 5L for displaying information about processes and the system activities in general: The **topas** command. This tool is similar to the **top** command utility that is typically used in HP-UX environments.

Example 12-4 on page 417 shows output from the **topas -d 0 -n 0 -p 15** command, which means that you want to monitor only the top 15 processes without monitoring any disk and network activities. For detailed information about the **topas** command, please refer to the **topas** man page.

Example 12-6   The topas command

```
Topas Monitor for host:    i19962c           EVENTS/QUEUES      FILE/TTY
Thu May  2 11:01:38 2002    Interval:  2      Cswitch    175   Readch      0
                                              Syscall    182   Writech    27
Kernel    0.1  |                            | Reads        0   Rawin       0
User      0.0  |                            | Writes       0   Ttyout      0
Wait      0.0  |                            | Forks        0   Igets       0
Idle     99.8  |###########################| Execs        0   Namei       7
                                              Runqueue   0.0   Dirblk      0
Name              PID CPU% PgSp Owner        Waitqueue  0.0
topas           19196  0.1  1.8 root
```

```
syncd         5728  0.0  0.3 root      PAGING              MEMORY
dtexec       19892  0.0  1.7 root      Faults       0      Real,MB    1023
dtscreen     20934  0.0  1.6 root      Steals       0      % Comp     15.8
ksh          18480  0.0  0.7 root      PgspIn       0      % Noncomp   6.6
i4llmd       17290  0.0  1.9 root      PgspOut      0      % Client    0.5
telnetd      16928  0.0  0.7 root      PageIn       0
X             3656  0.0  3.2 root      PageOut      0      PAGING SPACE
rpc.lockd    10328  0.0  0.0 root      Sios         0      Size,MB    1024
gil           2580  0.0  0.0 root                         % Used      0.8
dtsession     6744  0.0  2.9 root      NFS (calls/sec)    % Free      99.1
dtterm        9864  0.0  2.5 root      ServerV2     0
dtwm         14472  0.0  2.9 root      ClientV2     0      Press:
ttsession    14296  0.0  2.0 root      ServerV3     0      "h" for help
init             1  0.0  1.8 root      ClientV3     0      "q" to quit
```

Note: You should have the bos.perf.tools fileset installed in order to use the **topas** command. The command location is /usr/bin/topas.

Finally, you can also use the command line in AIX 5L to display information about processes. You should use the **ps** command. For detailed information about the available options, please refer to the **ps** man page.

The following examples show how to use the **ps** command in AIX 5L to obtain required information about processes.

► To display all processes, enter:

```
ps -e -f
```

► To list processes owned by specific users, enter:

```
ps -f -l -ujim,jane,su
```

► To list processes that are associated with the /dev/console and /dev/tty1 ttys, enter:

```
ps -t console,tty/1
```

► To list processes not associated with a terminal, enter:

```
ps -t -
```

► To display a specified format with field specifiers, enter:

```
ps -o ruser,pid,ppid=parent,args
```

The output is:

```
RUSER   PID     parent  COMMAND
helene  34      12      ps -o ruser,pid,ppid=parent,args
```

► To display a specified format with field descriptors, enter:

```
ps -o "< %u > %p %y : %a"
```

The output is:

```
< RUSER >        PID    TT :    COMMAND
< helene >        34    pts/3 : ps -o < %u > %p %y : %a
```

► To display information about processes and kernel threads controlled by the current terminal, enter:

```
ps -lm
```

The output is similar to:

```
F S UID  PID PPID  C PRI NI ADDR  SZ WCHAN    TTY  TIME  CMD
240003 A  26 8984 7190  1  60 20 2974 312      pts/1 0:00  -ksh
400 S    -    -    - 1  60  -    -   -          -     - -
200005 A  26 9256 8984 15  67 20 18ed 164      pts/1 0:00  ps
0 R      -    -    - 15  67  -    -   -          -     - -
```

► To display information about all processes and kernel threads, enter:

```
ps -emo THREAD
```

The output is similar to:

```
USER   PID  PPID  TID S  C PRI SC   WCHAN   FLAG   TTY BND CMD
jane  1716 19292    - A 10  60  1      * 260801 pts/7  -  biod
-     -       - 4863 S  0  60  0 599e9d8   8400  -    - -
-     -       - 5537 R 10  60  1 5999e18   2420  -    3 -
luke 19292 18524    - A  0  60  0 586ad84 200001 pts/7  -  -ksh
-     -       - 7617 S  0  60  0 586ad84    400  -    - -
luke 25864 31168    - A 11  65  0      - 200001 pts/7  -  -
-     -       - 8993 R 11  65  0      -      0  -    - -
```

12.3 Sending signals to processes

For sending signals to processes, you should use the **kill** command in HP-UX 11i and AIX 5L. Typically, the **kill** command is used for terminating processes, but it is a much more powerful command. You can send any signal a process and thus handle them the way you want to do. The sending process (or shell) must have the permission to kill another process.

For a basic list of signals for HP-UX 11i see the kill (1M) and signal (5M) manual pages.

The basic list of signals for AIX 5L is listed below:

SIGHUP	**1**	Hangup, generated when terminal disconnects
SIGINT	**2**	Interrupt, generated from terminal special char
SIGQUIT	**3**	Quit, generated from terminal special char
SIGILL	**4**	Illegal instruction (not reset when caught)
SIGTRAP	**5**	Trace trap (not reset when caught)

SIGABRT	6	Abort process
SIGEMT	7	EMT instruction
SIGFPE	8	Floating point exception
SIGKILL	9	Kill (cannot be caught or ignored)
SIGBUS	10	Bus error (specification exception)
SIGSEGV	11	Segmentation violation
SIGSYS	12	Bad argument to system call
SIGPIPE	13	Write on a pipe with no one to read it
SIGALRM	14	Alarm clock timeout
SIGTERM	15	Software termination signal
SIGURG	16	Urgent condition on I/O channel
SIGSTOP	17	Stop (cannot be caught or ignored)
SIGTSTP	18	Interactive stop
SIGCONT	19	Continue (cannot be caught or ignored)
SIGCHLD	20	Sent to parent on child stop or exit
SIGTTIN	21	Background read attempted from control terminal
SIGTTOU	22	Background write attempted to control terminal
SIGIO	23	I/O possible, or completed
SIGXCPU	24	CPU time limit exceeded
SIGXFSZ	25	File size limit exceeded
SIGMSG	27	Input data in the ring buffer
SIGWINCH	28	Window size changed
SIGPWR	29	Power-fail restart
SIGUSR1	30	User defined signal 1
SIGUSR2	31	User defined signal 2
SIGPROF	32	Profiling time alarm
SIGDANGER	33	System crash imminent; frees up some page space
SIGVTALRM	34	Virtual time alarm
SIGMIGRATE	35	Migrates process
SIGPRE	36	Programming exception
SIGVIRT	37	AIX 5L virtual time alarm
SIGALRM1	38	m:n condition variables (reserved)
SIGWAITING	39	m:n scheduling (reserved)
SIGCPUFAIL	59	Predictive De-configuration of Processors (reserved)
SIGKAP	60	Keep alive poll from native keyboard
SIGGRANT	SIGKAP	Monitor mode granted
SIGRETRACT	61	Monitor mode should be relinquished
SIGSOUND	62	Sound control has completed
SIGSAK	63	Secure attention key

Unless you create software, you will only use a few of these signals in day-to-day work. In this chapter we focus only on killing, stopping, and terminating processes.

12.3.1 Killing a process

Sometimes it is necessary to stop (kill) a process. The process may be in an endless loop, or you may have started a large job that you want to stop before it is completed. You can kill any process that you own, and superuser can kill any processes in the system except for a few processes such as init, fsflush, and so on.

In both the HP-UX 11i and AIX 5L operating systems, you should use the `kill` command to stop a process. The usage of the `kill` command is the same in both systems. For example:

```
kill [ -s { SignalName | SignalNumber } ] ProcessID ...
```

or

```
kill [ - SignalName | - SignalNumber ] ProcessID ...
```

The `kill` command sends a signal (by default, the SIGTERM signal) to a running process. This default action normally stops processes. If you want to stop a process, specify the process ID (PID) in the ProcessID variable. The shell reports the PID of each process that is running in the background (unless you start more than one process in a pipeline, in which case the shell reports the number of the last process). You can also use the **ps** command to find the process ID number of commands.

A root user can stop any process with the `kill` command. If you are not a root user, you must have initiated the process you want to stop.

HP-UX 11i

In HP-UX 11i, you can also use SAM.

Use the following SAM hierarchy: Process Management → Process Control, then mark some process and select Actions → Safe Kill using SIGTERM, or Forced (Unsafe) Kill using SIGKILL. You can only use these signs by SAM.

AIX 5L

In AIX 5L, you have the following possibilities to chose from:

► The Web-based System Manager
► The `smitty kill` fast path
► The `kill` command

To use the Web-based System Manager to kill a process, follow the steps listed below:

1. Display all the processes, as shown in Figure 12-3 on page 416.

2. Select the process or processes you want to remove.

3. Chose **Delete** from the selected menu shown in Figure 12-4 on page 417. The screen shown in Figure 12-5 should appear.

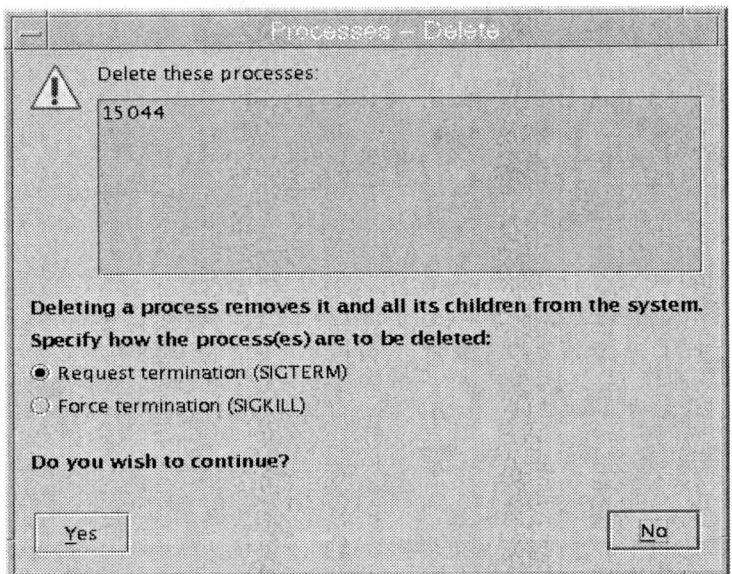

Figure 12-5   Terminating a process using Web-based System Manager

4. Chose what type of signal you want to use (SIGTERM or SIGKILL).

5. Click **Yes**.

Alternatively, you can go through the SMIT hierarchy:

1. Type **smitty kill** at the command line. It opens the menu shown in Example 12-7.

Example 12-7   smitty kill command

```
                         Remove a Process

Type or select values in entry fields.
Press Enter AFTER making all desired changes.

                                              [Entry Fields]
    SIGNAL type                               SIGTERM               +
  * PROCESS ID                                []
  +#
```

```
F1=Help          F2=Refresh       F3=Cancel        F4=List
F5=Reset         F6=Command       F7=Edit          F8=Image
F9=Shell         F10=Exit         Enter=Do
```

2. In the SIGNAL type field, chose the signal you want to send by using the F4 and arrow keys, and press Enter.

3. In the PROCESS ID fields, chose the process to be affected by using the F4 and arrow keys, and press Enter.

4. Press Enter again and wait for an OK prompt.

You can also use the command line. The following examples show the use the **kill** command in AIX 5L, along with a description of each task.

► To stop a given process, enter:

   kill 1095

   This stops process 1095 by sending it the default SIGTERM signal. Note that process 1095 might not actually stop if it has made special arrangements to ignore or override the SIGTERM signal.

► To stop several processes that ignore the default signal, enter:

   kill -KILL 2098 1569

   This sends signal 9, the SIGKILL signal, to processes 2098 and 1569. The SIGKILL signal is a special signal that normally cannot be ignored or overridden.

► To stop all of your processes and log yourself off, enter:

   kill -KILL 0

   This sends signal 9, the SIGKILL signal, to all processes having a process group ID equal to the sender's process group ID. Because the shell cannot ignore this SIGKILL signal, this also stops the login shell and logs you off.

► To stop all processes that you own, enter:

   kill -9 -1

   This sends signal 9, the SIGKILL signal, to all processes owned by the effective user, even those started at other work stations and that belong to other process groups. If a listing that you requested is being printed, it is also stopped.

► To send a different signal code to a process, enter:

   kill   -USR1   1103

   The name of the **kill** command is misleading because many signals, including SIGUSR1, do not stop processes. The action taken on SIGUSR1 is defined by the particular application you are running.

Note: To send signal 15 (the SIGTERM signal) with this form of the `kill` command, you must explicitly specify -15 or SIGTERM.

12.4 Changing the priority of a process

You can raise or lower the priority of a command or a process by changing the nice number. You have two options to chose from:

▶ Invoke a command with an altered scheduling priority (using the **nice** command).

▶ Alter the priority of running processes (using the **renice** command).

HP-UX 11i

In HP-UX 11i, to lower the priority of a process use:

`/usr/bin/nice` *command_name*	Increases the nice number by ten units (the default).
`/usr/bin/nice -10` *command_name*	Increases the nice number.
`/usr/bin/nice - -10` *command_name*	Raises the priority of the command by lowering the nice number. The first minus sign is the option sign, and the second minus sign indicates a negative number.

Use the **renice** command to alter the priority of running process:

```
renice [-n offset] [ -g | -p | -u ] ID...
```

The **renice** command alters the scheduling priority of one or more running processes. By default, the processes to be affected are specified by their process IDs. For information about the available options of the **renice** command, please refer to the **renice** man page.

The following examples show the use of the **renice** command in HP-UX 11i:

▶ To adjust the system scheduling priority so that group IDs 224 and 68 would have a higher scheduling priority, if the user has the appropriate privileges to do so, enter:

```
renice -n -4 -g 224 68
```

▶ To adjust the system scheduling priority so that numeric user ID 9 and user smith would have a lower scheduling priority, use:

```
renice -n 4 -u 9 smith
```

AIX 5L

In AIX 5L, you can also use the **nice** and **renice** commands to change the priority of a process. The **nice** command runs another command at a different priority, while the **renice** command changes the priority of an already running process. The root user can increase or decrease the priority of any process. Other users can only decrease the priority of processes they own.

The **nice** and **renice** commands reside in /usr/bin and are part of the bos.rte.control fileset, which is installed by default from the AIX 5L base installation media.

The following examples show how to use the **nice** and **renice** commands in AIX 5L.

▶ To run the **cc** command at a lower priority, type:

```
nice -n 15 cc -c *.c
```

▶ To specify a very high priority, enter:

```
nice --10 wall <<end
System shutdown in 2 minutes!
end
```

This example runs the **wall** command at a higher priority than all user processes, which slows down everything else running on the system. The <<end and end portions of the example define a document here, which uses the text entered before the end line as standard input for the command.

> **Note:** If you do not have root user authority when you run this command, the **wall** command runs at the normal priority.

▶ To run a command at low priority, enter:

```
nice cc -c *.c
```

This example runs the **cc** command at low priority.

> **Note:** This does not run the command in the background. The workstation is not available for doing other things.

▶ To run a low-priority command in the background, enter:

```
nice cc -c *.c &
```

This example runs the **cc** command at low priority in the background. The workstation is free to run other commands while the **cc** command is running.

► To alter the system scheduling priority so that process IDs 987 and 32 have lower scheduling priorities, enter:

```
renice -n 5 -p 987 32
```

► To alter the system scheduling priority so that group IDs 324 and 76 have higher scheduling priorities (if the user has the appropriate privileges to do so), enter:

```
renice -n -4 -g 324 76
```

► To alter the system scheduling priority so that numeric user ID 8 and user smith have lower scheduling priorities, enter:

```
renice -n 4 -u 8 smith
```

You can also use the Web-based System Manager to change the priority of a process, as shown in Figure 12-6.

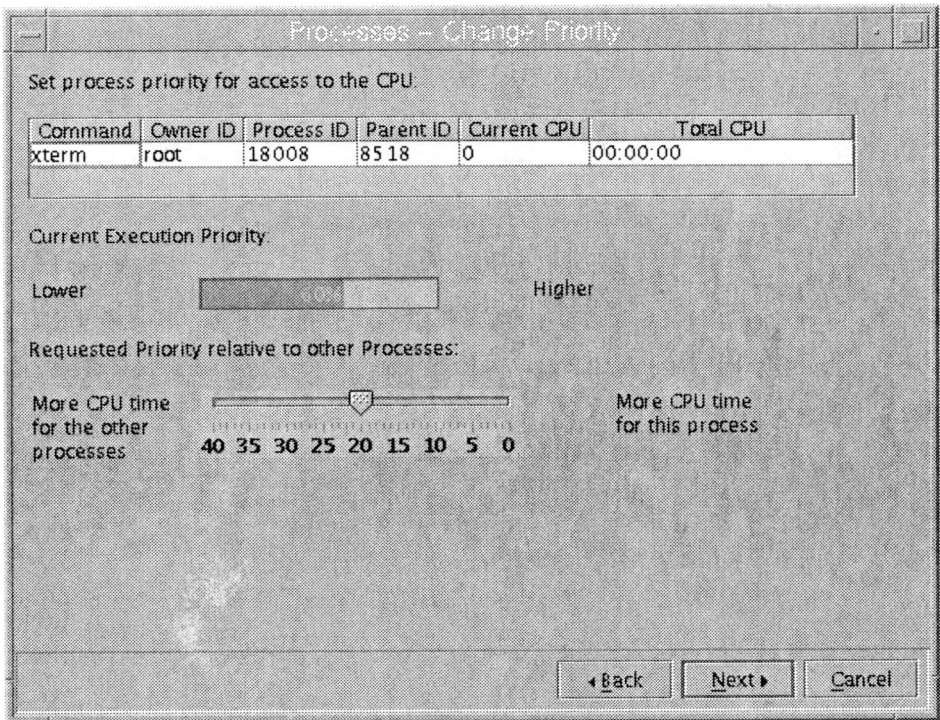

Figure 12-6   Changing priority of a process using Web-based System Manager

Alternatively, you can use the **smitty nice** and **smitty renice** fast paths.

To run a command with altered priority using **smitty**, follow this procedure:

1. Type **smitty nice** at the command line and press Enter. It opens the menu shown in Example 12-8.

Example 12-8   smitty nice command

```
                    Set Initial Priority of a Process

Type or select values in entry fields.
Press Enter AFTER making all desired changes.

                                                [Entry Fields]
    PRIORITY number                             [10]                    +
  * COMMAND name                                []




F1=Help            F2=Refresh         F3=Cancel         F4=List
F5=Reset           F6=Command         F7=Edit           F8=Image
F9=Shell           F10=Exit           Enter=Do
```

2. Enter the priority number you wish to set, then use the arrow keys to move to the COMMAND name option.

3. Enter the command name you want to run. Press Enter.

4. Wait for an OK prompt, which means the command successfully completed.

To change the priority of a running process using **smitty**, follow this procedure:

1. Type **smitty renice** at the command line and press Enter. It opens the menu shown in Example 12-9.

Example 12-9   smitty renice command

```
                  Alter the Priority of a Running Process

Type or select values in entry fields.
Press Enter AFTER making all desired changes.

                                                [Entry Fields]
  * PRIORITY increment                          [0]                     +
  * PROCESS ID                                  []                      +




F1=Help            F2=Refresh         F3=Cancel         F4=List
F5=Reset           F6=Command         F7=Edit           F8=Image
```

2. Enter the priority increment that you want to set and use the arrow keys to move down to the PROCESS ID option.

3. Use the F4 key and the arrow keys to select the process and press Enter.

4. Press Enter again and wait for an OK prompt, which means the command successfully completed.

12.5 Working with jobs

The general concept of working with jobs is the same in both the HP-UX 11i and AIX 5L operating systems. There are only small differences, depending on which shell you are using. For more information about these differences, see the appropriate man pages for the **bg**, **fg**, and **jobs** commands. In this chapter, we assume that the way the systems handle the jobs is the same in HP-UX 11i and AIX 5L, so we will only briefly describe the concept.

12.5.1 Foreground and background processes

Processes that are started from and require a user's interaction are called foreground processes. Processes that are run independently of a user are referred to as background processes. Programs and commands run as foreground processes by default. To run a process in the background, place an ampersand (&) at the end of the command name that you use to start the process.

12.5.2 Daemons

Daemons are processes that run unattended. They are constantly in the background and are available at all times. Daemons are usually started when the system starts and run until the system stops. A daemon process performs system services and is available at all times to more than one task or user. Daemon processes are started by the root user or root shell and can be stopped only by the root user. For example, the qdaemon process provides access to system resources, such as printers. Another common daemon is the sendmail daemon.

12.5.3 Zombie process

A zombie process is a dead process that is no longer executing but is still recognized in the process table (in other words, it has a PID number). It has no other system space allocated to it. Zombie processes have been killed or have exited and continue to exist in the process table until the parent process dies or the system is shut down and restarted. Zombie processes show up as <defunct> when listed by the **ps** command.

12.5.4 Starting and stopping a process

You start a foreground process from a display station by either entering a program name or command name at the system prompt. Once a foreground process has started, the process interacts with you at your display station until it is complete. This means no other interaction (for example, entering another command) can take place at the display station until the process is finished or you halt it.

To start a process in the foreground

To run a process in the foreground, type the name of the command with all the appropriate parameters and flags:

```
$ CommandName
```

Press Enter.

To start a process in the background

To run a process in the background, type the name of the command with all the appropriate parameters and flags, followed by an ampersand (&), and press Enter:

```
$ CommandName&
```

When the process is running in the background, you can perform additional tasks by entering other commands at your display station.

Generally, background processes are most useful for commands that take a long time to run. However, because they increase the total amount of work the processor is doing, background processes also slow down the rest of the system.

Most processes direct their output to standard output, even when they run in the background. Unless redirected, standard output goes to the display station. Because the output from a background process can interfere with your other work on the system, it is usually good practice to redirect the output of a background process to a file or a printer. You can then look at the output whenever you are ready. As long as a background process is running, you can check its status with the **ps** command.

Canceling a foreground process

If you start a foreground process and then decide you do not want to let it finish, you can cancel it by pressing INTERRUPT. This is usually done by pressing Ctrl+C or Ctrl+Backspace.

Note: INTERRUPT (Ctrl+C) does not cancel background processes. To cancel a background process, you must use the **kill** command.

Stopping a foreground process

It is possible for a process to be stopped, but not have its process ID (PID) removed from the process table. You can stop a foreground process by pressing Ctrl+Z.

Note: Ctrl+Z works in the Korn shell (ksh) and C shell (csh), but not in the Bourne shell (bsh).

Restarting a stopped process

This procedure describes how to restart a process that has been stopped with Ctrl+Z.

Note: To restart a stopped process, you must either be the user who started the process or have root user authority.

To show all the processes running or stopped but not killed on your system, type:

```
ps -ef
```

You might want to pipe this command through a **grep** command to restrict the list to those processes most likely to be the one you want to restart. For example, if you want to restart a vi session, you could type:

```
ps -ef | grep vi
```

Press Enter. This command would display only those lines from the **ps** command output that contained the word vi. The output would look something like this:

```
UID    PID   PPID  C       STIME     TTY  TIME  COMMAND
root   1234  13682 0       00:59:53  -    0:01  vi test
root   14277 13682 1       01:00:34  -    0:00  grep vi
```

In the **ps** command output, find the process you want to restart and note its PID number. In the example, the PID is 1234.

To send the CONTINUE signal to the stopped process, type:

```
kill -19 1234
```

Substitute the PID of your process for the 1234. The -19 indicates the CONTINUE signal. This command restarts the process in the background. If it is okay for the process to run in the background, you are finished with the procedure. If the process needs to run in the foreground (as a vi session would), you must proceed with the next step.

To bring the process in to the foreground, type:

```
fg 1234
```

Once again, substitute the PID of your process for the 1234. Your process should now be running in the foreground. (You are now in your vi edit session.)

12.5.5 Scheduling a process for later operation (the at command)

You can set up a process as a batch process to run in the background at a scheduled time. The **at** and **smit** commands let you enter the names of commands to be run at a later time and allow you to specify when the commands should be run.

The **at** command is the same in both the HP-UX 11i and AIX 5L operating systems. For more information about the **at** command in HP-UX 11i, see the appropriate man pages for the **at**.

> **Note:** The /var/adm/cron/at.allow and /var/adm/cron/at.deny files control whether you can use the **at** command. A person with root user authority can create, edit, or delete these files. Entries in these files are user login names with one name to a line. The following is an example of an at.allow file:
>
> ```
> root
> nick
> dee
> sarah
> ```

If the at.allow file exists, only users whose login names appear in it can use the **at** command. A system administrator can explicitly stop a user from using the **at** command by listing the user's login name in the at.deny file. If only the at.deny file exists, any user whose name does not appear in the file can use the **at** command.

You cannot use the **at** command if one of the following items is true:

► The at.allow file and the at.deny file do not exist (allows root user only).
► The at.allow file exists but the user's login name is not listed in it.
► The at.deny file exists and the user's login name is listed in it.

If the at.allow file does not exist and the at.deny file does not exist or is empty, only someone with root user authority can submit a job with the **at** command.

The **at** command syntax allows you to specify a date string, a time and day string, or an increment string for when you want the process to run. It also allows you to specify which shell or queue to use. The following examples show some typical uses of the command.

The at command

As an example, if your login name is joyce and you have a script named WorkReport that you want to run at midnight, do the following:

1. Type in the time you want the program to start running:

   ```
   at midnight
   ```

2. Type the names of the programs to run, pressing Enter after each name. After typing the last name, press the end-of-file character (Ctrl+D) to signal the end of the list:

   ```
   WorkReport^D
   ```

   After pressing Ctrl+D, the system displays information similar to the following:

   ```
   job joyce.741502800.a at Fri Jul  6 00:00:00 CDT 2001.
   ```

   The program WorkReport is given the job number joyce.741502800.a and will run at midnight July 6.

To list the programs you have sent to be run later, type:

```
at -l
```

The system displays information similar to the following:

```
joyce.741502800.a      Fri Jul  6 00:00:00 CDT 2001
```

To cancel a program you have set up to run later, first list the job numbers assigned to your programs with **at -l**. Once you know the job number of the program you want to cancel, type:

```
at -r joyce.741502800.a
```

This cancels job joyce.741502800.a.

See the **at** command in the *AIX 5L Version 5.3 Commands Reference, SC23-4888-02*, for the exact syntax.

You can also use the **smitty at** and **smitty sjat** commands to perform this task. The **smitty at** command opens the menu shown in Example 12-10.

Example 12-10   smitty at command

```
                            Schedule Jobs

Move cursor to desired item and press Enter.

   List All Jobs Scheduled
   Schedule a Job
   Remove a Job from the Schedule




F1=Help               F2=Refresh            F3=Cancel            F8=Image
F9=Shell              F10=Exit              Enter=Do
```

The **smitty sjat** command opens the menu shown in Example 12-11.

Example 12-11   smitty sjat command

```
                            Schedule a Job

Type or select values in entry fields.
Press Enter AFTER making all desired changes.

                                                [Entry Fields]
   YEAR                                         [02]
   MONTH                                        [May]                  +
   DAY (1-31)                                   [03]
 * HOUR (0-23)                                  []
 * MINUTES (0-59)                               []
 # SHELL to use for job execution              Korn (ksh)             +
 * COMMAND or SHELL SCRIPT (full pathname)      []




F1=Help               F2=Refresh            F3=Cancel            F4=List
F5=Reset              F6=Command            F7=Edit              F8=Image
F9=Shell              F10=Exit              Enter=Do
```

12.5.6 Listing all the scheduled processes (at or atq commands)

You can list all scheduled processes with the -l flag of the **at** command or with the **atq** command.

Both commands give the same output, but the **atq** command can order the processes by the time the **at** command was issued and can display just the number of processes in the queue.

You can list all scheduled processes in the following ways:

▶ With the **at** command from the command line
▶ With the **atq** command

The at command
To list the scheduled processes, type:

```
at -1
```

This command lists all the scheduled processes in your queue. If you are a root user, this command lists all the scheduled processes for all users.

The atq command
To list all scheduled processes in the queue, type:

```
atq
```

If you are a root user, you can list the scheduled processes in a particular user's queue by typing:

```
atq UserName
```

To list the number of scheduled processes in the queue, type:

```
atq -n
```

12.5.7 Removing a process from the schedule (the at command)

You can remove a scheduled process with the **at** command using the -r flag.

From the command line
To remove a scheduled process, you must know the process number. You can obtain the process number using the **at -1** command or the **atq** command. See 12.5.6, "Listing all the scheduled processes (at or atq commands)" on page 435, for details.

When you know the number of the process you want to remove, type:

```
at -r ProcessNumber
```

You can also use the **smitty rmat** command to perform this task. It opens the screen shown in Example 12-12.

Example 12-12 smitty rmat command

```
                        Remove a Job from the Schedule

Type or select values in entry fields.
Press Enter AFTER making all desired changes.


                                                    [Entry Fields]
* JOB NUMBER to remove                                                      +



F1=Help            F2=Refresh         F3=Cancel          F4=List
F5=Reset           F6=Command         F7=Edit            F8=Image
F9=Shell           F10=Exit           Enter=Do
```

12.6 Binding or unbinding a process

On multiprocessor systems, you can bind a process to a processor or unbind a previously bound process. Only AIX 5L has this function by default.

AIX 5L

In AIX 5L, to bind or unbind a process you may use:

► The Web-based System Manager
► SMIT or the **smitty bindproc** and **smitty ubindproc** fast paths
► The command line (the **bindprocessor** command)

You must have root user authority to bind or unbind a process you do not own.

> **Note:** While binding a process to a processor might lead to improved performance for the bound process (by decreasing hardware-cache misses), overuse of this facility could cause individual processors to become overloaded while other processors are underused. The resulting bottlenecks could reduce overall throughput and performance. During normal operations, it is better to let the operating system assign processes to processors automatically, distributing system load across all processors. Bind only those processes that you know can benefit from being run on a single processor.

When using the Web-based System Manager, follow these steps:

1. Display all the processes, as shown in Figure 12-3 on page 416.

2. Select the process you want to bind.

3. Chose the Bind to a CPU options from the menu shown in Figure 12-4 on page 417. The pop-up box shown in Figure 12-7 will appear.

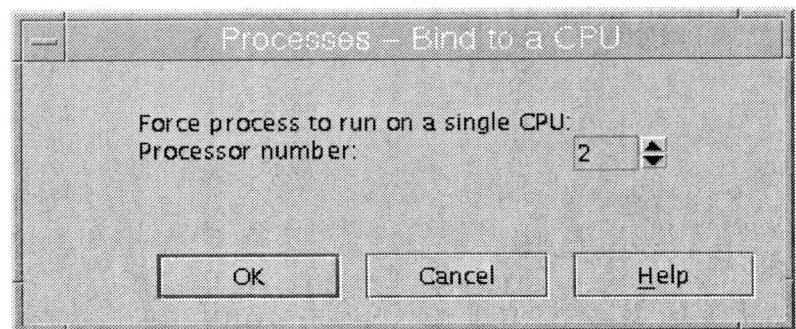

Figure 12-7   Binding a process using the Web-based System Manager

4. Chose the processor number.

5. Click **OK**.

To unbind a process, chose the Unbind from a CPU option from the menu shown in Figure 12-4 on page 417, and it will do it without any further confirmation.

When using **smitty**, follow these steps:

1. Type **smitty bindproc** at the command line. It opens the screen shown in Example 12-13.

Example 12-13   smitty bindproc

```
                        Bind a Process to a Processor

Type or select values in entry fields.
Press Enter AFTER making all desired changes.

                                                          [Entry Fields]
* PROCESS ID                                             []
+#
  PROCESSOR ID                                                             +


F1=Help            F2=Refresh        F3=Cancel         F4=List
F5=Reset           F6=Command        F7=Edit           F8=Image
```

```
F9=Shell          F10=Exit            Enter=Do
```

2. Chose the process ID using the F4 and arrow keys. Press Enter.

3. Chose the processor ID using the F4 and arrow keys. Press Enter.

4. Press Enter again and wait for an OK prompt.

To unbind a process:

1. Type **smitty ubindproc** at the command line. It opens the screen shown in Example 12-14.

Example 12-14   smitty ubindproc

```
                            Unbind a Process

Type or select values in entry fields.
Press Enter AFTER making all desired changes.

                                                   [Entry Fields]
* PROCESS ID                                       []
+#

F1=Help            F2=Refresh          F3=Cancel          F4=List
F5=Reset           F6=Command          F7=Edit            F8=Image
F9=Shell           F10=Exit            Enter=Do
```

2. Chose the process ID using the F4 and arrow keys. Press Enter.

3. Press Enter again and wait for an OK prompt.

Alternatively, you can use the **bindprocessor** command to bind or unbind a process. The syntax of the command is:

```
bindprocessor Process [ ProcessorNum ] | -q | -u Process
```

The **bindprocessor** command binds or unbinds the kernel threads of a process or lists available processors. The Process parameter is the process identifier of the process whose threads are to be bound or unbound, and the ProcessorNum parameter is the logical processor number of the processor to be used. If the ProcessorNum parameter is omitted, the process is bound to a randomly selected processor.

The -q flag of the **bindprocessor** command lists the available logical processor numbers. You can use the logical numbers given as values for the ProcessorNum parameter. The -u flag unbinds the threads of a process, allowing them to run on any processor.

The following examples show how to use the **bindprocessor** command in AIX 5L Version 5.x to bind or unbind a process to the processor:

► To see which processors are available (possible ProcessorNum values), enter:

```
bindprocessor -q
```

For a four-processor system, the output is similar to:

```
The available processors are: 0 1 2 3
```

► To bind the threads in process 19254 to processor 1, enter:

```
bindprocessor 19254 1
```

► To unbind the process 16324 use:

```
bindprocessor -u 16342
```

12.7 Quick reference

Table 12-1 displays the tasks, commands, and location of files or information that is needed to perform process management in HP-UX 11i and AIX 5L.

Table 12-1   Quick reference for process management

Task/locations	AIX 5L	HP-UX 11i
Running multiple tasks in a GUI environment	Chose one of the following: ► **wsm** ► smit or smitty ► The **smitty process** fast path	**sam**
Listing information about processes	**ps** or **topas**	**ps** or **top**
Sending signals to processes	**kill**	**kill**
Changing the priority of a process	**nice** or **renice**	**nice** or **renice**
Binding a process	**bindprocessor**	N/A
Unbinding a process	**bindprocessor**	N/A
Scheduling a process for later execution	**at**	**at**

Task/locations	AIX 5L	HP-UX 11i
Listing scheduled processes	at -l or atq	at -l
Removing a process from the schedule	at -r	at -r

13

Security

This chapter is about some of the differences in securing both HP-UX 11i and AIX 5L. Both of these systems provide many security features that can be used to improve security. This chapter attempts to emphasize the practical use of these security features, why they are necessary, and how they can be used in your environment. We also provide some recommend guidelines and best practices when there are many different ways to achieve a secure system.

We discuss most important security-related issues, but we also look at various ways that the systems may be comprised followed by an example of how to secure these platforms to minimize the risk. The practical examples for both operating systems are given, the differences are described, and the important files are referenced.

This chapter is *not* a be all and end all of how to secure either an HP-UX or an AIX 5L system. There are many guides found easily on the Internet or at your local technical book store. The idea is to provide an administrator in one flavor of UNIX with a quick jump-start in securing the other.

The following topics are covered in this chapter:

13.1 Overview

When thinking about security, you first need to identify the threats and the kind of vulnerabilities that your system is exposed to. We do not complete a formal analysis here, but simply walk through examples of threats.

There are a myriad of ways to get unauthorized access to a system, where root access is the ultimate aim, for example:

- ▶ Use a Trojan Horse on a careless administrator to create a back door.
- ▶ Use a well-known exploit on an unfixed system.
- ▶ Use a little known exploit on a "supposedly fixed" system.
- ▶ Use a new exploit on a "supposedly fixed" system.

There are exploits for local access, such as permission problems. There are also exploits for network access, such as service configuration errors. Since, in a way, UNIX security is based on trust, it actually is easy enough to find exploits, and easy enough to disable them.

A user can convince (through guile perhaps) a system administrator to run a program that the user has written or modified to capture root's password, create a SUID shell, install a backdoor, and so on. Once a user has root access, the user can install a *root kit* that will attempt to remove him or her from the process table, connection list, auditing files, accounting system, and so forth. The hacker can then even establish other accounts, or backdoors to your system. With this established, a hacker can do whatever they want to your system, and return later.

A hacker can also convince certain network service programs to run files. The sendmail utility was notorious for having holes in it. There were ways that this program might be convinced to run either an interactive program or perhaps a predefined program by a hacker. This could then be used to install their backdoor or create a root account.

A hacker can use IP spoofing by telling everyone he or she is someone else, someone that you trust, and then walking right in the front door.

There are other types of attacks that can happen as well—attacks aimed at your network to disable your communications with other computers. These are called Denial of Service (DOS). There is also an extension to this form of attack—hacking several computers and using them to mount a DOS on a different system. This has been dubbed Distributed Denial of Service (DDOS).

Also, you should keep in mind one important principle: There are no absolutely secure systems. Remember that hackers are never satisfied with yesterday's exploits. They are always trying to find new ways to break into systems or to bring them down. Hacking is constantly evolving and growing. Stay informed by reading the news at:

```
http://www.cert.org
```

13.2 Hardware security

There are several security mechanisms that HP hardware systems provide—the Guardian Service Processor (GSP) or Management Processor (MP), depending on the HP model. The GSP/MP can provide password-protected access to hardware system configuration and, depending on the model, may also provide password protection to the physical system console.

The AIX 5L Version 5.3 operating system runs on IBM @server pSeries (RS/6000) machines exclusively. Using AIX 5L Version 5.3 security features in conjunction with IBM @server pSeries (RS/6000) hardware security features, you can improve your system security. IBM @server pSeries (RS/6000) provides the following three hardware (including firmware) security features: Cover lock key, power-on password, and privileged-access password.

13.2.1 HP hardware security features

The HP hardware security features differ by model, so for more detailed information please see the documentation accompanying your hardware.

GSP or MP

The GSP/MP is a mandatory install on a separate processor (sometimes on a separate card for some platform cases) to the main CPUs, which is always the monitoring system's power and cooling, and provides system configuration and console access.

The terms *GSP* and *MP* are often used rather interchangeably—though it seems that an MP is installed on those models where N-Pars (*hard* partitions) are available, where the term GSP is used for the remainder.

An MP provides optional password protection to access to each OS's system console; that is, if the MP has had password protection enabled, then you *need* to enter a password to access any of the system consoles in the complex. Depending on the users and authorities assigned, you may need a different user ID/password pair to perform any MP configuration tasks.

This contrasts with a GSP in that, by default, you are already connected to the OS's system console. You need to enter GSP mode by issuing the command sequence Ctrl+B. You may now need to provide a user ID/password that provides access to different GSP configuration menus.

It is strongly advised that a GSP/MP user ID and password be configured and set, especially considering the fact that modern GSP/MP systems provide Ethernet connections that can be configured into the LAN for network access to the console. It is said that the GSP password cannot be retrieved once set, but there are methods documented by HP that can provide the clearing of all GSP/MP user ID/password information in case of a lost or forgotten password. All of these methods require access to either the physical machine or, at a minimum, the physical console.

Considering that from the GSP you can initiate some machine or complex-wide actions (for example, initiate a Transfer Of Control (TOC), which is really a core dump of the running system, or perform a full system reset or power down), limiting access to the console is definitely a priority.

For more information about configuring the GSP/MP, please refer to either the documentation that was supplied with your system or the *Service Processors Users Guide*, which can be found at:

```
http://www.docs.hp.com
```

Physical security

Some HP models provide a physical key lock, which limits access to opening the casing of the machine. Most of the newer models do not provide easy access to the internals and require special tools to gain access to the internals.

The different physical security aspects of the different models can vary quite a bit, so there is no easy one-stop-fits-all description that can be adequately applied. Please see the particular model documentation for details:

```
http://www.docs.hp.com
```

13.2.2 IBM @server pSeries (RS/6000) hardware security features

The IBM @server pSeries (RS/6000) provides the following hardware (including firmware) security features:

Cover lock key
This security feature prevents the cover from being removed. You need a physical key to access the inside hardware components.

Power-on password
This password helps protect information stored in your system. Every time you power on or reset your system, this password is required to continue the operation.

When the system is powered on, it checks whether a power-on password (POP) is present. If there is one present, and the *unattended start mode* is not set, it means the machine's owner does not want the system to be used unless the POP is supplied. In this case, the system will prompt for the POP. The user is given three attempts to enter the correct password. If the user fails to supply the correct password, the system will go into a *hung* state and must be powered off before continuing. This password helps protect information stored in your system. NB: For servers controlled via an *HMC*, the power-on password is effectively replaced by the *hscroot* password needed to log onto the HMC and logically power up the machine.

Unattended start mode

To use this mode, a power-on password must be previously specified. If unattended start mode is enabled, the system will boot from the defined boot device without requiring the user to enter the power-on password. While the system can be booted without entering the POP, the keyboard controller will be programmed to lock up until the POP is provided. This mode is ideal for servers that run unattended. After an electrical power failure, for example, the operating system will be rebooted without waiting for a user to enter the power-on password.

Privileged-access password

This password protects against the unauthorized starting of System Management Services (SMS). SMS is built-in firmware that provides system management tools that include setting or resetting power-on/privileged-access passwords. When the user presses one of the keys to access SMS, the system will check to see if a privileged access password exists; if it does, the user is prompted to enter the privileged access password. The user is given three attempts to supply the correct password. If the user fails to do so, the system will go into a hung state and must be powered off before continuing.

If you set both power-on and privileged-access passwords, only the privileged-access password is required to start SMS. Password setting and the required password to start AIX 5L or SMS are summarized in Table 13-1.

Table 13-1   Password setting and required passwords

Password setting	Starting AIX 5L	Starting SMS
None	Not required	Not required
Power-on	Power-on	Power-on
Privileged-access	Not required	Privileged-access
Both power-on and privileged-access	Power-on	Privileged-access

In case you do not have a machine's password, the only way to get access to the system is by removing the system's battery. You must be aware that this procedure will erase all firmware configuration data maintained in NVRAM, such as the error log and any IP addresses configured to interfaces for network boot. In this case, you need the cover lock key to open the cover.

Note: Power-on passwords only apply to PCI-based RS/6000 machines. The implementation of these hardware security features is slightly different between IBM @server pSeries (RS/6000) models. For more precise information, refer to the User's Guide distributed with your system.

The cover lock key must be available when it is needed for software or hardware maintenance.

Depending on your system application, you may not need to use the power-on password. Even in such a case, a privileged-access password should be set. Nevertheless, with just a privileged-access password anyone can start SMS and bypass all security and access any file on the disks.

If you decide not to use a power-on password, we recommend that you change the boot device sequence. As distributed, server searches for operating systems start up code in the following sequence (if available):

1. Diskette drive
2. CD-ROM drive
3. Hard disk drive
4. Network device

This means anyone can boot your system from their own startup code provided by a diskette or CD-ROM. Such a code could bypass all security and access any file on the disks (actually, if you forget root's password, you may need to use a variation on this procedure). Therefore, we recommend that you specify only the hard disk drive as a boot device. Setting it this way allows your server to boot from only AIX 5L on the hard disk.

13.3 Securing HP-UX and AIX 5L platforms

This section takes a practical approach to what needs to be done to secure HP-UX and AIX 5L platforms. We look at various ways that the systems may be compromised followed by an example of how to secure the platforms.

There are six general steps in securing a platform and ensuring its validity during operational use:

1. Install and secure an operating system (including patches and fixes).
2. Install and secure applications (including patches and fixes).
3. Install filters and/or IPSec (optional).
4. Pre-deployment testing.
5. Operational deployment.
6. Regular monitoring.

We do not cover all of the above steps. Some steps, such as installation, have already been separately covered. Instead, this chapter focuses on the installation and configuration of HP-UX 11i and AIX 5L Version 5.3 systems, effectively hardening them. The first and most important step is to have a secure platform to work on.

We walk through a typical process to create a secure platform. Note that this chapter is securing a sample platform. Do not follow these steps without knowing their impact on the operational usage. It is a good idea to perform these lockdown procedures first on a test machine before actual rollout to live use.

It is good to keep in mind the security principles throughout the whole securing process. Whenever you remove a package, a fileset, or limit a functionality, a decision needs to be made about the security versus convenience.

13.3.1 Installation and patching

Every bit of software has bugs; some of these bugs can be used to gain elevated privileges to your system. Vendors of both the operating system and application software are continually providing patches to close down possible exploits. A best practice is to subscribe to your vendors' patch mailing list and the CERT:

```
http://www.us-cert.gov/cas/techalerts/
```

Do not just subscribe and read the alerts that come out, but also be proactive in actually installing the fixes at regular intervals.

The following steps should be taken to help secure the system:

1. Install a new system with the latest version of the operating system (either HP-UX or AIX 5L). Each new release of the system includes security improvements and additional features to enhance system security. Always use the latest version of the operating system that your applications will support. Do not perform an upgrade to an existing install if possible.

   AIX 5L   It is recommended to perform the install with the TCB option selected. This is different from the same acronym in HP-UX. The AIX 5L TCB is referred to as the Trusted Computing Base, but its intent is quite different than the HP-UX TCB. Please see:

```
http://publib.boulder.ibm.com/infocenter/pseries/index.jsp?topic=/com.ib
m.aix.doc/aixbman/security/installing_configuring_tcb.htm
```

   also refer to 13.4, "Trusted Computing Base (TCB)" on page 471.

   Some useful man pages are **tsh** and **tcbck**.

2. At installation time, reduce the installation down to the minimum number of packages necessary to support the application to be hosted. This reduction in services, libraries, and applications helps increase security by reducing the number of subsystems that must be disabled, patched, and maintained. For example, if you have no need for the X-Windows environment, do not install it at all.

3. Set the password for root as soon as you can.

   HP-UX   You have the choice of setting the password during the install phase or on first boot.

   AIX 5L   The Installation Assistant launches when you first install a machine. You can set the password there.

4. Immediately after a system is installed, all recommended, security, and Y2K patches should be applied.

   For HP-UX these patches are available from the ITRC at:

```
http://www.itrc.hp.com/service/patch/releaseIndexPage.do
```

and for AIX 5L at:

```
http://www.ibm.com/eserver/support/fixes/fcgui.jsp
```

Care must be taken when applying patches to a system. Some patches modify the system initialization scripts and may disable security changes made to a system. It does not affect us here, but after you have locked the machine down be aware that when patching, scripts that were deleted from the init run level directories (or /etc/inittab, /etc/rc.*) to disable services could be replaced during the patch installation process, enabling the service once more. Be sure to examine all system init scripts and test all patches on non production systems to discover any such configuration changes.

> **Tip:** It is a very good idea to install all the latest patches during the initial server build and *before* you perform the system lockdown. This way, a patch will not unexpectedly undo some of your lockdown work.

13.3.2 Disabling services

One of the keys to a more secure system is limiting what is installed or running on the system to the minimum required. For example, many Linux distributions enable a DNS server during an install, but it is more than likely that only a DNS client is required to be configured.

If the software is bundled in such a way that it is easy to either un-install, or better yet, to not install at all, that is the best solution. Otherwise, disabling services from running on startup is the next best way forward.

Disabling services in HP-UX and AIX 5L

There are three primary locations that provide startup for processes or daemons. Each of these should be checked for services that can be disabled.

inetd

Disable (by commenting out or removing the line) all unnecessary services provided by inetd. Both HP-UX and AIX 5L use /etc/inetd.conf as the configuration file, though AIX 5L also provides the command `lssrc -ls inetd` to list what the service's current inetd process is actively providing.

Do not forget to refresh the inetd daemon once you have made any changes to the configuration file. In both HP-UX and AIX 5L, you can use `kill -HUP <PID>`, where *PID* is the process ID of inetd.

In AIX 5L, you can also use `refresh -s inetd`. While in HP-UX you can use `inetd -c`.

In a base installed version of HP-UX 11i there are about 27 services active by default, while in AIX 5L there are about 16.

For many systems, you should be able to remove nearly all the services provided by inetd, especially if you install and use ssh/scp/sftp as a replacement for telnet/login/ftp.

As mentioned previously, there are a myriad of well thought out guides available on these topics. This is really just to let you know that, in this case, HP-UX and AIX 5L are configured in the same way.

inittab

The /etc/inittab file on both HP-UX and AIX 5L allows the OS to start up and maintain tasks at boot time.

inittab and HP-UX

The HP-UX inittab is edited directly. You then run **init q** to have the init process re-read the configuration file. It uses the pound sign (#) as the comment character, so one way to disable a service is to comment it out. The other way is to change the *action* to *off.*

inittab and AIX 5L

In AIX 5L it is recommended to use the **chitab** command, or you can modify the file directly.

To use **chitab**, the easiest way is to basically list the line you want to modify with **lsitab**, and copy and paste with the changes into the **chitab** command, as below.

Example 13-1   AIX 5L changing the inittab with chitab

```
jumpingjim # lsitab tty1
tty1:0123456789:respawn:/usr/sbin/getty /dev/tty1
jumpingjim # chitab 'tty1:0123456789:off:/usr/sbin/getty /dev/tty1'
```

By using **chitab** you do not need to ask init to re-read the configuration file. If you edit the file manually, you will need to use **init q**.

Note that in the AIX 5L inittab the comment character is a colon (:).

General startup

Please refer to Chapter 4, "System startup and shutdown" on page 83, for a more detailed description of the differences between HP-UX and AIX 5L startups.

Disabling processes during startup on HP-UX

A well behaved daemon in HP-UX will have its configuration files in /etc/rc.config.d. These files will not usually be overwritten on patch upgrades and are therefore the best location to disable daemons for startup.

Most daemons have a variable that is set in /etc/rc.config.d/<daemon>, which tells the start and stop scripts whether this daemon should be started, for example, the *sendmail* daemon, which can be disabled if all you are doing is sending and not receiving e-mails, as shown in Example 13-2.

Example 13-2   HP-UX's disabling sendmail daemon

```
snowymountains # grep SENDMAIL_SERVER= /etc/rc.config.d/mailsrvs
export SENDMAIL_SERVER=1
## So, just modify the SENDMAIL_SERVER=1 to SENDMAIL_SERVER=0 ##
```

The other way to disable boot time daemons from starting is to change the /sbin/rcX.d/SXXX<daemon> to have a name that does not start with S. The convention most commonly used is to disable appropriate start scripts so that they start with an "_" instead. Refer to Example 13-3.

Example 13-3   HP-UX disabling sendmail from starting

```
snowymountians # ls  /sbin/rc*/*mail*
/sbin/rc1.d/K460sendmail  /sbin/rc2.d/S540sendmail
snowymountians # mv /sbin/rc2.d/S540sendmail /sbin/rc2.d/_S540sendmail
```

This means that the **/sbin/rc** command during startup will not attempt to execute the daemons and that if needed, it will be easy to change things back to the way that they were.

Seeing as security is best practiced by having multiple layers, it is a good idea to both "turn off" a daemon via its rc.config.d variables and also change it so that it does not even attempt to start by modifying the name of /sbin/rcX.d/S<daemon>.

Disabling processes during startup on AIX 5L

Several daemons and services are started if you install the server filesets, such as:

► bos.net.tcp.server
► bos.net.nfs.server
► bos.net.nis.server

We do not recommend the installation of these filesets unless necessary (and in many cases it really is not necessary at all).

bos.net.tcp.server includes the **securetcpip** command, which disables extremely risky servers started from inetd. This disables tftp, utftp, tftpd, rcp, rlogind, rlogind, rsh, and rshd. This command is /etc/securetcpip (please have a browse of the man page).

In general it is better to deliberately disable all your network services, then explicitly configure and enable specific services that are required by the applications and users.

By default AIX 5L does not use the same style of centralized startup script environment as HP-UX. It effectively runs particular "rc" scripts as directed via /etc/inittab and cfgmgr. These scripts usually live in /etc/rc.<name>.

Looking at the /etc, we discover the startup scripts for the following services:

► rc.C2
► rc.CC
► rc.bsdnet
► rc.d
► rc.dacinet
► rc.dt
► rc.ha_star
► rc.ike
► rc.net
► rc.net.serial
► rc.nfs
► rc.powerfail
► rc.qos
► rc.startaacct
► rc.stopaacct
► rc.tcpip

We recommend you rename the following dangerous services to prevent them from starting (this is something that you should only do on your test machine to verify there are no unexpected consequences):

```
# mv rc.dt Xrc.dt
# mv rc.net.serial Xrc.net.serial
```

Next, drill inside rc.tcpip, which is responsible for starting the network daemons. In this case, disable all appropriate daemons by commenting them out using #. In our case, we were able to disable all the daemons apart from **syslogd**.

Options can also be added to daemons to provide additional security. The only daemon we have allowed to start is syslogd, and we add a -r option to suppress logging for remote hosts:

```
start /usr/sbin/syslogd "$src_running" -r
```

13.3.3 Disabling NFS

NFS is just a set of processes that are started on machine boot. To disable NFS in particular, please see 9.7.5, "Disabling NFS services" on page 320. Unless there is an ongoing need for NFS, it is possible to have NFS normally shut down and to only start it up when it is required.

13.3.4 Adjusting default network settings for security

The most common network is TCP/IP. There are some different TCP/IP options that can affect the security of your system or the security of the networks that your system connects to.

HP-UX   Configure different options in /etc/rc.config.d/nddconf and use the **ndd -c** command to apply them immediately.

To display information about different parameters use **ndd -h supported** and for detailed information **ndd -h <parameter>**, as shown in Example 13-4.

Example 13-4   HP-UX using ndd to disable ip_forwarding

```
firefly # ndd -h supported|head -10

SUPPORTED ndd tunable parameters on HP-UX:

IP:
    ip_def_ttl            - Controls the default TTL in the IP header
    ip_forward_directed_broadcasts -  Controls subnet broadcasts packets
    ip_forward_src_routed -  Controls forwarding of source routed packets
    ip_forwarding         -  Controls how IP hosts forward packets
    ip_fragment_timeout   -  Controls how long IP fragments are kept
    ip_icmp_return_data_bytes -  Maximum number of data bytes in ICMP
firefly # ndd -h ip_forwarding
ip_forwarding:

    Controls how IP hosts forward packets: Set to 0 to inhibit
    forwarding; set to 1 to always forward; set to 2 to forward
    only if the number of logical interfaces on the system is 2
    or more. [0,2] Default: 2

firefly # ndd -get /dev/tcp ip_forwarding
2
firefly # ndd -set /dev/tcp ip_forwarding 0
```

AIX 5L   Configure different options using the **no** command or **smitty tuning** or by editing /etc/tunables/nextboot, as shown in Example 13-5 on page 454.

Example 13-5 AIX 5L using no to re-disable ipforwarding

```
no -a |head -10
                arpqsize = 12
              arpt_killc = 20
             arptab_bsiz = 7
               arptab_nb = 73
               bcastping = 0
      clean_partial_conns = 0
                 delayack = 0
            delayackports = {}
         dgd_packets_lost = 3
            dgd_ping_time = 5
# no -h ipforwarding
Help for tunable ipforwarding:
Specifies whether the kernel should forward packets. The default value of 0
prevents forwarding of IP packets when they are not for the local system. A
value of 1 enables forwarding. ipforwarding is a Dynamic boolean attribute.

# no -L ipforwarding
--------------------------------------------------------------------------
NAME           CUR   DEF   BOOT   MIN   MAX   UNIT           TYPE
  DEPENDENCIES
--------------------------------------------------------------------------
ipforwarding   1     0     0      0     1     boolean        D
--------------------------------------------------------------------------
# no -p -o ipforwarding=0
Setting ipforwarding to 0
Setting ipforwarding to 0 in nextboot file
```

Some things to look at in HP-UX

The following changes are what Bastille B.02.01.03 will change to lock down the network stack:

ip_forward_directed_broadcasts=0 Disables subnet broadcasts packets

ip_forward_src_routed=0 Disables forwarding of source routed packets

ip_forwarding=0 Disables the server from acting like a router

ip_ire_gw_probe=0 Disables dead gateway detection

ip_pmtu_strategy=1 Sets the Path MTU Discovery strategy

ip_send_source_quench=0 Disables *source quench* sending

tcp_conn_request_max=4096 Max number of outstanding inbound connection requests

| tcp_syn_rcvd_max=1000 | Max suspect connections allowed to persist in SYN_RCVD state |

Some things to look at in AIX 5L

They are:

ipsrcrouteforward=0	Denies forwarding of source-routed packets
ip6srcrouteforward=0	Denies forwarding of source-routed packets
udp_pmtu_discover=0	Stops autodiscovery of MTU in the network interface
tcp_pmtu_discover=0	Stops autodiscovery of MTU in the network interface
ipsendredirects=0	Disables sending redirect signals
clean_partial_conns=1	Clears incomplete partial connections if required
bcastping=0	Disables responses to broadcast pings (default)
directed_broadcast=0	Disables directed broadcast to a gateway (default)
ipignoreredirects=1	Disables processing IP redirects (default)
ipsrcrouterecv=0	Discards source-routed packets (default)
icmpaddressmask=0	Ignores any ICMP address mask request (default)
nonlocsrcroute=0	Disallows addressing to outside hosts (default)
ipforwarding=0	Disables the server from acting like a router (default)

13.3.5 Kernel adjustments - HP-UX 11i only

Some security exploitation programs take advantage of the HP-UX 11i kernel executable system stack to attack the system. These attack programs attempt to overwrite parts of the program stack of a privileged program in an attempt to control it.

In HP-UX 11i, some of these exploits can be avoided by making the system stack non-executable. This may break some programs, for example, Java 1.2 programs will fail if using JDK/JRE 1.2.2 versions older than 1.2.2.06, which were designed to execute code off of the stack. However, you can run "`chatr +es <executeable_file>`" to override this for individual programs if they break.

Enable protection for buffer overflow exploits by setting the executable_stack kernel parameter to 0, recompiling the kernel and rebooting.

13.3.6 Secure the root login

Securing access to the root account is something handled differently on both platforms. There are generally two parts to securing the root login:

▶ Prohibiting remote root logins or prohibiting all root logins. It is good practice to be able to work out *who* was logged in as root at which times. Ensuring that the only way of accessing the root account is via the **su** command enables logging of root access via the file.

▶ Limiting *who* can actually **su** to root further strengthens the system, as then even if someone who generally does have access to the machine finds out the root password in some way, unless they are in the authorized group, they will be denied access.

Secure the root login on HP-UX

First, make sure that you can log onto the machine via some other user.

Prohibit remote root logins

Prohibit root from logging on to the system from anything other than *specified* physical terminals. You do this by creating a /dev/securetty file (see the man page for `login`) that contains the authorized tty's (without the /dev prefix) one per line. An empty file means that root cannot directly log on at all; all access to root would be via **su** or some other means.

> **Warning:** If you have installed **ssh**, then even though you have configured the /etc/securetty file, root could still **ssh** into the machine. To prohibit this, you must change the sshd_config file such that PermitRootLogin is denied and refresh **sshd**.

Limit who can su to root

There is a little mentioned file in HP-UX that was introduced in HP-UX 11.0 via a patch. When it was first introduced, no documentation was supplied. This was rectified in HP-UX 11i, and you can now learn all about it via the **security** man page.

To limit the users who can **su** to root, just add the line:

```
SU_ROOT_GROUP=<groupname>
```

> **Note:** Only one group is allowed. If the file /etc/default/security does not exist, create it with world readable, root writable permissions.

> **Tip:** Read the **man security** information for details on parameters like SU_ROOT_GROUP, MIN_PASSWORD_LENGTH, NUMBER_OF_LOGINS_ALLOWED, PASSWORD_HISTORY_DEPTH, and PASSWORD_MIN_<type>_CHARS.
>
> Remember that you should include root in the /etc/ftpd/ftpusers file, so that root cannot **ftp** into the machine. See "Restricting FTP logins" on page 463.

Secure the root login on AIX 5L

First, make sure that you can log onto the machine via some other user.

Prohibit remote root logins

Prohibit root from logging on to the system from anything other than *any* physical terminal. You can do this for any user you like. Just use the **chuser** command or the **smitty chuser** and set rlogin=false as shown in Example 13-6.

Example 13-6   AIX 5L prohibit remote root logins

```
giggles # lsuser -a rlogin root
root rlogin=true
giggles # chuser  rlogin=false root
giggles # lsuser -a rlogin root
root rlogin=false
```

If you want to ensure that the root cannot even log on from a physical terminal, you also need to set login=false using the same methods. This will mean that root cannot directly log on at all; all access to root would be via **su** or some other means.

> **Warning:** Even with rlogin=false (login=false if you have installed **ssh**), then by default, root will still be able to **ssh** into the machine. To prohibit this, you must change the sshd_config file such that PermitRootLogin is denied and refresh **sshd**.
>
> Remember that you should include root in the /etc/ftpusers file, so that root cannot **ftp** into the machine. See "Restricting FTP logins" on page 463.

Limit who can su to root

In AIX 5L there is a definable user attribute on all users (not just root) that allows you to specify which groups are able to **su** to a user.

You can set the *sugroups* attribute via any of the standard methods of modifying a user. Example 13-7 shows an example of the **chuser** command.

Example 13-7   AIX 5L limit who can su to a user

```
bamboo # chuser sugroups=aixadmin root
bamboo # lsuser -a sugroups root
root sugroups=aixadmin
```

13.3.7 Customize the environment

There are a handful of environmental things that should be checked for correctness on both platforms:

- ► "Login herald and message" on page 458
- ► "PATH variable" on page 460
- ► "Default umask" on page 461
- ► "Automatic inactivity timeout for shell logins" on page 462
- ► "Restricting FTP logins" on page 463
- ► "Restricting at and cron access" on page 463
- ► "Default password attributes" on page 464
- ► "syslog configuration" on page 467
- ► "Log in the logins" on page 468

Login herald and message

When someone **telnets** into the machine, by default, both HP-UX and AIX 5L tell the user (via a *login herald*) just that little bit more information than is required. You can also provide a privacy/security message to the users after they have logged on. This is generally performed by updating /etc/motd.

It is recommended to change both of these to both include a warning that only authorized users should attempt to log in, as well as to not display any operating system identifiable information (hostname, OS type/level).

Modifying the default login herald on HP-UX

Example 13-8 shows the HP-UX default herald.

Example 13-8   HP-UX default herald

```
HP-UX brazil B.11.11 U 9000/889 (tb)
```

```
login:
```

The login herald is specified in HP-UX by the addition of the -b <filename> flag on the **telnetd** entry in /etc/inetd.conf, as shown in Example 13-9.

Example 13-9   HP-UX specifying a login herald

```
telnet      stream tcp nowait root /usr/lbin/telnetd  telnetd  -b /etc/issue
```

The /etc/issue file is, by default, read only by the **getty** command for a physical terminal herald.

> **Tip:** By symbolically linking /etc/issue to /etc/motd you limit the number of locations that need updating and keep the message consistent no matter what login style, for example, **ln -s /etc/motd /etc/issue**.

Modifying the default login herald on AIX 5L

Example 13-10 shows how to modify the default logging herald on AIX 5L.

Example 13-10   AIX 5L default herald

```
AIX Version 5
(C) Copyrights by IBM and by others 1982, 2005.
login:
```

Either use the **chsec** command or update /etc/security/login.cfg and change the login herald as shown in Example 13-11.

Example 13-11   AIX 5L example login herald definition

```
myAIX # chsec -f /etc/security/login.cfg -s default -a herald="Unauthorized use
of this system is prohibited.\n\nlogin: "

   OR update the login.cfg file

   herald = "\r\n\n\n\n\n\n\n\n\n\n\n\n\n\n\ NOTICE TO
   USERS\r\n\r\nUse of this machine waives all rights to your
   privacy,\r\n\r\n and is consent to be monitored.\r\n\r\nUnauthorized
   use prohibited.\r\n\r\n\r\nlogin: "
```

While we are here, we may as well as modify the logindelay parameter. This makes it much slower on a brute force attack on a system. Refer to Example 13-12 on page 460.

Example 13-12 AIX 5L updating the logindelay for failed logins

```
AIXme # chsec -f /etc/security/login.cfg -s default -a logindelay=2
```

Modifying the default CDE message

If you have CDE installed, you have an additional place to configure its equivalent of the **telnetd** login herald. If CDE is installed, replace the default CDE welcome greeting. If the /etc/dt/config/C directory does not exist, create the directory structure and copy the default configuration file:

```
mkdir -p /etc/dt/config/C
chmod -R a+rX /etc/dt/config
cp -p /usr/dt/config/C/Xresources /etc/dt/config/C
```

Add the following lines to /etc/dt/config/C/Xresources:

```
Dtlogin*greeting.labelString:      %LocalHost%
Dtlogin*greeting.persLabelString:  login: %s
```

(This assumes that your default LANG is C.)

Message of the day (/etc/motd)

During the login process both systems provide the same mechanism to allow a message to be displayed to the users. This is done via the /etc/motd file, as shown in Example 13-13.

Example 13-13 Simple example /etc/motd

```
NOTICE TO USERS
Use of this machine waives all rights to your privacy,
and you are consenting to be monitored. Unauthorized use prohibited.
```

PATH variable

The system's default PATH should *not* contain the current working directory. Everyone knows that it is convenient, but it is still a security risk to allow your PATH environment variable to contain your current directory. This is even more risky for the *root* user and therefore even more discouraged. It is recommended to never include the period (.) anywhere in the PATH, as this can allow for deliberate attempts at subverting commands.

PATH Variable in HP-UX

There a couple locations commonly used to set the PATH. The first two can be used to set PATH system wide.

/etc/PATH   Used by /etc/profile to set the PATH.

/etc/profile	Not recommended, but sometimes administrators or installation programs add in additional PATH entries at the end of /etc/profile.
/etc/skel/.profile	The profile that is copied into newly created home directories. By default this appends "." to the PATH.
~/.profile	An existing users profile.

Of course, unless the user is running some form of restricted shell, they can always modify their own PATH variable after login on or via the appropriate user level startup script (usually ~/.profile).

PATH variable in AIX 5L

The AIX 5L PATH also has some commonly used locations, the first two can be used for setting the PATH system wide.

/etc/environment	The login command grabs the PATH variable from this file.
/etc/profile	Not recommended, but sometimes administrators or installation programs add in additional PATH entries at the end of /etc/profile.
/etc/security/.profile	The profile that is copied across to newly created home directories. By default this overwrites the PATH variable and includes a "." at the end.
~/.profile	A existing users profile.

Again, the user can most likely modify their own PATH just like in the HP-UX case above.

Default umask

The umask is the way of deciding what the default permissions are on newly created files or directories. For a secure environment, it is a good idea to restrict the default file and directory creation permissions to the tightest allowed. That would mean only the user who created the file would be able to read it (umask 077); for something a bit more generous, you would permit the other users in the group to read it as well (umask 027).

Both HP-UX and AIX 5L have the umask command to set the default file/directory creation permissions. There are a couple of differences though when you come to want to secure your system.

Default umask and HP-UX

There is no one place where you can set a umask that will be used each and every time a user process executes. For example, make sure that all the daemons that are running also have an appropriate umask configured. Note, though, that it is possible that some programs may assume that files are created with certain permissions, without checking this to be the case. If that is the case, then setting the **umask** for these programs to 077 may break them.

To set a default umask for all the daemons see Example 13-14.

Example 13-14   HP-UX setting default umask for starting daemons

```
echo "umask 022" > /sbin/init.d/umask
 for d in /sbin/rc?.d
 do
    ln /sbin/init.d/umask $d/S000umask
 done
```

To set a umask for each user as they log on add/update the following line to /etc/profile.

```
umask 027
```

Default umask and AIX 5L

AIX 5L, on the other hand, has the umask= parameter in /etc/security/user, either in the default stanza or you can override this on a per-user basis. The default umask in the AIX 5L world is 022. To modify this for all users who do not have an overridden umask, just update the umask value /etc/security/user to your desired value. This will also take care of those daemons that start on system startup.

Automatic inactivity timeout for shell logins

This is not really anything OS specific, but is related to the *shell* your users are using.

In POSIX style shells (like ksh, sh, bash), the variable that you can use to log someone off after a predefined time period of shell inactivity is one of:

► TMOUT
► TIMEOUT

To enable automatic logoff, all you do is update /etc/profile to contain:

```
TMOUT=600 ; TIMEOUT=600 ; export TMOUT TIMEOUT; readonly TMOUT TIMEOUT
```

Setting the variable readonly prohibits users from disabling this mechanism.

For more information you will need to read of your own shell's man page, as even different implementations have different variable names.

Restricting FTP logins

By default both HP-UX and AIX 5L use a ftpusers file that contains all the users who you *do not* wish to be able to **ftp** into the system. The only difference is in the location:

HP-UX	/etc/ftpd/ftpusers
AIX 5L	/etc/ftpusers

Taking the approach that you should deny everything and then allow only those who need it, you could do something like creating an /etc/ftpusers file:

```
cut -f1 -d: /etc/passwd > /etc/ftpusers or /etc/ftpd/ftpusers
chown root /etc/ftpusers
chmod 600 /etc/ftpusers
```

Then remove any users that require ftp access from the ftpusers file.

Apart from the bulk standard simple functions of FTP, both HP-UX 11i and AIX 5L have quite a bit more that can be done to secure an FTP server if you must run one.

For some good information about the HP-UX 11i FTP daemon, there are details on the WU-FTPD in the HP-UX 11i release notes.

For AIX 5L FTP changes that were introduced in AIX 5L Version 5.2 you can refer to Chapter 8 of the *AIX 5L Differences Guide Version 5.2,* SG24-5765-02.

Restricting at and cron access

Both HP-UX and AIX 5L have the UNIX system scheduling service **cron** enabled by default. So anyone who has access to **at** or **crontab** on the system can make use of this service to schedule commands for later running—perhaps after they have left the company.

On both HP-UX 11i and AIX 5L, the default configuration of **cron** is that not all users are able to use it.

Once again, taking the *deny all* approach, you can deny everyone from using **at** and **cron** and then selectively allow those who need it (which is often only root).

Restricting at and cron access on HP-UX

The extract from the **crontab** man page, as shown in Example 13-15 on page 464, shows information about how to restrict access.

Example 13-15   HP-UX crontab man page extract

```
You can execute crontab if your name appears in the file
/usr/lib/cron/cron.allow.  If that file does not exist, you can use
crontab if your name does not appear in the file
/usr/lib/cron/cron.deny.  If only cron.deny exists and is empty, all
users can use crontab.  If neither file exists, only the root user can
use crontab.  The allow/deny files consist of one user name per line.
```

The default /usr/lib/cron/cron.allow file contains only root, adm, and uucp. The same is true for the default /usr/lib/cron/at.allow. So this of course means that on HP-UX 11i, root, uucp, and adm are the only authorized users of **cron** or **at**.

Restricting at and cronaccess on AIX 5L

The extract from the AIX 5L **crontab** man page, as shown in Example 13-16, shows information about how to restrict access.

Example 13-16   AIX 5L crontab man page extract

```
A user cannot use the crontab command if one of the following is true:
*    The cron.allow file and the cron.deny file do not exist (allows root user
                                                                 only).
*    The cron.allow file exists but the user's login name is not listed in it.
*    The cron.deny file exists and the user's login name is listed in it.
```

In the AIX 5L case, the default installation is that there *is* a /var/adm/cron/cron.deny, but it is *empty,* so as per the man page, this means that *anyone* with a log on to the system can schedule commands. The same (emptyness) is true for the /var/adm/cron/at.deny file.

It would be recommended that you delete the cron.deny and at.deny files (for simplification) and that you create a /var/adm/cron/cron.allow and /var/adm/cron/at.allow file that only contain the users (root, for example) that require access to **cron**.

Default password attributes

By default, both HP-UX and AIX 5L have lower than ideal password defaults applied for a secure environment.

Default password attributes and HP-UX

First, read the man page associated with /etc/default/security as it details information about the following configurable parameters:

► ABORT_LOGIN_ON_MISSING_HOMEDIR
► MIN_PASSWORD_LENGTH
► NOLOGIN

- ▶ NUMBER_OF_LOGINS_ALLOWED
- ▶ PASSWORD_HISTORY_DEPTH
- ▶ SU_ROOT_GROUP
- ▶ SU_DEFAULT_PATH
- ▶ PASSWORD_MIN_UPPER_CASE_CHARS
- ▶ PASSWORD_MIN_LOWER_CASE_CHARS
- ▶ PASSWORD_MIN_DIGIT_CHARS
- ▶ PASSWORD_MIN_SPECIAL_CHARS
- ▶ SU_KEEP_ENV_VARS

We do not go into any detail here, as more and more options are being added via patches. Also, HP-UX 11i V1.6 (Itanium) has more options available to it than HP-UX 11i V1.

As part of having tighter password security in HP-UX it would be advisable to convert the system to a trusted system. In part, this removes the encrypted passwords from /etc/passwd and places them in a restricted directory structure under /tcb/files/auth.

The other option is to convert to a "traditional" *shadow* password file. This option was introduced with HP-UX 11i v1.6. For more information about shadow passwords see:

```
http://www.docs.hp.com/hpux/onlinedocs/5187-0701/00/00/82-con.html#shadowpasswo
rds>
```

To convert the system to a TCB system use the **tsconvert** command, as shown in Example 13-17.

Example 13-17   HP-UX converting to a TCB trusted system configuration

```
# /usr/lbin/tsconvert
Creating secure password database...
Directories created.
Making default files.
System default file created...
Terminal default file created...
Device assignment file created...
Moving passwords...
secure password database installed.
Converting at and crontab jobs...
At and crontab files converted.
# passwd
Changing password for root
Old password:
Last successful password change for root: NEVER
Last unsuccessful password change for root: NEVER
```

```
Do you want (choose one letter only):
        pronounceable passwords generated for you (g)
        a string of letters generated (l) ?
        to pick your passwords (p) ?

Enter choice here: p
New password:
Re-enter new password:
Passwd successfully changed
```

For more information about the differences between HP-UX TCB and the AIX 5L implementation of the same three letter acronym, please see "Trusted Computing Base (TCB)" on page 471.

> **Warning:** After converting to a trusted system, all passwords are *expired* and users will be prompted to change their password on next login. This can have side effects for batch programs or ftp style of automated processes.
>
> Always change the root password after converting to a trusted system so that it is reset to a known password.
>
> You can always *unconvert* with **/usr/lbin/tsconvert -r**.

Default password attributes and AIX 5L

You can set the default password attributes in AIX 5L by changing the default stanza values in /etc/security/user, as shown in Example 13-18.

Example 13-18   AIX 5L example default password attributes
```
minage=0
maxage=12
maxexpired=4
minalpha=4
minother=1
minlen=6
mindiff=3
maxrepeats=3
histexpire=26
histsize=8
pwdwarntime=14
tpath=on
```

syslog configuration

It is always useful to be able to review what has happened on your system. There are two parts to this:

▶ Standard system logs
▶ Auditing

We touch on auditing in 13.4.4, "Auditing and HP-UX" on page 473, and 13.4.9, "Auditing and AIX 5L" on page 482.

The primary creator of log files in both HP-UX and AIX 5L is **syslogd**. Both systems use the /etc/syslog.conf file to control the configuration of the daemon, but the capabilities of the two **syslogd**'s are different. From a general administrative point of view, handling of alerts is performed in the same way—it is just when you come down to the housekeeping level that they differ.

syslog.conf and HP-UX

As you can see from Example 13-19, the HP-UX syslog uses /var/adm/syslog/syslog.log as its default log file, and sends all messages with a priority of *info* and above to this file.

syslogd is started by /sbin/rc2.d/S220syslogd, which moves /var/adm/syslog/syslog.log to /var/adm/syslog/OLDsyslog.log and recreates syslog.log with world readable permissions. Otherwise, by default, there is no housekeeping performed on any of the HP-UX syslog files—they can grow without bounds.

It is recommended to archive your syslog files to maintain a history, as in HP-UX many of the system messages are sent to syslog and it can be a very helpful tool for troubleshooting or later analysis.

Example 13-19   HP-UX default /etc/syslog.conf

```
mail.debug              /var/adm/syslog/mail.log
*.info;mail.none        /var/adm/syslog/syslog.log
*.alert                 /dev/console
*.alert                 root
*.emerg                 *
```

Note: The -r flag in HP-UX's syslogd overrides the default function of suppressing duplicated messages. See the HP-UX man page for more details on both of the different parameters that **syslogd** takes, as well as /etc/syslog.conf.

AIX 5L, on the other hand, comes shipped with an empty /etc/syslog.conf configuration, though there are some very good examples commented out in the file. The AIX 5L syslog provides for automatic housekeeping, both on size or time.

To log all facility messages at the debug level or above to the file /tmp/syslog.out, and have the file rotated when it gets larger then 500 kilobytes or if a week passes, limit the number of rotated files to 10, use compression, and also use /syslogfiles as the archive directory. Type:

```
*.debug /tmp/syslog.out rotate size 500k time 1w files 10 compress archive
/syslogfiles
```

Log in the logins

Of course, you would also like to know who was logged in, tried to log in, or switched users when. Both systems use the /var/adm/sulog to capture **su** success or failures. Both systems will create the sulog file, with appropriate permissions, if it does not exist. See the respective **su** man pages.

The good ones

Aside from switching users, keeping track of who was logged on is also quite handy. This is handled via the wtmp file on both systems.

On both systems, if this file does not exist, then it will *not* be created and logins will not be tracked. So make sure that there is a non-world writable file called /var/adm/wtmp.

To access this file, you can use the **last** command, as shown in Example 13-20. In HP-UX there is an additional option of -R, which also shows the IP address that the user logged in from (not displayed by default). In AIX 5L, there is a -t <[CC]YY]MMDDhhmm> flag, which will show you *who* was logged on at the specified time and date.

Example 13-20   Some last commands

```
myHPUX # last -4 -R
root     pts/tg       10.1.1.197         Mon Jul 11 16:11 - 16:49  (00:37)
root     pts/te       11.12.13.32        Mon Jul 11 15:45    still logged in
root     ftp          localhost          Mon Jul 11 15:32 - 15:32  (00:00)
root     ftp          localhost          Mon Jul 11 15:32 - 15:32  (00:00)

myAIX # last -t 200507091800 -3
root     pts/4        localhost              Jul 06 21:07 - 21:41 (1+00:34)
root     pts/3        tot198.itso.ibm.com    Jul 06 21:05 - 21:41 (1+00:35)
root     pts/5        localhost              Jul 06 20:45 - 21:05  (00:19)
```

Both systems have the **fwtmp** command, which will help you manipulate the contents of the wtmp accounting records.

The bad ones

We know how to track friendly logins, but what about people who tried to log on but could not?

In HP-UX if you have a file called /var/adm/btmp, all the invalid login attempts get logged here. This file is of the same format as the wtmp file and you can read it with the same commands, though there is a special `lastb` command equivalent to `last`, as shown in Example 13-21. If the /var/adm/btmp file does not exist, all you need to do is **touch** it.

> **Tip:** For HP-UX, unlike the wtmp file, you definitely *do not* want this file to be world readable, as it will often actually contain user passwords accidently entered as login names.

Example 13-21   HP-UX lastb command

```
myHPUX # lastb -3
mypass   pts/tg        Mon Jul 11 17:20
jimmy    pts/tg        Mon Jul 11 17:20
jimmy    pts/tg        Mon Jul 11 17:20
```

In the world of AIX 5L you have the /etc/security/failedlogin file, which is created by default, again, in the same format as wtmp. One way to read this file is to use the `last -f <filename>`, as shown Example 13-22.

Example 13-22   /etc/security/failedlogin file

```
hometime # last -f /etc/security/failedlogin  -3
UNKNOWN_  pts/5         localhost              Jul 10 20:24    still logged in.
UNKNOWN_  pts/5         localhost              Jul 10 20:24 - 20:24  (00:00)
root      pts/5         localhost              Jul 10 18:29    still logged in.
```

Notice how in the AIX 5L case, you have an "UNKNOWN_" user. This is what is logged if the login name is not known to AIX 5L, while in the HP-UX case, the string that was typed would have been logged. (This can sometimes be the user's password if they were not paying attention to the screen and got a bit excited about logging on.)

Unlike the HP-UX btmp file, the AIX 5L /etc/security/failedlogin file will be created for you if it does not exist.

13.3.8 Regular system review

The following section is a list of recommended day-to-day tasks.

Recommended day-to-day tasks

We recommend doing these activities on an on-going basis. For example:

► Change the root password on the first Monday of the month on all your systems and make them all individuals.

► Create a bootable mksysb or make_tape_recovery image of your system weekly. Keep your tapes for at least eight weeks.

► Maintain and enforce your security policy. Make sure all your users know what your security policy is and remind them quarterly of what their responsibilities are in protecting the assets.

► Monitor your log files as appropriate:

```
/var/adm/sulog
/var/adm/wtmp
/etc/utmp
/var/adm/btmp or /etc/security/failedlogin
```

► Monitor your **cron** and **at** jobs to ensure there are no unexpected entries.

On AIX 5L the **cronadm** command is used by a root user to list or remove all users **crontab** or **at** jobs.

```
cronadm at -l
cronadm cron -l
```

Otherwise, you can go and look in /var/spool/cron/crontabs and /var/spool/cron/atjobs on both flavors.

► If you enabled auditing or accounting, monitor these files weekly.

We recommend that you review your system for certain things on a scheduled basis. This will help you find security holes, and it will help you keep your system documented when changes happen.

Regularly review the following:

► Run **tcbck -n tree** manually once a month so you see the output. Also, at this time, manually compare the sysck.cfg file with the backup on your write-protected media with the **diff** command.

► Ensure that any security fixes are applied in a timely manner.

► Verify your LPPs (**lppchk/swverify**) once a month. This will show you other information about your files compared to the installed filesets.

► Verify your user configuration once a month.

For HP-UX:

```
pwck [-sl]
grpck
```

For AIX 5L these commands verify consistency in the standard authentication methods:

```
pwdck -n ALL
grpck -n ALL
usrck -n ALL
```

► Verify that the customizing that you did when you installed your computer is still in place, that is, disabling things in /etc/rc.tcpip, /sbin/rcX.d, inetd.conf, etc.

► Run an internal security audit tool, such as tiger, to verify that you do not have a file or directory with insecure permissions.

► Run an external security audit tool, such as strobe, against your system to verify that you do not have any external security holes.

13.4 Trusted Computing Base (TCB)

Both HP-UX and AIX 5L have something called the *Trusted Computing Base*. These are two different things, with different core purposes and functions.

This section describes the Trusted Computing Base as it is in HP-UX and then as it is in AIX 5L.

13.4.1 The HP-UX 11i TCB

More often than not, a machine with the HP-UX TCB enabled is referred to as a *trusted system*.

In HP-UX 11i v1, you cannot pre-configure the HP-UX TCB environment during install time, though in HP-UX 11i V1.6 (Itanium) there is the *Install-Time Security* product, which allows you to pick out a predefined security option.

When HP-UX is running in *standard* mode, the encrypted password files reside in /etc/passwd. This is the basic UNIX standard (where everyone can read the encrypted passwords), though not considered very secure, as nowadays with fast computers, the passwords can be broken with brute force in a reasonable amount of time.

To overcome this limitation, there are two options provided in different versions of HP-UX 11i. There is trusted system and also shadow passwords. Here we shall talk about the trusted system environment.

The TCB conversion is bi-directional, that is, it is a fairly undisruptive task to convert or unconvert, though on conversion *to* the TCB environment, all the users passwords are expired and they will be prompted to change them on the next log in.

13.4.2 Differences between trusted and non-trusted systems

An extract from the HP-UX FAQ can be found at:

```
http://www.faqs.org/faqs/hp/hpux-faq/section-68.html
```

Trusted systems have improved password management.

Below is a list of password management features:

► Specification of a grace period and expiration period for passwords.
► The ability to specify system-wide password aging.
► The ability to specify an absolute account life.
► The ability to disable accounts after repeated login failures.
► Passwords lengths of up to forty (40) characters.
► The ability to access a random password generator.

A trusted system allows system auditing to be turned on. System auditing enables the ability to trace every system call issued by each user on the system. Non-trusted systems run with system auditing disabled.

Trusted systems have additional login restrictions, while non-trusted systems do not.

► In addition to account disabling, the account may also be locked.

► Setting accounts to be accessed only at certain times of the day.

► The ability to specify account location access. In other words, account access at specific devices, workstations, and so on.

► The ability to specify a single-user boot password.

Password defaults

Prior to patch PHCO_24606 (or base HP-UX 11i V1.6), the only way to provide greater granularity of password strength attributes was to convert to a trusted system. When you had converted from the standard environment to the trusted environment, HP-UX imposed more stringent password setting rules for a user (though precisely what these were was scantily documented)—things like disallowing null passwords, requiring uppercase/special characters, and excluding the user ID or a dictionary word from being in the password.

With the installation of PHCO_24606, some of these items have been addressed, even at the non-trusted configuration level. For example, you can now specify the number of upper/lower/digit/special characters (see `man security` for more information).

Trusted system commands in HP-UX 11i

There are some additional commands that are used for managing the TCB environment in a trusted system. Some of them are:

`/usr/lbin/modprpw`	Modify protected password database properties (for example, lock/unlock a user)
`/usr/lbin/getprpw`	Display protected password database properties
`authck`	Verify protected password database
`prpwd`	Not a command, but the man page describes the files and layout of the protected password database

13.4.3 Converting to a trusted system in HP-UX 11i

It is very straightforward to convert both to and from using the trusted system in HP-UX 11i. You can either use SAM → Auditing and Security → System Security Policies, which will ask if you would like to convert your system, or use `tsconvert`.

To unconvert a system from having the TCB, you just use `tsconvert -r`, as shown in Example 13-23.

Example 13-23   HP-UX unconverting a trusted system

```
kangaroo # /usr/lbin/tsconvert -r
Restoring /etc/passwd...
/etc/passwd restored.
Deleting at and crontab audit ID files...
At and crontab audit ID files deleted.
```

13.4.4 Auditing and HP-UX

To be able to provide system call level auditing, the HP-UX system needs to be running in trusted mode. If you attempt to enter any of the SAM panels that require a TCB environment, SAM will give you the option of converting before permitting you to proceed.

There is quite good information about HP-UX auditing in the section 5man page of audit, that is, `man 5 audit`.

To display and/or change the current status of auditing in HP-UX use the `audsys` command as shown in Example 13-24 on page 474.

Example 13-24   HP-UX displaying the audit status and turning off

```
lollypop # audsys
auditing system is currently on
current file: /.secure/etc/audfile2
next    file: none
statistics-     afs Kb  used Kb  avail %   fs Kb   used Kb  avail %
current file:    1000      19       98    143360   130936       9
next    file: none
lollypop # audsys -f
auditing system halted
lollypop # audsys
auditing system is currently off
current file: /.secure/etc/audfile2
next    file: none
statistics-     afs Kb  used Kb  avail %   fs Kb   used Kb  avail %
current file:    1000      19       98    143360   130936       9
next    file: none
```

Example 13-25 shows the last 10 lines of the current audit file.

Example 13-25   HP-UX displaying the audit file

```
unclebob # audisp /.secure/etc/audfile2 |tail -10
050711 11:17:58  6715 S     15    2882     -1        0        0        0
0 ?????
[ Event=chmod; User=????????; Real Grp=root; Eff.Grp=root;  ]

        RETURN_VALUE 1 = 0;
        PARAM #1 (file path) = 0 (cnode);
                             0x40000003 (dev);
                             2060 (inode);
                (path) = /etc/opt/resmon/log/registrar.log
        PARAM #2 (int) = 420
```

There is some good information in Chapter 8 of the *Managing systems and Workgroups, A Guide for* HP-UX *Administrators,* 5990-8172, which can be found at:

```
http://docs.hp.com
```

The AIX 5L TCB

TCB in AIX 5L provides something similar to a lightweight version of *tripwire,* being able to verify that a subset of some of the operating system files remain in their trusted installation state. It also introduces the concept of a *trusted path.* This is something that is accessed through a *trusted shell* (**man tsh**), in which you can only execute commands that are in your trusted PATH. The whole point being that you know that you are only executing commands that you are meant to be, and that someone cannot have snuck in and subverted them.

TCB is a good tool to detect penetrations and configuration changes. TCB stores information about files, which can later be used to verify that the files have not been modified. TCB is not installed by default. You have the option to install TCB during the initial installation. It cannot be added without reinstalling AIX 5L. For more information about installing AIX 5L with TCB enabled, refer to Chapter 3, "Installing and upgrading tasks" on page 29.

You can do a *Preservation Install* and include TCB. However, if you have done any customizing in rootvg, this may remove your changes. Always do a backup of your system before you try this. We cannot guarantee that Preservation Install will keep all your changes, since Preservation Install does not preserve everything. Try it out on a test system if you can.

TCB monitors over 600 files, plus the devices (/dev), by default. It stores these files in an ASCII file, /etc/security/sysck.cfg. Make a backup of this file and write protect it immediately.

13.4.5 Checking the Trusted Computing Base in AIX 5L

The **tcbck** command audits the security state of the Trusted Computing Base. The security of the operating system is jeopardized when the TCB files are not correctly protected or when configuration files have unsafe values. The **tcbck** command audits this information by reading the /etc/security/sysck.cfg file. This file includes a description of all TCB files, configuration files, and trusted commands.

> **Note:** If the Trusted Computing Base option was not selected during the initial installation, the **tcbck** command is disabled. The command can be correctly enabled only by reinstalling the system.

13.4.6 Using the tcbck command in AIX 5L

The **tcbck** command is normally used to:

► Assure the proper installation of security-relevant files.

► Assure that the file system tree contains no files that clearly violate system security.

► Update, add, or delete trusted files.

The **tcbck** command can be used in three ways:

► Normal use

- Noninteractive at system initialization
- With the **cron** command

▶ Interactive use

- Useful for checking out individual files and classes of files

▶ Paranoid use

- Stores the sysck.cfg file offline and restores it periodically to check out the machine

Checking trusted files in AIX 5L TCB

Run the **tcbck** command to check the installation of trusted files at system initialization. To perform this automatically and produce a log of what was in error, add the following command to the /etc/rc file:

```
tcbck -y ALL
```

This causes the **tcbck** command to check the installation of each file described by the /etc/security/sysck.cfg file.

Checking the file system in AIX 5L TCB

Run the **tcbck** command to check the file system any time you suspect the integrity of the system might have been compromised. This is done by issuing the following command:

```
tcbck -t tree
```

When the **tcbck** command is used with the tree parameter, all files on the system are checked for correct installation (this could take a long time). If the **tcbck** command discovers any files that are potential threats to system security, you can alter the suspected file to remove the offending attributes. In addition, the following checks are performed on all other files in the file system:

▶ If the file owner is root and the file has the setuid bit set, the setuid bit is cleared.

▶ If the file group is an administrative group, the file is executable, and if the file has the setgid bit set, the setgid bit is cleared.

▶ If the file has the tcb attribute set, this attribute is cleared.

▶ If the file is a device (character or block special file), it is removed.

▶ If the file is an additional link to a path name described in /etc/security/sysck.cfg file, the link is removed.

▶ If the file is an additional symbolic link to a path name described in /etc/security/sysck.cfg file, the symbolic link is removed.

> **Note:** All device entries must have been added to the /etc/security/sysck.cfg file prior to execution of the **tcbck** command or the system is rendered unusable. Use the -l flag to add trusted devices to /etc/security/sysck.cfg.

Adding a trusted program to AIX 5L TCB

To add a specific program to the /etc/security/sysck.cfg file, type:

```
tcbck -a PathName [attribute=value]
```

Only attributes whose values are not deduced from the current state of the file need be specified on the command line. All attribute names appear in the /etc/security/sysck.cfg file. For example, the following command registers a new setuid-root program named /usr/bin/setgroups, which has a link named /usr/bin/getgroups:

```
tcbck -a /usr/bin/setgroups links=/usr/bin/getgroups
```

After installing a program, you might not know which new files are registered in the /etc/security/sysck.cfg file. These can be found and added with the following command:

```
tcbck -t tree
```

This command displays the name of any file that is to be registered in the /etc/security/sysck.cfg file.

Deleting a trusted program from AIX 5L TCB

If you remove a file described in the /etc/security/sysck.cfg file, also remove the description of this file. For example, if you have deleted the /etc/cvid program, the following command causes an error message to be shown:

```
tcbck -t ALL
```

The error message shown is:

```
3001-020 The file /etc/cvid was not found.
```

The description of this program can be removed with the following command:

```
tcbck -d /etc/cvid
```

13.4.7 Configuring the tcbck program in AIX 5L

The **tcbck** command reads the /etc/security/sysck.cfg file to determine which files to check. Each trusted program on the system is described by a stanza in the /etc/security/sysck.cfg file:

class
Name of a group of files. This attribute allows several files with the same class name to be checked by specifying a single argument to the **tcbck** command. More than one class can be specified, with each class being separated by a comma.

owner
User ID or name of the file owner. If this does not match the file owner, the **tcbck** command sets the owner ID of the file to this value.

group
Group ID or name of the file group. If this does not match the file owner, the **tcbck** command sets the owner ID of the file to this value.

mode
Comma-separated list of values. The allowed values are SUID, SGID, SVTX, and TCB. The file permissions must be the last value and can be specified either as an octal value or as a 9-character string. For example, either 755 or rwxr-xr-x are valid file permissions. If this does not match the actual file mode, the **tcbck** command applies the correct value.

links
Comma-separated list of path names linked to this file. If any path name in this list is not linked to the file, the **tcbck** command creates the link. If used without the tree parameter, the **tcbck** command prints a message that there are extra links but does not determine their names. If used with the tree parameter, the **tcbck** command also prints any additional path names linked to this file.

symlinks
Comma-separated list of path names symbolically linked to this file. If any path name in this list is not a symbolic link to the file, the **tcbck** command creates the symbolic link. If used with the tree argument, the **tcbck** command also prints any additional path names that are symbolic links to this file.

program
Comma-separated list of values. The first value is the path name of a checking program. Additional values are passed as arguments to the program when it is executed.

acl   Text string representing the access control list for the file. It must be of the same format as the output of the **aclget** command. If this does not match the actual file ACL, the **sysck** command applies this value using the **aclput** command.

source   Name of the file this source file is to be copied from prior to checking. If the value is blank, and this is either a regular file, directory, or a named pipe, a new empty version of this file is created if it does not already exist. For device files, a new special file is created for the same type device.

The **tcbck** command provides a way to define and maintain a secure software configuration. The **tcbck** command also ensures that all files maintained by its database are installed correctly and have not been modified.

Restricting access to a terminal in AIX 5L TCB

The **getty** and **shell** commands change the owner and mode of a terminal to prevent untrusted programs from accessing the terminal. The operating system provides a way to configure exclusive terminal access.

Using the trusted communication path in AIX 5L TCB

A trusted communication path is established by pressing the SAK reserved key sequence (Ctrl+X, Ctrl+R). A trusted communication path is established under the following conditions:

► When logging in to the system.

   After you press the SAK:

   – If a new login screen scrolls up, you have a secure path.

   – If the trusted shell prompt is displayed, the initial login screen was an unauthorized program that might have been trying to steal your password. Learn who is currently using this terminal with the who command and then log off.

► When you want the command you enter to result in a trusted program running. Some examples of this include:

   – Running as root user. Run as root user only after establishing a trusted communication path. This ensures that no untrusted programs are run with root user authority.

   – Running the **su**, **passwd**, and **newgrp** commands. Run these commands only after establishing a trusted communication path.

> **Attention:** Use caution when using SAK; it kills all processes that attempt to access the terminal and any links to it (for example, /dev/console can be linked to /dev/tty0).

Configuring the Secure Attention Key for AIX 5L TCB

Each terminal can be independently configured so that pressing the Secure Attention Key (SAK) at that terminal creates a trusted communication path. This is specified by the sak_enabled attribute in the /etc/security/login.cfg file. If the value of this attribute is true, recognition of the SAK is enabled.

If a port is to be used for communications (for example, by the **uucp** command), the specific port used has the following line in its stanza of the /etc/security/login.cfg file:

```
sak_enabled = false
```

This line or no entry disables the SAK for that terminal.

To enable SAK on a terminal, add the following line to the stanza for that terminal:

```
sak_enabled = true
```

13.4.8 Understanding the tcbck report in AIX 5L

The **tcbck** report can be difficult to understand. The following explains how to read output from the **tcbck -t tree** or **tcbck -t ALL** command:

```
3001-023 The file /dev/pts/0 has the wrong file mode.
3001-075 Change the file modes for /dev/pts/0? (yes, no) no
```

A pts is a Pseudo Terminal Slave. It will take on the ownership of whoever is logged on through that device. This will always be incorrect if someone is logged on when you run **tcbck**. Therefore, if you want to avoid getting this message, run (in ksh):

```
for i in $(ls /dev/pts/* )
do
tcbck -a ${i} mode=""
done
```

```
3001-041 The file /dev/rhdisk0 has too many links.
```

Find the links to this file, and verify them.

► If the file does not have the TCB bit set, you will have to manually find the links (with **find** or **ncheck**). Substitute your file for /dev/rhdisk0, and the i-node number from your **ls -i**:

```
# ls -i /dev/rhdisk0
195 /dev/rhdisk0
# ncheck -i 195 /
/:
/dev/rhdisk0
    /dev/ipldevice
```

► If the file does have the TCB bit set, TCB will tell you the link (and prompt you to delete or add it):

```
3001-032 The link from the file <new file>
to <TCB file> should not exist.
3001-069 Remove the file <new file>? (yes, no) no
3001-095 Add the new link for <new file>? (yes, no) yes
```

If you had answered yes to deleting the link, TCB would not have prompted you to add it.

► /dev/ipldevice is a valid file and was not added maliciously, so add it to the links section of /etc/security/sysck.cfg. If this were not the case, you would need to edit the i-node and remove the extra links.

► If /dev/rhdisk0 was linked to /hacker/rawdisk then we would be concerned and take appropriate action.

```
3001-089 The symbolic link from the file /usr/local/bin/rksh.test2 to
         /usr/bin/rksh should not exist.
```

If you have the TCB bit set, **tcbck -[ntpy] tree** will find unauthorized symbolic links. TCB will take the same action for symbolic links as it does for hard links.

```
3001-020 The file /dev/tty0 was not found.
```

This shows that a file that TCB is attempting to monitor no longer exists. If it was a device file, it probably is not a security problem. It may, however, be a hardware problem. In this case, the machine does not have a tty0 defined. There is one included in the sysck.cfg, so it reports the error. This can be fixed with **tcbck -d /dev/tty0** or by adding the device with **mkdev**.

13.4.9 Auditing and AIX 5L

AIX 5L's auditing subsystem has a quite straightforward set of commands. For example, to start auditing, you would just use **audit on** and to stop it **audit off**.

The Security Administration Guide has a good section on auditing. It can be found here:

```
http://publib.boulder.ibm.com/infocenter/pseries/index.jsp?topic=/com.ibm.a
ix.doc/aixbman/security/setting_up_auditing.htm
```

Examples of using the auditing commands are shown in Example 13-26.

Example 13-26 Auditing commands

```
samson # audit query |head -6
auditing on
audit bin manager is process 19804
audit events:
        general -
USER_SU,PASSWORD_Change,FILE_Unlink,FILE_Link,FILE_Rename,FS_Chdir,FS_Chroot,PO
RT_Locked,PORT_Change,FS_Mkdir,FS_Rmdir
        objects -
AUD_CONFIG_WR,S_USER_WRITE,S_PASSWD_READ,S_PASSWD_WRITE,S_LOGIN_WRITE,S_LIMITS_
WRITE,S_GROUP_WRITE,S_ENVIRON_WRITE
        SRC -
SRC_Start,SRC_Stop,SRC_Addssys,SRC_Chssys,SRC_Delssys,SRC_Addserver,SRC_Chserve
r,SRC_Delserver
samson # auditpr -v -hhelrtRpPTc < /audit/bin1|head -10
host            event           login    real     time
status      process  parent   thread   command
--------------- ---------------- -------- -------- -----------------------
----------- -------- -------- -------- -------------------------------
000197AA4C000000 FS_Chroot     root     root     Sun Jul 10 18:29:36 2005 OK
10688    10316    24011    sshd
        change root directory to: /var/empty
000197AA4C000000 FS_Chdir      root     root     Sun Jul 10 18:29:36 2005 OK
10688    10316    24011    sshd
        change current directory to: /
000197AA4C000000 FILE_Unlink   root     root     Sun Jul 10 18:29:36 2005 OK
12368    5638     29315    compress
        filename /audit/tempfile.00005638
```

```
000197AA4C000000 S_PASSWD_READ  root    root    Sun Jul 10 18:29:36 2005 OK
10316     18086    56347    sshd
          audit object read event detected /etc/security/passwd
```

13.5 Useful tools

As mentioned at the start of this chapter, there is currently a version of Bastille for HP-UX. This tool provides a fast and easy way of *helping* lock down your system.

There are a couple of useful things to know that, generically, apply to both HP-UX and AIX 5L, which will assist tightening up your (primarily) network security.

netstat is an often underutilized utility. It can provide information about who is connected to your system from where, as well as what you are providing to others. As mentioned, the less you provide, the lower the possible problems.

lsof (List Open Files) is a freeware utility that is extremely powerful, both for network connections and general troubleshooting anything that uses files (and everything is a file in UNIX).

13.5.1 Some uses of the netstat command

The following shows the output of **netstat -a -f inet**. Each service listening (LISTEN) can be a potential security vulnerability.

Example 13-27   AIX 5L what is LISTENing with netstat

```
# netstat -a -f inet|grep -E "^Acti|^Prot|LISTEN"| head -10
Active Internet connections (including servers)
Proto Recv-Q Send-Q  Local Address          Foreign Address        (state)
tcp4     0      0    *.daytime              *.*                    LISTEN
tcp      0      0    *.ftp                  *.*                    LISTEN
tcp4     0      0    *.ssh                  *.*                    LISTEN
tcp      0      0    *.telnet               *.*                    LISTEN
tcp4     0      0    *.smtp                 *.*                    LISTEN
tcp4     0      0    *.time                 *.*                    LISTEN
tcp4     0      0    *.sunrpc               *.*                    LISTEN
tcp4     0      0    *.smux                 *.*                    LISTEN
tcp4     0      0    *.dpclSD               *.*                    LISTEN
```

The best way to eliminate such vulnerabilities is to disable the services that start them.

13.5.2 Some uses of the lsof command

A useful program to learn about the programs that start these services mentioned above is the **lsof** program. **lsof** is a GNU freeware and not a part of AIX 5L but can be found on the Linux Compatibility toolkit.

Let us take the last line of Example 13-28, the dpclSD daemon.

Example 13-28 grep dpcl /etc/services

```
yeehaa # grep dpcl /etc/services
dpclSD          7895/tcp          # DPCL Super Daemon
yeehaa # lsof -i :dpclSD
lsof: WARNING: compiled for AIX version 5.1.0.0; this is 5.3.0.0.
COMMAND    PID USER    FD    TYPE      DEVICE SIZE/OFF NODE NAME
inetd    24548 root    21u  IPv4 0x70254600      0t0  TCP *:dpclSD (LISTEN)
yeehaa # grep dpcl /etc/inetd.conf
dpclSD        stream  tcp       nowait   root     /etc/dpclSD dpclSD /etc/dpcld
/tmp/dpclSD01 /tmp/dpclsd
```

We can see from Example 13-28 that this service is served from **inetd** and that is where we would need to turn it off if appropriate.

14

Performance management

In this chapter we provide the basic performance concepts and explain the common tools between AIX 5L and HP-UX 11i.

This chapter contains the following:

14.1 Overview

Before we can even begin analyzing or tuning performance, some basic definitions need to be understood. The performance of a computer is referred to as how well the computer responds to the user and applications requests. So we can say that performance is dependent on a combination of throughput and response times. Throughput is the measure of the amount of work over a period of time and response time is the elapsed time between when a job or request is submitted to when the response of that request is returned.

On both AIX 5L and HP-UX 11i, we have two areas of system performance:

► System management

 – Allocation of resources
 – Establishment of system policies
 – Continuous system monitoring

► Application development

 – Design aspects
 – System considerations

In the first case, the system administrator or system manager is responsible for monitoring the system. Also, she helps to establish the policies that govern the use of resources. On the other hand, the application developer must be able to leverage the resources of the system for a particular application while maintaining a balance with other applications running on the system.

So, in order to get a better idea of performance tuning, we will use the following definition:

"Performance tuning is the application and allocation of system resources to best meet the defined requirements and goals."

As you can see, this definition sounds simple and straightforward, but there is actually a complex process behind. First of all, we need to define which are our goals and our resources.

When defining our goals, a balance of response time for users and total system throughput must be achieved. When we talk about resources, we refer to:

► Hardware resources

 – CPU
 – Memory (RAM speed and amount of memory)
 – I/O (disk space, I/O bus, adapters technology, number of disks, and so on)
 – Network (adapter performance and network bandwidth)

- Logical resources
  - Logical Volume Manager (AIX 5L LVM and VERITAS Volume Manager)
  - File systems (organization and fragmentation)
  - Memory buffers (virtual memory manager)
  - Load balancing (AIX 5L Workload Manager, HP-UX Process Resource Manager)

In order to achieve the goal of this chapter, we follow Figure 14-1.

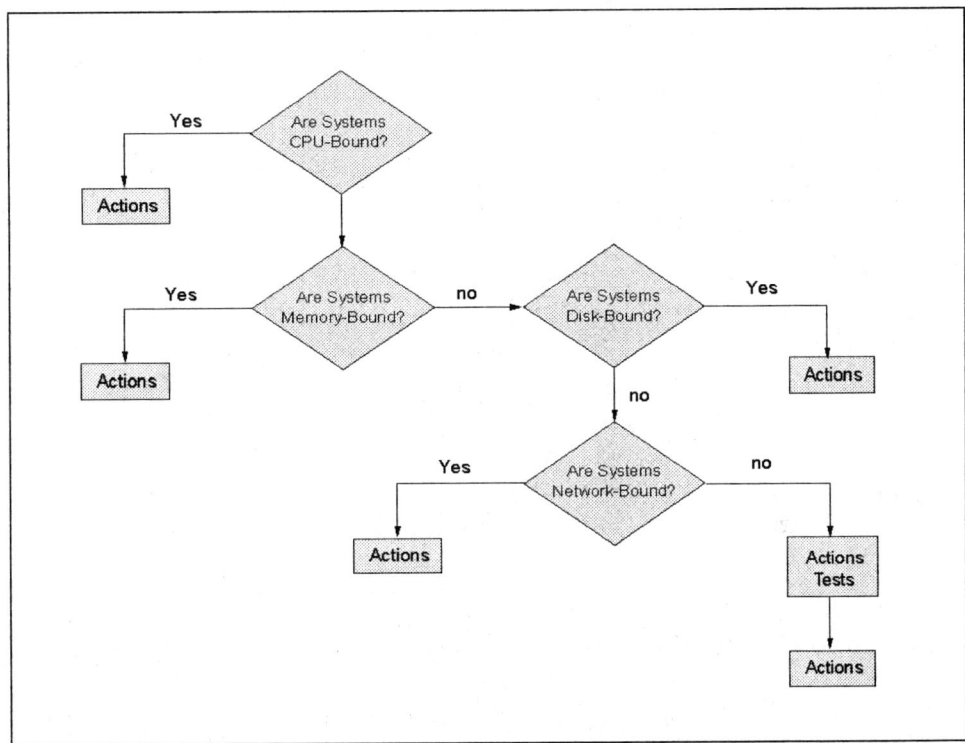

Figure 14-1   Performance tuning flowchart

14.2 CPU concepts and performance analysis

In this section we discuss the way in which AIX 5L and HP-UX 11i treat the processes. First of all, we will define a process as an activity that is started by a command, a shell, an application, and so on. As we talk about in Chapter 12, "Process management" on page 409, any process has a lot of properties, such as file descriptors, PID, PPID, and environment. Every process in both operating systems are multithreaded, which means that the process is divided into small entities called *threads*.

A thread is a single sequential flow of control. Multiple threads of control allow an application to overlap operations, such as reading from a terminal and writing to a file; these capabilities are provided without causing system overhead.

A thread by itself has its own properties, such as scheduling policy, scheduling priority, stack, pending signals, and some thread specific data.

14.2.1 The lifetime of a process

In AIX 5L, when a process starts, it create multiple threads. Each of its threads has multiple states, as shown in Figure 14-2.

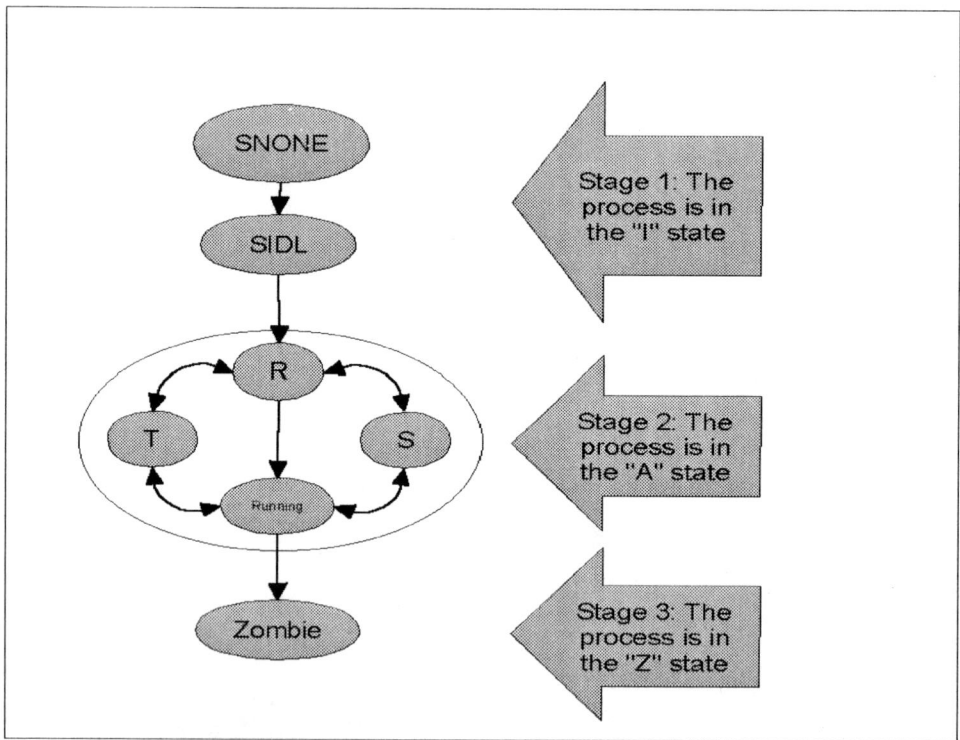

Figure 14-2   Process and thread states

Let us explain each of the states:

► State I (Idle) for a process

- SNONE: Before a process is created, it needs a slot in the process and thread tables. This state is known as SNONE.
- SIDL: When the process is waiting for resources (memory) to be allocated, it is in the SIDL state (at this time, the process occupies a slot process and as many thread slots as needed).

▶ State A (Active) for a process

- R (Ready to run): When the process gets into the A state, one or more of its threads gets in the "ready to run" state, contending for the CPU with other "ready to run" threads. Only one thread has the use of the CPU at a time; with SMP models, each processor would be running a different thread, as part of the same process or as independent threads from different processes.
- S (Sleep): If a thread is waiting for an I/O or other event, it sleeps instead of wasting CPU. When the I/O operation is completed, the thread is awakened and placed in the "ready to run" state to compete with the other threads for the processor.
- T (stopped): A thread can be stopped via the SIGSTOP signal, and started again with the SIGCONT signal, which brings the thread into the "ready to run" state. This is the only way in which the T state for a thread can be achieved.
- Running: When a thread in the "ready to run state" access to the processor, it gets into the running state.

▶ State Zombie for a process

Z (Zombie): This is the normal state of a process; when a process ends or dies, the process goes into the zombie state. In this state, the threads do not use CPU time or memory space; they only use the slot in the process and thread table. A zombie exists for a very short time until the parent process receives a signal that they have terminated. Parent processes that are programmed in such a way that they ignore this signal, or even die before the child processes they have created do, can leave zombies on the system. The only way to remove existing zombies from the system is by rebooting the system.

In order to monitor the state of a process, we use the **ps** command as shown in Example 14-1 and Example 14-2 on page 490.

Example 14-1   Monitoring the process state in a HP-UX system

```
# ps -el | more
F    S   UID   PID  PPID C PRI NI   ADDR      SZ  WCHAN   TTY  TIME COMD
1003 S    0     0     0  0 128 20     bf1d88    0  -       ?    0:14 swapper
1003 S    0     8     0  0 100 20   4c659040    0  d0a178  ?    0:00 supsched
1003 S    0     9     0  0 100 20   4c659180    0  bf1658  ?    0:00 strmem
```

```
1003 S    0     2     0  0 128 20  4c659540    0 d4bef0 ?   0:16 vhand
1003 S    0     3     0  0 128 20  4c659680    0 a19064 ?  31:19 statdaemon
1003 S    0     4     0  0 128 20  4c6597c0    0 ca68a4 ?   1:33 unhashdaemon
1003 S    0    12     0 37 -32 20  4c659900    0 be9f80 ?  37:36 ttisr
1003 R    0    13     0  0 152 20  4c659a40    0 -      ?   0:01 ioconfigd
 141 S    0     1     0  0 168 20  4c659b80  112 ff0000 ?   0:00 init
1003 S    0    19     0  0 147 20  4c659cc0    0 beb338 ?   0:01 lvmkd
1003 S    0    25     0  0 148 20  4c698580    0 75b5a0 ?   0:00 lvmschedd
1003 S    0    26     0  0 100 20  4c6986c0    0 -      ?   0:00 smpsched
 003 S    0    31     0  0 100 20  4c698d00    0 -      ?   0:00 sblksched
   1 S    0  2691     1  0 156 20  4c76b040   19 47aa00 ?   0:00 getty
   1 S    0 20450     1  0 154 20  4ce24840    0 c9f8e0 ?   0:00 biod
   1 R    0   365     1  0 152 20  4c8ba0c0   16 -      ?   0:56 syncer
1003 R    0    37     0  0 152 20  4c76b180    0 -      ?  55:27 vxfsd
   1 S    0   457     1  0 155 20  4cbd5080   19 cce434 ?   0:00 ptydaemon
   1 S    0 20521 20520  0 154 20  4de54180   66 415100 ?   0:00 nfsd
   1 S    0   454     1  0 154 20  4c8ba840   20 af61a0 ?   0:02 syslogd
```

In Example 14-1 on page 489 and Example 14-2, the display and flags "-el" of
the **ps** command are the same for AIX 5L and HP-UX 11i.

Example 14-2   Monitoring the process state on an AIX 5L system

```
# ps -el | more
     F S UID    PID  PPID  C PRI NI ADDR    SZ     WCHAN    TTY  TIME CMD
200003 A   0     1     0  0  60 20 18038  1864            -    0:00 init
240001 A   0  3502  5960  0  60 20 1c23c   552            -    0:00 syslogd
240001 A   0  3656  5504  0  60 20 91a9   5752 310b7e10    -    0:01 X
 40001 A   0  3932 17290  0  60 20 1a3da  3784 31010198    -    0:00 i4llmd
340001 A   0  4178  5960  0  60 20 102f0  2980 ea002820    -    0:00 rmcd
240001 A   0  4784  5960  0  60 20 2362   3040      *      -    0:00 IBM.ERrm
240401 A   0  4928     1  0  60 20  100     76            -    0:00 ssa_daemon
 40001 A   0  5504     1  0  60 20 1d19d  1640            -    0:00 dtlogin
240001 A   0  5728     1  0  60 20 5205    320 312e6858    -    0:00 syncd
240001 A   0  5960     1  0  60 20 18218   696            -    0:00 srcmstr
 40001 A   0  6460  5504  0  60 20 1a1ba  1604 30d5bc2c    -    0:00 dtlogin
240001 A   0  6740  6460  0  60 20 151d5  2708            -    0:03 dtgreet
200001 A   0  7038  8256  0  60 20 d44d   1100            -    0:00 telnetd
240001 A   0  7506  5960  0  60 20 c24c   1776            -    0:00 portmap
240001 A   0  7766  5960  0  60 20 7247   3024            -    0:00 sendmail
 40401 A   0  8036     1  0  60 20 17217   624    1909bc    -    0:00 errdemon
240001 A   0  8256  5960  0  60 20 6246    620            -    0:00 inetd
240001 A   0  8514  5960  0  60 20 e24e   1280            -    0:00 snmpd
240001 A   0  8772  5960  0  60 20 1261    744            -    0:00 dpid2
240001 A   0  9030  5960  0  60 20 a26a    980            -    0:00 hostmibd
240001 A   0  9318  5960  0  60 20 12292   460 c0042100    -    0:00 qdaemon
200005 A   0  9908 18600  2  61 20 b46b    272 30d5b068 pts/1 0:00 more
```

The S column shows the state of a process. If we look at the AIX 5L processes, every process is in the active state, but we do not know exactly if it is running, sleeping, stopped, or ready to run. On the other hand, the HP-UX system shows us some process in the S state (sleeping), which also means that it is active but waiting.

In AIX 5L, you can also see the status of each running thread by typing the following command:

```
# ps -elmo THREAD
```

14.2.2 The process queues

Fundamentally, the scheduler is a thread dispatcher, based on the priority of each thread. Only those threads in the ready to run state can be dispatched to the processor. Starting with AIX 5L, there are 256 priority values for a range of 0 through 255. Before AIX 5L Version 5.1, there were only 128 priority levels, as shown in Figure 14-3 on page 492. Each priority level is associated with a run queue. On SMP systems, there is a separate set of these queues for each processor. So, when a thread is launched by a process, it has a priority, and the scheduler assigns this thread to the corresponding queue.

This method makes it easier for the scheduler to determine which thread is most favored to run without having to examine a single large run queue. The scheduler consults a bit on each queue; when the bit is ON, it indicates the presence of a ready to run thread in the corresponding run queue.

In AIX 5L, there is also a full set of run queues, called the Global Run Queue, which can feed any processor for fixed priority threads. The use of this Global Run Queue by a process can be done by setting the environment variable RT_GRQ=ON. This will cause all threads of the process to use any available processor when they reach the ready to run state.

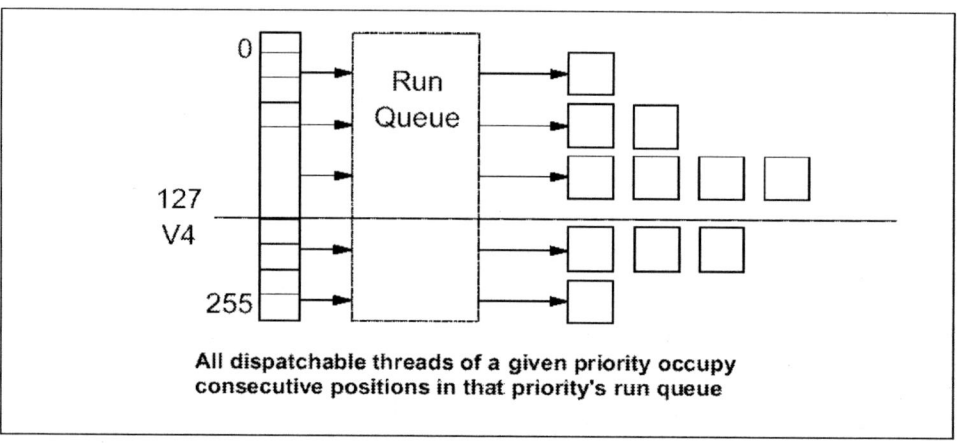

Figure 14-3   Run queues

14.2.3 CPU time slice and process priority

Every processor on the system is shared among all the existing threads by giving each thread a certain slice of time to run. This is called a *time slice*, this unit is measured in clock ticks (1 clock tick = 10 ms). By default, a time slice = 1 tick, in AIX 5L and HP-UX 11i. But if you want to change this value, in AIX 5L you need to change by tick and in HP-UX 11i by milliseconds. For example:

HP-UX 11i
The better way to change this value in the HP-UX 11i, it is with SAM.

sam, Kernel Configuration, Configurable Parameters and to change time slice parameter. It is necessary to reboot the system.

AIX 5L Version 5.x
`schedo -p -o timeslice='ticks'`

or by `smitty TunSchedo`

No reboot is necessary.

In some situations, when there is too much context switching, there could be an overhead when dispatching threads. In these cases, increasing the time slice may have a positive impact on performance.

The scheduler performs a context switch when:

► A thread has to wait for a resource.
► A higher priority thread wakes up.
► A thread has used up its time slice.

14.2.4 CPU monitoring using sar

The `sar` command reports the use of CPU during an interval, or it also can collect data into a file for future examination and extraction.

The way to collect information into a file is by running:

```
sar -o filename <interval> <# of intervals> >/dev/null
```

To extract the information of the file, we use the following command:

```
sar -u -f filename -s <starting time> -e <ending time>
```

Here is an example of `sar` execution within an interval:

```
# sar -u 10 3
AIX i19962c 1 5 000321944C00      05/01/02
17:17:39    %usr    %sys    %wio    %idle
17:17:49       0       1       0      99
17:17:59       0       0       0     100
17:18:09       0       0       0     100
Average        0       0       0     100
```

The syntax for AIX 5L and HP-UX 11i is exactly the same; the parameters on the example indicate:

-u	Collect CPU usage data
10	Interval in seconds
3	Number of intervals

The columns of the output provide the following information:

%usr	Reports the percentage of time the CPU spent at the user level.
%sys	Reports the percentage of time the CPU spent in execution of system functions.
%wio	Reports the percentage of time the CPU was idle waiting for I/O to complete.
%idle	Reports the percentage of time the CPU was idle, with no outstanding for I/O requests.

Tip: In AIX 5L, we can make some interpretations about the output of the `sar` -u command; if %usr+%sys>80%, the system is CPU bound.

When the CPU always has outstanding disk I/O (%wio), you must further investigate this area.

In order to get more information of what could be happening on the system, we are going to review the process queues with **sar -q**.

In Figure 14-4, we are extracting the information of the process queue from a previously created file (system1, system2, and system3). The -q option can indicate whether you have too many jobs running (runq-sz) or have a potential paging bottleneck.

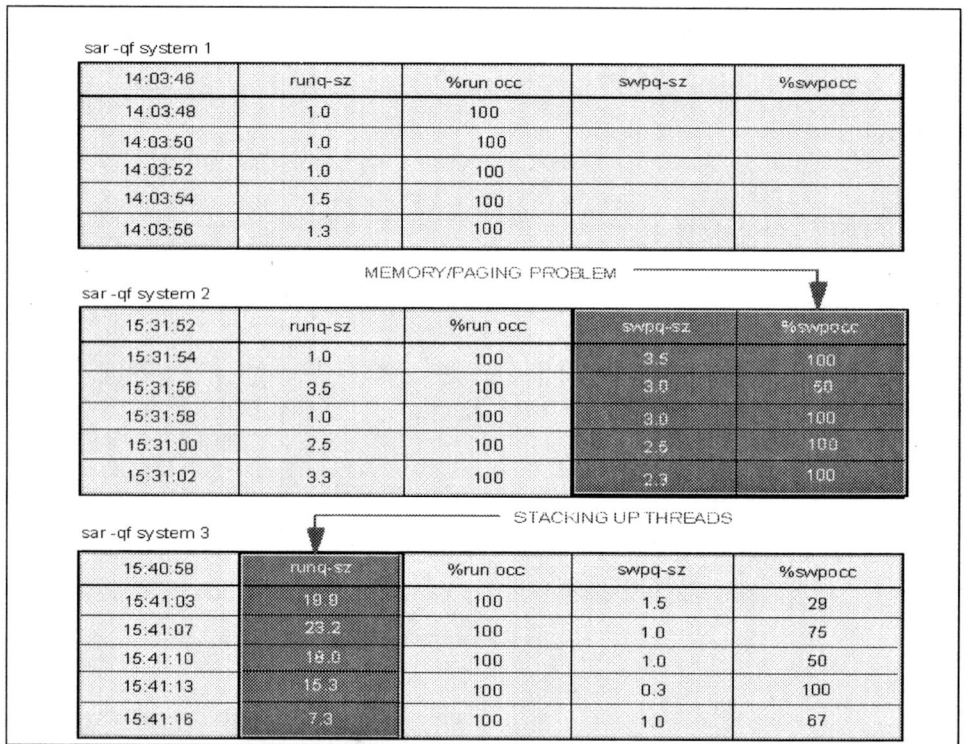

Figure 14-4   Process queue (sar -q)

The relevant terms are as follows:

runq-sz
The average run-queue size, average number of processors running, and the percentage of time that the run queue was occupied.

swapq-sz
The average number of processes waiting for a page fault resolution and the percentage of time that the swap queue was occupied.

You also can use **tprof** command and other commands for CPU monitoring in AIX 5L, see **tprof** man page for details.

For more information about this topic, refer to *AIX 5L Practical Performance Tools and Tuning Guide* Edition, SG24-6478-00.

14.3 Memory concepts and performance analysis

In this section we explain the basic virtual memory concepts in AIX 5L and the issues that affect performance. Then we use and interpret `vmstat` reports for AIX 5L and HP-UX 11i systems. By the end of this section we see some advanced tools for AIX 5L.

14.3.1 The AIX 5L Virtual Memory Manager

Virtual memory is a method by which real memory appears larger than its true size. Basically, the virtual memory subsystem is composed of real memory plus physical disk space, where portions of files and programs that are not being used are stored.

The VMM divides the physical storage segments into three types of segments. Each one, and the real memory, is divided by the VMM into 4 KB pages, When a page is needed from a disk location, it is loaded into a frame in real memory.

The following list show us the segment types for the physical storage:

Client segment   This segment resides in a remote server, such as NFS, or it could also be data on a CD-ROM.

Persistent segment   Local file systems are also known as a persistent segment.

Working segment   This kind of segment is transitory and exists only during use by their process. They do not have a permanent disk storage location. If free pages in real memory are needed, then some inactive pages are moved to the working segment.

14.3.2 The page stealer

When the number of available real memory frames (4 KB pages) on the free list becomes low, the page stealer is automatically invoked by the VMM. The page stealer looks into the Page Frame Table (PFT) for candidate pages to steal. Look at Figure 14-5 on page 496 to get a graphical explanation.

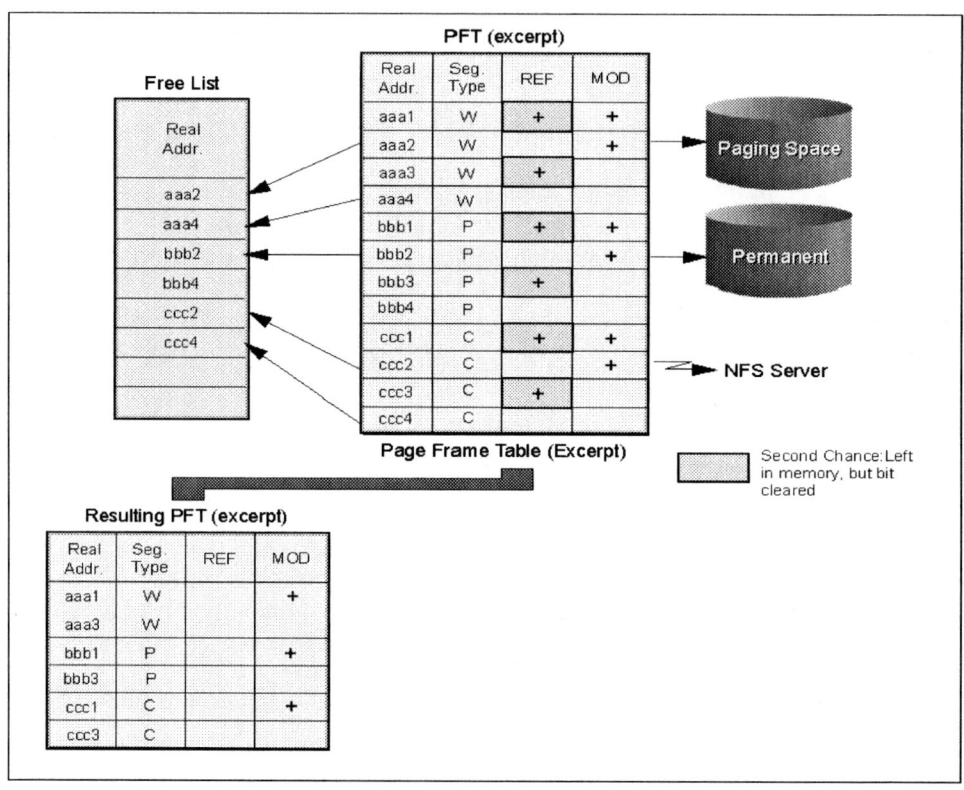

Figure 14-5   The page stealer

As shown in Figure 14-5, the PFT includes flags to signal which pages have been referenced and which have been modified. When the page stealer encounters a page that has been referenced, it does not steal that page, but instead resets the reference flag for that page. The next time it passes and the reference bit on that page is turned off, that page is stolen. A page that was not referenced in the first pass is immediately stolen.

VMM attempts to keep the size of the free list (the number of free pages in real memory) within a fixed range. The high threshold for this range is computed as two frames (8 KB) per megabyte of real memory and the low threshold is set at eight frames (32 KB) below the high threshold. These two values are known as *minfree* and *maxfree* and can be tuned with the **vmtune** command.

Table 14-1 on page 497 illustrates some differences between AIX 5L and HP-UX 11i systems for the page stealer.

Table 14-1   VMM differences between AIX 5L and HP-UX 11i

Concept	AIX 5L	HP-UX 11i
Page size	4 KB	4 KB
Memory table	PFT (page frame table).	pfdat (Page Frama Data Table).
Page stealer algorithm	Controlled by VMM.	Controlled by vhand daemon.
High threshold for free list	maxfree. Tuned by `# vmo -p -o maxfree='new_value'` Not is necessary reboot.	lotsfree Kernel parameter. For you to change this value, it is necessary to reboot in the system.
Low threshold for free list	minfree. Tuned by `# vmo -p -o minfree='new_value'` Not is necessary reboot	minfree. Kernel parameter. For you to change this value, it is necessary reboot in the system.

14.3.3 Memory monitoring: vmstat

Before we can proceed with **vmstat**, let us make some useful definitions:

page-in   A page-in occurs whenever a page is returned to real memory from a paging space. This action will cause a process thread to stop until the read operation from disk is done.

page-out   This operation occurs when the total amount of free pages on the free list is less than minfree, or when a new process starts and it does not find enough real memory to run. A page-out is always done by the page stealer algorithm.

Reclaimed page   A reclaim is done when a page that was just put on the free list is needed again before that page frame has been occupied by another page.

Page fault   It occurs when a page that is known to have been referenced recently is referenced again, and is not found in memory because the page has been replaced (an perhaps written to disk) since it was last accessed.

vmstat overview

The **vmstat** command reports statistics about virtual memory, CPU activity, and disks. If the **vmstat** command is invoked without flags, the report will contain the virtual memory activity since system startup. If you are using intervals, they are specified in seconds. Also, the first report shown contains statistics for the time since system startup. Subsequent reports contain statistics collected during the interval since the previous report. The basic syntax for **vmstat** is the same for AIX 5L and HP-UX 11i:

```
# vmstat <interval> <# of intervals>
```

For this command, the interval is measured in seconds.

Interpreting vmstat in HP-UX 11i

In HP-UX 11i, as in AIX 5L, the **vmstat** command sends a report about the virtual memory.

As you can see in Example 14-3, the **vmstat** command has the same syntax that AIX 5L. For this output, the first thing to mention is that **vmstat** reports averaged rates, based on two measures of kernel counters; the first line shows us the report of virtual memory activity since last boot. Beginning with the second line, the results are based on the interval (in our case, 10 seconds).

Example 14-3   Using vmstat in HP-UX 11i

```
# vmstat 10 5
procs       memory              page                     faults      cpu
 r  b  w     avm     free  re  at  pi  po  fr  de  sr   in      sy   cs  us sy id
 2  0  0  135382  198527   0   0   0   0   0   0   0  978   96258  227  13 22 65
 2  0  0  135382  198527   0   0   0   0   0   0   0  980   96227  236  15 21 64
 2  0  0  135382  198527   0   0   0   0   0   0   0  974   96093  244  21 23 55
 2  0  0  134670  198527   0   0   0   0   0   0   0  973   96141  240  15 20 65
 2  0  0  134670  198527   0   0   0   0   0   0   0  974   96159  238  12 22 66
 2  0  0  134670  198527   0   0   0   0   0   0   0  976   96197  235  16 19 65
 2  0  0  134670  198527   0   0   0   0   0   0   0  976   96174  234  17 17 66
```

The main difference between the AIX 5L and HP-UX 11i output of **vmstat** is the disk section. The following list describes each column:

r/b/w   Each column defines the size of the running queue, the waiting queue (processes block for I/O waiting), and idle processes that have been swapped at some time.

avm   The total number of active pages at the time of the interval.

free   This is the size of the free list.

re   Number of pages reclaimed from the free list.

at	Number of address translation fault.
pi/po	Number of page-ins or page-outs from file system or swap space.
fr	Number of freed pages.
de	Number of pages freed after write.
sr	Number of pages that were examined by clock algorithm.
in/sy/cs	Interrupts/system calls/CPU context switches per second during the interval.
cpu	These columns (us, sy, and id) represent the same output as `sar -u`.

Interpreting vmstat in AIX 5L

In this section we discuss the use and interpretation of the **vmstat** command. The syntax used for AIX 5L is the same as for HP-UX 11i, as shown in Example 14-4.

Example 14-4   Using vmstat

```
#vmstat 5 7
kthr      memory               page                faults         cpu
----- ----------- ------------------------ ------------ -----------
 r  b   avm   fre re pi po  fr   sr cy  in   sy  cs us sy id wa
15  1 49472 197594  0  0  0   0    0  0 444 1527 217  2  1 96  1
41  0 48146 198920  0  0  0   0    0  0 432 48227 664 63 37  0  0
32  0 44792 202274  0  0  0   0    0  0 431 49658 653 63 37  0  0
12  0 42007 205059  0  0  0   0    0  0 431 45009 720 66 34  0  0
 7  0 40189 206877  0  0  0   0    0  0 431 35177 411 45 29 27  0
 0  0 40189 206877  0  0  0   0    0  0 432  546 178  0  0 99  0
 0  1 40189 206877  0  0  0   0    0  0 514  575 181  0  2 94  4
```

Example 14-4 shows us the basic use of the **vmstat** command for an AIX 5L system; each column is described below:

kthr	This heading is used to measure the kernel thread changes per second over the sampling interval.
r or b	Number of kernel threads per second placed on the runq or waitq during the interval (waiq= awaiting resources or waiting on I/O).
memory	Information about VMM.
fre	It is used to monitor the total amount of free page frames in the memory.
avm	The total number of active pages at the time of the interval.

page	Information about page faults and paging activity, it is measured in units per second.
re	Number of page reclaims per second observed in the sample interval.
pi or po	Number of page-ins or page-outs per second during the interval.
fr	Number of pages per second that were freed.
sr	Number of pages that were examined by the page replacement algorithm.
cy	Number of cycles per second of the replacement algorithm.
faults	Interrupt average per second during the sampling.
in/sy/cs	Number of device interrupts/system calls/kernel thread context switches per second observed in the interval.
CPU	Same output as `sar -u`.

> **Tip:** In AIX 5L, we can make the following interpretations:
>
> ► If the free column is at a low threshold (2 times the number of MB of real memory minus 8) and the pi rate is more than five per second, then it is quite likely your memory is over-committed.
>
> ► A high page scan (sr) to page steal (fr) ratio also indicates a more active memory subsystem.

The `vmstat` command can also be used with the -s flag, which shows a summary of the VMM. Let us take a look at the following example:

Example 14-5   vmstat command with -s flag

```
#vmstat -s
              1949454 total address trans. faults
                16766 page ins
                67388 page outs
                    0 paging space page ins
                    0 paging space page outs
                    0 total reclaims
              1096931 zero filled pages faults
                 5512 executable filled pages faults
                    0 pages examined by clock
                    0 revolutions of the clock hand
                    0 pages freed by the clock
                82711 backtracks
                    0 lock misses
```

```
        0 free frame waits
        0 extend XPT waits
    11460 pending I/O waits
    73632 start I/Os
    73631 iodones
 42373064 cpu context switches
101956035 device interrupts
        0 software interrupts
        0 traps
128114594 syscalls
```

The -s option of the **vmstat** command sends a summary report to STDOUT;
starting from system initialization, the output represents the count of various
events. The -s option is exclusive of other options.

14.3.4 Advanced memory tools: svmon

svmon will give us a more in-depth analysis of memory. **svmon** captures a
snapshot of the current state of memory. The information can be analyzed using
different reports.

The options for **svmon** include:

-G   This flag gives us a global report, describing the real
               memory in use and paging space in use for whole system.

-P   This option displays the memory usage for active
               processes.

-S   Displays the memory usage for the specified segments or
               the top ten.

-D   Displays detailed information about a specified segment.

-U   Displays user statistics.

-C   Displays commands statistics.

-W   Displays statistics by Workload Manager classes.

How much memory is in use

svmon can be used to show how is the memory in use, as shown in
Example 14-6.

Example 14-6   Using svmon

```
# svmon -G -i 7 5
               size      inuse       free       pin    virtual
memory       262119      70135     191984     12761      54302
pg space     262144       1091
```

```
              work         pers        clnt       lpage
pin          12761            0           0           0
in use       54300        15835           0           0
              size        inuse        free         pin    virtual
memory      262119        70638      191481       12761      54805
pg space    262144         1091

              work         pers        clnt       lpage
pin          12761            0           0           0
in use       54803        15835           0           0
              size        inuse        free         pin    virtual
memory      262119        71235      190884       12761      55402
pg space    262144         1091

              work         pers        clnt       lpage
pin          12761            0           0           0
in use       55400        15835           0           0
```

Example 14-6 on page 501 shows a global report (-G) repeated five times at a 7 second interval (-i 7 5).

The row headings in a global report are:

► memory

This row describes memory statistics shown in 4 KB pages. The columns for this row are:

size	Number of memory frames (real memory size).
inuse	This value represents detailed statistics of the subset of real memory.
free	Number of frames free of all memory pools.
pin	Number of frames containing pinned pages.
virtual	Number of pages allocated in the system virtual space.
stolen	Number of frames stolen by rmss and made unusable by VMM. This field only appears if memory size is actually simulated by rmss.

Note: The rmss (Real Memory Size Simulator) command simulates various memory sizes without having to extract and replace memory boards. Also, it can run applications over a range of memory sizes. It is mostly used as a capacity planning tool. Its syntax is:

```
# rmss -c <memory size in MB>
```

► in use

This row specifies statistics on the subset of real memory in use. The columns for this row are:

work   Number of frames containing working segment pages.

pers   Number of frames containing persistent segment pages.

clnt   Number of frames containing client segment pages.

► pin

This row specifies statistics on the subset of real memory containing pinned pages. the columns for this row are:

work   Number of frames containing working segment pinned pages.

pers   Number of frames containing persistent segment pinned pages.

clnt   Number of frames containing client segment pinned pages.

► pg space

This row specifies statistics describing the use of paging space. The columns for this row are:

size   Size of paging space.

inuse   Number of paging space pages used.

Remember:

► 1 frame = 1 page, but a frame is a page located in real memory.

► Working segment: Data that resides in real memory.

► Persistent segment: Data that actually is in the disk (file system and paging space).

► Client segment: Data from an NFS server or a CD-ROM.

► Pinned page: A page that resides on real memory and cannot be taken out from real memory.

Who are the memory users

To find the memory users, use the following command:

```
# svmon -Put 10
```

Where:

-P	Allows you to search processes.
-u	This option sorts in reverse order.
-t	Number of top processes to show.

Example 14-7   Finding the top 10 memory consuming processes

```
# svmon -Put 10
---------------------------------------------------------------------
     Pid Command         Inuse    Pin   Pgsp  Virtual 64-bit Mthrd LPage
   35866 ls              3696    2025   2005    10348      N     N     N

    Vsid     Esid Type Description          LPage  Inuse   Pin Pgsp
Virtual
       0        0 work kernel seg              -   3217   2023 1965 4878
   1d01d        d work shared library text     -    355      0   30 5339
   120b3        2 work process private         -     86      2    9   95
   150b4        f work shared library data     -     34      0    1   36
   162b6        1 pers code,/dev/hd2:6891      -      4      0    -    -
   175b7        - pers /dev/hd2:21103          -      0      0    -    -


---------------------------------------------------------------------
     Pid Command         Inuse    Pin   Pgsp  Virtual 64-bit Mthrd LPage
   19878 svmon           3670    2025   1995    10291      N     N     N

    Vsid     Esid Type Description          LPage  Inuse   Pin Pgsp
Virtual
       0        0 work kernel seg              -   3217   2023 1965 4878
   1d01d        d work shared library text     -    355      0   30 5339
   170b6        2 work process private         -     47      2    0   47
   140b5        f work shared library data     -     27      0    0   27
   19f39        1 pers code,/dev/hd2:18457     -     24      0    -    -
   180b9        - pers /dev/hd4:8305           -      0      0    -    -


---------------------------------------------------------------------
     Pid Command         Inuse    Pin   Pgsp  Virtual 64-bit Mthrd LPage
   14778 -ksh            3665    2025   2054    10320      N     N     N

    Vsid     Esid Type Description          LPage  Inuse   Pin Pgsp
Virtual
       0        0 work kernel seg              -   3217   2023 1965 4878
   1d01d        d work shared library text     -    355      0   30 5339
    c0ac        1 pers code,/dev/hd2:6215      -     40      0    -    -
   1fdbf        2 work process private         -     30      2   51   78
   1e7de        f work shared library data     -     20      0    8   25
    a06a        - pers /dev/hd2:21059          -      2      0    -    -
    3723        - pers /dev/hd4:8198           -      1      0    -    -
```

In Example 14-7 on page 504, we use **svmon** to locate the top 10 memory consuming processes. The information provided by the command is divided into paragraphs; each one contains information detailed by the process.

The first section of each paragraph displays the general information for the process:

Pid	Process ID.
Command	Command that the process is running.
Inuse	Total number of pages in real memory that the process is using.
Pin	Total number of pinned pages used by the process.
Virtual	Total number of pages of virtual space used by the process.

The second section of each paragraph displays detailed information of the memory usage by the process.

Vsid	Virtual segment ID.
Esid	Effective segment ID.
Type	Type of the segment.
Description	This is a textual description of the segment, including the logical volume name and i-node of the file that is being used.
Inuse	Number of real memory pages for this segment.
Pin	Number of pages pinned from this segment.
Pgspace	Number of pages in paging space for this segment.

Tip: If you would like to know the file associated with the i-node, use any of the following commands:

```
# find / -name "*" -inum XXXX
```

where **XXXX** represents the number of i-node indicated by the svmon output

or

```
# ncheck -i <i-node number> <lv name>
```

For example:

```
# ncheck -i 6891 /dev/hd2
```

14.3.5 Paging space and Swap space

When memory gets over-committed, many pages have to be moved into a secondary area, called paging space in AIX 5L or swap space in HP-UX 11i.

HP-UX 11i

In HP-UX 11i, the primary swap space is defined in logical volume (/dev/vg00/lvol2).

The **swapinfo** command is used to list swap space configured in HP-UX 11i.

Example 14-8   swapinfo command

```
# swapinfo
              Kb        Kb        Kb   PCT  START/       Kb
TYPE       AVAIL      USED      FREE  USED  LIMIT RESERVE  PRI  NAME
dev      1048576         0   1048576    0%      0       -    1  /dev/vg00/lvol2
reserve        -    267696   -267696
memory   1445308    747432    697876   52%
```

The **swapon** command enable a logical volume to secondary swap area.

AIX 5L

In AIX 5L, the paging space is defined by default in a logical volume (/dev/hd6).

There are two paging space allocation policies:

► Early page space allocation
► Late page space allocation

AIX 5L uses late page space allocation by default, which means that paging space is not actually allocated unless the pages are touched (being touched means the page was modified somehow). This policy provides better performance and prevents processes from unnecessarily using too much paging space.

If a process wants to ensure that it will not be killed due to low paging conditions, this process can pre-allocate paging space by using the early page space allocation policy. This is done by setting an environment variable called *PSALLOC*. This can be done within the process or at the command line (#PSALLOC=early).

Characteristics of paging space

In AIX 5L, the paging space is implemented as a logical volume, which allows you to easily add/remove additional paging spaces. Here we have some of its characteristics:

► Implemented as a logical volume (could be spread across multiple physical volumes).

► VMM can use as many paging spaces as needed.

> **Tip:** Follow these rules of thumb to calculate the paging space allocation area. You need to check the application requirements:
>
> ► If real memory is less than 256 MB, paging space is two times real memory.
>
> ► If real memory is greater than 256 MB, paging space is 512 MB + (real memory - 256) times 1.25.
>
> ► It is better to create a second paging space than to extend an existing one.
>
> ► A paging space cannot use more than 20 percent of total disk space.
>
> ► Use the lsps -a command to monitor the use of paging space.
>
> ► If the %used for a paging space is greater than 85 percent, it is quite likely you are running out of paging space. Many applications use a great deal of paging space. Ensure that the problem is not related to real memory by using the vmstat command.

Understand that paging space never substitutes real memory, but if you run out of paging space, any new process can be started, and many running processes will be killed in order to free the paging space. A paging space cannot be deleted online, so it should be deactivated for the next boot, and then you could delete it. Use the following commands to delete it:

```
# chps -a 'n' pagingxx (where xx represents the umber of the paging space you
want to delete)
# shutdown -Fr
# rmps pagingxx
```

Allocation policy

AIX Version 4.3.2 introduced the deferred paging space allocation policy, which ensures that no disk block is allocated for paging until it becomes necessary to pageout a given memory page. This allocation policy was a modification and enhancement to the existing late allocation policy which initiated a disk block allocation once a memory page was requested and accessed, regardless of the need to pageout that frame. The early paging space allocation policy offers an alternative to the deferred paging space allocation policy. If the former policy is chosen the paging space is allocated when memory is requested – even before the frame is accessed or scheduled for pageout. The deferred allocation policy reduces the amount of required paging space substantially.

AIX 5L implements two paging space garbage collection (PSGC) methods for deferred allocation working segments:

► Garbage collect paging space on re-pagein
► Garbage collect paging space scrubbing for in-memory frames

Garbage collect paging space on re-pagein

This garbage collection method is also referred to as the re-pagein disk block free mechanism. This mechanism only applies to the deferred page space allocation policy. Normally, the deferred page space allocation policy will, upon paging a page back in from disk, retain its disk block, and leave the page unmodified in memory. If the page does not get modified then, when it is selected for replacement by the VMM it does not have to be written to disk again. This is a performance advantage for pages that are not modified after being paged back in from disk. The re-pagein disk block free mechanism allows the system administrator to specify that the operating system should free a page's disk block after pagein. The page will be left modified in memory. If the page gets selected for replacement by the VMM, it will have a new disk block allocated for it, and it will be written to disk.

Garbage collect paging space scrubbing for in-memory frames

The re-paging disk block free mechanism is supplemented by a more powerful but less granular method. Instead of, or in addition to the re-pagein disk block free mechanism, a system administrator might want to try and reclaim paging space disk blocks for pages that are already in memory. When using the deferred page space allocation policy, pages that are paged in from paging space retain their paging space disk block while they are in memory. If the page does not get modified, then when it is selected for replacement by the Virtual Memory Manager, it does not have to be written to disk again. This is a performance advantage for pages that are not modified after being paged back in from disk. Over time, however, after many pageins, it is possible that there could be many pages in memory that are consuming paging space disk blocks. This could cause paging space to become low. To address this problem, the system administrator, through the vmo command, can enable a mechanism to free paging space disk blocks from pages in memory that have them. This is referred to as garbage collection, or scrubbing of these disk blocks.

For more information about Paging space garbage collection, refer to *AIX 5L Differences Guide Version 5.2 Edition*, SG24-5765.

14.4 I/O concepts and performance analysis

Most of the time, many of the performance problems in our systems are found on the physical disk; for that reason, this section will cover the issues about disk monitoring, interpreting results of the most useful commands (`iostat`), and discussing the tuning techniques available in AIX 5L. For detailed information about the Logical Volume Manager and the storage concepts, refer to Chapter 6, "Logical Volume Manager and disk management" on page 141.

14.5 Disk and LVM monitoring

The following section describes disk and LVM monitoring tools.

14.5.1 iostat command

The following sections describe the `iostat` command.

In HP-UX

In HP-UX the `iostat` command reports on the disk I/O statistics as shown in Example 14-19 on page 524. The statistics are displayed for each disk device that is active on the system. The following details are displayed with the command:

device   Disk device

bps   Kilobytes transferred per second

sps   Number of seeks per second

msps   Milliseconds per average seek

Example 14-9   Example of iostat command in HP-UX 11i

```
# iostat 2 5

    device    bps    sps    msps

    c1t3d0     0     0.0    1.0
    c1t4d0     0     0.0    1.0

    c1t3d0     1     0.5    1.0
    c1t4d0     0     0.0    1.0

    c1t3d0     0     0.0    1.0
    c1t4d0    24     3.0    1.0

    c1t3d0     0     0.0    1.0
```

c1t4d0	0	0.0	1.0

c1t3d0	4	0.5	1.0
c1t4d0	0	0.0	1.0

Example 14-15 displays the disk I/O statistics every two seconds for a count of five and then stops.

The -t options displays the tty and CPU statistics in addition to the disk statistics as shown in Example 14-15.

Example 14-10   Example of iostat command with -t option in HP-UX 11i

```
# iostat -t 2 3
                        tty               cpu
                    tin tout        us  ni  sy  id
                     0    7          5   0·  9  86

        device   bps      sps    msps

        c1t3d0    0      0.0     1.0
        c1t4d0    0      0.0     1.0

                        tty               cpu
                    tin tout        us  ni  sy  id
                     0   91         12   0  21  67

        device   bps      sps    msps

        c1t3d0    4      0.5     1.0
        c1t4d0    0      0.0     1.0

                        tty               cpu
                    tin tout        us  ni  sy  id
                     0   94         17   0  18  65

        device   bps      sps    msps

        c1t3d0    0      0.0     1.0
        c1t4d0    0      0.0     1.0
```

In AIX 5L

The **iostat** tool will provide data on the activity of physical volumes, but not file systems or logical volumes. The **iostat** command is used for monitoring system input/output device load by observing the time the physical disks are active in relation to their average transfer rates. The **iostat** command generates reports that can be used to determine an imbalanced system configuration to better balance the I/O load between physical disks and adapters.

Remember that the first set of data represents all activity since the system start-up.

The first line of the **iostat** output reports statistics for the time since the reboot and the subsequent lines displays the statistics for the last interval. When monitoring, consistent high transfers rates and low CPU idle states could indicate disk I/O bottlenecks. But further investigating will be required as there are many factors that contribute to performance problems.

The Example 14-11 shows the number of characters read from and written to terminals. This shown by the tin and tout values. The CPU statistics show the percentage of time the system spent in the different modes: user (us), user at low-priority processes (ni), system (sy), and idle (id).

Example 14-11 Example of iostat command in AIX 5L

```
#iostat 5 10

System configuration: lcpu=2 drives=6 paths=9 vdisks=0

tty:      tin        tout   avg-cpu:  % user    % sys    % idle   % iowait
          0.1        2.1              2.8       1.6      95.4      0.2
                " Disk history since boot not available. "

tty:      tin        tout   avg-cpu:  % user    % sys    % idle   % iowait
          0.0        0.0              62.8      36.9      0.3      0.0

Disks:        % tm_act     Kbps      tps    Kb_read    Kb_wrtn
hdisk3          0.0        0.0       0.0        0          0
hdisk2         81.9     1319.2      93.6      108       6488
hdisk0         24.5      496.8      28.4       72       2412
hdisk1         17.2      501.6      29.8       84       2424
hdisk4          0.0        0.0       0.0        0          0
cd0             0.0        0.0       0.0        0          0
tty:      tin        tout   avg-cpu:  % user    % sys    % idle   % iowait
          0.0        0.0              63.8      36.2      0.0      0.0
Disks:        % tm_act     Kbps      tps    Kb_read    Kb_wrtn
hdisk3          0.0        0.0       0.0        0          0
hdisk2         51.2      822.4      54.6      164       3948
hdisk0         25.4      387.2      30.8      144       1792
hdisk1         16.4      389.6      29.8      140       1808
hdisk4          0.0        0.0       0.0        0          0
cd0             0.0        0.0       0.0        0          0
tty:      tin        tout   avg-cpu:  % user    % sys    % idle   % iowait
          0.0        0.0              63.8      35.7      0.3      0.1
```

```
Disks:       % tm_act      Kbps      tps   Kb_read   Kb_wrtn
hdisk3          0.0         0.0       0.0         0         0
hdisk2         56.4      1157.6      60.8       112      5676
hdisk0         30.0       536.8      35.8       108      2576
hdisk1         19.4       528.0      35.2        80      2560
hdisk4          0.0         0.0       0.0         0         0
cd0             0.0         0.0       0.0         0         0
```

In Example 14-11 on page 511, the first report is the summary since the last boot and shows the overall balance. The system maintains a history of a disk activity; if the history is disabled, the following message will appear when you run the **iostat** command:

```
Disk history since boot not available.
```

This is only for the first report; the interval disk I/O statistics are unaffected by this. If you would like to enable the disk history, you can use the smitty screen shown in Example 14-12. We need to select true in the "Continuously maintain DISK I/O history" field. Run # **smitty chgsys** to get the screen.

Example 14-12   Enabling disk I/O history

```
                Change / Show Characteristics of Operating System
Type or select values in entry fields.
Press Enter AFTER making all desired changes.

                                                   [Entry Fields]
System ID                                       0X036FC090202E2200
Partition ID                                    0X036FC090202E2201
Maximum number of PROCESSES allowed per user    [8128]                  +#
Maximum number of pages in block I/O BUFFER CACHE  [20]                 +#
Maximum Kbytes of real memory allowed for MBUFS [0]                     +#
Automatically REBOOT system after a crash        true                   +
Continuously maintain DISK I/O history           false                  +
HIGH water mark for pending write I/Os per file [0]                     +#
LOW water mark for pending write I/Os per file  [0]                     +#
Amount of usable physical memory in Kbytes       4194304
State of system keylock at boot time             normal
Enable full CORE dump                            false                  +
Use pre-430 style CORE dump                      false                  +
Pre-520 tuning compatibility mode                disabl                 +
Maximum login name length at boot time          [9]                     +#
ARG/ENV list size in 4K byte blocks             [6]                     +#
CPU Guard                                        enable                 +
Processor capacity increment                     1.00
Partition is capped                              true
Partition is dedicated                           true
Entitled processor capacity                      2.00
```

```
Minimum potential processor capacity          1.00
Maximum potential processor capacity          4.00
Variable processor capacity weight            0

F1=Help         F2=Refresh      F3=Cancel       F4=List
F5=Reset        F6=Command      F7=Edit         F8=Image
F9=Shell        F0=Exit         Enter=Do
```

Here we have the column definitions for the output of the **iostat** command shown in Example 14-12 on page 512.

A header row with number of CPUs and the number of disks that are currently active in the system are printed at the beginning of the output.

► TTY report

The tin and tout columns show the number of characters read and written by all TTY devices, including real TTY devices connected to an asynchronous port or pseudo TTY devices (telnet sessions, aixterm windows, and so on). Because the processing of input and output characters consumes CPU resources, look for a correlation between increased TTY activity and CPU utilization.

► CPU report

The statistics of this column present the same output as **sar -u**.

► Drive report

When you suspect a disk I/O performance problem, use the **iostat** command with the -d option to avoid the information about TTY and CPU. You can also see the system-wide throughput summary of these disk statistics by specifying the -s option.

► Disks report

This section shows the name of the physical volumes. They are either hdisk or cd followed by a number. If the physical volume name is specified within **iostat**, only that name specified is displayed. The subheadings are:

%tm_act   Indicates the percentage of time the physical disk was active (bandwidth utilization for the drive), in other words, the total time disk requests are outstanding. As disk use increases, performance decreases and response time increases.

Kbps   Indicates the amount of data transferred (read or written) to the drive in KB per second during the interval.

| tps | Indicates the number of transfers per second that were issued to the physical disk. |
| Kb_read/Kb_written | Reports the total of data in KB read/written to the physical volume during the interval. |

> **Tip:** Here we have some useful considerations about the `iostat` output:
>
> ► If I/O wait time is greater than 20 percent, you might have a disk or I/O bound situation.
>
> ► If tm_acct is greater than 75 percent, you might have a disk or I/O bound situation.

In AIX 5L Version 5.3, the `iostat` command has been enhanced to include the following:

► Shared processor partitions

On micro-partitioning/simultaneous multi-threaded environments, the `iostat` command now reports:

– Number of physical processors consumed (physc)
– Percentage of entitlement consumed (% entc)

► Asynchronous I/O (AIO) monitoring

The `iostat` command now has new monitoring features and flags for getting the AIO and the POSIX AIO statistics.

-A	Reports historic AIO statistics along with utilization metrics.
-P	Reports POSIX AIO statistics along with utilization metrics.
-q	Reports each AIO queue's request count.
-Q	Reports AIO queues associated with each mounted file system and the queue request count.
-l	Displays the data in a 132 column width. This flag is simply a formatting flag.

From AIX 5L Version 5.2, the `iostat` also included the following enhancements:

► The -s flag added a new line to the header of each statistic's data that reports the sum of all activity on the system.

► The -a flag produces an adapter throughput report.

► The -m flag displays statistics about the path activities with the hdisk associated to the path. This was an *iostat* enhancement for multipath I/O (MPIO).

For further information and enhancements on the *iostat* command, refer to:

► *AIX 5L Differences Guide Version 5.2 Edition, SG24-5765*
► *AIX 5L Differences Guide Version 5.3 Edition, SG24-7463-00*

14.5.2 Conclusions for iostat

Taken alone, there is no unacceptable value for any of the fields of the *iostat* output, because statistics are too closely related to application characteristics, system configuration, and type of physical disk drives. Therefore, when you are evaluating data, look for patterns and relationships. The most common relationship is between disk utilization (%tm_act) and the transfer rate (tps).

To draw a valid conclusion from this data, you have to understand the application's disk data access patterns, such as sequential, random, or a combination of both. For example, if an application reads/writes sequentially, you should expect a high disk transfer rate (Kbps) when you have a high disk busy rate (%tm_act). Columns Kb_read and Kb_wrtn can confirm an understanding of an application's read/write behavior.

Generally, you do not need to be concerned about a high disk busy rate as long as the disk transfer rate is also high. However, if you get a high disk busy rate and low disk transfer rate, you may have a fragmented logical volume, file system, or individual file.

A discussion about disk, logical volume, and file system performance sometimes leads you to the conclusion that the more drives you have on your system, the better the I/O is. This is not always true, because there is a limit to the amount of data that can be handled by a disk adapter. The disk adapter can also become a bottleneck.

14.6 Advanced tools: filemon

At this point we can identify which disk is overloaded, or which adapter is getting close to becoming over-committed, but we do not know which logical volumes or which files are the most used and which could be hotspots. This information is really useful in balancing the load between disks and adapters; in order to know that information, we use the **filemon** command.

Using filemon

The filemon tool collects and presents trace data on the various layers of file system utilization, including logical file systems, virtual memory segments, LVM, and the physical disk layer.

The **filemon** command monitors file and I/O activity at four levels:

Logical file system
The **filemon** command monitors logical I/O operations on logical files. The monitored operations include all read, write, open, and lseek system calls, which may or may not result in actual physical I/O depending on whether the files are already buffered in memory. I/O statistics are kept on a per-file basis.

Virtual memory system
The **filemon** command monitors physical I/O operations (that is, paging) between segments and their images on disk. I/O statistics are kept on a per-segment basis.

Logical volumes
The **filemon** command monitors I/O operations on logical volumes. I/O statistics are kept on a per-logical-volume basis.

Physical volumes
The **filemon** command monitors I/O operations on physical volumes. At this level, physical resource utilizations are obtained. I/O statistics are kept on a per-physical-volume basis.

Any combination of the four levels can be monitored, as specified by the command-line flags. By default, the **filemon** command only monitors I/O operations at the virtual memory, logical volume, and physical volume levels. These levels are all concerned with requests for real disk I/O.

Let us take a look at the syntax of the **filemon** command:

```
filemon [ -d ] [ -i Trace_File -n Gennames_File] [ -o File] [ -O Levels] [ -P ]
[ -T n] [ -u ] [ -v ]
```

Where:

-o	Name of the output file
-i	Name of the input file
-d	Defer trace until trcon
-T*n*	Set buffer size (default is 32000 bytes)
-v	Verbose output
-u	Print unnamed file activity

-O		Additional options to select trace; valid -O options are:
	lf	Monitor logical file I/O.
	vm	Monitor virtual memory.
	lv	Monitor logical volumes.
	pv	Monitor physical volumes.
	all	Select everything.
-P		Pins monitor process in memory

Normally, filemon runs in the background while other applications are running and being monitored. The **filemon** command will collect all the information in the output file only when you enter the **#trcstop** command. By default, only the top 20 logical files and segments are reported, unless the -v option is used.

In Example 14-13, we have the logical file reports; by default, only the top 20 most used files are reported. If the verbose option is used, then the activity for all files will be reported.

Example 14-13   Using filemon

```
filemon -o filemon.out -O lf < Monitor started >
# ksh io.sh < This shell script produces some overload on some files >
# trcstop < Monitor stopped >
# more filemon.out

Wed Jul  6 16:50:30 2005
System: AIX p650n04 Node: 5 Machine: 000197AA4C00
Cpu utilization:  6.5%

Most Active Files
------------------------------------------------------------------------
  #MBs  #opns  #rds  #wrs  file                    volume:inode
------------------------------------------------------------------------
   1.6      7   3255     0  unix                    /dev/hd2:2247
   1.0     54      0  1976  null
   0.4     52    103     0  ksh.cat                 /dev/hd2:21059
   0.1      9     18     0  limits                  /dev/hd4:41
   0.1      8     16     0  qconfig                 /dev/hd4:4154
   0.0      9      8     0  cat.cat                 /dev/hd2:20894
   0.0      4      4     0  find.cat                /dev/hd2:20984
   0.0      1      2     0  pid=0_fd=86694
```

In the first section of the files report, you will find the name of the file, including the logical volume in which it resides and its inode.

The report continues with a detailed report of each file, as shown in Example 14-14. Some fields report single values, while others show a distribution as with the read requests.

Example 14-14   Using filemon (cont. detailed output for file usage)

```
------------------------------------------------------------------------
Detailed File Stats
------------------------------------------------------------------------

FILE: /unix  volume: /dev/hd2 (/usr)  inode: 2247
opens:                   7
total bytes xfrd:        1666560
reads:                   3255    (0 errs)
  read sizes (bytes):  avg    512.0 min     512 max     512 sdev     0.0
  read times (msec):   avg    0.065 min   0.009 max  66.650 sdev   1.716

FILE: /dev/null
opens:                   54
total bytes xfrd:        1011712
writes:                  1976    (0 errs)
  write sizes (bytes): avg    512.0 min     512 max     512 sdev     0.0
  write times (msec):  avg    0.027 min   0.004 max  28.079 sdev   0.671

FILE: /usr/lib/nls/msg/en_US/ksh.cat  volume: /dev/hd2 (/usr)  inode: 21059
opens:                   52
total bytes xfrd:        421888
reads:                   103     (0 errs)
  read sizes (bytes):  avg   4096.0 min    4096 max    4096 sdev     0.0
  read times (msec):   avg    0.050 min   0.013 max   0.166 sdev   0.036
lseeks:                  255
```

The *read sizes* and *write sizes* will give you an idea of how efficiently your application is reading or writing information.

Not all the measures that we obtain from these tools are deterministic; we have to make some interpretations about the results. Here we have some useful recommendations to keep in mind for the I/O performance analysis:

► Look for most active files/file systems/logical volumes:

  – Can a hot file system be better placed on a physical drive?

  – Can a hot file system be spread across multiple physical drives?

  – Does paging dominate disk utilization? (filemon)

  – Are there enough memory pages to cache the file pages being used by the running processes? (svmon)

► Look for heavy physical volume utilization:
  – Is the type of drive causing a bottleneck? (filemon)
  – Is the SCSI the bottleneck? (iostat)

14.7 Network concepts and performance analysis

In this section we do not discuss any kinds of configuration issues. We cover the main topics that affect the performance in the network (network memory buffers and adapter queue size); for detailed information about network configuration refer to Chapter 9, "Network management" on page 279.

The goal for a network or system administrator should be to balance the demands of users against resource constraints to ensure acceptable network performance. In order to reach this goal we use the following steps:

1. Characterize workload, configuration, bandwidth, and so on.

2. Measure performance:

   – Run tools (**netstat**, **netpmon**, and **tcpmon**).
   – Identify bottlenecks.
   – Tune network parameters (**no**, **ifconfig**, and **chdev**).

Before we proceed, let us define some terms for AIX 5L Version 5.3:

thewall   This is a tunable parameter that represents the maximum size of the network real memory pool in KBs.

mbuf   A pinned memory space of 256 bytes that is used to store data for inbound and outbound network traffic. The amount of mbufs can be tuned using the high and low water marks.

                 To hold data less than 228 bytes, a single 256 bytes mbuf will be used.

cluster   A group of mbufs used to allocate a large amount of data. Its size must not be greater than 16 KB.

MTU   Maximum Transmission Unit. Network data in a network travels in frames, so the network interface places an upper limit on the maximum data that can be transferred in one frame; this value is the MTU.

14.7.1 Network monitoring: netstat

The **netstat** command provides information about the amount of input packets, output packets, collisions, and information related to the network memory buffers (mbufs). It also shows statistics about protocols, and the contents of the various network-related data structures.

The **netstat** command in HP-UX gives you similar information as in other UNIX flavors. The example below shows the output of the **netstat** command with the -I option for a specific interface, lan3. The first line of the report shows summary information since the last system reboot.

Example 14-15   Using netstat -I in HP-UX

```
# netstat -I lan3 5
(lan3)-> input      output      (Total)-> input      output
        packets     packets               packets     packets
        422560      390267                426418      394125
             4           3                     4           3
             3           1                     3           1
             1           1                     1           1
             1           1                     1           1
             3           1                     3           1
             1           1                     1           1
```

In Example 14-16 we use the **netstat** command in AIX 5L Version 5.3 with the -i option, which gave us the summary of the packets transferred for each interface defined in the system. In our case, en0 (Ethernet) and en1 (Ethernet), lo0 is the loopback address used by local processes.

Example 14-16   Using netstat -i

```
# netstat -i
Name  Mtu    Network    Address          Ipkts Ierrs   Opkts Oerrs Coll
en0   1500   link#2     0.2.55.3a.7.db   407076    0   71125    0    0
en0   1500   192.168.100 p650n04_en0     407076    0   71125    0    0
en1   1500   link#3     0.2.55.6f.1f.ef   29572    0   11666    0    0
en1   1500   10.1.1     p650n04           29572    0   11666    0    0
lo0   16896  link#1                         784    0     860    0    0
lo0   16896  127        localhost           784    0     860    0    0
lo0   16896  localhost                      784    0     860    0    0
```

The columns are defined as follows:

MTU The value for the frame size is, by default, 1500 in an Ethernet adapter.

Network Displays the network address of the network that the interface is connected to.

Address	Specifies the MAC address or hardware address.
Ipkts	Number of total input packets since the last boot.
Opkts	Number of total transmitted packets since the last boot.
Ierrs/Oerrs	Input/output errors.
Coll	Collisions; this count is not available for Ethernet interfaces (en).

> **Tip:** In AIX 5L Version 5.3, if the Oerrs column from `netstat -i` is greater than 1 percent of Opkts, the send (transmit) queue size (tx_que_size) for that interface should be increased.
>
> If Oerrs is greater than 1 percent of Ipkts, then execute the # `netstat -m` command to check for a lack of memory.

Another useful option for the `netstat` command is -I, which can be used to monitor the packet transmission for one interface within an interval. Look at Example 14-17 for the use of this command.

Example 14-17   Using netstat -I

```
[p650n04][/]> netstat -I en0 5
    input   (en0)      output            input   (Total)    output
packets  errs  packets  errs colls   packets  errs  packets  errs colls
594187     0   255912     0     0    625681     0   269443     0     0
 20532     0    20525     0     0     20575     0    20584     0     0
 19540     0    19530     0     0     19581     0    19586     0     0
 19540     0    19533     0     0     19581     0    19590     0     0
 20538     0    20529     0     0     20581     0    20588     0     0
 19533     0    19526     0     0     19573     0    19581     0     0
 20537     0    20528     0     0     20580     0    20588     0     0
 19554     0    19546     0     0     19596     0    19603     0     0
 20487     0    20480     0     0     20528     0    20537     0     0
 19554     0    19546     0     0     19597     0    19606     0     0
 19528     0    19516     0     0     19571     0    19574     0     0
 20536     0    20530     0     0     20579     0    20590     0     0
```

The output and interpretation for each column is the same as for the -i option.

14.7.2 Network tuning techniques and commands

In this section we review some commands and techniques that are going to help us improve our network performance.

Tuning commands

In this section we discuss tuning commands in HP-UX and AIX 5L.

HP-UX

The **ndd** command is used to do network tuning in HP-UX. It allows you to display and change network tunable parameters. The file /etc/rc.config.d/nddconf is used to make permanent changes to the tunable network parameters that will be used at system reboots.

The following are some examples of the **ndd** command:

► Displays all the tunable parameters:

```
# ndd -h supported
```

► Displays a detailed description of the parameter and the allowed values:

```
# ndd -h ip_forwarding
```

► To get a value of a parameter:

```
# ndd -get /dev/ip ip_forwarding
```

► To set a value of a parameter:

```
# ndd -set /dev/ip ip_forwarding 1
```

AIX 5L

This section illustrates the tuning options for AIX 5L.

no (network options)

With the **no** command, you can configure network tuning parameters and display or change the current network options, such as thewall, tcp_sendspace, and tcp_receivespace. You can use the command to set or display the current or the next boot values. This command can also make permanent changes or defer changes until the next reboot.

Let us review some of its flags:

-a	Displays current values for tunable parameters. Displays reboot or permanent values ID used together with the -r or -p options.
-d	Resets tunable back to its default value.
-o option=NewValue	Displays or changes the value for the specified option or attribute to NewValue.
-L	Displays the values of specific or all the tunable parameters.

Example 14-18   Example of no command

```
# no -a
          extendednetstats = 0
                  thewall = 1048576
              sockthresh = 85
                  sb_max = 1048576
               somaxconn = 1024
            tcp_recvspace = 16384
            tcp_sendspace = 16384
      clean_partial_conns = 0
        net_malloc_police = 0
                  rto_low = 1
```

Example 14-18 only presents some of the possible parameters that can be modified. The following list shows the commonly used parameters that can be tuned in order to obtain better network performance:

thewall   Allows you to increase the total amount of real memory (in KB) that can be designated to networking processes.

tcp_recvspace   This kernel value is used as the default socket receive buffer size when an application opens a TCP socket.

tcp_sendspace   This is the kernel value that controls the default socket send buffer. The send buffer controls how much data an application can write to a socket before it is blocked.

udp_recvspace   Establishes the receive socket buffer size for a UDP connection.

udp_sendspace   Defines the send socket buffer size for a UDP connection.

sb_max   This parameter controls the maximum size that a buffer can reach. That means that TCP/UDP receive and send buffers must be less than or equal to this value. If you want larger values for the buffers, then you need to modify this kernel variable also.

The following are some examples of using the **no** command:

▶ To display the maximum size of the mbuf pool:

```
# no -o thewall
```

▶ To change the size of the mbuf pool to a new value:

```
# no -o thewall=630000
```

▶ To list the current and reboot value, range, unit, type, and dependencies of all tunables parameters managed by the **no** command:

```
no -L
```

► To display help information about:

```
# no -h tcp_sendspace
```

> **Note:** Be careful when you use this command. If used incorrectly, the **no** command can cause your system to become inoperable.
>
> Before modifying any tunable parameter, you should first carefully read about all the characteristics of a tunable.
>
> For more information about tunable parameters and options of the **no** command, see the **no** command man pages.

Changing the transmit queue size value

The transmit queue size is a value that is totally dependent on the type/model of the adapter; refer to your network adapter manual to learn the supported values. When changing the value, the resource (adapter) must not be in used. Example 14-19 shows the way to change this attribute for the Ethernet adapter of our system. This process can also be issued by smitty.

Example 14-19 Changing the transmit queue size

```
# rmdev -l en0
en0 Defined
# rmdev -l ent0
ent0 Defined
# chdev -l ent0 -a tx_que_size=16384
ent0 changed
# mkdev -l ent0
ent0 Available
# mkdev -l en0
en0 Available
```

Let us describe each of the commands:

rmdev -l en0	Changes the status of the Ethernet interface (from available to defined)
rmdev -l ent0	Changes the status of the Ethernet adapter (from available to defined)
chdev -l	When the interface and the adapter are defined, changes the value of the transmit queue size:
-l	Indicates the logical device (ent0)
-a	Indicates the attribute we want to modify (tx_que_size=16384)
mkdev -l ent0	Changes the adapter into the available state

```
mkdev -l en0          Returns the interface to the available state
```

If we do not change the interface and adapter status from available to defined, we would receive the following output for the **chdev** command:

```
# chdev -l ent0 -a tx_que_size=16384
Method error (/usr/lib/methods/chgent):
        0514-062 Cannot perform the requested function because the
                 specified device is busy.
```

14.8 Introduction to workload management

This section describes some of the features included in AIX 5L with Workload Manager (WLM) and in HP-UX 11i with Process Resource Manager (PRM) to manage workload. Workload management, as you know, is vital because the conflicting pressures of costs, a lack of skilled support people, fast-growing server farms, and the need of competitive advantage, are forcing clients to look for proactive solutions design.

For resource management in HP-UX, Process Resource Manager (PRM) is used. The PRM tool controls system resources, for example, memory, cpu, and disk. This software not is included with the base HP-UX operating system.

For more information about Process Resource Manager, refer to *HP Process Resource Manager User's Guide HP Part Number,* B8733-90011 at:

```
http://docs.hp.com/en/B8733-90011/index.html
```

In AIX 5L

Workload Manager (WLM), which is included with the operating system, allows you to manage workloads. This feature has been available since AIX Version 4.3.3. Some of its functions are listed below:

► Management of I/O bandwidth in addition to the already existing CPU cycles
► Graphical display of resource utilization
► Fully dynamic reconfiguration

WLM gives the system administrator the ability to create different classes of services for jobs, and to specify attributes for those classes. These attributes specify minimum and maximum amounts of CPU, physical memory usage, and disk I/O throughput. WLM automatically assigns the jobs to the defined class using the rules provided by the system administrator.

The components of WLM are:

Classes   This is the main concept in WLM, which is a collection of processes that has a set of resource limits applied to it. A hierarchy of classes exists, which includes the *superclass* and *subclass*. In the superclass level, the determination of the resource is based on the resource shares and limits. In the subclass level, the resource shares and limits are based on the amount of each resource allocated to the parent superclass.

Tiers Defines the relative priority of groups of classes to each other. There are 10 available tiers, from 0 to 9, where tier 0 is the most important and 9 is the least important.

As a result, those classes in tier 0 will get resource allocation priority over classes in tier 1 and so on. The tier applies to both superclass and subclasses.

Users An admin user for WLM must be a valid system user (defined in /etc/passwd or NIS), and this is the person that performs administration tasks on the superclass. The Admingroup is a group of users allowed to perform administration tasks on the superclass.

There are two ways to assign a process to a class: Automatic or manual.

The automatic assignment is done when a process calls the system call exec, using the assignment rules specified by the WLM administrator. Manual means that a selected process or group of processes is assigned to a class by a user that has the required authority on both the process and target classes. This manual assignment can be done using the command line, smitty, or WSM.

As we mentioned, the class has its own rules in order to make automatic assignment of classes by WLM. An example of the class assignment rules is shown in Table 14-2.

Table 14-2 Example of class assignment rules

Class	Reserved	User	Group	Application	Type	Tag
System	-	root	-	-	-	-
db1	-	-	-	/usr/oracle/bin/db*	-	_db1

Where:

Class name This field must contain the name of a class that is defined in the class file corresponding to the level of the rules file.

Reserved Reserved for future use and must have a hyphen (-).

Users	The user name of the user-owning process, which must be a system user or an NIS-defined user.
Groups	List of one or more groups separated by commas (,).
Application	The full path name for an application can be used to determine the class to which a process belongs.
Process types	Introduced in AIX 5L Version 5.1. This is also a comma-separated list, which can define the class of a process. Here are possible attributes for this field: 32-bit, 64-bit, plock, and fixed.
Tags	Introduced in AIX 5L Version 5.1. This field must have one or more application tags separated.

As you can see, WLM can help with the management of workload on our systems. Let us review some tasks with smitty.

The fast path for WLM in SMIT is:

```
# smitty wlm
```

The main menu is shown in Example 14-20.

Example 14-20   Workload management screen

```
                    Workload Management

Move cursor to desired item and press Enter.
  Manage time-based configuration sets
  Work on alternate configurations
  Work on a set of Subclasses
  Show current focus (Configuration, Class Set)
  List all classes
  Add a class
  Change / Show Characteristics of a class
  Remove a class
  Class assignment rules
  Start/Stop/Update WLM
  Assign/Unassign processes to a class/subclass

F1=Help          F2=Refresh        F3=Cancel        F8=Image
F9=Shell         F0=Exit           Enter=Do
```

The fast path to start WLM is:

```
# smitty wlmstart
```

The dialog screen can be seen in Example 14-21 on page 528.

Example 14-21   Starting WLM

                         Start Workload Manager
Type or select values in entry fields.
Press Enter AFTER making all desired changes.

                                                      [Entry Fields]
* Configuration, or for a set: set name/currently   current   +
        applicable configuration
  Management mode   Active   +
  Enforce Resource Set bindings   Yes   +
  Disable class total limits on resource usage   Yes   +
  Disable process total limits on resource usage   Yes   +
  Start now, at next boot, or both ?   Now   +

F1=Help   F2=Refresh   F3=Cancel   F4=List
F5=Reset   F6=Command   F7=Edit   F8=Image
F9=Shell   F10=Exit   Enter=Do

By default, WLM is not started any time the systems restarts; in this screen, you
can decide if you would like to start it only for this session or when the system
restarts. The management mode line has the following options:

Active mode   Activates classification of processes and regulation of
                         resources.

Passive mode   Activates classification of processes without regulation of
                         resources.

The smit fast path to move processes between classes is:

```
# smitty wlmassign
```

The dialog screen looks like Example 14-22.

Example 14-22   Moving a process in WLM

                  Assign/Unassign processes to a class/subclass

Type or select values in entry fields.
Press Enter AFTER making all desired changes.

                                                         [Entry Fields]
  Assign/Unassign to/from Superclass/Subclass/Both   Assign Superclass
  Class name (for assignment)   []
  List of PIDs   []
  List of PGIDs   []

F1=Help   F2=Refresh   F3=Cancel   F4=List

```
F5=Reset       F6=Command     F7=Edit        F8=Image
F9=Shell       F0=Exit        Enter=Do
```

In this dialog screen, you can decide whether to remove a process from a superclass or a subclass or to assign it.

You need to select a list of processes (PIDs) in order to move/remove them into the specified class. When you assign a process to a class, all the values (cpu time, memory, and I/O) defined for that class are assigned to the process.

14.9 Quick reference

Table 14-3 shows the command comparison between AIX 5L and HP-UX 11i for performance management.

Table 14-3   Quick reference for performance management

Tasks	AIX 5L	HP-UX 11i
Changing the CPU time slice	`schedo`	Change `time slice` kernel parameter
CPU monitoring	`sar` and `tprof`	`sar`
Memory monitoring	`vmstat`	`vmstat`
Paging/swap space monitoring	`lsps`	`swapinfo`
Finding the memory users	`ps`, `svmon`, and `ipcs`	`ps` and `ipcs`
Disk monitoring	`iostat` and `sar`	`iostat` and `sar`
Locating the most used files	`filemon`	N/A
Network monitoring	`netstat` and `netpmon`	`netstat`
Tuning network parameters	`no`	`ndd`
Managing workload	WLM (Workload Manager) You can choose: ► `smitty wlm` ► `wsm`	PRM (Process Resource Manager)

Troubleshooting

This chapter contains the following:

15.1 Overview

Troubleshooting system problems is one of the most important and challenging tasks for system administrators. Although we cannot cover everything about troubleshooting in this chapter, we discuss the basic tools provided in AIX 5L and HP-UX 11i. We discuss error logging, system dumps, event tracing, and the LED codes.

15.2 Error logging

In this section we discuss the error logging facility that is available in HP-UX 11i and AIX 5L Version 5.x and also show how to work with the syslogd daemon.

15.2.1 Error logging in HP-UX 11i

The following section describes the error logging in HP-UX 11i.

Syslog

In HP-UX 11i, system messages and errors related to system problems, alerts, and notices are logged in the /var/adm/syslog/syslog.log file. The syslogd daemon reads the configuration file /etc/syslog.conf and logs the messages and errors to the files as specified in the configuration file. The configuration file determines the messages and destination files where the messages will be logged based on selectors, priorities, and facilities specified in the file. For more details on the configuration file, refer to the *syslogd (1M) manual page*.

dmesg

The `dmesg` command looks in the system buffer for recent diagnostic messages and displays them. These are unusual system event occurrences. To view the recent messages, use the `dmesg` command.

15.2.2 Error logging in AIX 5L

The error logging process begins when the AIX 5L operating system module detects an error. The error-detecting segment of code then sends error information to either the errsave kernel service and errlast kernel service for pending system crash, or to the errlog subroutine to log an application error, where the information is, in turn, written to the /dev/error special file. The errlast preserves the error record in the NVRAM. Therefore, in the event of a system crash, the last logged error is not lost.

This process then adds a time stamp to the collected data. The errdemon daemon constantly checks the /dev/error file for new entries, and when new data is written, the daemon conducts a series of operations.

Before an entry is written to the error log, the errdemon daemon compares the label sent by the kernel or application code to the contents of the error record template repository. If the label matches an item in the repository, the daemon collects additional data from other parts of the system.

To create an entry in the error log, the errdemon daemon retrieves the appropriate template from the repository, the resource name of the unit that detected the error, and detailed data. Also, if the error signifies a hardware-related problem and the Vital Product Data (VPD) hardware exists, the daemon retrieves the VPD from the Object Data Manager (ODM). When you access the error log, either through SMIT or with the **errpt** command, the error log is formatted according to the error template in the error template repository and presented in either a summary or detailed report. Most entries in the error log are attributable to hardware and software problems, but informational messages can also be logged.

Generating the error log

You can generate the error reports using smitty or through the **errpt** command.

Using smitty

You can use the System Management Interface Tool (SMIT) with a fast path to run the **errpt** command. To use the SMIT fast path, enter:

```
# smitty errpt
```

After completing a dialog about the destination of the output and concurrent error reporting, you will see a panel similar to that shown in Example 15-1.

Example 15-1   Generate an error report screen

```
                        Generate an Error Report

Type or select values in entry fields.
Press Enter AFTER making all desired changes.

[TOP]                                              [Entry Fields]
  CONCURRENT error reporting?                      no
  Type of Report                                   summary             +
  Error CLASSES (default is all)                   []                  +
  Error TYPES   (default is all)                   []                  +
  Error LABELS (default is all)                    []                  +
  Error ID's      (default is all)                 []                  +X
  Resource CLASSES (default is all)                []
```

```
Resource TYPES    (default is all)              []
Resource NAMES    (default is all)              []
SEQUENCE numbers  (default is all)              []
STARTING time interval                          []
ENDING time interval                            []
Show only Duplicated Errors                     [no]                              +
[MORE...5]

F1=Help            F2=Refresh          F3=Cancel          F4=List
F5=Reset           F6=Command          F7=Edit            F8=Image
F9=Shell           F10=Exit            Enter=Do
```

In Example 15-1 on page 533, the fields can be specified as:

CONCURRENT error reporting

Yes means you want errors displayed or printed as the errors are entered into the error log.

Type of Report

DETAILED gives comprehensive information, SUMMARY displays one line per error, and INTERMEDIATE generates a shortened version of the detailed report.

Error CLASSES

Values are H (hardware), S (Software), O (operator messages created with errlog), and U (undetermined). You can specify more than one error class.

Resource CLASSES

Classes specified by user (for hardware, class is device class).

ERROR TYPES

The following are the error types:

PEND

The lost device or component availability is imminent.

PERF

The performance of the device or component has degraded to below an acceptable level.

TEMP

Recovered from condition after several attempts.

PERM

Unable to recover from error condition. Error types with this value are usually the most severe errors and imply that you have a hardware or software defect. Error types other than PERM usually do not indicate a defect, but they are recorded so that they can be analyzed for the diagnostic problems.

UNKN	The severity of the error cannot be determined.
INFO	The error type is used to record informational entries.
Resource TYPES	Generates a report for resource types specified by the user. For hardware it is a device type.
Resource NAMES	Common device name (for example, hdisk0).
ID	The error identifier.
STARTING and ENDING time	The format mmddhhmmyy (month, day, hour, minute, and year) can be used to select only errors from the log that are timestamped between the two values.

errpt command

The **errpt** command generates a report of logged errors. Three types of reports can be produced depending upon the options you use. The types are:

Summary report	This is the default report. It gives an overview and contains one line of data for each error.
Detailed report	This shows a detailed description of all of the errors that are logged. You need to use the -a option to generate this report.
Intermediate report	Displays a shortened version of the detailed report. Use the -A option to generate this report.

The **errpt** command queries the /var/adm/ras/errlog error log file to produce the error report.

Let us see some examples:

► If you use the **errpt** command without any options, it generates a summary report similar to Example 15-2 on page 536. In the output, the C column represents the error class and T represents the error type. Refer to "Using smitty" on page 533 for an explanation of these columns.

Example 15-2   errrpt summary report

```
# errpt
IDENTIFIER TIMESTAMP   T C RESOURCE_NAME  DESCRIPTION
A6DF45AA   0705122205  I O RMCdaemon      The daemon is started.
2BFA76F6   0704211105  T S SYSPROC        SYSTEM SHUTDOWN BY USER
9DBCFDEE   0705122105  T O errdemon       ERROR LOGGING TURNED ON
192AC071   0704211005  T O errdemon       ERROR LOGGING TURNED OFF
BC3BE5A3   0704173405  P S SRC            SOFTWARE PROGRAM ERROR
E18E984F   0630203005  P S SRC            SOFTWARE PROGRAM ERROR
BA431EB7   0630203005  P S SRC            SOFTWARE PROGRAM ERROR
BA431EB7   0630203005  P S SRC            SOFTWARE PROGRAM ERROR
1BA7DF4E   0630203005  P S SRC            SOFTWARE PROGRAM ERROR
BA431EB7   0630203005  P S SRC            SOFTWARE PROGRAM ERROR
BA431EB7   0630203005  P S SRC            SOFTWARE PROGRAM ERROR
```

► To display the detailed error report, use the following command. An extract of a detailed report is shown in Example 15-3.

```
# errpt -a
```

Example 15-3   errpt detailed report

```
---------------------------------------------------------------------------
LABEL:          RMCD_INFO_0_ST
IDENTIFIER:     A6DF45AA

Date/Time:      Tue Jul  5 12:22:21 CDT 2005
Sequence Number: 145
Machine Id:     000197AA4C00
Node Id:        p650n04
Class:          O
Type:           INFO
Resource Name:  RMCdaemon

Description
The daemon is started.

Probable Causes
The Resource Monitoring and Control daemon has been started.

User Causes
The startsrc -s ctrmc command has been executed or
the rmcctrl -s command has been executed.

        Recommended Actions
        Confirm that the daemon should be started.

Detail Data
DETECTING MODULE
```

```
RSCT,rmcd.c,1.48,209
ERROR ID
6eKoraOB5gmO/f3E.qE4e.1..................
REFERENCE CODE
```

```
---------------------------------------------------------------------------
```

▶ To display errors of a particular class, for example, for the Hardware class, use the following command:

```
#errpt -d H
IDENTIFIER TIMESTAMP  T C RESOURCE_NAME  DESCRIPTION
BFE4C025   0628103005 P H sysplanar0     UNDETERMINED ERROR
E142C6D4   0627182205 T H sysplanar0     EEH temporary error for adapter
BFE4C025   0613200005 P H sysplanar0     UNDETERMINED ERROR
BFE4C025   0608190405 P H sysplanar0     UNDETERMINED ERROR
```

▶ To display a detailed report of all errors logged for a particular error identifier, enter the following command:

```
# errpt -a -j identifier
```

Where *identifier* is the eight-digit hexadecimal unique error identifier. To clear all entries from the error log, enter the following command:

```
# errclear 0
```

▶ To stop error logging, enter the following command:

```
#/usr/lib/errstop
```

▶ To start error logging, enter the following command:

```
# /usr/lib/errdemon
```

▶ To list the current setting of the error log file and buffer size and duplicate information, enter the following command:

```
# /usr/lib/errdemon -l
Error Log Attributes
--------------------------------------------
Log File               /var/adm/ras/errlog
Log Size               1048576 bytes
Memory Buffer Size     32768 bytes
Duplicate Removal      true
Duplicate Interval     10000 milliseconds
Duplicate Error Maximum 1000
```

15.2.3 syslogd daemon

The syslogd daemon works in a similar way as in HP-UX 11i. It logs the system messages from different software components (kernel, daemon processes, and system applications). When started, syslogd reads the /etc/syslog.conf configuration file. Whenever you change this file, you need to refresh the syslogd subsystem:

```
# refresh -s syslogd
```

/etc/syslog.conf file

The general format of the /etc/syslog.conf file is:

```
selector          action
```

The selector field names a *facility* and a *priority level*. Separate facility names with a comma (,). Separate the facility and priority level portions of the selector field with a period (.). Separate multiple entries in the selector field with a semicolon (;). To select all the facilities, use an asterisk (*).

The action field identifies a destination (file, host, or user) to receive the messages. If routed to a remote host, the remote system will handle the message indicated in its own configuration file. To display messages on a user's terminal, the destination field must contain the name of a valid, logged-in system user. If you specify an asterisk (*) in the action field, a message is sent to all logged-in users.

These are the facilities that are used in selector field:

kern	Kernel
user	User level
mail	Mail subsystem
daemon	System daemons
auth	Security or authorization
syslog	syslogd messages
lpr	Line-printer subsystem
news	News subsystem
uucp	uucp subsystem
*	All facility levels

You can use the following priority levels in the selector field. Messages of the specified level and all levels above it are sent as directed:

emerg	Specifies emergency messages. These messages are not distributed to all users.
alert	Specifies important messages, such as a serious hardware error. These messages are distributed to all users.

crit	Specifies critical messages not classified as errors, such as improper login attempts.
err	Specifies messages that represent error conditions.
warning	Specifies messages for abnormal, but recoverable, conditions.
notice	Specifies important informational messages. Messages without a priority designation are mapped into this priority message.
info	Specifies informational messages. These messages can be discarded, but are useful in analyzing the system.
debug	Specifies debugging messages. These messages may be discarded.
none	Excludes the selected facility. This priority level is useful only if preceded by an entry with an asterisk (*) in the same selector field.

The following example shows sample lines from /etc/syslog.conf:

```
auth.debug          /dev/console
mail.debug          /tmp/mail.debug
daemon.debug        /tmp/daemon.debug
auth.debug          /dev/console
*.debug;mail.none   @system1
```

Let us see what each line represents:

auth.debug /dev/console	Specifies that all security messages are directed to the system console
mail.debug /tmp/mail.debug	Specifies that all mail messages are collected in the /tmp/mail.debug file
*.debug;mail.none @system1	Specifies that all other messages, except messages from the mail subsystem, are sent to the syslogd daemon on host system1

Note: Whenever you modify the /etc/syslog/conf file, you need to restart the syslogd daemon; only then will the changes come into effect. In AIX 5L, you can restart using the `refresh -s syslogd` command. In HP-UX 11i, you can make the daemon re-read its configuration file by sending it a hang-up signal, `kill -HUP `cat /var/run/syslog.pid`,` or you can stop and start the syslog daemon by running the `/sbin/init.d/syslogd stop/start` command.

15.3 Hardware diagnostics

In this section we discuss how to run the hardware diagnostics on HP-UX 11i and AIX 5L.

In HP-UX 11i

The following describes the Support Tools Manager for HP-UX 11i.

Support Tools Manager (STM)

STM is a toolset that you can use to get system and device information and run diagnostics. It has three different interfaces: X-Windows (xstm), menu interface (mstm), and command-line interface (cstm). When started, the system map is displayed. You can then select any device to test, run diagnostics, display the logs, update firmware, and get further information.

For more details refer to the *stm (1M) manual page*.

In AIX 5L

Whenever a hardware problem occurs in AIX 5L, use the **diag** command to diagnose the problem. The **diag** command allows you to analyze the error log. It provides information that is very useful for the service representative.

The diag command

The **diag** command offers different ways to test hardware devices or the complete system.

Let us see one method of testing of hardware devices using the **diag** command:

1. Start the **diag** command. A welcome screen appears. Press Enter. You will see a screen similar to Example 15-4.

Example 15-4   diag function selection menu

```
FUNCTION SELECTION                                                   801002

Move cursor to selection, then press Enter.

   Diagnostic Routines
      This selection will test the machine hardware. Wrap plugs and
      other advanced functions will not be used.
   Advanced Diagnostics Routines
      This selection will test the machine hardware. Wrap plugs and
      other advanced functions will be used.
   Task Selection (Diagnostics, Advanced Diagnostics, Service Aids, etc.)
      This selection will list the tasks supported by these procedures.
      Once a task is selected, a resource menu may be presented showing
```

```
      all resources supported by the task.
   Resource Selection
      This selection will list the resources in the system that are supported
      by these procedures. Once a resource is selected, a task menu will
      be presented showing all tasks that can be run on the resource(s).


F1=Help              F10=Exit              F3=Previous Menu
```

2. To test hardware devices, the next menu you see on the screen is
   DIAGNOSTIC MODE SELECTION. You can select two options:

   System verification   Will test the system, but will not analyze the error
                              log. This option is used to verify that the machine
                              is functioning correctly after completing a repair or
                              an upgrade.

   Problem determination Tests the system and analyzes the error log if one
                              is available. This option is used when a problem is
                              suspected on the machine. Do not use this option
                              after you have repaired a device, unless you
                              remove the error log entries of the broken device.

   You can select either of the options, depending upon your requirement.

3. The next menu you will see on the screen is similar to Example 15-5. In this
   menu, you can select any listed hardware device to run the diagnostics. If you
   want to test the complete system, select All Resources. To select any
   hardware device, move the cursor to the particular device and press Enter. In
   our example, we have selected rmt0 (notice the + symbol before rmt0). To
   start diagnostics, press F7.

   If you press F4, the diag tool displays all the diagnostic tasks that are
   supported by the selected device.

Example 15-5   Diagnostic selection

```
DIAGNOSTIC SELECTION                                             801006

From the list below, select any number of resources by moving
the cursor to the resource and pressing 'Enter'.
To cancel the selection, press 'Enter' again.
To list the supported tasks for the resource highlighted, press 'List'.

Once all selections have been made, press 'Commit'.
To exit without selecting a resource, press the 'Exit' key.


  [MORE...23]
    tty2          01-S3-00-00     Serial Port
    scsi0         10-60           Wide SCSI I/O Controller
```

```
    cd0             10-60-00-4,0    SCSI Multimedia CD-ROM Drive (650 MB)
  + rmt0            10-60-00-5,0    SCSI 8mm Tape Drive (20000 MB)
    tok0            10-68           IBM PCI Tokenring Adapter (14101800)
    ssa0            10-70           IBM SSA Enhanced RAID Adapter (14104500)
    ent0            10-78           IBM 10/100/1000 Base-T Ethernet PCI
                                    Adapter (14100401)
[MORE...1]

F1=Help             F4=List         F7=Commit         F10=Exit
F3=Previous   Menu
```

If the device is busy, the diag tool does not permit testing the device or analyzing the error log. Example 15-6 shows that the selected Ethernet adapter ent0 was not tested because it was in use (but you can test these devices using other diagnostic modes). The diagnostic modes are described in "Diagnostic modes" on page 542.

Example 15-6   Diagnostic menu

```
ADDITIONAL RESOURCES ARE REQUIRED FOR TESTING                        801011

No trouble was found. However, the resource was not tested because
the device driver indicated that the resource was in use.

The resource needed is
- ent0              U0.1-P2/E1      10/100 Mbps Ethernet PCI Adapter II
                                    (1410ff01)

To test this resource, you can do one of the following:
   Free this resource and continue testing.
   Shut down the system and reboot in Service mode.

Move cursor to selection, then press Enter.

   Testing should stop.
   The resource is now free and testing can continue.

F3=Cancel           F10=Exit
```

Diagnostic modes

There are three different diagnostic modes available. They are concurrent, maintenance, and stand-alone modes.

Concurrent mode

Concurrent mode means that the diagnostic programs are executed during normal system operation. Certain devices can be tested (for example, a tape device that is currently not in use), but the number of resources that can be tested is very limited.

Maintenance mode

Maintenance is single-user mode. To expand the list of devices that can be tested, take the system down to maintenance mode with the `shutdown -m` command. Run the `diag` command. In this mode, all the user programs are stopped. All the user volume groups are inactive, which extends the number of devices that can be tested in this mode.

Stand-alone mode

The stand-alone mode offers the greatest flexibility. You can test systems that do not boot or that have no operating system installed (the latter requires a diagnostic CD-ROM). You can follow these steps to start up the diagnostics in stand-alone mode:

1. If you have a diagnostic CD-ROM (or a diagnostic tape), insert it into the system. (If you do not have a diagnostic CD-ROM, you boot diagnostics from the hard disk.)

2. Shut down the system. When AIX 5L is down, turn off the system power.

3. On a micro channel system, set the key switch to service.

4. Turn on the power.

5. On a PCI system, press F6 on a graphic console or press 6 on an ASCII console when an acoustic beep is heard and icons (or words) are shown on the display. This simulates booting in service mode (logical key switch). (Not all PCI models support this.)

6. The `diag` command will be started automatically, either from the hard disk or the diagnostic CD-ROM.

> **Note:** The `diag` command offers a wide number of additional tasks that are hardware related. All these tasks can be found after starting the `diag` main menu and selecting Task Selection.
>
> The tasks that are offered are hardware (or resource) related. For example, if your system has a service processor, you will find service processor maintenance tasks, which you do not find on machines without a service processor. Or, on some systems, you find tasks to maintain RAID and SSA storage systems.

Supported platforms

All current PCI models support the **diag** command. The following machines support the **diag** command:

► All current PCI systems: 43Ps with LED, F-models, H-models, M-models, and S-models

► All micro channel systems

The **diag** command is not supported on the following platforms:

► Old PCI systems: 40Ps, 43Ps without LED

If **diag** is not supported on your platform, you must use the System Management Service (SMS) to test the hardware.

15.3.1 System dumps in HP-UX 11i

In HP-UX 11i, the **crashconf** command is used to configure and to fetch the information from the dump device. By default, the crash dump area is the same as the swap area (/dev/vg00/lvol2), but you can create another dump area, and change the dump area or add this dump area.

The default directory that it will put the memory image in is /var/adm/crash. This directory can be changed in the /etc/rc.config.d/savecrash file.

The following commands can be used for system dumps in HP-UX 11i:

```
crashconf
savecrash
crashutil
lvlnboot
lvrmboot
```

For more information about the crash dump commands, refer to the commands' man pages.

Some examples of system dump commands are:

► To display the current dump device information, use the following command:

```
# crashconf -v

Crash dump configuration has been changed since boot.

CLASS         PAGES      INCLUDED IN DUMP   DESCRIPTION
--------      ----------  ----------------
--------------------------------------
UNUSED        133863  no,  by default    unused pages
USERPG         52592  no,  by default    user process pages
```

```
BCACHE      208285  no,  by default    buffer cache pages
KCODE         2525  no,  by default    kernel code pages
USTACK        1050  yes, by default    user process stacks
FSDATA         222  yes, by default    file system metadata
KDDATA      101553  yes, by default    kernel dynamic data
KSDATA       24193  yes, by default    kernel static data

Total pages on system:          524283
Total pages included in dump:   127018

DEVICE          OFFSET(kB)   SIZE (kB)   LOGICAL VOL.   NAME
------------    ----------   ----------  ------------
--------------------------
 31:0x013000        310112     1048576   64:0x000002   /dev/vg00/lvol2
                                ----------
                                  1048576
```

► To change the primary dump device to /dev/vg00/lv_dump, use the following commands:

```
# lvcreate -L 500 -n lv_dump -r n -C y vg00
# lvlnboot -d /dev/vg00/lv_dump
# lvrmboot -d /dev/vg00/lvol2
# crashconf -ar /dev/vg00/lv_dump
```

► To create the secondary dump device use the following commands:

```
# lvcreate -L 500 -n lv_dump -r n -C y vg00
# lvlnboot -d /dev/vg00/lv_dump
# crashconf /dev/vg00/lv_dump
```

15.3.2 System dumps in AIX 5L

In AIX Version 4.3.3 and earlier, the paging space is used as the default dump device created at installation time. AIX 5L servers with a real memory size larger than 4 GB will, at installation time, have a dedicated dump device created. This dump device is automatically created and no user intervention is required. The default name of the dump device is lg_dumplv and the directory default in rootvg is /var/adm/ras.

The sysdumpdev command

In AIX 5L, the **sysdumpdev** command is used to manage the system crash dumps. With this command, you can display the dump device information, change the destination of the dump, and estimate the size of the system dump.

Let us see some examples:

► To estimate the size of the system dump, use the following command:

```
# sysdumpdev -e
```

```
0453-041 Estimated dump size in bytes: 26004684
```

► To display the current dump device information, use the following command:

```
# sysdumpdev -l
primary                /dev/lg_dumplv
secondary              /dev/sysdumpnull
copy directory         /var/adm/ras
forced copy flag       TRUE
always allow dump      FALSE
dump compression       ON
```

► To change the primary dump device to /dev/hd7, use the following command:

```
# sysdumpdev -P -p'/dev/lv_dump'
primary /dev/lv_dump
secondary /dev/sysdumpnull
copy directory /var/adm/ras
forced copy flag TRUE
always allow dump FALSE
```

► To change the secondary dump device, use the following command:

```
# sysdumpdev -P -s'dev/lv_dump'
primary /dev/lg_dumplv
secondary /dev/lv_dump
copy directory /var/adm/ras
forced copy flag TRUE
always allow dump FALSE
```

► To display the most recent dump statistics, use the following command:

```
# sysdumpdev -L
0453-039
Device name: /dev/lg_dumplv
Major device number: 10
Minor device number: 2
Size:                76737536 bytes
Date/Time:           Sun Oct 21 16:48:34 CDT 2004
Dump status:         0
dump completed successfully
```

To check that the dump is readable, start the **kdb** command on the dump file. The **kdb** command needs a kernel file (UNIX) to match the dump file. If you do not specify a kernel file, **kdb** uses the /usr/lib/boot/unix file by default.

Collecting the dump and related information

The easiest way to copy a dump and other system information to be used in analyzing the problem is by using the **snap** command. The **snap** command gathers system configuration information and compresses the information into a tar file that can then be downloaded to some other media. The **snap** command automatically creates the /tmp/ibmsupt directory, and several subdirectories are created below this.

The snap command

The **snap** command is a general purpose utility for gathering information about a system.

In general, it is better to run the **snap -a** command when building a snap image for sending to IBM. Also, the -o option is useful for writing the information collected by the **snap** command to removable media, such as a tape. For example:

```
# snap -o /dev/rmt0
```

Forcing a dump

You only force a dump on a machine that is completely hung. There are several ways of initiating a dump. You can choose one of these methods depending on the status of your machine.

Forcing a dump on MCA systems

To force a dump, use one of the following options.

Option 1

The steps of the first option are:

1. Turn the key mode switch to the service position.

2. Press the Reset button once.

3. The system will start a dump and the LED panel will display LED 0c2.

Option 2

For the second option:

1. Turn the key mode switch to the Service position.

2. Press the Function keys Ctrl+Alt+Num_Pad 1.

Option 3

Use the **sysdumpstart** command or use the **smitty dump** fast path.

Forcing a dump on PCI systems

In PCI systems, the key switch is not available. Forcing a dump varies from model to model. You can refer to the Hardware Service Guide of your system, or you can use the `sysdumpstart` command to force the dump, or use the `smitty dump` fast path. A menu similar to that shown in Example 15-7 will be displayed. Select the Start a Dump to the Primary Dump Device option to force the dump.

> **Note:** Keep in mind that, when you force a dump with either `sysdumpstart` or smitty, the system comes down. Once the dump completes, you can restart the system. If there is not enough space in the /var file system, the system prompts you for the tape.

Example 15-7   smitty dump

```
                          System Dump

Move cursor to desired item and press Enter.

    Show Current Dump Devices
    Show Information About the Previous System Dump
    Show Estimated Dump Size
    Change the Primary Dump Device
    Change the Secondary Dump Device
    Change the Directory to which Dump is Copied on Boot
    Start a Dump to the Primary Dump Device
    Start a Dump to the Secondary Dump Device
    Copy a System Dump from a Dump Device to a File
    Always ALLOW System Dump
    System Dump Compression
    Check Dump Resources Utility

    Esc+1=Help          Esc+2=Refresh        Esc+3=Cancel        Esc+8=Image
    Esc+9=Shell         Esc+0=Exit           Enter=Do
```

15.3.3 LED codes in AIX 5L

While booting, you can observe the different LED codes on the LED panel of the machine, at different boot stages. These codes will be useful to debug any problem while booting. The boot procedures are implemented in different ways, depending on the type of AIX 5L machine.

There are mainly two types of machines:

► The RS/6000 family of machines was launched in 1990 and, over the years, has changed to adopt new technology as it becomes available. The first RS/6000 machines were based around the Micro Channel Architecture

(MCA) and had a number of features common to each machine in the range, in particular, a three-digit LED and a three-position key mode switch.

► In recent years, the RS/6000 family has migrated to Peripheral Component Interconnect (PCI) bus technology. Initial machines of this type (7040 and 7248) did not have the three-digit LED or three-position key mode switch of the previous MCA machines. Subsequent PCI machines have a LED or LCD display, but none have the three-position key mode switch.

Here are some of the LED codes that are displayed on MCA systems:

292   Initializing a SCSI adapter. Needed to run the disk containing AIX 5L.

252   Locating the diskette drive or reading from a bootable diskette media.

243 or 233   Booting from a device listed in the NVRAM boot list. Usually hdisk0, a bootable CD-ROM, or a mksysb tape.

551   This is an indication that all devices in the machine are configured correctly and the machine is ready to vary on the root volume group.

517 or 553   Once these two LEDs has been displayed. Any problem experienced after this point is more than likely going to be AIX 5L-related as opposed to hardware-related.

581   TCP/IP configuration is taking place. If this number stays on the LED panel for a very long time, you should perhaps look at your TCP/IP settings and routing information once you are able to log in to the system.

c31   This code indicates the system is awaiting input from you on the keyboard. This is usually encountered when booting from a CD-ROM or mksysb tape. This is normally the dialogue to select the system console.

c32 or c33   These codes tell you that the boot process is nearly complete. Shortly afterwards, you should see output on the panel from the AIX 5L boot process starting various software subsystems.

551, 555, or 557 If the system hangs at these LED codes, the known causes might be:

       ► A corrupted file system.

       ► A corrupted journaled file system (JFS or JFS2) - log device.

- A failing fsck (file system check) caused by a bad file system helper.
- A bad disk in the machine that is a member of the rootvg.

552, 554, or 556   If the system hangs at these LED codes, the known causes might be:

- A corrupted file system.
- A corrupted journaled file system (JFS or JFS2) - log device.
- A bad IPL-device record or bad IPL-device magic number. (The magic number indicates the device type.) A corrupted copy of the Object Data Manager (ODM) database on the boot logical volume.
- A hard disk in the inactive state in the root volume group.

For a complete list of LED and other error and information codes, refer to the AIX 5L Message Center at:

```
http://publib.boulder.ibm.com/infocenter/pseries/index.jsp
```

The following publication also contains a listing of the codes: *eServer pSeriesDiagnostic Information for Multiple Bus Systems Version 5.3,* SA38-0509.

15.4 Event tracing on AIX 5L

In this topic, we discuss tracing the events and generating reports of event tracing in AIX 5L.

The trace system is a tool allowing you to capture the sequential flow of system activity or system events. Unlike a stand-alone kernel dump that provides a static snapshot of a system, the trace facility provides a more dynamic way to gather problem data.

Tracing can be used to isolate system problems and also to measure the system performance by observing the system and application execution.

All the traced events are written to /var/adm/ras/trcfile. The trace facility generates a huge amount of data. The amount of data it generates depends on what events you trace.

All the events traced are referenced by hook identifiers (Hook IDs). Events that can be traced are identified by a unique hook ID. You can trace a particular event that is more relevant to your problem by selecting the appropriate event or hook ID.

To display the defined event IDs, use the **trcrpt** command. Refer to Example 15-8.

Example 15-8 Listing hook IDs

```
# trcrpt -j | more
004 TRACEID IS ZERO
3A8 SCSESDD
2A4 kentdd
2A5 kentdd
2A6 kentdd
2A7 stokdd
2A8 stokdd
2A9 stokdd
2AA stokdd
2EA gxentdd
2EB gxentdd
2EC gxentdd
409 STTY SF
707 LFTDD:
709 INPUTDD:
2FA ethchandd
```

15.4.1 Starting the trace

You can start the trace by using the **trace** command. The trace can be started either in interactive or in background mode.

If you issue the **trace** command without the -a option, it runs in interactive mode.

If you run the **trace** command with the -a option, it runs in the background mode. Once the trace is started in background mode, you use the **trcon**, **trcoff**, and **trcstop** commands to start tracing, stop tracing, and exit tracing, respectively.

Using the trace command

You can run the **trace** command with the **smitty trcstart** fast path.

In interactive mode, to trace the EXEC system call event when running the **pwd** command, use the following commands:

```
# trace -j 134
-> !pwd
```

```
/
-> quit
#
```

> **Tip:** To get the hook ID or event ID of the EXEC system call, use the **trcrpt** **-j** command.

To trace the same command in non-interactive mode, use the following commands:

```
# trace -a -j 134
# pwd
/
# trcstop
```

15.4.2 Trace report

The output of the **trace** command will be in binary format and is dumped into the /var/adm/ras/trcfile file. To generate the report from this file, you can use the **trcrpt** command.

Let us see some of the examples of using the **trcrpt** command.

If you run the **trcrpt** command without any options, it displays the output on the standard output, as in Example 15-9.

Example 15-9 trcrpt command

```
# trcrpt

Sun Jul 10 19:36:42 2005
System: AIX 5.3 Node: p650n04
Machine: 000197AA4C00
Internet Address: 0A0101C7 10.1.1.199
At trace startup, the system contained 2 cpus, of which 2 were traced.
Buffering: Kernel Heap
This is from a 32-bit kernel.
Tracing only these hooks, 134


trace -a -j 134


ID    ELAPSED_SEC     DELTA_MSEC     APPL    SYSCALL KERNEL   INTERRUPT

001   0.000000000     0.000000                       TRACE ON channel 0
                                                      Sun Jul 10 19:36:42 2005
```

```
134    13.809465602    13809.465602           exec:   cmd=trcstop pid=-1
tid=20081
002    13.815905568        6.439966           TRACE OFF channel 0000 Sun
Jul 10 19:36:56 2005
```

To redirect the output to a file, use the **trcrpt -o** *file_name* command.

15.5 Quick reference

Table 15-1 shows some troubleshooting command comparisons between AIX 5L and HP-UX 11i.

Table 15-1   Quick reference for troubleshooting

Tasks	AIX 5L	HP-UX 11i command
Displaying error log	errpt -a	dmesg and view /var/adm/syslog/syslog.log
Controlling system dump	sysdumpdev	crashconf
Hardware diagnostics	diag	stm
Stopping/starting syslog daemon	refresh -s syslogd	kill -HUP `cat /var/run/syslog.pid` or /sbin/init.d/syslogd stop/start
Examining the crash dump	kdb	
Event tracing	trace trcrpt	
Display a snapshot of virtual memory	svmon	N/A
Capturing and analyzing a snapshot of virtual memory	vmstat	vmstat
Displaying I/O statistics	iostat or filemon	iostat
Reporting system activity	sar	sar
Displaying simple and complex lock contention information	lockstat	lockstat
Reporting CPU usage	tprof or topas	top
Displaying paging/swapping space	lsps -l	swapinfo

Tasks	AIX 5L	HP-UX 11i command
Providing interface level packet tracing for Internet protocols	`iptrace`	`nettl` and `netfmt`
Displaying NFS and RPC statistics	`nfsstat`	`nfsstat`
Specifying users who have access to cron	`/var/adm/cron/cron.allow`	`/var/adm/cron/cron.allow`
Specifying users who have no access to cron	`/var/adm/cron/cron.deny`	`/var/adm/cron/cron.deny`
Specifying remote users and hosts that can execute commands on the local host	`/etc/hosts.equiv`	`/etc/hosts.equiv`
Default Super user log	`/var/adm/sulog`	`/var/adm/sulog`
Configuring syslogd daemon	`/etc/syslog.conf`	`/etc/syslog.conf`
Displaying physical RAM	`bootinfo -r` or `prtconf`	`dmesg | grep -i physical`

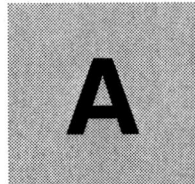

AIX 5L Object Data Manager (ODM)

This appendix describes the following characteristics about the AIX 5L ODM:

Overview

The ODM is a repository for information about the system. The ODM enables up to 1000 device configurations. The ODM is a very important component of AIX 5L and is one major difference from other UNIX systems. It contains device support, device vital product data, software support for these devices, and so on.

ODM components

There are three basic components of ODM: Object classes, objects, and descriptors.

Object classes

The ODM consists of many database files, where each file is called an object class.

Objects

Each object class consists of objects. Each object is one record in an object class.

Descriptors

The descriptors describe the layout of the objects. They determine the name and data type of the fields that are part of the object class.

ODM commands

The following is the list of the commands that you can use to access the ODM:

► You can create ODM classes using the **odmcreate** command. This command has the following syntax:

```
odmcreate descriptor_file.cre
```

The file descriptor_file.cre contains the class definition for the corresponding ODM class. Usually these files have the suffix .cre.

► To delete an entire ODM class, use the **odmdrop** command. This command has the following syntax:

```
odmdrop -o object_class_name
```

The name object_class_name is the name of the ODM class you want to remove. Be very careful with this command; it removes the complete class immediately.

► To view the underlying layout of an object class, use the **odmshow** command. The syntax is:

```
odmshow object_class_name
```

Table A-1 shows an extraction from ODM class PdAt, where four descriptors (uniquetype, attribute, deflt, and values) are shown.

Table A-1   Example of ODM class PdAt

uniquetype	attribute	deflt	values
tape/scsi/4mm4GB	block_size	1024	0-16777215,1
disk/scsi/1000mb	pvid	none	
tty/rs232/tty	login	disable	enable, disable

3. The system administrators usually work with objects. The **odmget** command queries objects in classes. Executing this command with only a class name as a parameter will list the complete classes' information in a stanza format. You can use the -q flag to list only specific records. To add new objects, use **odmadd**. To delete objects, use **odmdelete**. To change the objects, use **odmchange**. These commands are explained in the next section.

All the ODM commands use the ODMDIR environment variable, which is set in the /etc/environment file. The default value of ODMDIR is /etc/objrepos.

Changing attribute values

The ODM objects are stored in a binary format, which means you need to work with the ODM commands to query or change any objects.

Let us see how to change an object's attribute.

The **odmget** command in Example A-1 will pick all the records from the PdAt class, where uniquetype is equal to tape/scsi/8mm and attribute is equal to block_size. In this instance, only one record should be matched. The information is redirected into a file that can be changed using an editor. In our example, the default value for the block_size attribute is changed to 512 from 1024.

The **odmdelete** command in Example A-1 will delete the old object in order to add the new object, which has a 512 block_size attribute.

Example: A-1   Changing attributes

```
# odmget -q"uniquetype=tape/scsi/8mm and attribute=block_size" PdAt > file
# vi file
PdAt:
```

```
                uniquetype = "tape/scsi/8mm"
                attribute = "block_size"
                deflt = "1024"
                values = "0-245760,1"
                width = ""
                type = "R"
                generic = ""
                rep = "nr"
                nls_index = 0
# odmdelete -o PdAt -q"uniquetype=tape/scsi/8mm and attribute=block_size"
# odmadd file
```

Note: Before the new value of 512 can be added into the ODM, the old object (which has the block_size set to 1024) must be deleted; otherwise, you would end up with two objects describing the same attribute.

The final operation is to add the file into the ODM with the changed attribute.

Location and contents of ODM repository

The ODM contains two important types of device information. One is *predefined* device information, which describes all supported devices. The other is *customized device* information, which describes all devices that are actually attached to the system.

To support diskless, dataless, and other workstations, the ODM object classes are held in three repositories. They are:

▶ /etc/objrepos

   Contains the customized devices object classes and the four object classes used by the Software Vital Product Database (SWVPD) for the / (root) part of the installable software product. The root part of software contains files that must be installed on the target system. These files cannot be shared in an AIX 5L network. This directory also contains symbolic links to the predefined devices object classes, because the ODMDIR variable is set to /etc/objrepos.

▶ /usr/lib/objrepos

   Contains the predefined devices object classes, SMIT menu object classes, and the four object classes used by the SWVPD for the /usr part of the installable software product. The object classes in this repository can be shared across the network by /usr clients, dataless, and diskless workstations. Software installed in the /usr-part can be shared across a network by AIX 5L systems only.

▶ /usr/share/lib/objrepos

Contains the four object classes used by the SWVPD for the /usr/share part of the installable software product. The /usr/share part of a software product contains files that are not hardware dependent. They can be used on other UNIX systems as well. An example is terminfo files that describe terminal capabilities. As terminfo is used on many UNIX systems, terminfo files are part of the /usr/share part of a system product.

ODM device configuration

This topic explains the basics of device configuration in ODM. Support for the devices is implemented in ODM in different object classes. The predefined device class names start with Pd and the customized devices class names start with Cu.

The following sections describe different predefined and customized object classes.

Predefined Devices (PdDv)

The predefined devices object class contains entries for all devices supported by the system. A device that is not a part of this ODM class could not be configured on an AIX 5L system.

Example A-2 shows the sample PdDv information. You can get this information by running the **odmget PdDv** command.

Example: A-2 Predefined devices (PdDv)

```
PdDv:
        type = "150mb"
        class = "tape"
        subclass = "scsi"
        prefix = "rmt"
        devid = ""
        base = 0
        has_vpd = 1
        detectable = 1
        chgstatus = 0
        bus_ext = 0
        fru = 1
        led = 2417
        setno = 54
        msgno = 1
        catalog = "devices.cat"
        DvDr = "tape"
```

```
Define = "/etc/methods/define"
Configure = "/etc/methods/cfgsctape"
Change = "/etc/methods/chggen"
Unconfigure = "/etc/methods/ucfgdevice"
Undefine = "/etc/methods/undefine"
Start = ""
Stop = ""
inventory_only = 0
uniquetype = "tape/scsi/150mb"
```

The attributes you should know about are:

Type
Specifies the product name or model number (for example, 150 Mb tape).

Class
Specifies the functional class name. A functional class is a group of device instances sharing the same high-level function. For example, tape is a functional class name representing all tape devices.

Subclass
Device classes are grouped into subclasses. The subclass scsi specifies all tape devices that may be attached to a SCSI system.

Prefix
Specifies the assigned prefix in the customized database, which is used to derive the device instance name and /dev name. For example, rmt is the prefix name assigned to tape devices. Names of tape devices would then look like rmt0, rmt1, or rmt2.

Base
This descriptor specifies whether a device is a base device or not. A base device is any device that forms part of a minimal base system. During the system boot, a minimal base system is configured to permit access to the root volume group and hence to the root file system. This minimal base system can include, for example, the standard I/O diskette adapter and a SCSI hard drive. The device shown in the example is not a base device.

Detectable
Specifies whether the device instance is detectable or non-detectable. A device whose presence and type can be electronically determined, once it is actually powered on and attached to the system, is said to be detectable. A value of 1 means that the device is detectable, and a value of 0 means that it is not detectable. These values are defined in the /usr/include/sys/cfgdb.h file.

LED
Indicates the hexadecimal value displayed on the LEDs when the Configure method executes. These values are

stored in decimal, while the value shown on the LEDs is hexadecimal.

Catalog
Identifies the file name of the National Language Support (NLS) message catalog that contains all messages pertaining to this device.

setno and msgno
Each device has a specific description (for example, 150 MB tape drive) that is shown when the device attributes are listed by the **lsdev** command. These two descriptors are used to show the message.

DvDr
Identifies the base name of the device driver associated with all device instances belonging to the device type (for example, tape). Device drivers are usually stored in the /usr/lib/drivers directory.

Define
Names the Define method associated with the device type. All Define method names start with the def prefix. This program is called when a device is brought into a defined state.

Configure
Names the Configure method associated with the device type. All Configure method names start with the cfg prefix. This program is called when a device is brought into the available state.

Change
Names the Change method associated with the device type. All Change method names start with the chg prefix. This program is called when a device is changed via the **chdev** command.

Unconfigure
Names the Unconfigure method associated with the device type. All Unconfigure method names start with the ucfg prefix. This program is called when a device is unconfigured by **rmdef**.

Undefine
Names the Undefine method associated with the device type. All Undefine method names start with the *und* prefix. This program is called when a device is undefined by **rmdef**.

Start and Stop
Few devices support a stopped state (only logical devices). A stopped state means that the device driver is loaded, but no application can access the device. These attributes name the methods to start or stop a device.

uniquetype
A key that is referenced by the other object classes. Objects use this descriptor as pointer back to the device description in PdDv. The key is a concentration of the class, subclass, and type values.

Predefined Attributes (PdAt)

The Predefined Attribute object class contains an entry for each existing attribute or each device represented in the PdDv object class. An attribute is any device-dependent information, such as interrupt levels, bus I/O address ranges, baud rates, parity settings, or block sizes. The extract of PdAt in Example A-3 shows three attributes (blocksize, physical volume identifier, and terminal name).

Example: A-3   Predefined attributes (PdAt)

```
PdAt:
        uniquetype = "tape/scsi/1200mb-c"
        attribute = "block_size"
        deflt = "512"
        values = "1024,512,0"
        ...

PdAt:
        uniquetype = "disk/scsi/1000mb"
        attribute = "pvid"
        deflt = "none"
        ...

PdAt:
        uniquetype = "tty/rs232/tty"
        attribute = "term"
        deflt = "dumb"
        values = ""
        ...
```

Let us define the key fields that are shown in Example A-3:

uniquetype   This descriptor is used as a pointer back to the device defined in the PdDv object class.

attribute   Identifies the name of the device attribute. This is the name that can be passed to the **mkdev** and **chdev** configuration commands.

deflt   Identifies default values for an attribute. Non-default values are stored in CuAt.

values   Identifies the possible values that can be associated with the attribute name. For example, allowed values for the block_size attribute range from 0 to 245760, with an increment of 1.

Customized Devices (CuDv)

The Customized Devices object class contains entries for all device instances defined in the system. As the name implies, a defined device object is an object that a define method has created in the CuDv object class. A defined device object may or may not have a corresponding actual device attached to the system.

A CuDv object contains attributes and connections specific to a device. Each device, distinguished by a unique logical name, is represented by an object in the CuDv object class. The customized database is updated twice, during system boot and at runtime, to define new devices, remove undefined devices, or update the information for a device whose attributes have been changed.

Example A-4 shows part of the CuDv object.

Example: A-4   Customized devices

```
CuDv:
        name = "cd0"
        status = 1
        chgstatus = 2
        ddins = "scdisk"
        location = "10-60-00-4,0"
        parent = "scsi0"
        connwhere = "4,0"
        PdDvLn = "cdrom/scsi/scsd"

CuDv:
        name = "hdisk0"
        status = 1
        chgstatus = 2
        ddins = "scdisk"
        location = "20-60-00-8,0"
        parent = "scsi1"
        connwhere = "8,0"
        PdDvLn = "disk/scsi/scsd"
```

They key descriptors in CuDv are:

name   A Customized Device object for a device instance is assigned a unique logical name to distinguish the instance from other device instances. The above example shows two devices, a CDROM device (cd0) and a hard disk (hdisk0).

status	Identifies the current status of the device instance. The possible values are:

- ▶ Status =0 : Defined
- ▶ Status =1 : Available
- ▶ Status =2 : Stopped

chgstatus	This flag tells whether the device instance has been altered since the last system boot. The diagnostics facility uses this flag to validate system configuration. The flag can take these values:

- ▶ chgstatus =0 : New device
- ▶ chgstatus =1 : Do not Care
- ▶ chgstatus =2 : Same
- ▶ chgstatus =3 : Device is missing

l	This descriptor typically contains the same value as the Device Driver Name descriptor in the Predefined Devices (PdDv) object class. It specifies the device driver that is loaded into the kernel.
location	Identifies the location code of the device.
parent	Identifies the logical name of the parent device instance.

Customized Attributes (CuAt)

The Customized Attribute object class contains customized device-specific attribute information.

Devices represented in the Customized Devices (CuDv) object class have attributes found in the Predefined Attribute (PdAt) object class and the CuAt object class. There is an entry in the CuAt object class for attributes that take customized values. Attributes taking the default value are found in the PdAt object class. Each entry describes the current value of the attribute.

These objects out of the CuAt object class show two attributes that take customized values. The attribute login has been changed to enable. The attribute pvid shows the physical volume identifier that has been assigned to disk hdisk0.

Additional device object classes

The following are the additional device object classes:

PdCn	The Predefined Connection (PdCn) object class contains connection information for adapters (or sometimes called intermediate devices). This object class also includes

predefined dependency information. For each connection location, there are one or more objects describing the subclasses of devices that can be connected.

CuDep   The Customized Dependency (CuDep) object class describes device instances that depend on other device instances. This object class describes the dependence links between logical devices, exclusively. Physical dependencies of one device on another device are recorded in the Customized Device (CuDv) object class.

CuDvDr   The Customized Device Driver (CuDvDr) object class is used to create the entries in the /dev directory. These special files are used from applications to access a device driver that is a part of an AIX 5L kernel.

CuVPD   The Customized Vital Product Data (CuVPD) object class contains vital product data (manufacturer of device, engineering level, part number, and so on) that is useful for technical support. When an error occurs with a specific device, the vital product data is shown in the error log.

Abbreviations and acronyms

APAR	Authorized Program Analysis Report
BOS	Based Operating System
EFI	Extensible Firmware Interface
HWE	Hardware Enablement
IBM	International Business Machines Corporation
ISL	Initial System Loader
ITSO	International Technical Support Organization
JFS	Journaled File System
LPP	Licensed Program Product
MH	Mail Handler
ML	Maintenance Level
MU	Maintenance Update
NFS	Network File System (NFS)
NIM	Network Installation Manager
NIS	Network Information Services
NLS	National Language Support
ODM	Object Data Manager
OE	Operating Environments
PDC	Processor Dependent Code
PPP	Point-to-Point Protocol
QPK	Quality Pack
SAM	System Administration Manager
SMIT	System Management Interface Tool
TCP/IP	Transmission Control Protocol/Internet Protocol

Related publications

The publications listed in this section are considered particularly suitable for a more detailed discussion of the topics covered in this redbook.

IBM Redbooks

For information about ordering these publications, see "How to get IBM Redbooks" on page 570. Note that some of the documents referenced here may be available in softcopy only.

► *AIX 5L Practical Performance Tools and Tuning Guide*, SG24-6478

► *AIX 5L Differences Guide Version 5.2 Edition*, SG24-5765

► *AIX 5L Differences Guide Version 5.3 Edition*, SG24-7463

► *Certification Study Guide - AIX 5L Installation and System Recovery* SG24-6183

► *IBM @server Certification Study Guide - pSeries AIX System Administration*, SG24-6191

► *Introducing VERITAS Foundation Suite for AIX*, SG24-6619

Other publications

These publications are also relevant as further information sources:

► *eServer™ pSeries Diagnostic Information for Multiple Bus Systems Version 5.3*, SA38-0509

► *HP Process Resource Manager User's Guide*, HP Part Number B8733-90011

► *HP-UX 11i Installation and Updating Guide*, HP Part Number 5990-7279

► *Patch Management User Guide*, HP Part Number 5991-0686

► *Ignite-UX Administration Guide*, HP Number B2355-90872

► *Managing Systems and Workgroups*, HP Number 5990-8172

► *HP-UX 11i Version 1.6 Release Notes*, HP Number 5187-0701

► *Managing Superdome Complexes: A Guide for HP-UX System Administrators, HP9000 Computers, Edition 1*, Manufacturing Part Number: B2355-90702 E1200

- *Installing and Managing HP-UX Virtual Partitions (vPars), Third Edition,* Manufacturing Part Number: T1335-90018

Online resources

These Web sites and URLs are also relevant as further information sources:

- IBM Technical Support

  http://techsupport.services.ibm.com/server/support?view=pSeries

- HP Web Documentation

  http://www.docs.hp.com

- HP Process Resource Manager Documentation

  http://docs.hp.com/en/B8733-90011/index.html

- AIX 5L Message Center - The place to go for a centralized view of all the AIX 5L Documentation

  http://publib.boulder.ibm.com/infocenter/pseries/index.jsp

- HP Web Documentation

  http://www.software.hp.com

- HP IT Resource Center

  http://www.itrc.hp.com

How to get IBM Redbooks

You can search for, view, or download Redbooks, Redpapers, Hints and Tips, draft publications and Additional materials, as well as order hardcopy Redbooks or CD-ROMs, at this Web site:

ibm.com/redbooks

Help from IBM

IBM Support and downloads

ibm.com/support

IBM Global Services

ibm.com/services

Index

Symbols

.com 22
.compat 22
.diag 22
.ucode 23
/etc/default/security 464
/etc/dt/config/C 460
/etc/dumpdates 252
/etc/environment 357
    PATH 461
/etc/filesystems 197
/etc/fstab 217
/etc/group 363
/etc/inetd.conf
    HP-UX 307, 459
/etc/inittab 99
/etc/issue
    HP-UX 459
/etc/mnttab 220
/etc/motd 460
/etc/passwd 347, 359–361
    HP-UX 465
/etc/PATH 460
/etc/profile 357–358
    PATH
        AIX 461
        HP-UX 461
/etc/securetcpip 452
/etc/security/.profile
    PATH 461
/etc/security/environ 356–357
/etc/security/group 364
/etc/security/limits 370
/etc/security/login.cfg 459
/etc/security/passwd 359–361
/etc/security/sysck.cfg 475–477
    acl 479
    class 478
    group 478
    links 478
    mode 478
    owner 478
    program 478
    source 479
    symlinks 478
/etc/security/user 466
/etc/shadow 359
/etc/skel/.profile
    PATH 461
/etc/skel/local.cshrc 356
/etc/skel/local.login 356
/etc/skel/local.profile 356
/etc/swapspaces 233
/etc/syslog.conf 538
/etc/utmp 346
/etc/vfstab 193
/tcb/files/auth 465
~/.profile
    PATH
        AIX 461
        HP-UX 461

Numerics

32-bit 14
32-bit system 44
64-bit architecture 2
64-bit Kernel 46
64-bit kernel 2, 44
64-bit processor 13
64-bit RISC 14

A

Accounting in Workload Manager 4
aclget 479
aclput 479
action 538
activating/deactivating a volume group 163
adapter 383
Add a print queue 406
Add a printer 406
add a volume group 159
Adding a logical volume (AIX 5L) 169
Adding a serial terminal (TTY) in AIX 5L 127
Adding local print queue 381
adding users 341
address spaces 2

RS64-II 14
rspc 76
RT_GRQ variable 491
Run Levels 84, 100
Run multiple tasks in a GUI environment 406
RUNNING 9, 400
run-queue size 494

S

S80 12
SAK 479
Samba 389
SAP/R3 377
sar interpretations in AIX 493
sar -q 494
savevg 258–259
sb_max 523
Scalability 71
Secure Attention Key 480
securetcpip 452
securetty 456
SecureWay 3
Selectable Logical Track Group (LTG) 3
selector 538
Serial number 326
serial printers 381
Server consolidation 2
service boot lists 90
Service Guide 91
service update 35
Set up a client for network installation 81
Setting up a print server 390
shell 479
shutdown 102, 105–106, 113
Shutdown and reboot 113
SIGABRT 421
SIGALRM 421
SIGALRM1 421
SIGBUS 421
SIGCHLD 421
SIGCONT 421
SIGCPUFAIL 421
SIGDANGER 421
SIGEMT 421
SIGFPE 421
SIGGRANT 421
SIGHUP 420
SIGILL 420

SIGINT 420
SIGIO 421
SIGKAP 421
SIGKILL 421
SIGMIGRATE 421
SIGMSG 421
signals 420
SIGPIPE 421
SIGPRE 421
SIGPROF 421
SIGPWR 421
SIGQUIT 420
SIGRETRACT 421
SIGSAK 421
SIGSEGV 421
SIGSOUND 421
SIGSTOP 421
SIGSYS 421
SIGTERM 421
SIGTRAP 420
SIGTSTP 421
SIGTTIN 421
SIGTTOU 421
SIGURG 421
SIGUSR1 421
SIGUSR2 421
SIGVIRT 421
SIGVTALRM 421
SIGWAITING 421
SIGWINCH 421
SIGXCPU 421
SIGXFSZ 421
single interface 11
site initialization files 356
Slave Name Server 322
SMIT dialog screen 6
smit errpt 533
smitty alt_install 63
smitty at 434
smitty backfile 249
smitty backfilesys 253
smitty bindproc 436–437
smitty chfs 206
smitty chgroup 366
smitty chps 237, 239
smitty chuser 355
smitty crfs 190
smitty crjfs 225
smitty dump 547